ROOT

VOLUME ONE:
FAMILY BUSINESS

**DAVID F. WALKER,
CHUCK BROWN &
SANFORD GREENE**
creators

**RICO RENZI &
SANFORD GREENE**
color artists

CLAYTON COWLES
letterer

SANFORD GREENE
cover artist

HEATHER ANTOS
editor

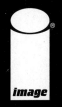

IMAGE COMICS, INC.

Robert Kirkman: Chief Operating Officer
Erik Larsen: Chief Financial Officer
Todd McFarlane: President
Marc Silvestri: Chief Executive Officer
Jim Valentino: Vice President

Eric Stephenson: Publisher / Chief Creative Officer
Corey Hart: Director of Sales
Jeff Boison: Director of Publishing Planning
& Book Trade Sales
Chris Ross: Director of Digital Sales
Jeff Stang: Director of Specialty Sales
Kat Salazar: Director of PR & Marketing
Drew Gill: Art Director
Heather Doornink: Production Director
Nicole Lapalme: Controller

IMAGECOMICS.COM

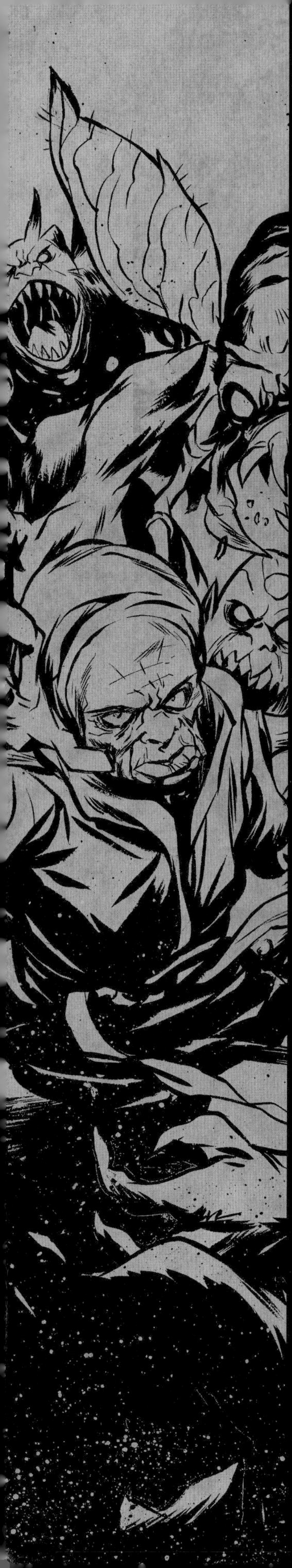

"For everyone who has stood up to the Jinoo. Keep fighting the monsters."

–David

"Dedicated to my big brothers for introducing me to a world of heroes, monsters, & magic. And to my wife & kids for their love, support."

–Chuck

"To my wife and children for the support and thanks to God for opportunity for me and my creative brothers to fight the good fight."

–Sanford

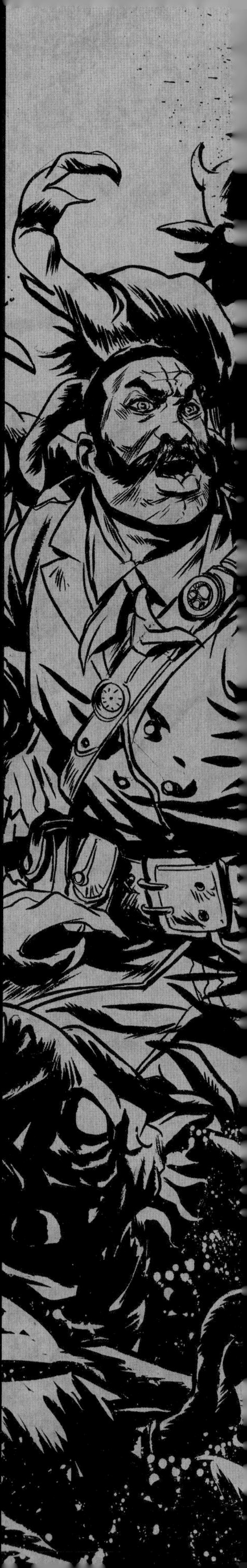

CHAPTER ONE

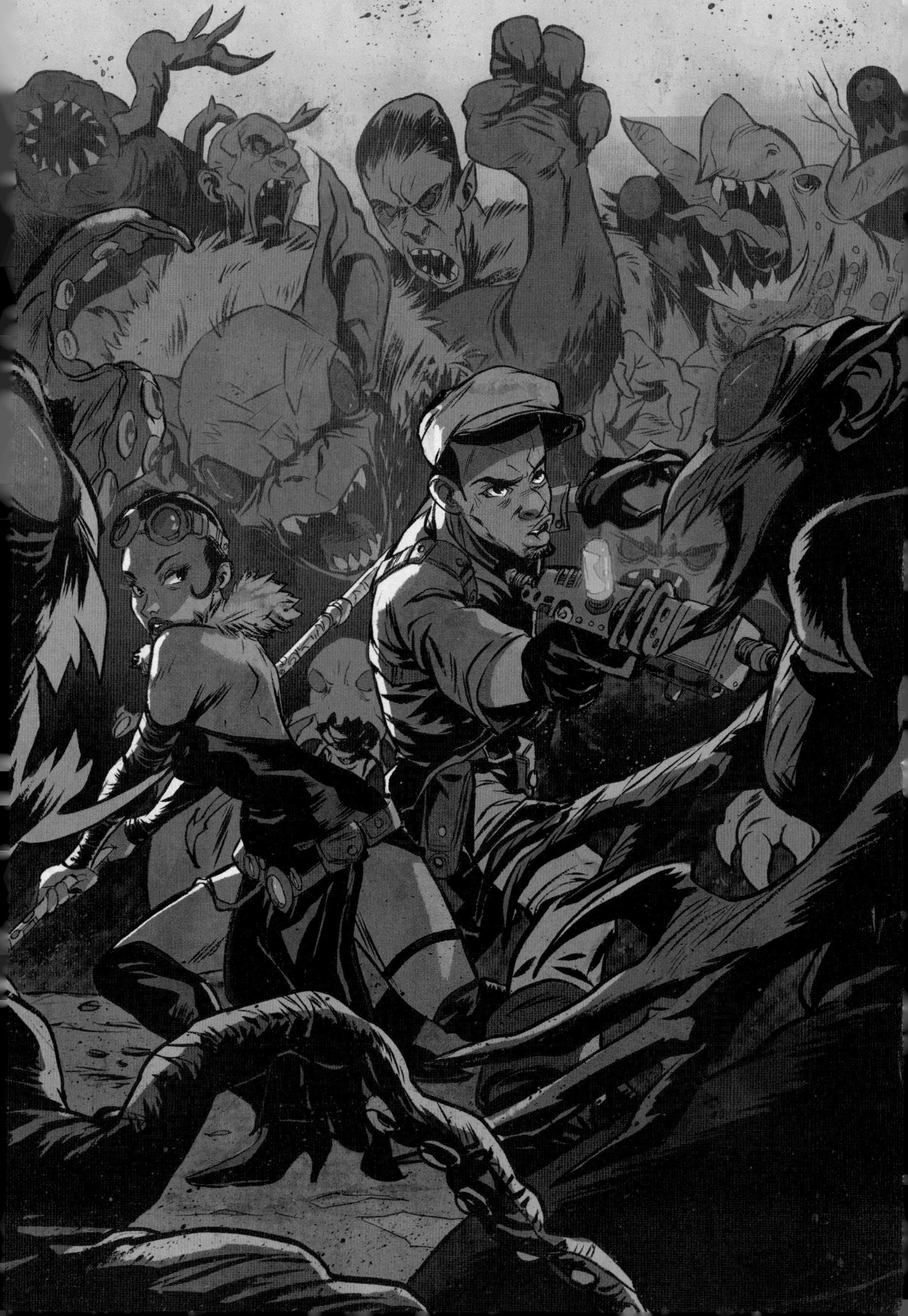

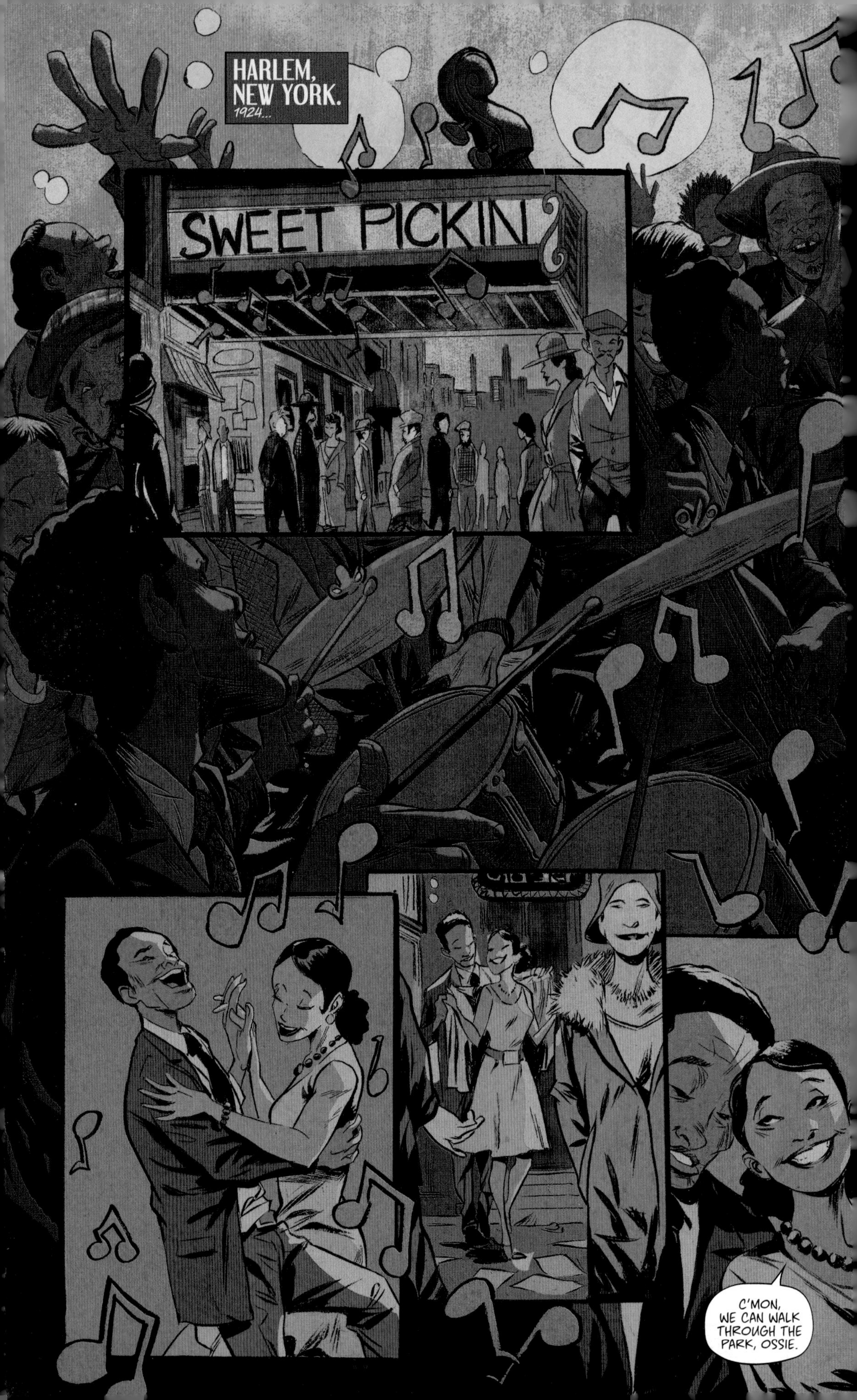
HARLEM, NEW YORK. 1924...
SWEET PICKIN
C'MON, WE CAN WALK THROUGH THE PARK, OSSIE.

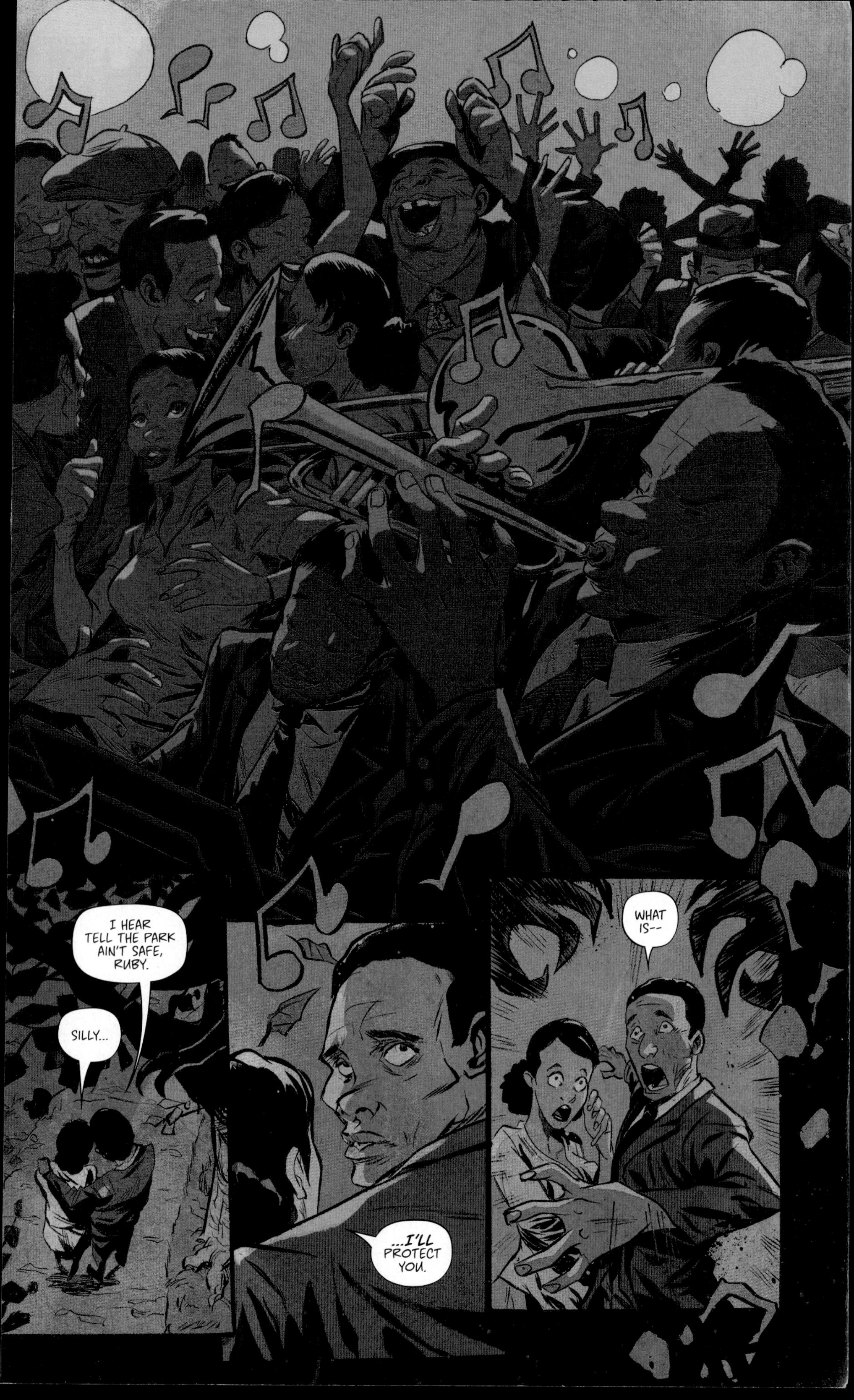
I HEAR TELL THE PARK AIN'T SAFE, RUBY.
SILLY...
...I'LL PROTECT YOU.
WHAT IS--

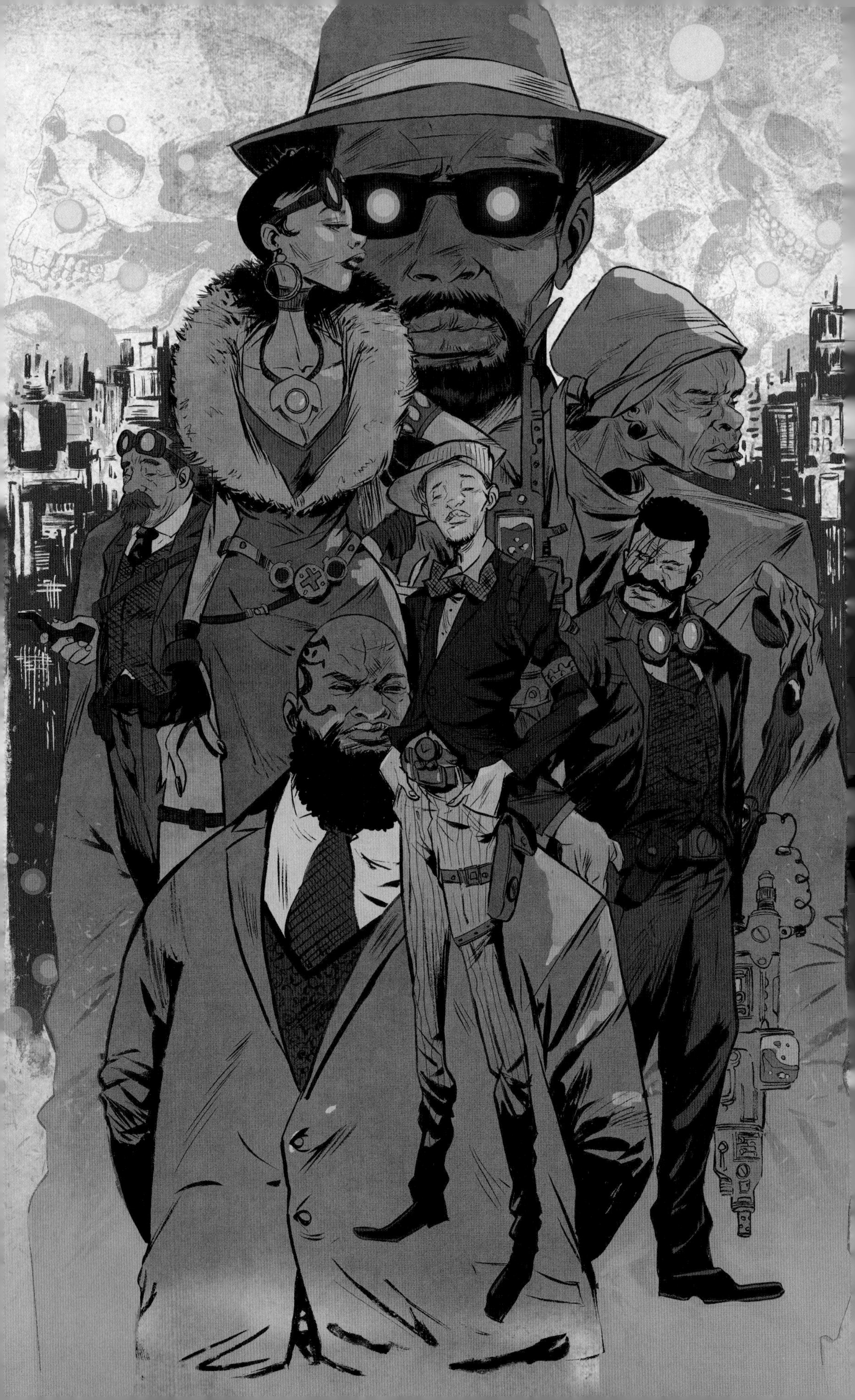

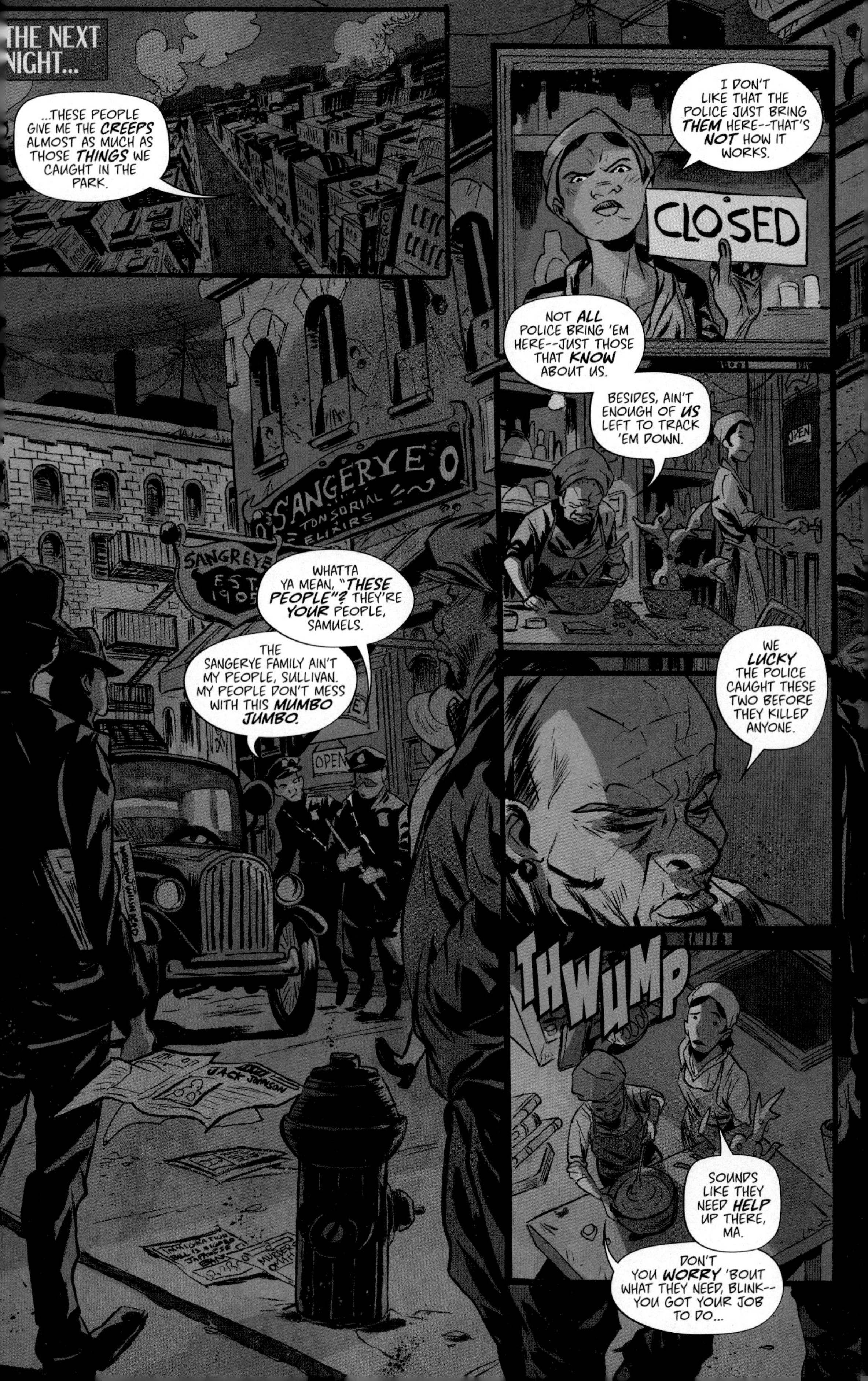
THE NEXT NIGHT...
...THESE PEOPLE GIVE ME THE CREEPS ALMOST AS MUCH AS THOSE THINGS WE CAUGHT IN THE PARK.
SANGERYE TONSORIAL ELIXIRS
SANGERYE EST. 1905
WHATTA YA MEAN, "THESE PEOPLE"? THEY'RE YOUR PEOPLE, SAMUELS.
THE SANGERYE FAMILY AIN'T MY PEOPLE, SULLIVAN. MY PEOPLE DON'T MESS WITH THIS MUMBO JUMBO.
OPEN
JACK JOHNSON
I DON'T LIKE THAT THE POLICE JUST BRING THEM HERE--THAT'S NOT HOW IT WORKS.
CLOSED
NOT ALL POLICE BRING 'EM HERE--JUST THOSE THAT KNOW ABOUT US.
BESIDES, AIN'T ENOUGH OF US LEFT TO TRACK 'EM DOWN.
OPEN
WE LUCKY THE POLICE CAUGHT THESE TWO BEFORE THEY KILLED ANYONE.
THWUMP
SOUNDS LIKE THEY NEED HELP UP THERE, MA.
DON'T YOU WORRY 'BOUT WHAT THEY NEED, BLINK--YOU GOT YOUR JOB TO DO...

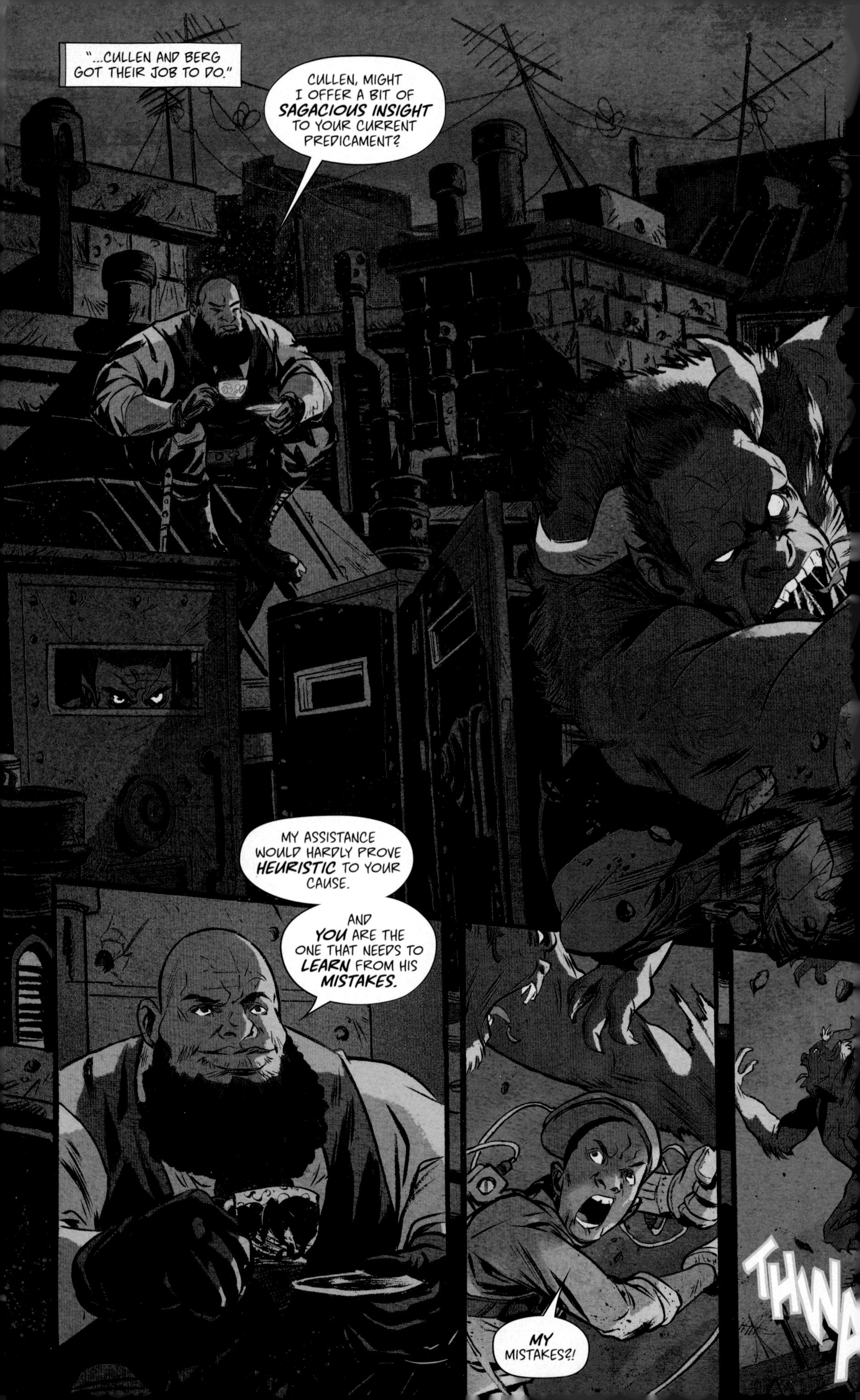
"...CULLEN AND BERG GOT THEIR JOB TO DO."
CULLEN, MIGHT I OFFER A BIT OF **SAGACIOUS INSIGHT** TO YOUR CURRENT PREDICAMENT?
MY ASSISTANCE WOULD HARDLY PROVE **HEURISTIC** TO YOUR CAUSE.
AND **YOU** ARE THE ONE THAT NEEDS TO **LEARN** FROM HIS **MISTAKES.**
MY MISTAKES?!
THWA

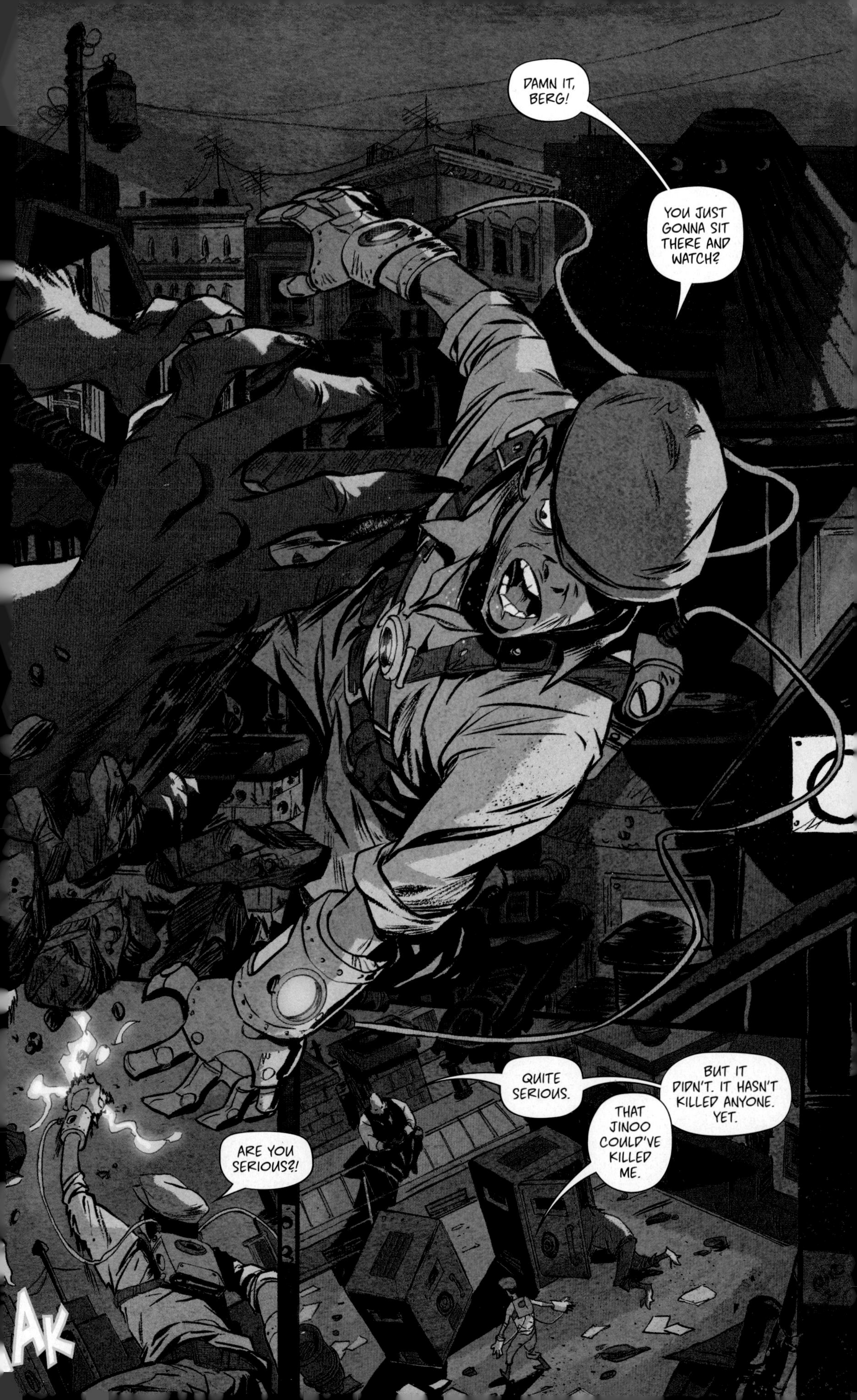
DAMN IT, BERG!
YOU JUST GONNA SIT THERE AND WATCH?
QUITE SERIOUS.
BUT IT DIDN'T. IT HASN'T KILLED ANYONE. YET.
THAT JINOO COULD'VE KILLED ME.
ARE YOU SERIOUS?!
AK

NOW, DISPENSE WITH THE **LOLLYGAGGING** AND PAY ATTENTION TO THE TASK AT HAND BEFORE YOU DO GET KILLED--WHICH WOULD BE MOST **INSALUBRIOUS.**

YOU THINK I'M NOT DOING THE **BEST** I CAN?

ROOOWR!

...AND **LOOK** AROUND YOU, CULLEN.

OH, **DAMN.**

DEAR COUSIN, YOU HAVE A **PREDILECTION** FOR **PRETERMITTING** THAT WHICH IS MOST **PERTINENT.** GET YOUR HEAD OUT OF THE CLOUDS...

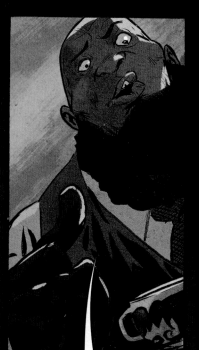

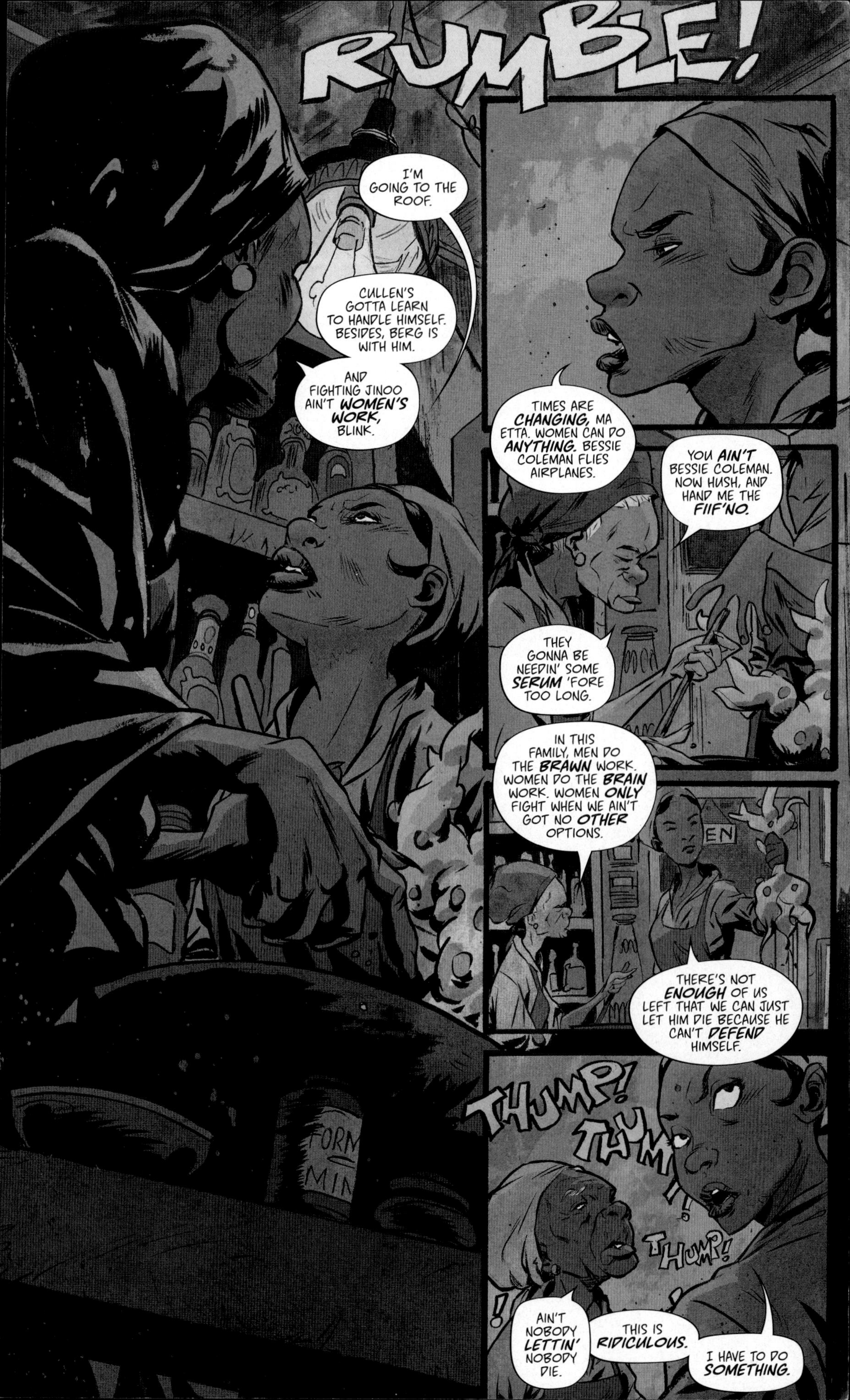
RUMBLE!
I'M GOING TO THE ROOF.
CULLEN'S GOTTA LEARN TO HANDLE HIMSELF. BESIDES, BERG IS WITH HIM.
AND FIGHTING JINOO AIN'T WOMEN'S WORK, BLINK.
TIMES ARE CHANGING, MA ETTA. WOMEN CAN DO ANYTHING. BESSIE COLEMAN FLIES AIRPLANES.
YOU AIN'T BESSIE COLEMAN. NOW HUSH, AND HAND ME THE FIIF'NO.
THEY GONNA BE NEEDIN' SOME SERUM 'FORE TOO LONG.
IN THIS FAMILY, MEN DO THE BRAWN WORK. WOMEN DO THE BRAIN WORK. WOMEN ONLY FIGHT WHEN WE AIN'T GOT NO OTHER OPTIONS.
THERE'S NOT ENOUGH OF US LEFT THAT WE CAN JUST LET HIM DIE BECAUSE HE CAN'T DEFEND HIMSELF.
THUMP! THUMP! THUMP!
AIN'T NOBODY LETTIN' NOBODY DIE.
THIS IS RIDICULOUS.
I HAVE TO DO SOMETHING.

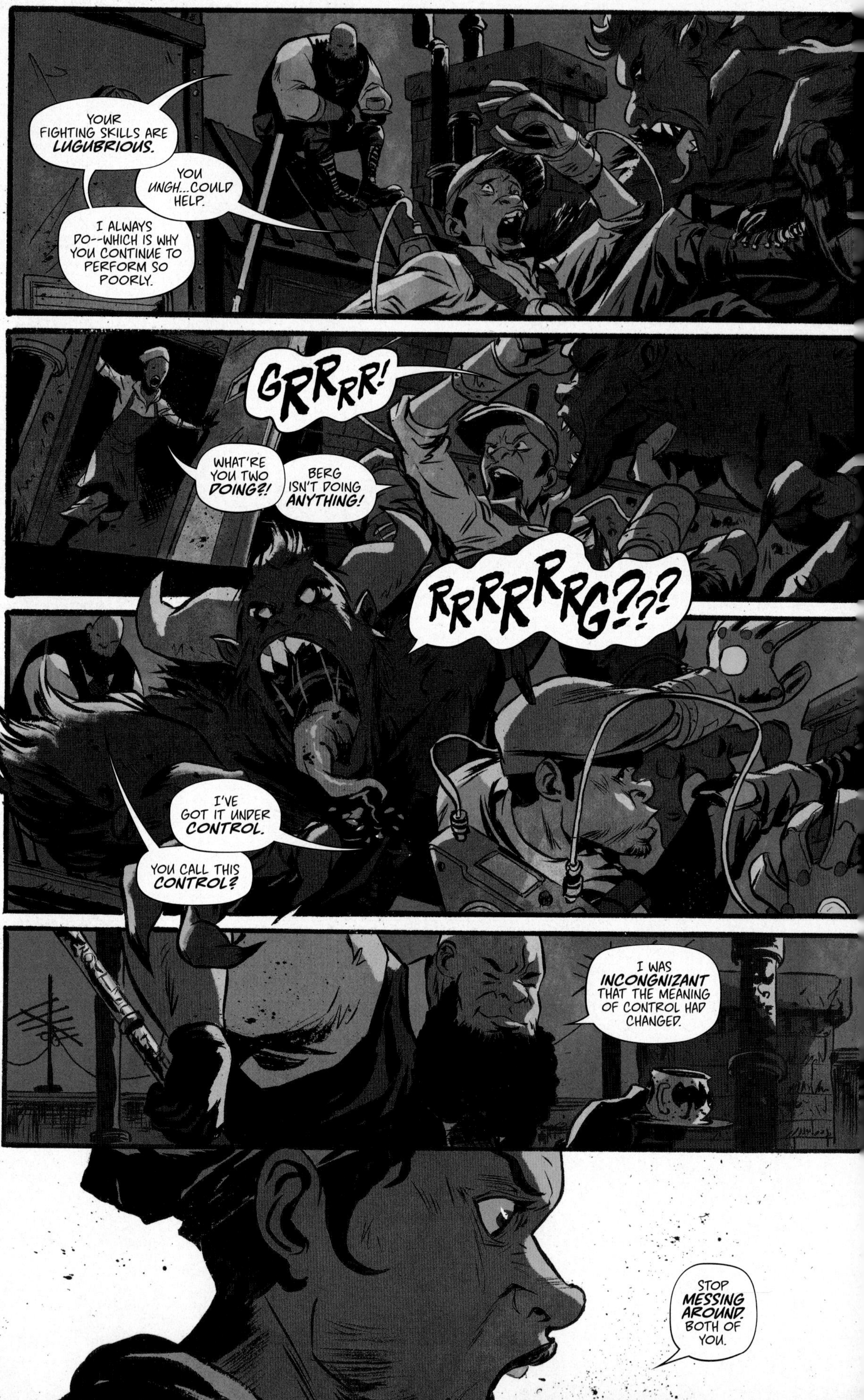
YOUR FIGHTING SKILLS ARE LUGUBRIOUS.
YOU UNGH...COULD HELP.
I ALWAYS DO--WHICH IS WHY YOU CONTINUE TO PERFORM SO POORLY.
GRRRR!
WHAT'RE YOU TWO DOING?!
BERG ISN'T DOING ANYTHING!
RRRRRRG???
I'VE GOT IT UNDER CONTROL.
YOU CALL THIS CONTROL?
I WAS INCONGNIZANT THAT THE MEANING OF CONTROL HAD CHANGED.
STOP MESSING AROUND. BOTH OF YOU.

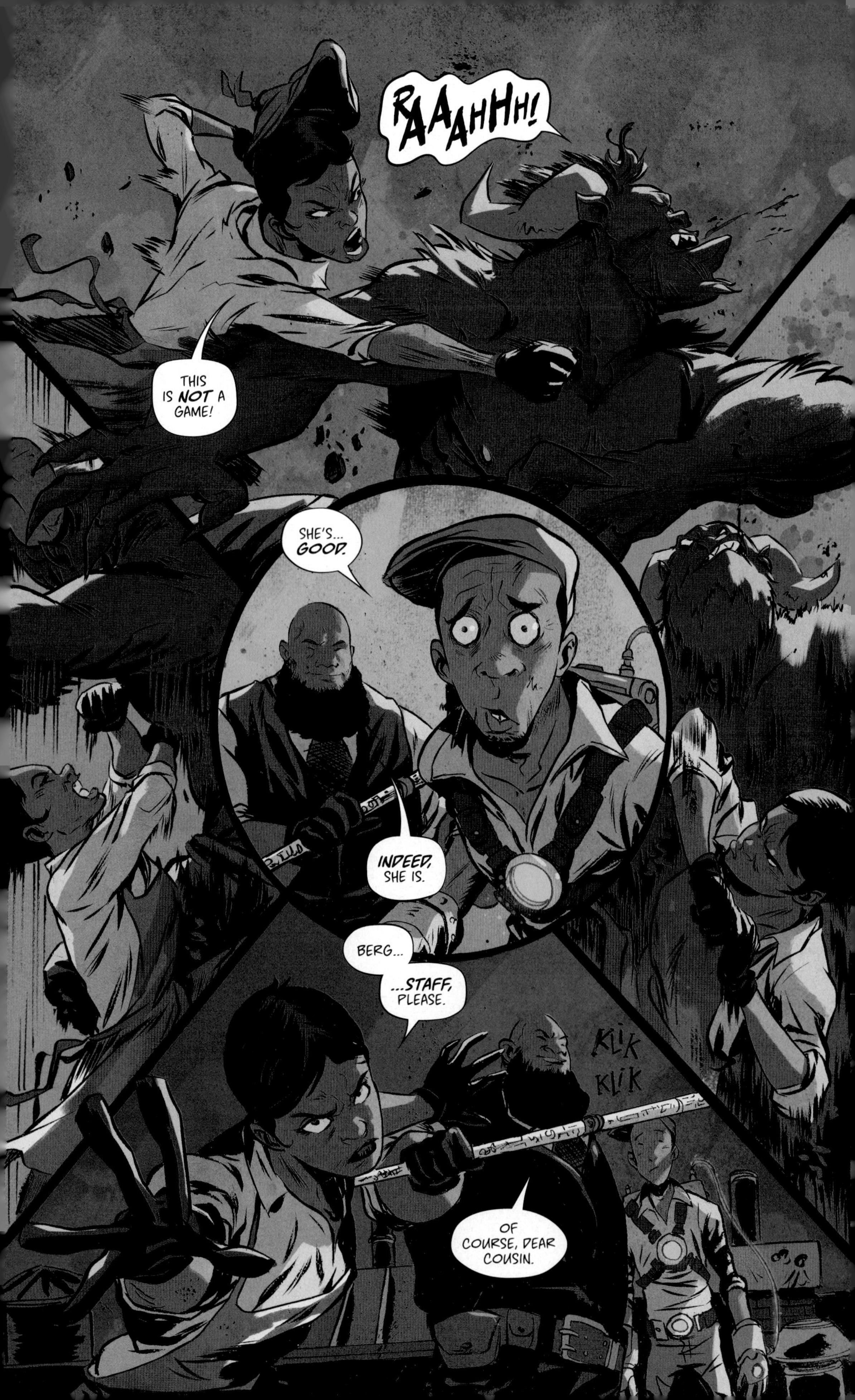
RAAAHHH!
THIS IS **NOT** A GAME!
SHE'S... **GOOD.**
INDEED, SHE IS.
BERG...
...STAFF, PLEASE.
KLIK KLIK
OF COURSE, DEAR COUSIN.

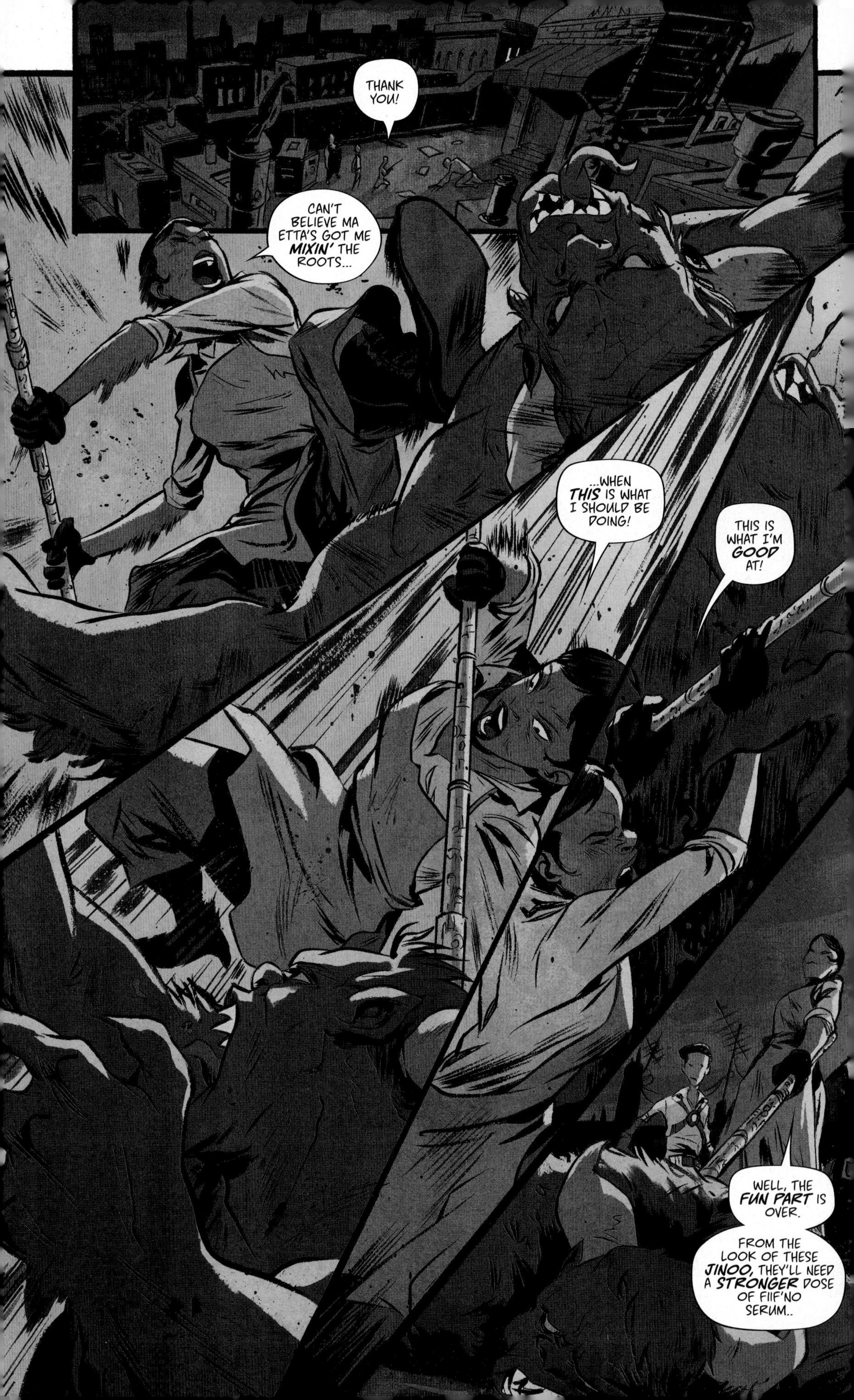
THANK YOU!
CAN'T BELIEVE MA ETTA'S GOT ME MIXIN' THE ROOTS...
...WHEN THIS IS WHAT I SHOULD BE DOING!
THIS IS WHAT I'M GOOD AT!
WELL, THE FUN PART IS OVER.
FROM THE LOOK OF THESE JINOO, THEY'LL NEED A STRONGER DOSE OF FIIF'NO SERUM..

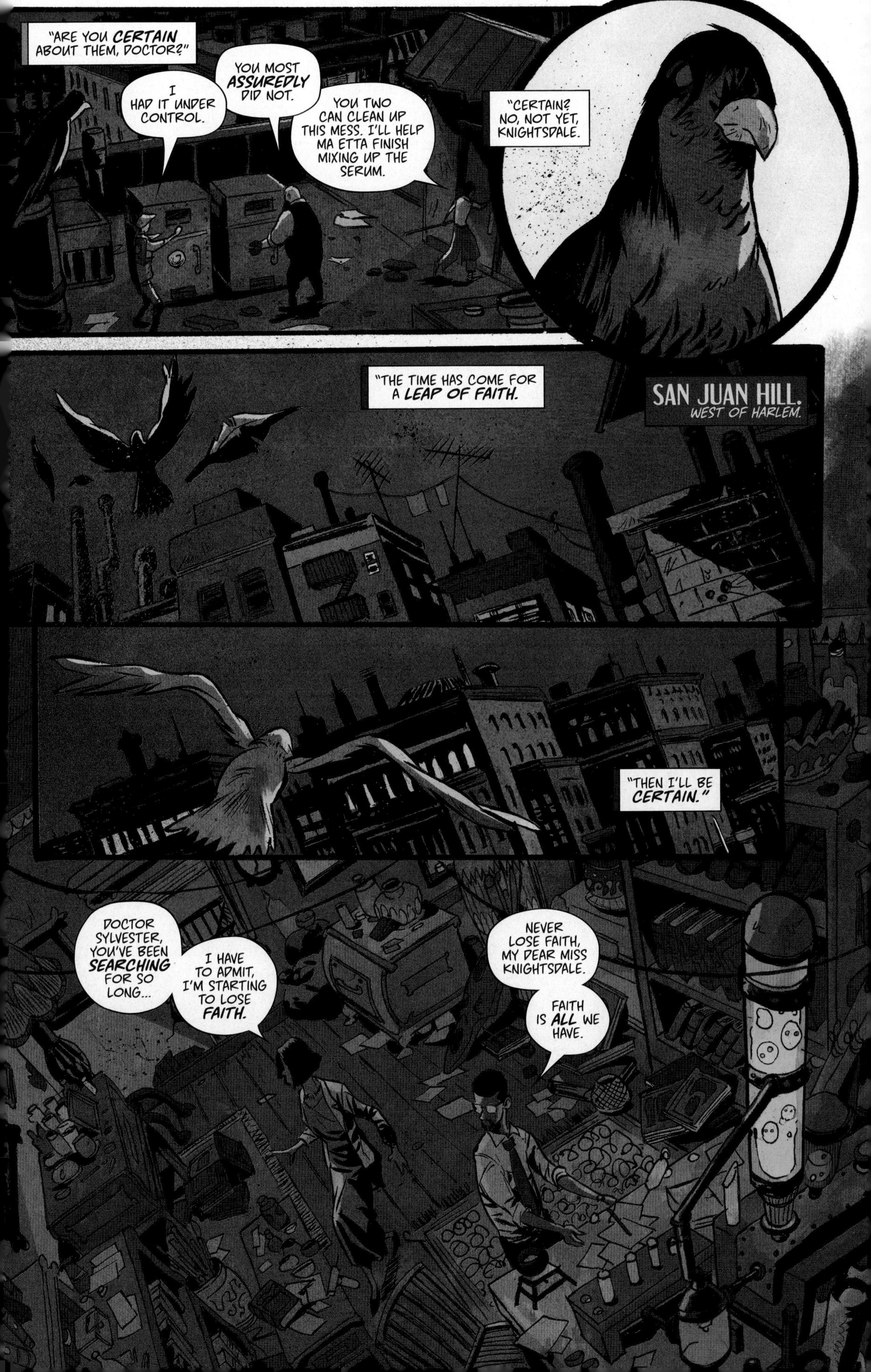
"ARE YOU CERTAIN ABOUT THEM, DOCTOR?"
I HAD IT UNDER CONTROL.
YOU MOST ASSUREDLY DID NOT.
YOU TWO CAN CLEAN UP THIS MESS. I'LL HELP MA ETTA FINISH MIXING UP THE SERUM.
"CERTAIN? NO, NOT YET, KNIGHTSDALE.
"THE TIME HAS COME FOR A LEAP OF FAITH.
SAN JUAN HILL.
WEST OF HARLEM.
"THEN I'LL BE CERTAIN."
DOCTOR SYLVESTER, YOU'VE BEEN SEARCHING FOR SO LONG...
I HAVE TO ADMIT, I'M STARTING TO LOSE FAITH.
NEVER LOSE FAITH, MY DEAR MISS KNIGHTSDALE.
FAITH IS ALL WE HAVE.

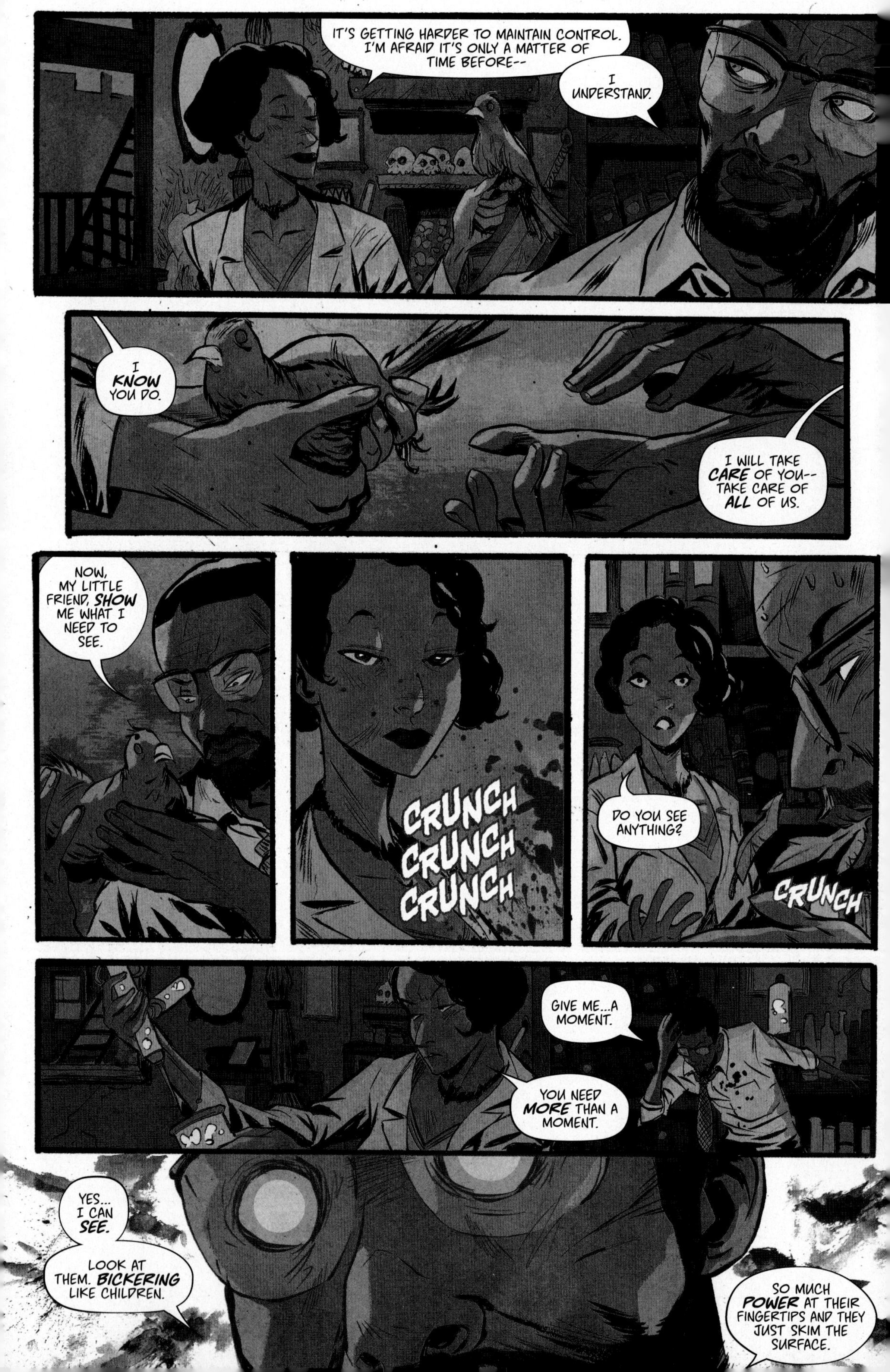
IT'S GETTING HARDER TO MAINTAIN CONTROL. I'M AFRAID IT'S ONLY A MATTER OF TIME BEFORE--
I UNDERSTAND.
I KNOW YOU DO.
I WILL TAKE CARE OF YOU-- TAKE CARE OF ALL OF US.
NOW, MY LITTLE FRIEND, SHOW ME WHAT I NEED TO SEE.
CRUNCH CRUNCH CRUNCH
DO YOU SEE ANYTHING?
CRUNCH
GIVE ME...A MOMENT.
YOU NEED MORE THAN A MOMENT.
YES... I CAN SEE.
LOOK AT THEM. BICKERING LIKE CHILDREN.
SO MUCH POWER AT THEIR FINGERTIPS AND THEY JUST SKIM THE SURFACE.

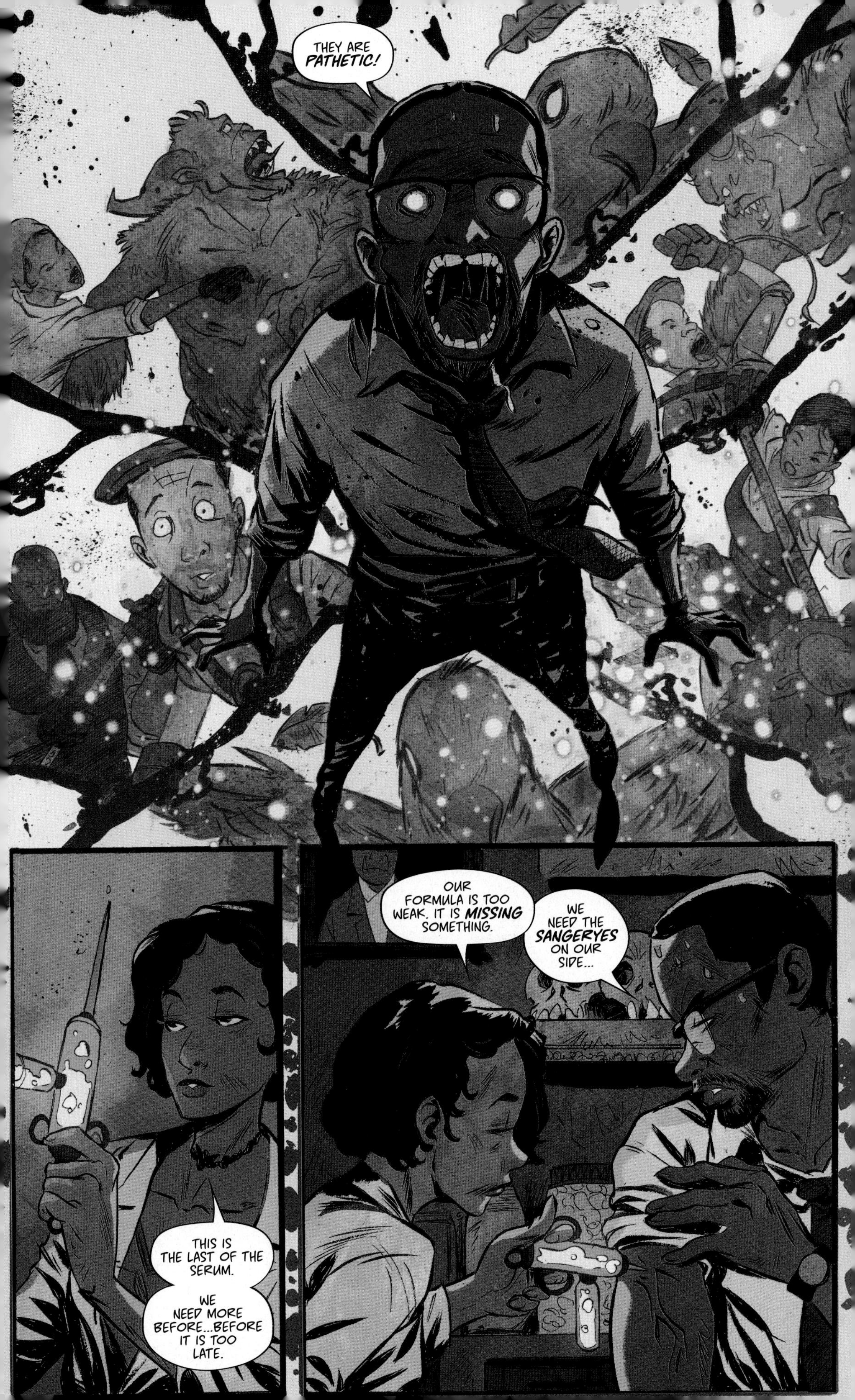

THEY ARE PATHETIC!
THIS IS THE LAST OF THE SERUM.
WE NEED MORE BEFORE...BEFORE IT IS TOO LATE.
OUR FORMULA IS TOO WEAK. IT IS MISSING SOMETHING.
WE NEED THE SANGERYES ON OUR SIDE...

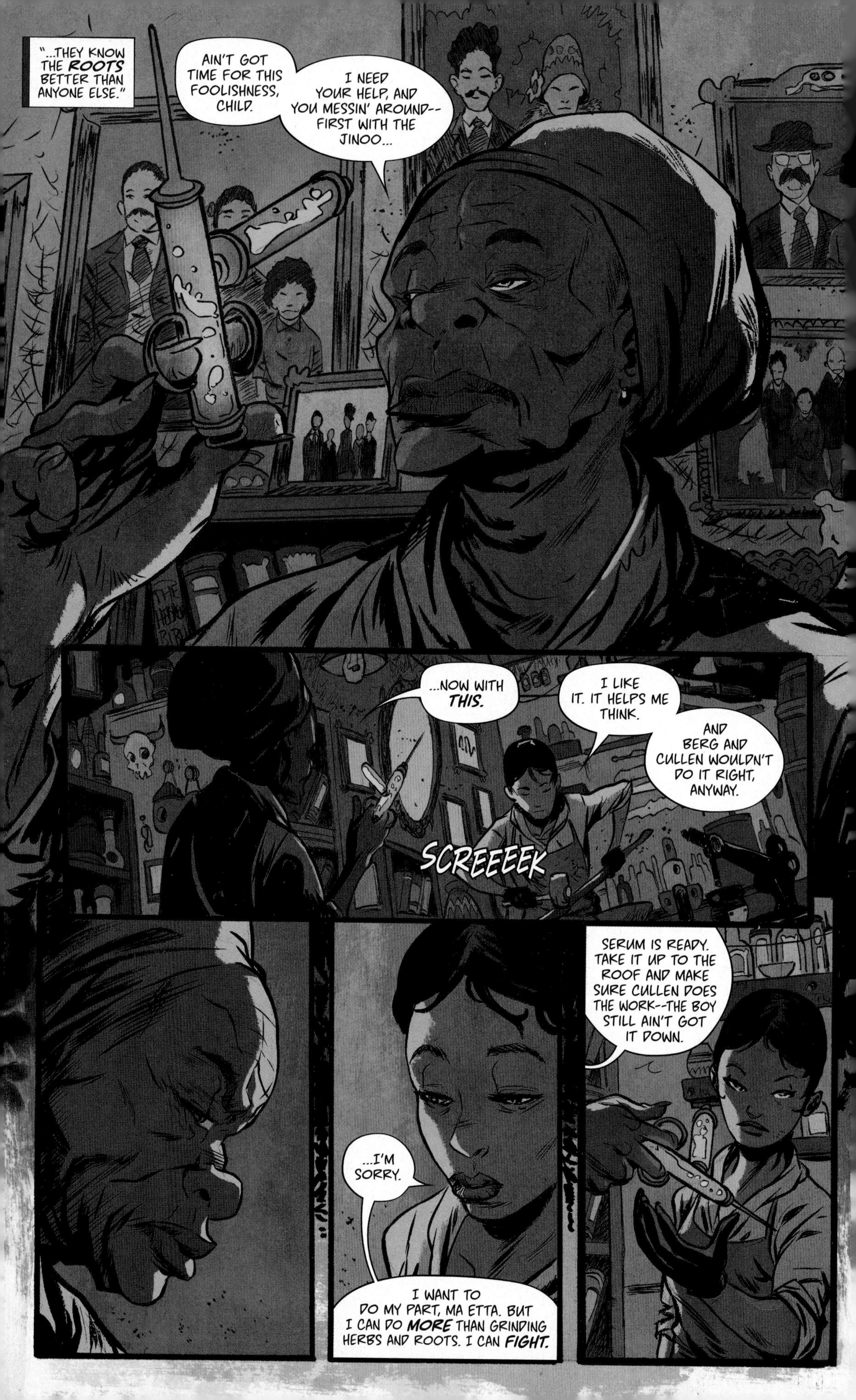
"...THEY KNOW THE **ROOTS** BETTER THAN ANYONE ELSE."
AIN'T GOT TIME FOR THIS FOOLISHNESS, CHILD.
I NEED YOUR HELP, AND YOU MESSIN' AROUND-- FIRST WITH THE JINOO...
...NOW WITH **THIS.**
I LIKE IT. IT HELPS ME THINK.
AND BERG AND CULLEN WOULDN'T DO IT RIGHT, ANYWAY.
SCREEEEK
SERUM IS READY. TAKE IT UP TO THE ROOF AND MAKE SURE CULLEN DOES THE WORK--THE BOY STILL AIN'T GOT IT DOWN.
...I'M SORRY.
I WANT TO DO MY PART, MA ETTA. BUT I CAN DO **MORE** THAN GRINDING HERBS AND ROOTS. I CAN **FIGHT.**

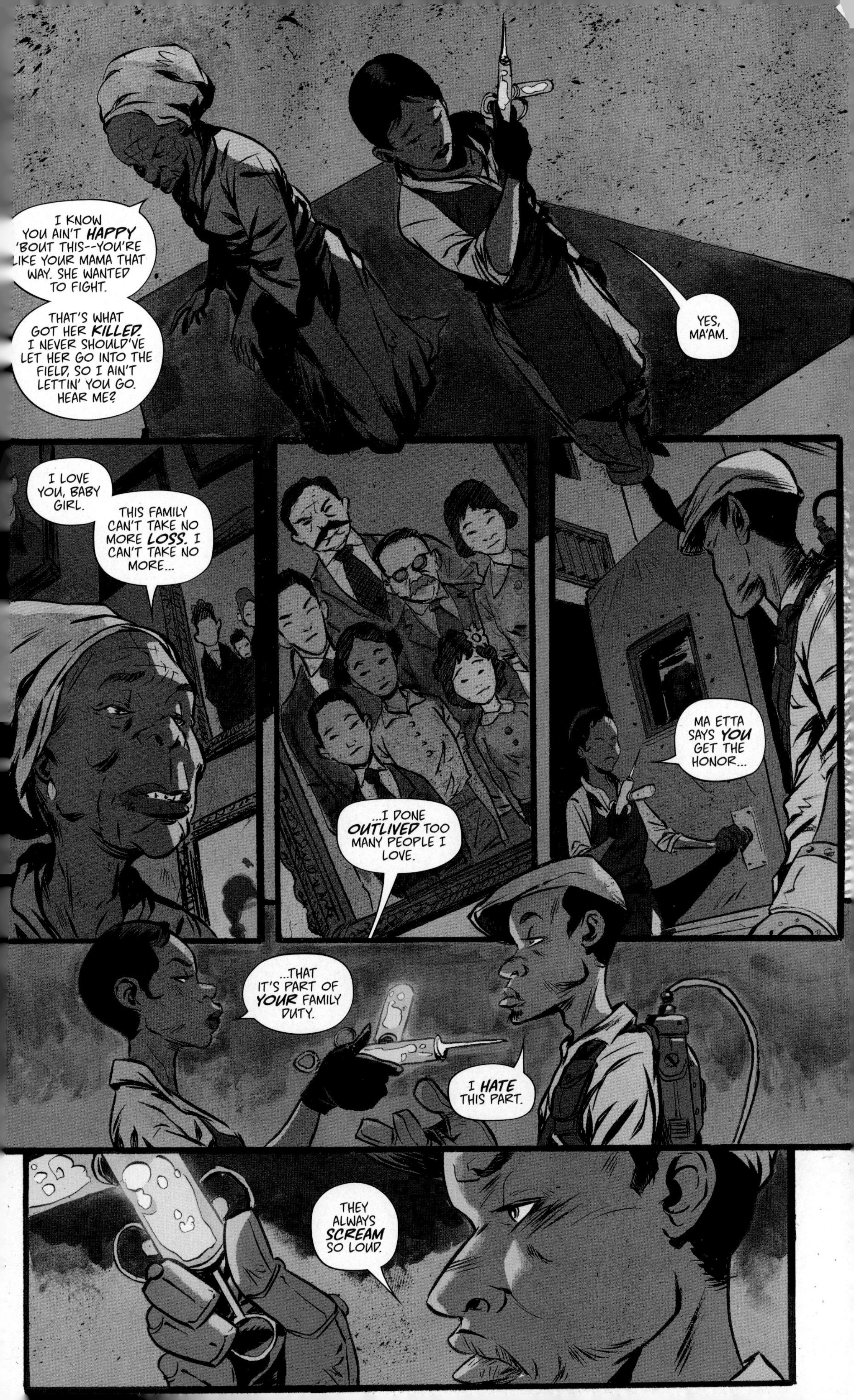
I KNOW YOU AIN'T HAPPY 'BOUT THIS--YOU'RE LIKE YOUR MAMA THAT WAY. SHE WANTED TO FIGHT.
THAT'S WHAT GOT HER KILLED. I NEVER SHOULD'VE LET HER GO INTO THE FIELD, SO I AIN'T LETTIN' YOU GO. HEAR ME?
YES, MA'AM.
I LOVE YOU, BABY GIRL.
THIS FAMILY CAN'T TAKE NO MORE LOSS. I CAN'T TAKE NO MORE...
...I DONE OUTLIVED TOO MANY PEOPLE I LOVE.
MA ETTA SAYS YOU GET THE HONOR...
...THAT IT'S PART OF YOUR FAMILY DUTY.
I HATE THIS PART.
THEY ALWAYS SCREAM SO LOUD.

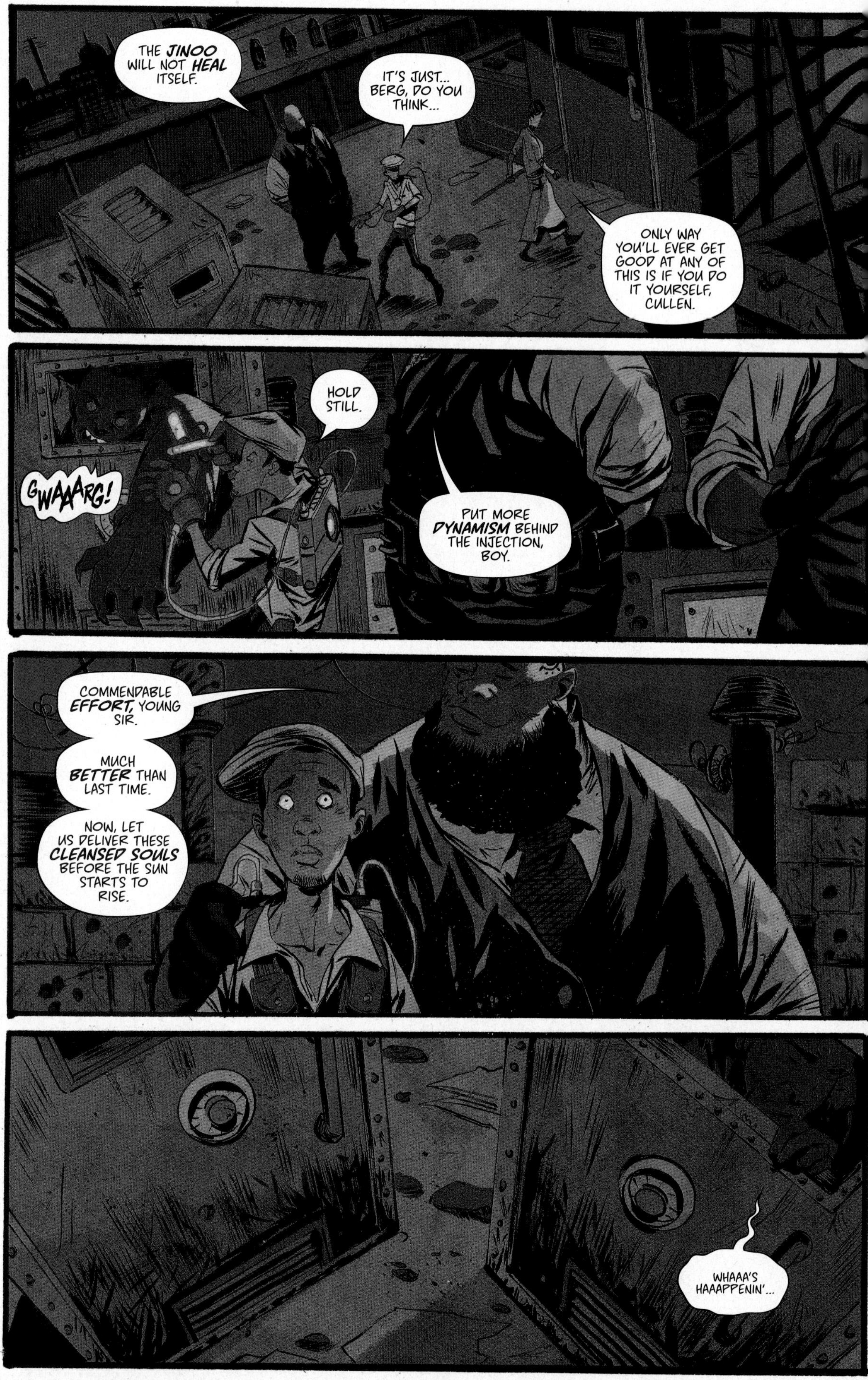
THE JINOO WILL NOT HEAL ITSELF.
IT'S JUST... BERG, DO YOU THINK...
ONLY WAY YOU'LL EVER GET GOOD AT ANY OF THIS IS IF YOU DO IT YOURSELF, CULLEN.
HOLD STILL.
GWAAARG!
PUT MORE DYNAMISM BEHIND THE INJECTION, BOY.
COMMENDABLE EFFORT, YOUNG SIR.
MUCH BETTER THAN LAST TIME.
NOW, LET US DELIVER THESE CLEANSED SOULS BEFORE THE SUN STARTS TO RISE.
WHAAA'S HAAAPPENIN'...

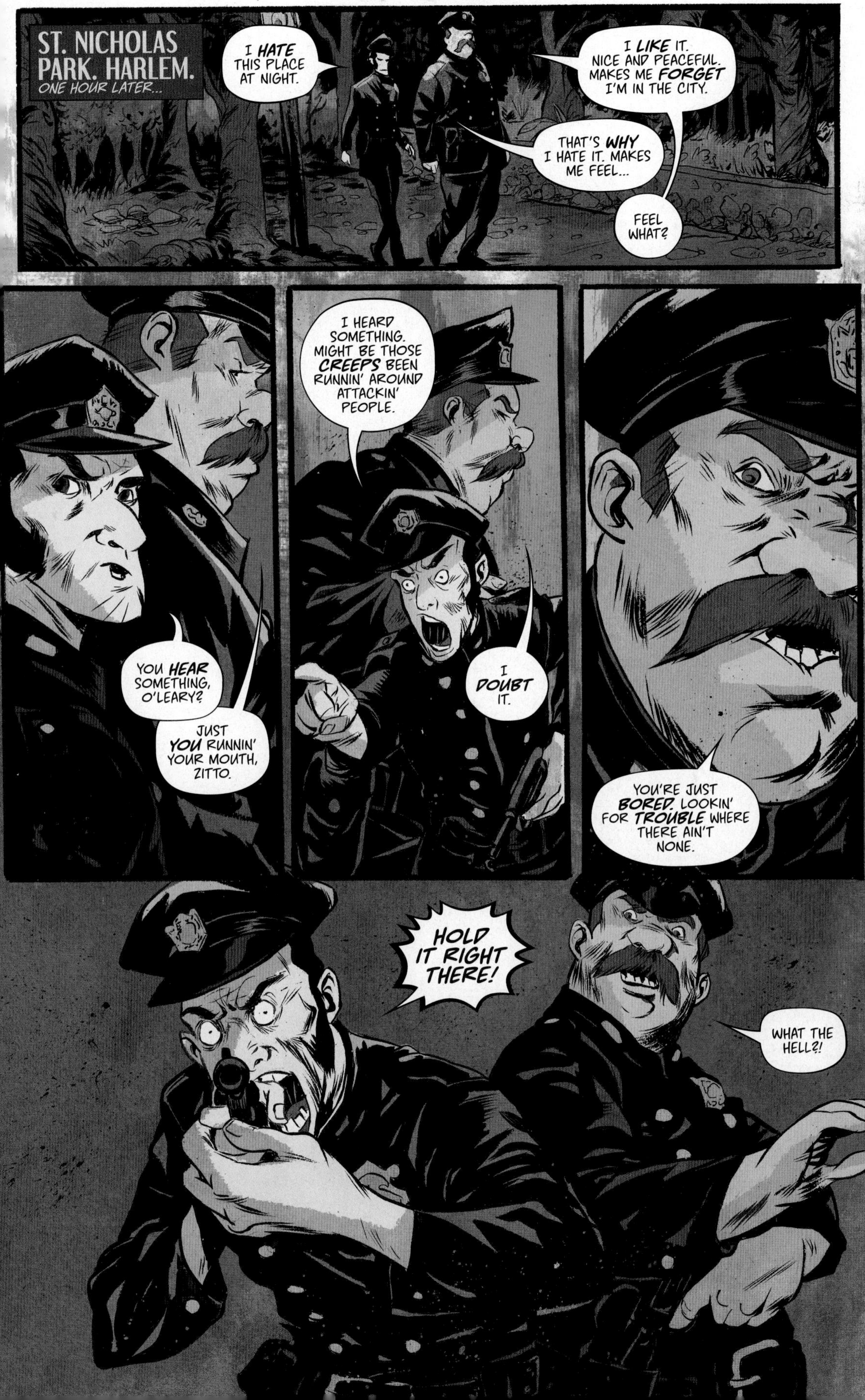
ST. NICHOLAS PARK. HARLEM.
ONE HOUR LATER...
I HATE THIS PLACE AT NIGHT.
I LIKE IT. NICE AND PEACEFUL. MAKES ME FORGET I'M IN THE CITY.
THAT'S WHY I HATE IT. MAKES ME FEEL...
FEEL WHAT?
YOU HEAR SOMETHING, O'LEARY?
JUST YOU RUNNIN' YOUR MOUTH, ZITTO.
I HEARD SOMETHING. MIGHT BE THOSE CREEPS BEEN RUNNIN' AROUND ATTACKIN' PEOPLE.
I DOUBT IT.
YOU'RE JUST BORED. LOOKIN' FOR TROUBLE WHERE THERE AIN'T NONE.
HOLD IT RIGHT THERE!
WHAT THE HELL?!

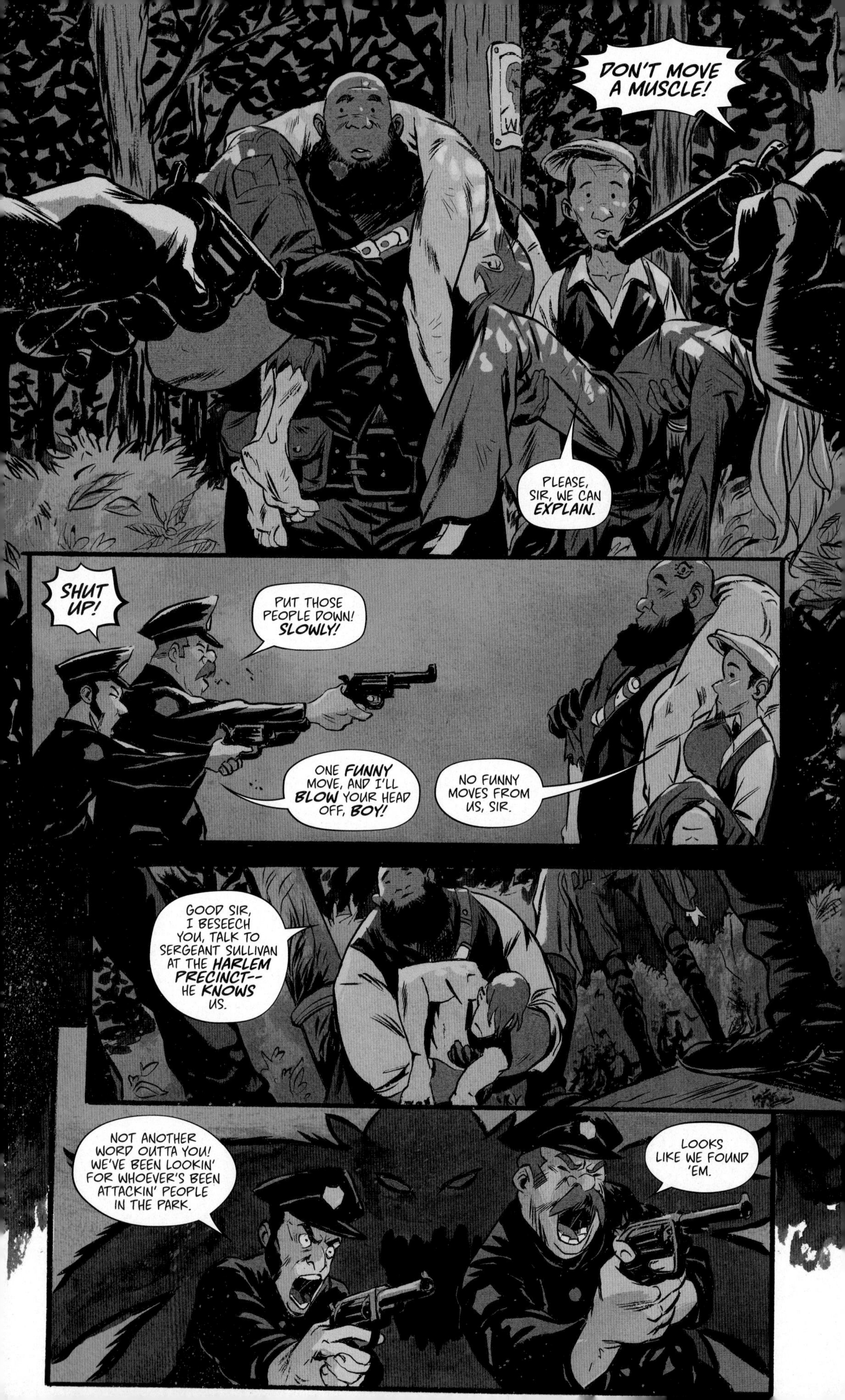
DON'T MOVE A MUSCLE!
PLEASE, SIR, WE CAN EXPLAIN.
SHUT UP!
PUT THOSE PEOPLE DOWN! SLOWLY!
ONE FUNNY MOVE, AND I'LL BLOW YOUR HEAD OFF, BOY!
NO FUNNY MOVES FROM US, SIR.
GOOD SIR, I BESEECH YOU, TALK TO SERGEANT SULLIVAN AT THE HARLEM PRECINCT-- HE KNOWS US.
NOT ANOTHER WORD OUTTA YOU! WE'VE BEEN LOOKIN' FOR WHOEVER'S BEEN ATTACKIN' PEOPLE IN THE PARK.
LOOKS LIKE WE FOUND 'EM.

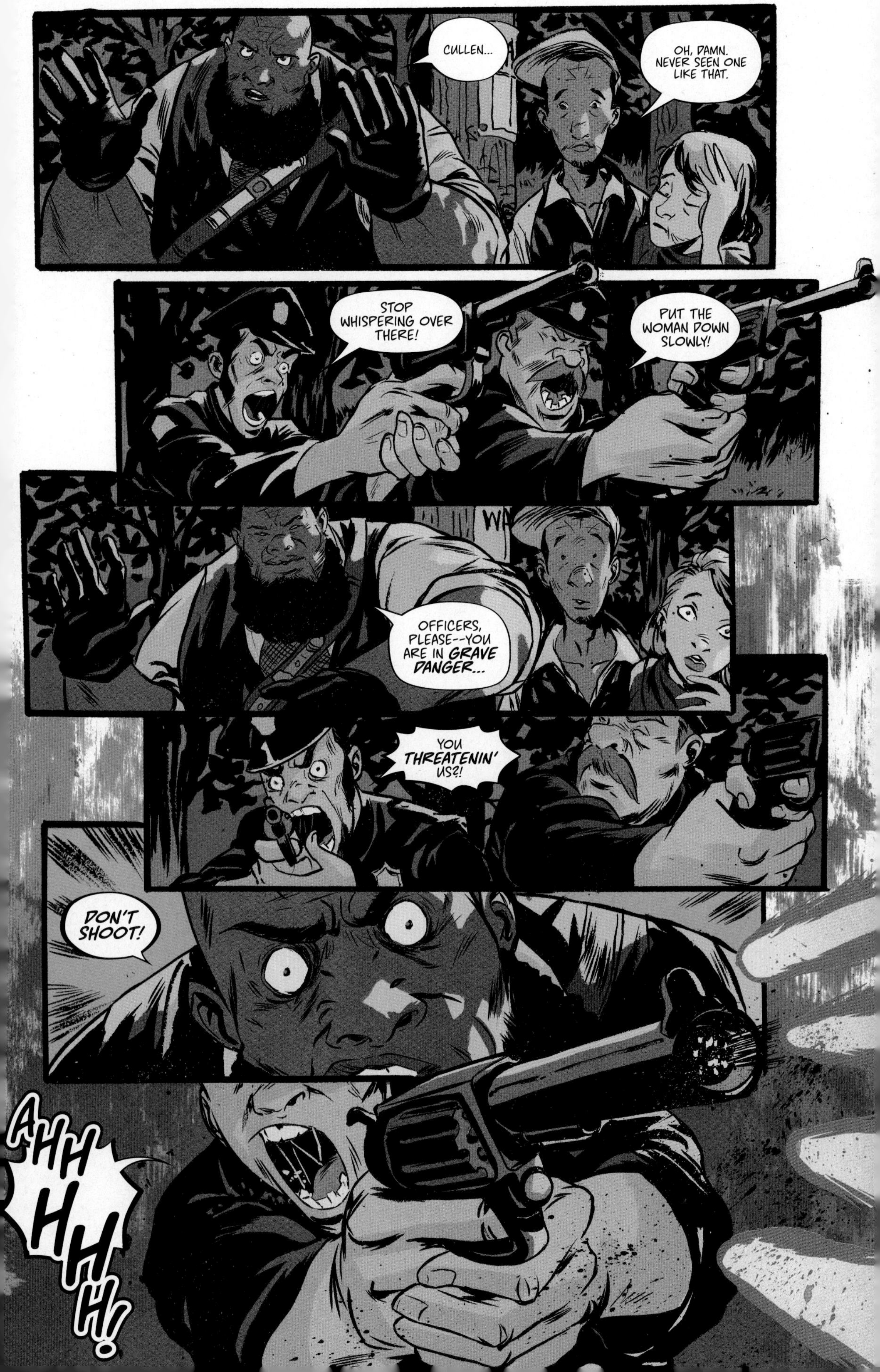
CULLEN...
OH, DAMN. NEVER SEEN ONE LIKE THAT.
STOP WHISPERING OVER THERE!
PUT THE WOMAN DOWN SLOWLY!
OFFICERS, PLEASE--YOU ARE IN GRAVE DANGER...
YOU THREATENIN' US?!
DON'T SHOOT!
AHHHHHH!

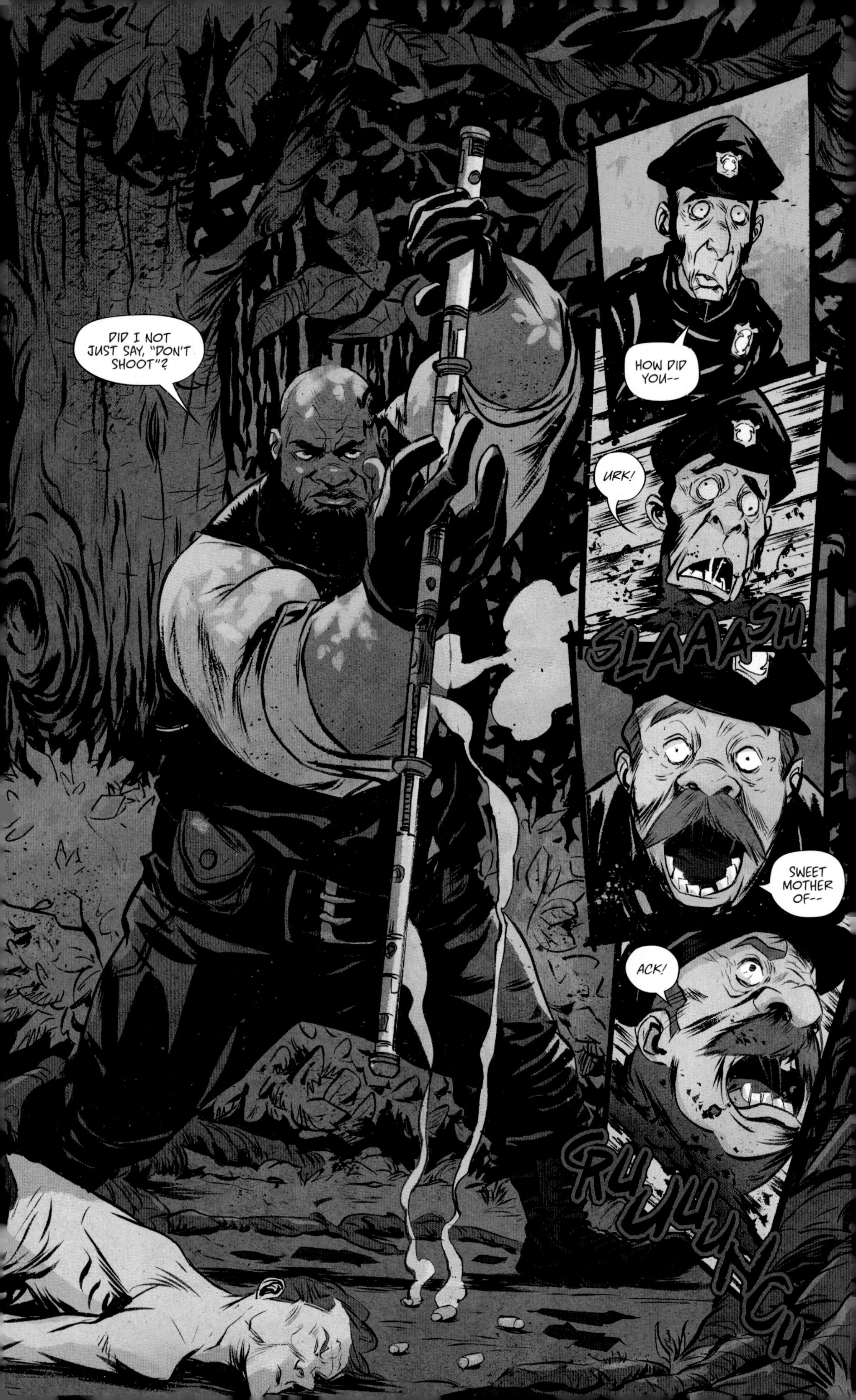
DID I NOT JUST SAY, "DON'T SHOOT"?
HOW DID YOU--
URK!
SLAAASH
SWEET MOTHER OF--
ACK!
CRUUUNCH

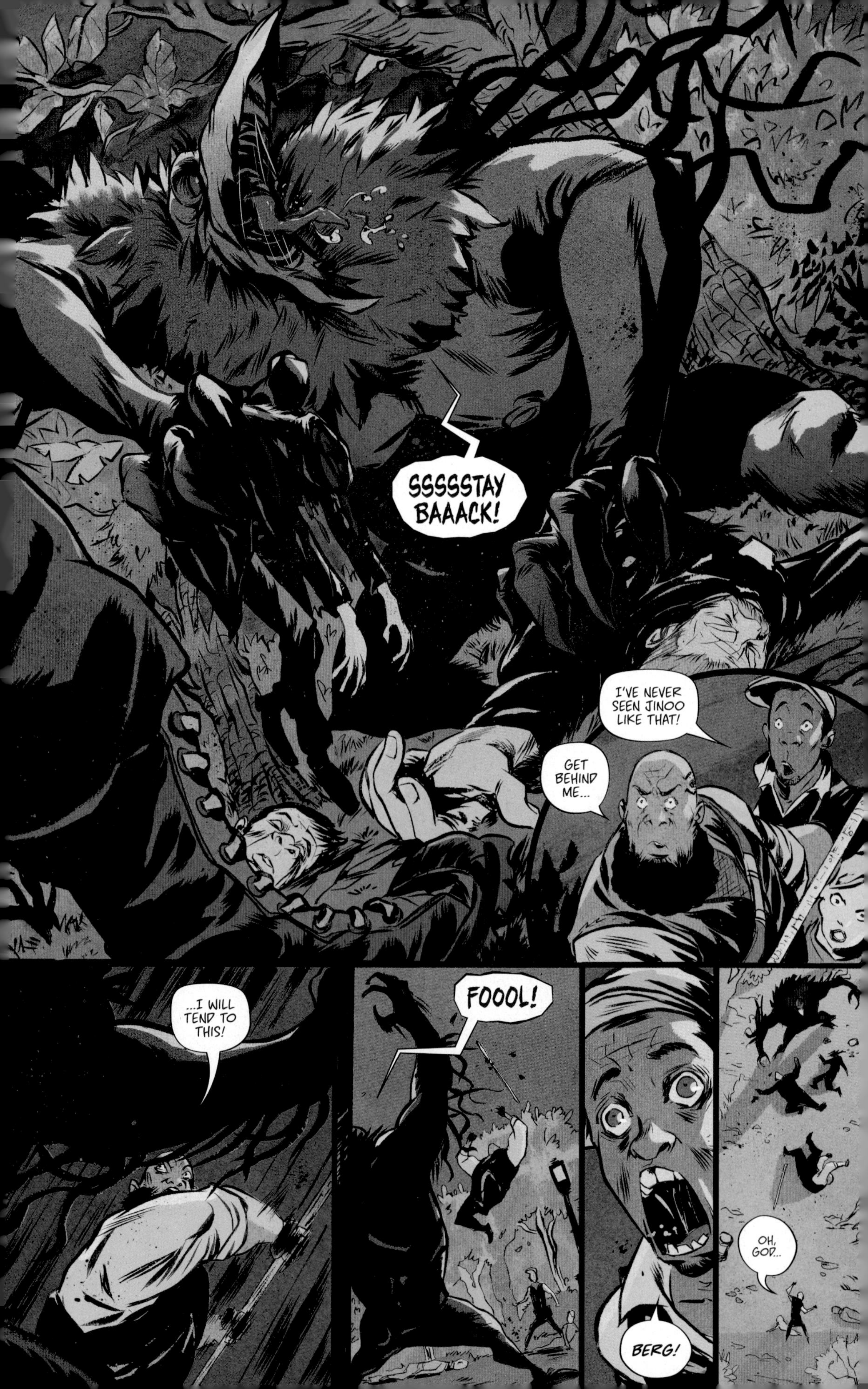
SSSSSTAY BAAACK!
I'VE NEVER SEEN JINOO LIKE THAT!
GET BEHIND ME...
...I WILL TEND TO THIS!
FOOOL!
BERG!
OH, GOD...

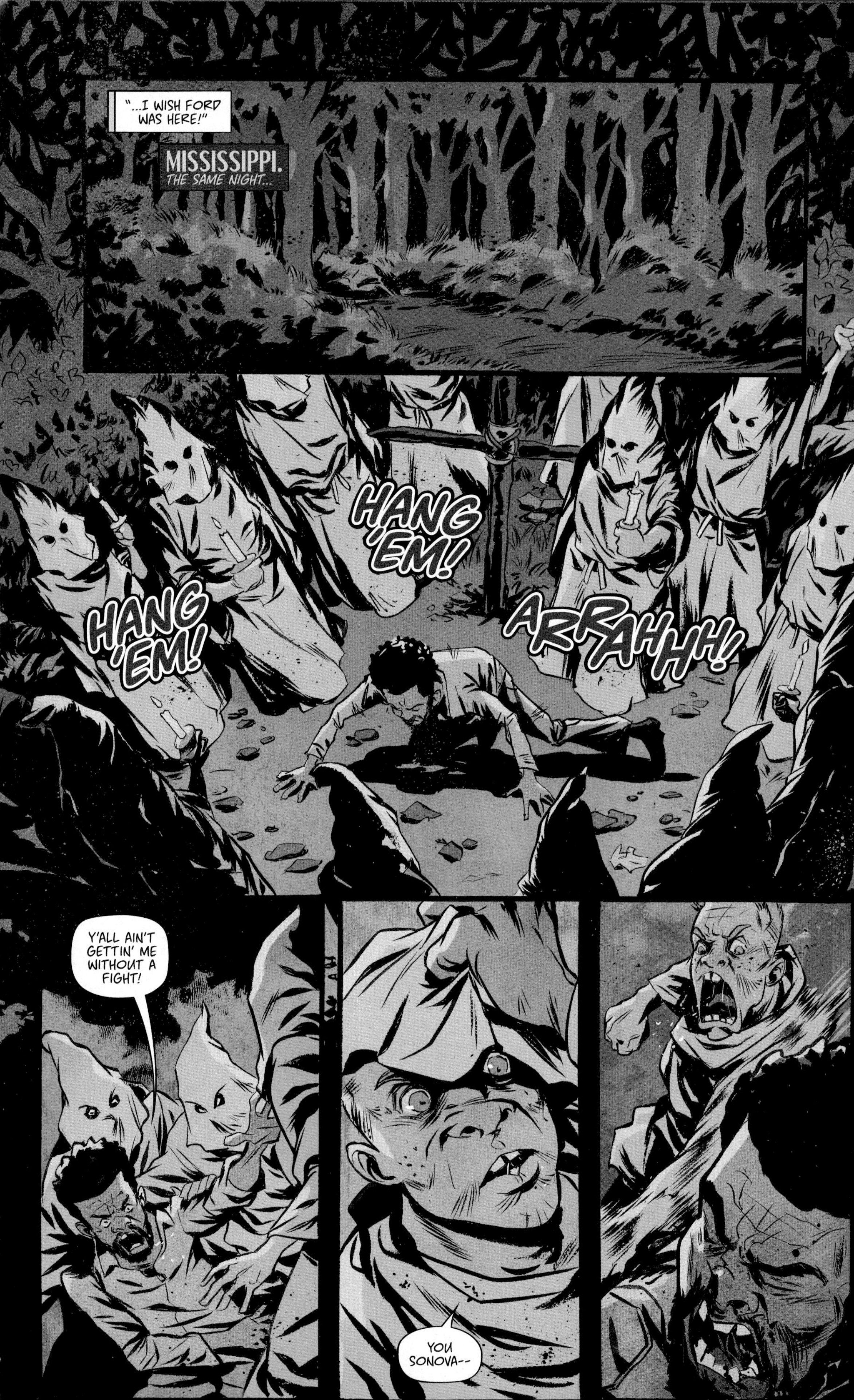
"...I WISH FORD WAS HERE!"
MISSISSIPPI.
THE SAME NIGHT...
HANG 'EM!
HANG 'EM!
ARRAHHH!
Y'ALL AIN'T GETTIN' ME WITHOUT A FIGHT!
YOU SONOVA--

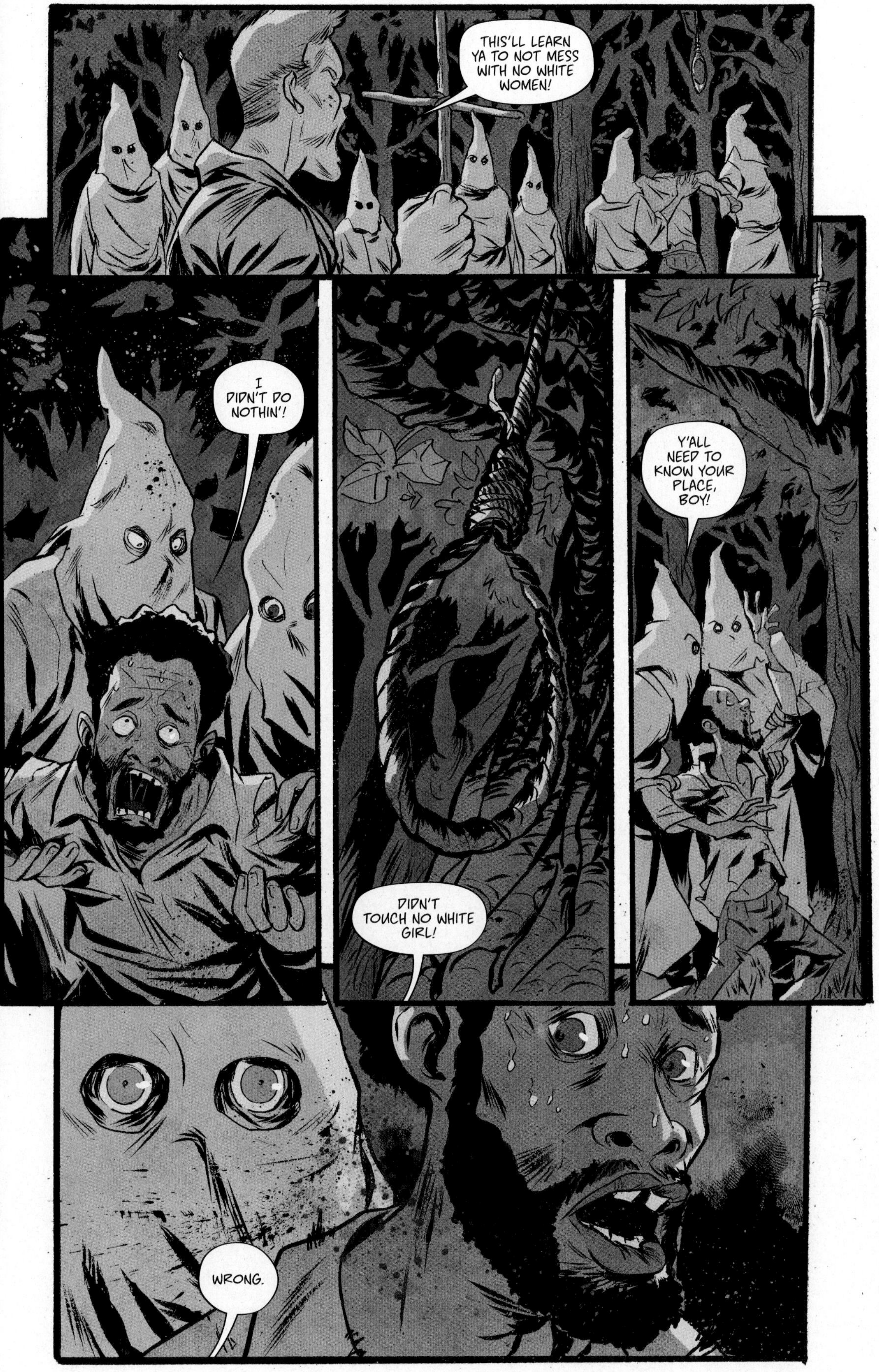
THIS'LL LEARN YA TO NOT MESS WITH NO WHITE WOMEN!
I DIDN'T DO NOTHIN'!
DIDN'T TOUCH NO WHITE GIRL!
Y'ALL NEED TO KNOW YOUR PLACE, BOY!
WRONG.

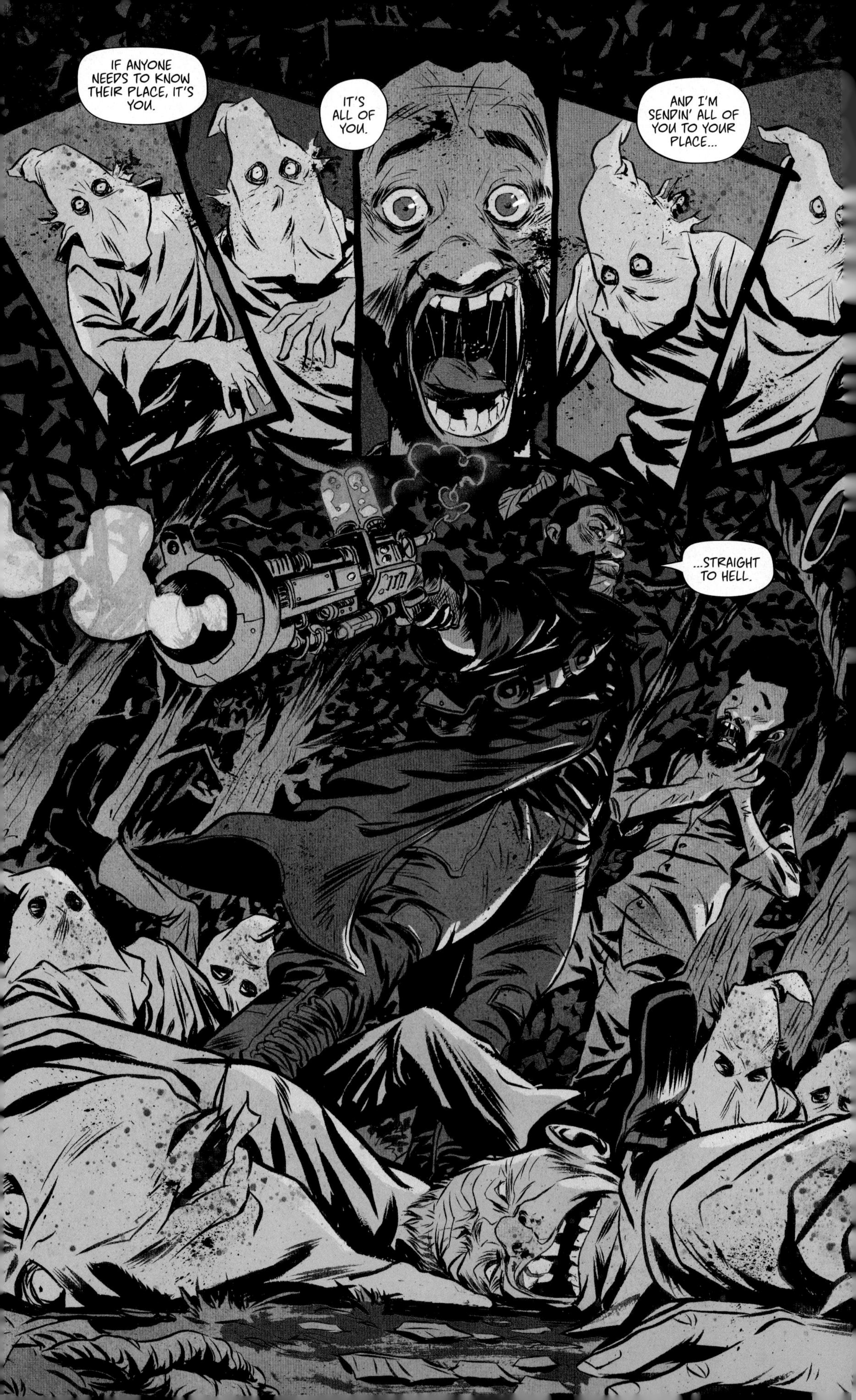
IF ANYONE NEEDS TO KNOW THEIR PLACE, IT'S YOU.
IT'S ALL OF YOU.
AND I'M SENDIN' ALL OF YOU TO YOUR PLACE...
...STRAIGHT TO HELL.

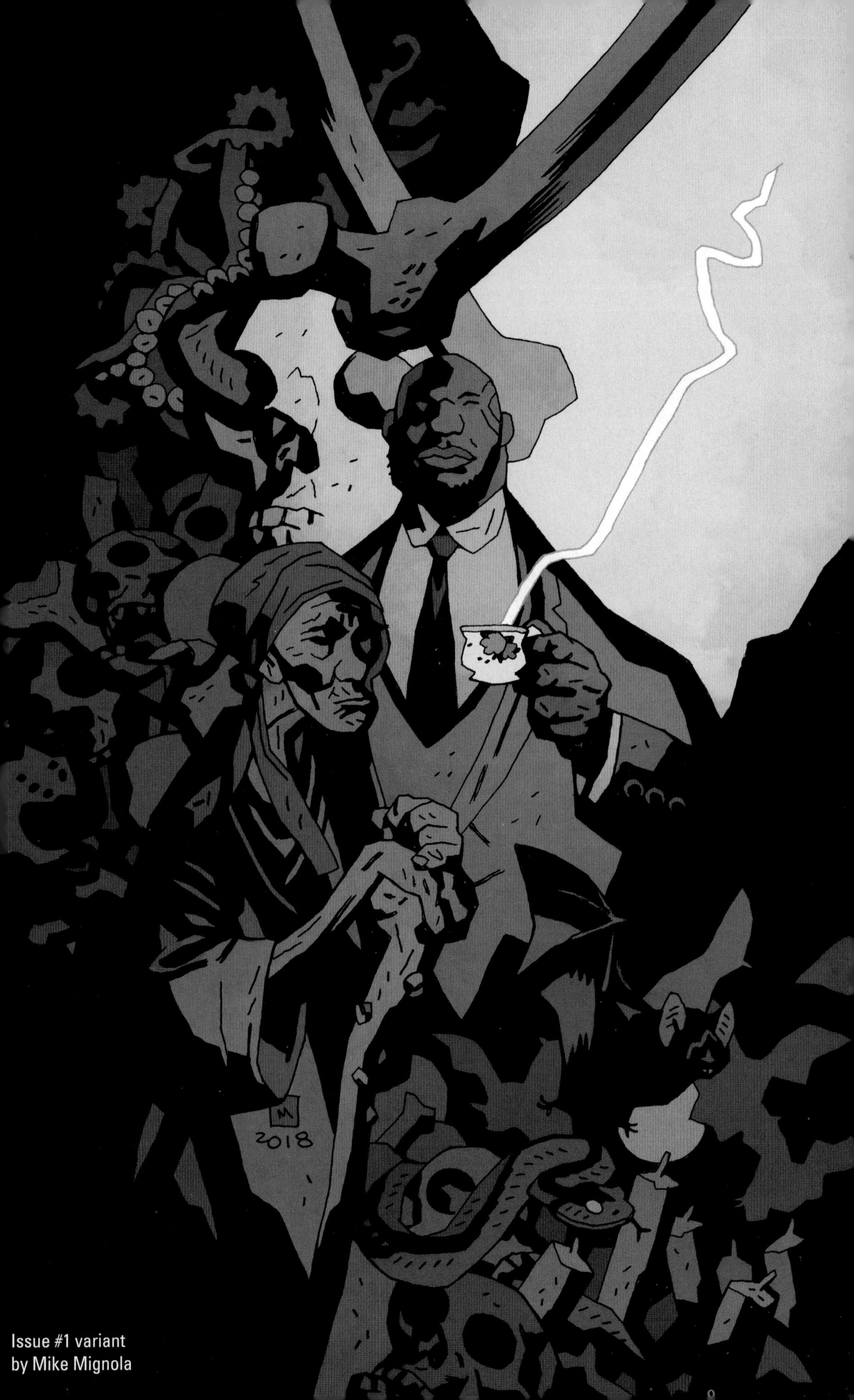
M
2018
Issue #1 variant
by Mike Mignola

CHAPTER TWO

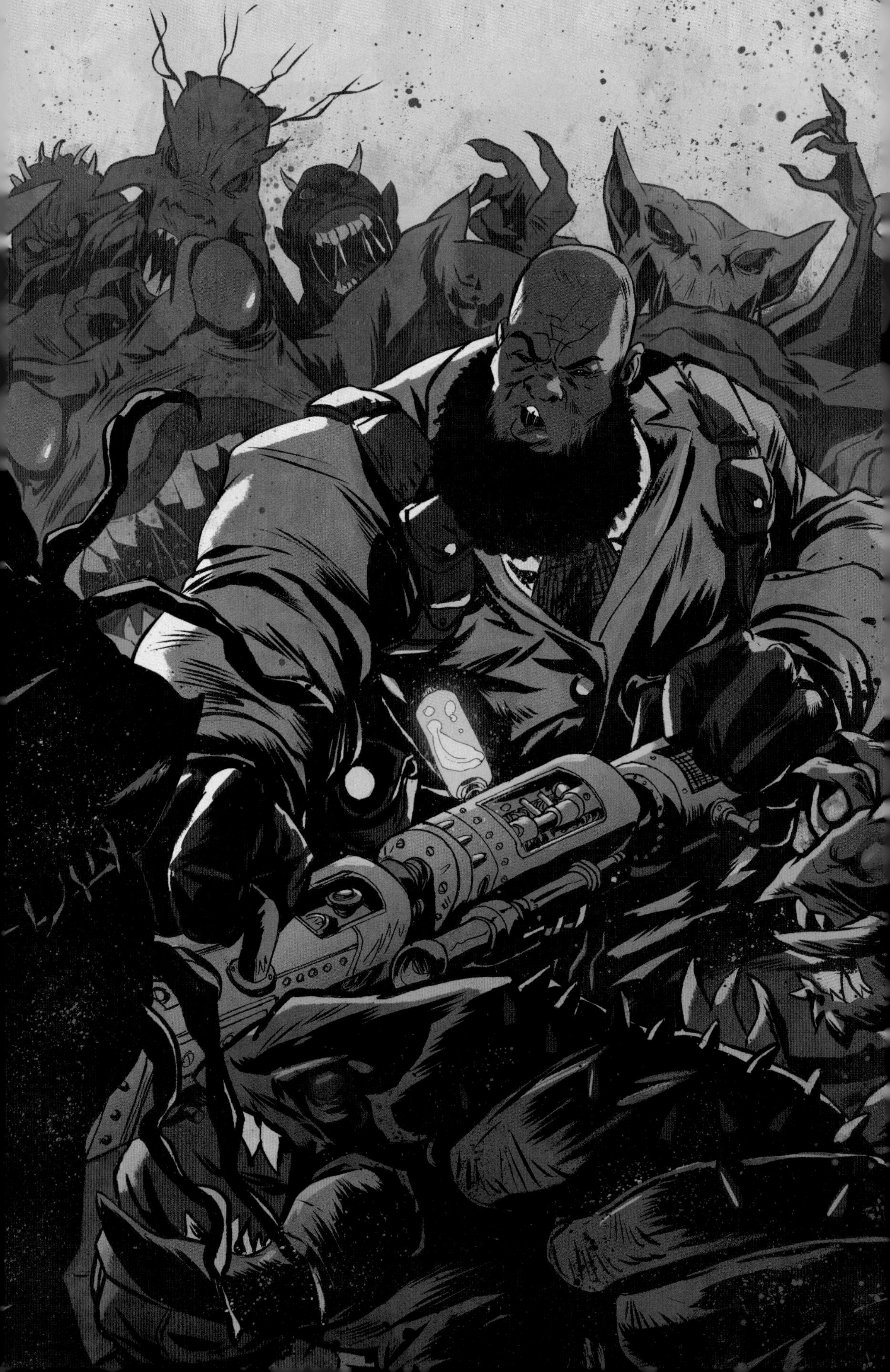

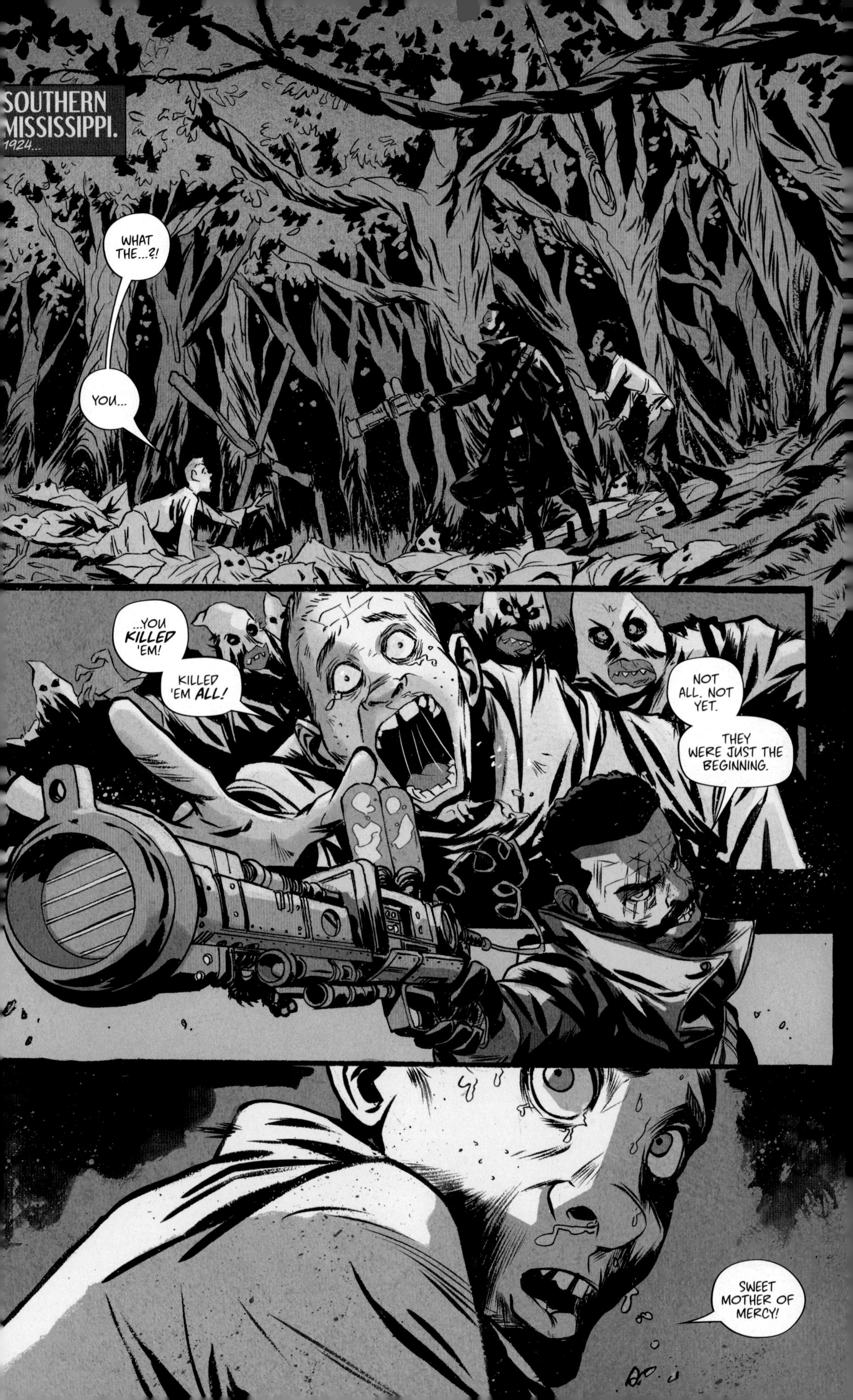
SOUTHERN MISSISSIPPI.
1924...
WHAT THE...?!
YOU...
...YOU KILLED 'EM!
KILLED 'EM ALL!
NOT ALL. NOT YET.
THEY WERE JUST THE BEGINNING.
SWEET MOTHER OF MERCY!

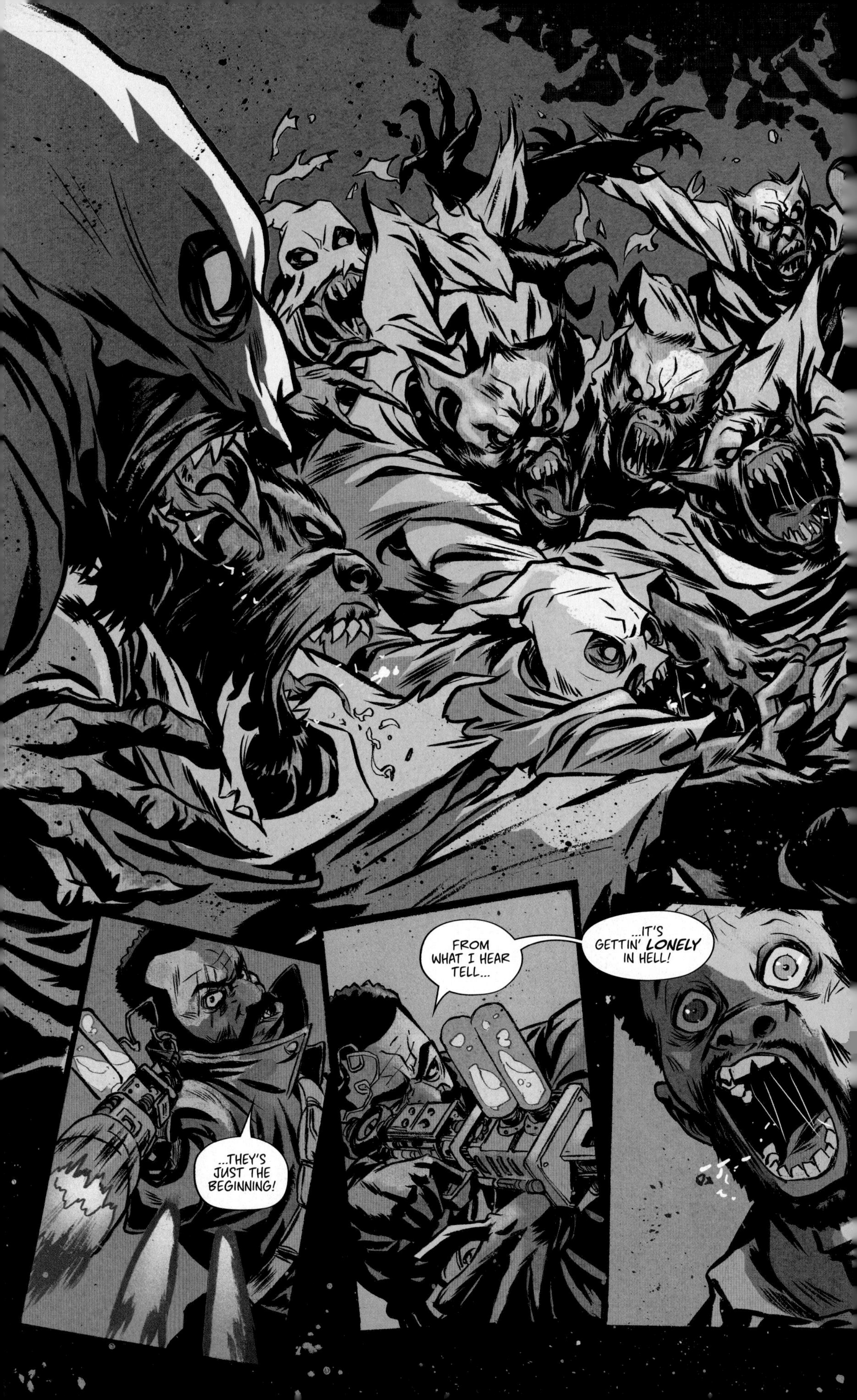
...THEY'S JUST THE BEGINNING!
FROM WHAT I HEAR TELL...
...IT'S GETTIN' LONELY IN HELL!

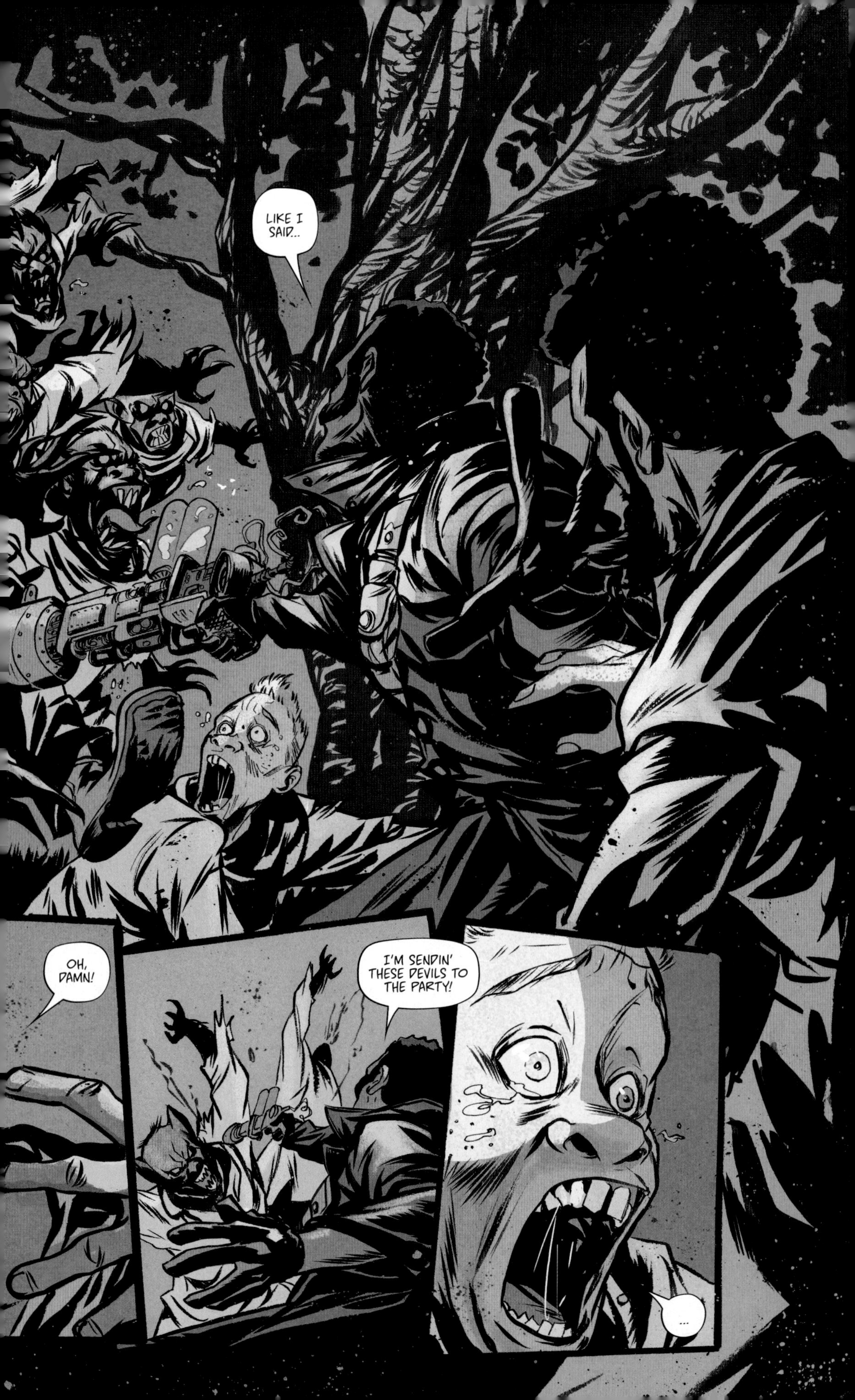
LIKE I SAID...
OH, DAMN!
I'M SENDIN' THESE DEVILS TO THE PARTY!
...

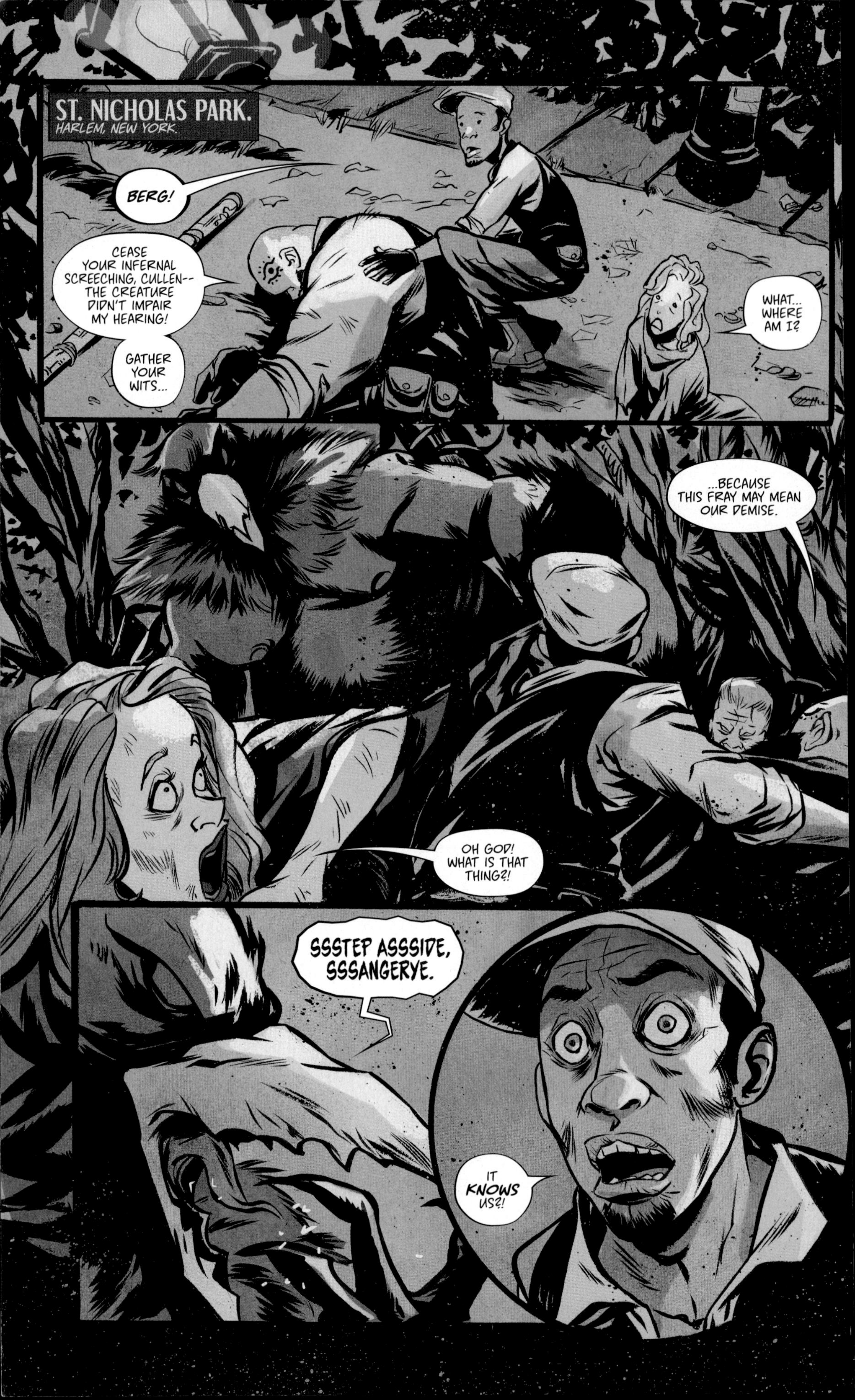
ST. NICHOLAS PARK.
HARLEM, NEW YORK.
BERG!
CEASE YOUR INFERNAL SCREECHING, CULLEN-- THE CREATURE DIDN'T IMPAIR MY HEARING!
GATHER YOUR WITS...
WHAT... WHERE AM I?
...BECAUSE THIS FRAY MAY MEAN OUR DEMISE.
OH GOD! WHAT IS THAT THING?!
SSSTEP ASSSIDE, SSSANGERYE.
IT KNOWS US?!

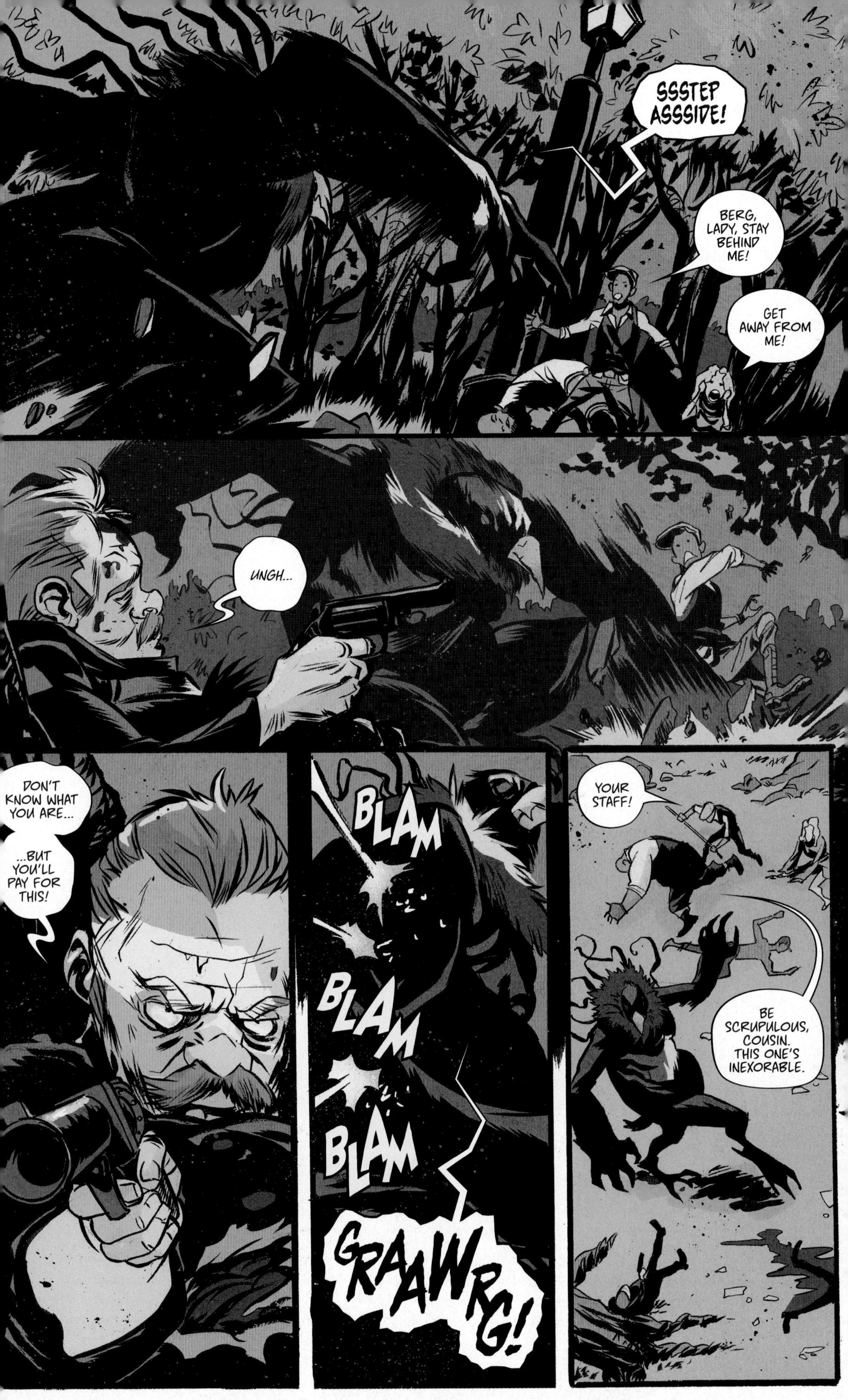
SSSTEP ASSSIDE!
BERG, LADY, STAY BEHIND ME!
GET AWAY FROM ME!
UNGH...
DON'T KNOW WHAT YOU ARE...
...BUT YOU'LL PAY FOR THIS!
BLAM
BLAM
BLAM
GRAAWRG!
YOUR STAFF!
BE SCRUPULOUS, COUSIN. THIS ONE'S INEXORABLE.

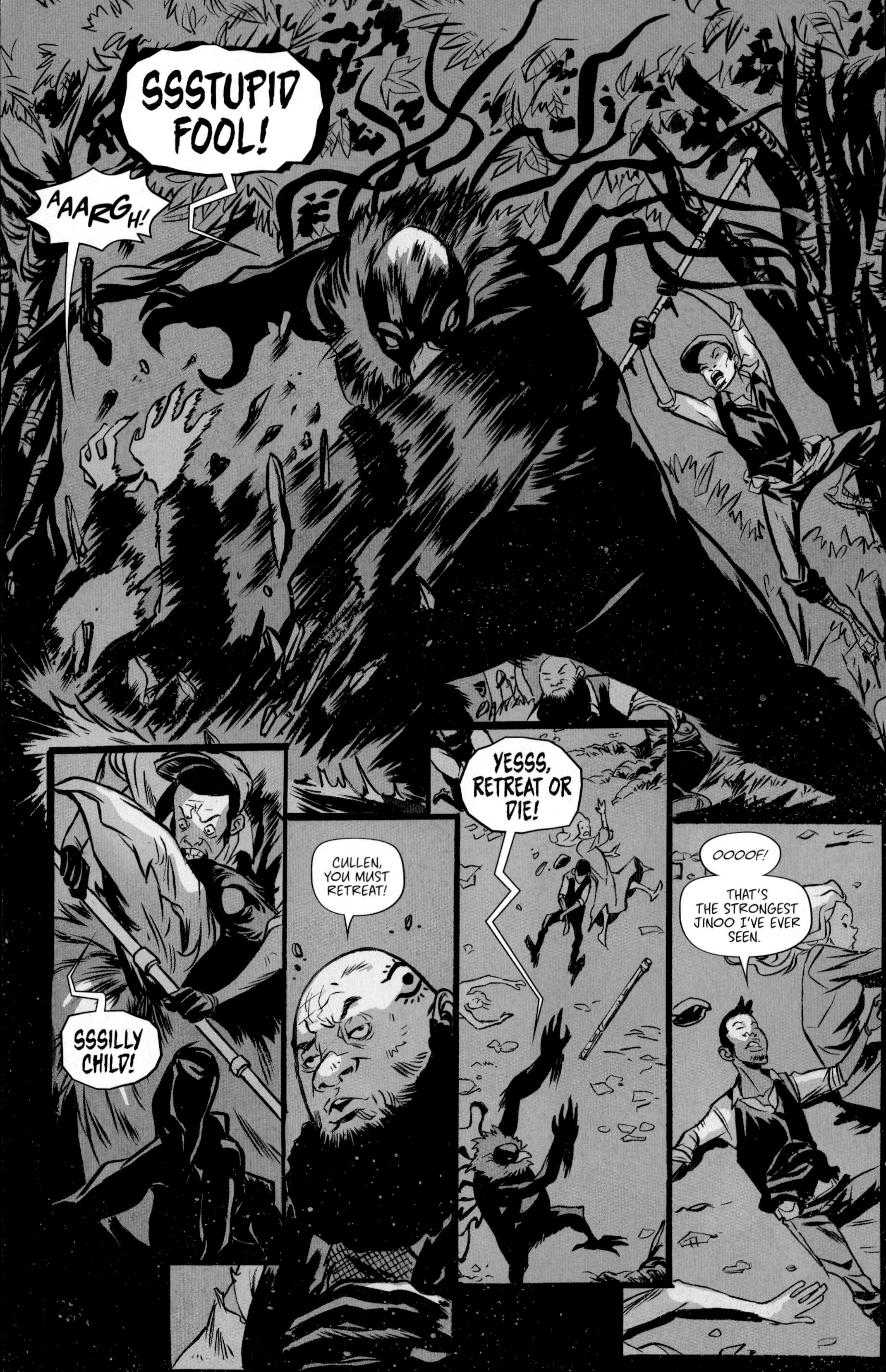
SSSTUPID FOOL!
AAARGH!
SSSILLY CHILD!
CULLEN, YOU MUST RETREAT!
YESSS, RETREAT OR DIE!
OOOOF!
THAT'S THE STRONGEST JINOO I'VE EVER SEEN.

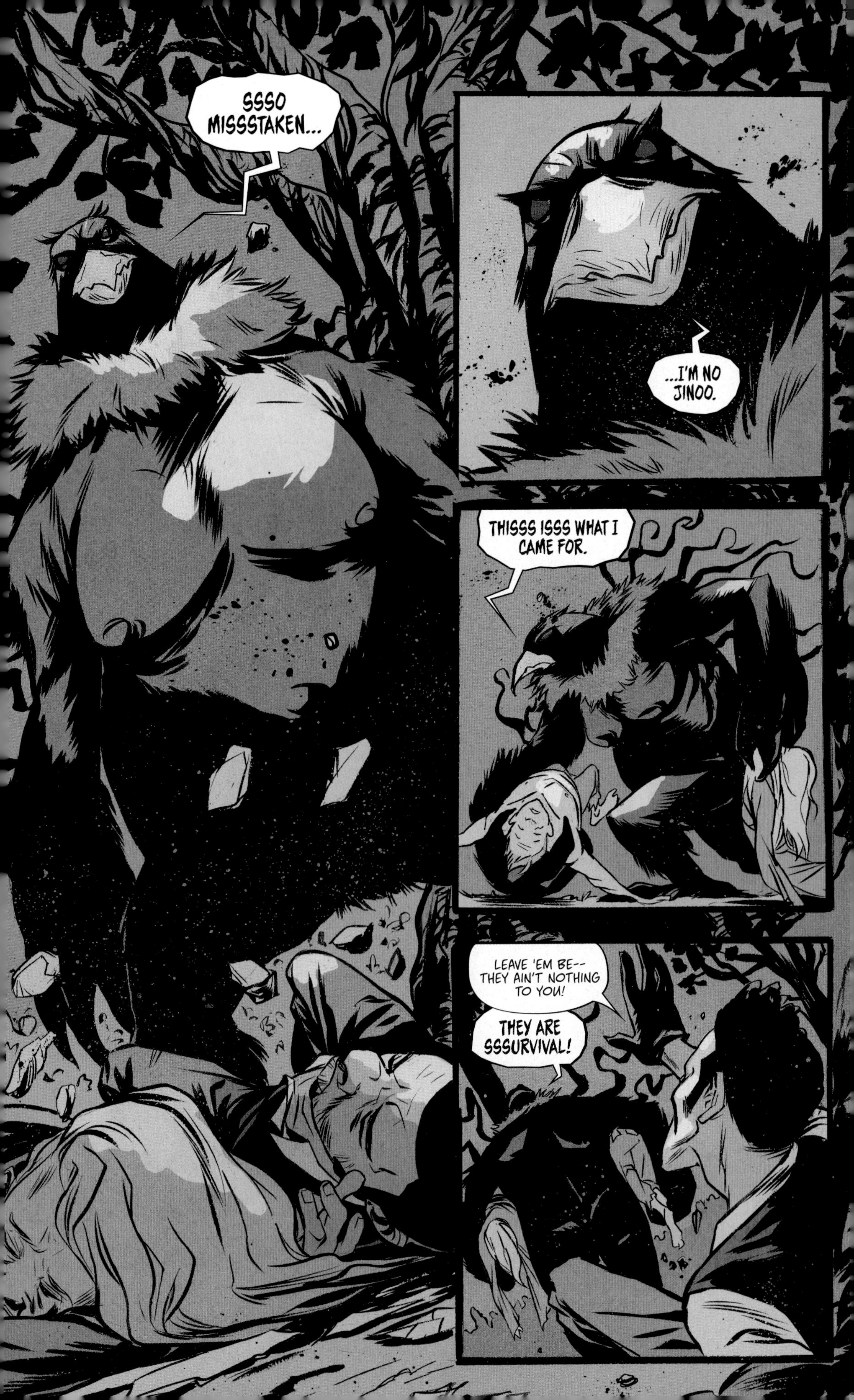
SSSO MISSSTAKEN...
...I'M NO JINOO.
THISSS ISSS WHAT I CAME FOR.
LEAVE 'EM BE-- THEY AIN'T NOTHING TO YOU!
THEY ARE SSSURVIVAL!

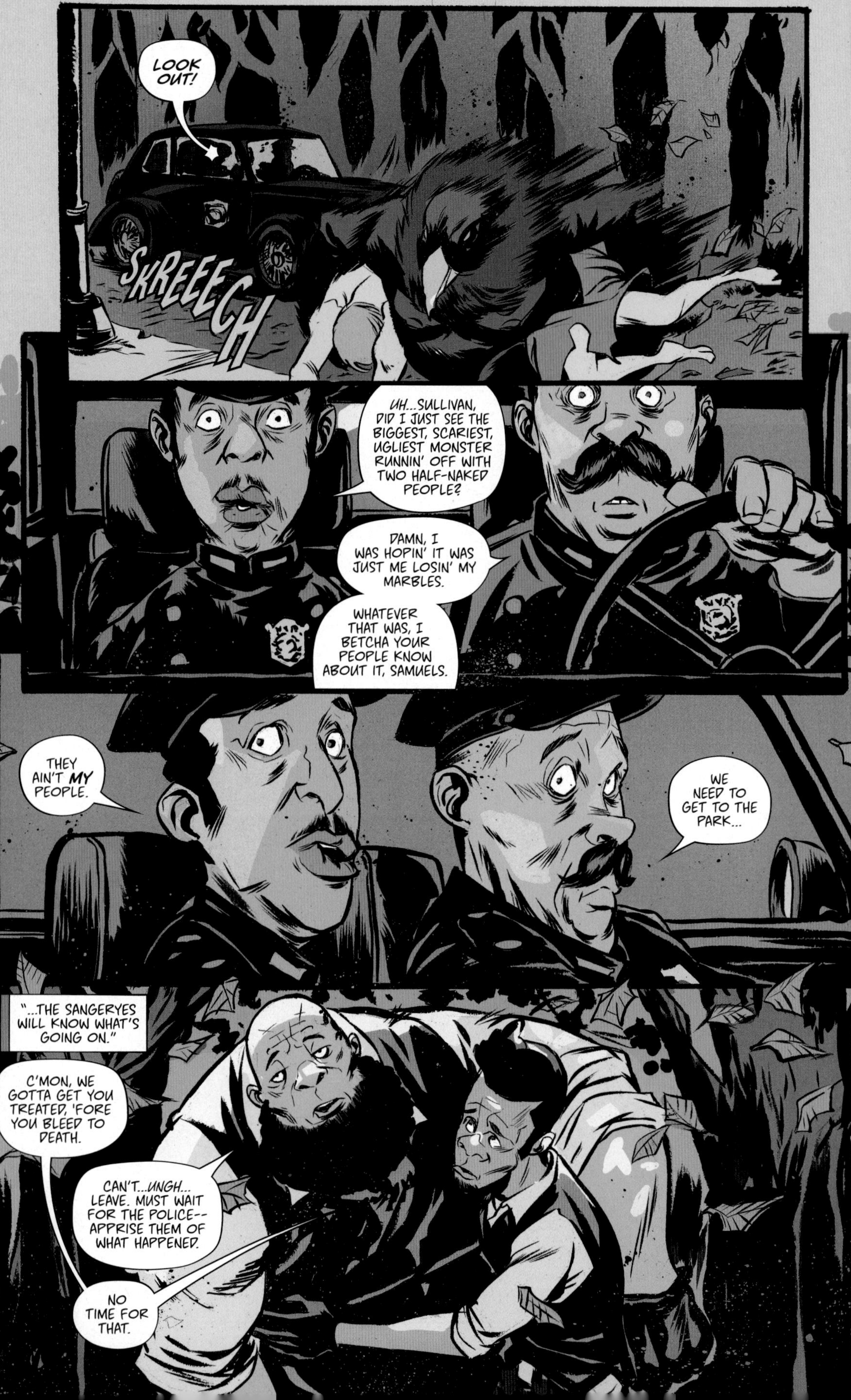
LOOK OUT!
SKREEECH
UH...SULLIVAN, DID I JUST SEE THE BIGGEST, SCARIEST, UGLIEST MONSTER RUNNIN' OFF WITH TWO HALF-NAKED PEOPLE?
DAMN, I WAS HOPIN' IT WAS JUST ME LOSIN' MY MARBLES.
WHATEVER THAT WAS, I BETCHA YOUR PEOPLE KNOW ABOUT IT, SAMUELS.
THEY AIN'T MY PEOPLE.
WE NEED TO GET TO THE PARK...
"...THE SANGERYES WILL KNOW WHAT'S GOING ON."
C'MON, WE GOTTA GET YOU TREATED, 'FORE YOU BLEED TO DEATH.
CAN'T...UNGH... LEAVE. MUST WAIT FOR THE POLICE-- APPRISE THEM OF WHAT HAPPENED.
NO TIME FOR THAT.

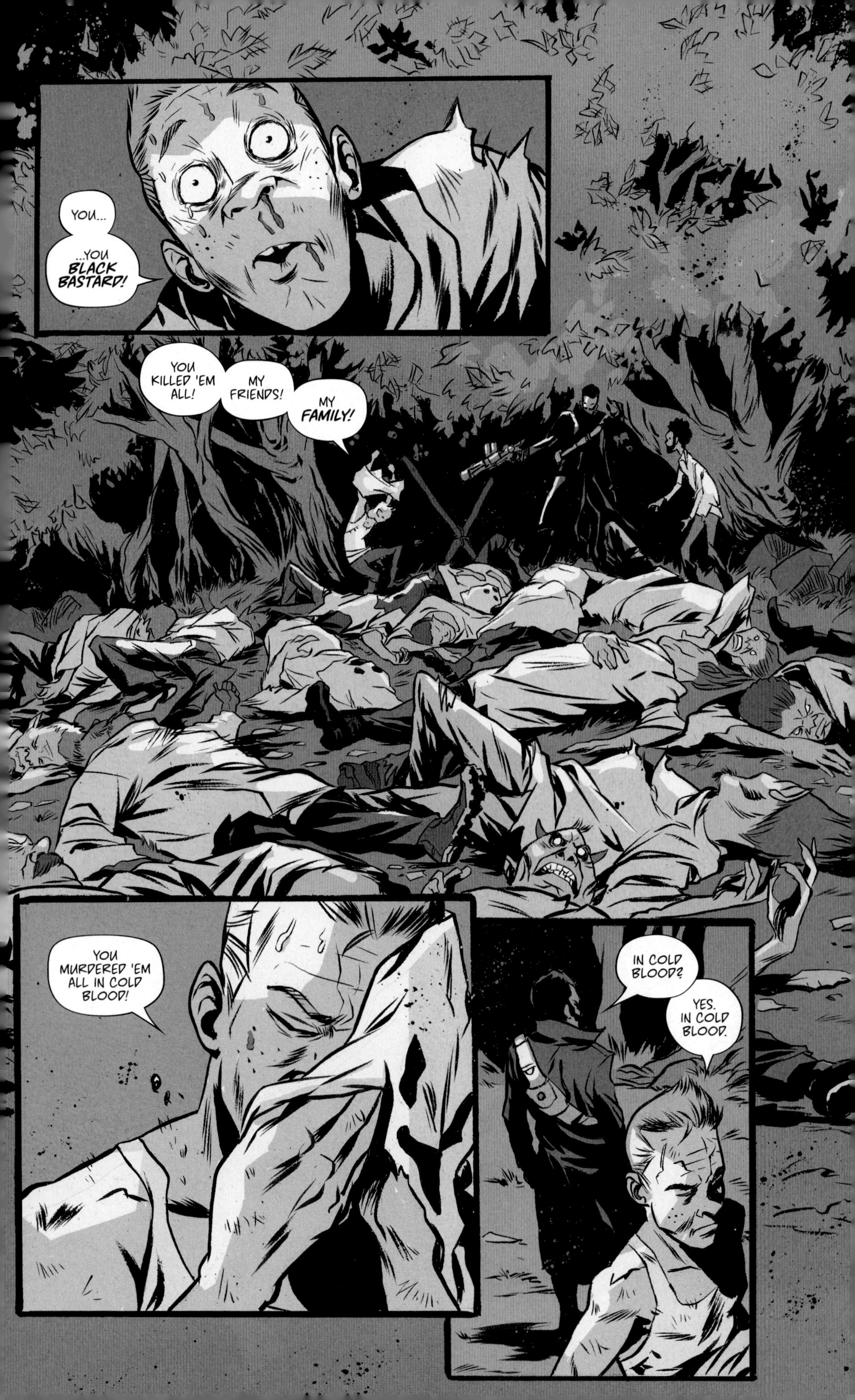
YOU...
...YOU BLACK BASTARD!
YOU KILLED 'EM ALL!
MY FRIENDS!
MY FAMILY!
YOU MURDERED 'EM ALL IN COLD BLOOD!
IN COLD BLOOD?
YES. IN COLD BLOOD.

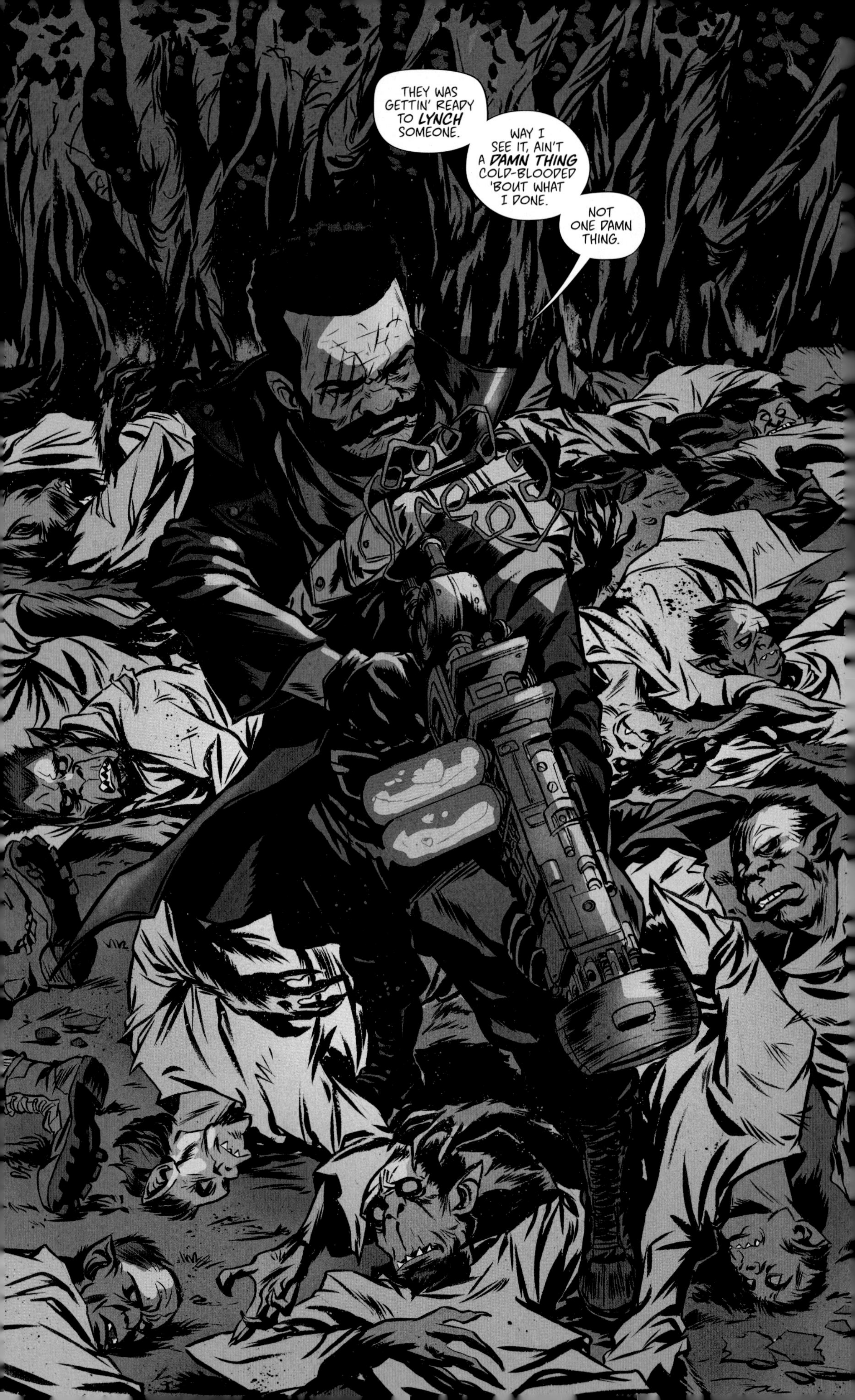
THEY WAS GETTIN' READY TO LYNCH SOMEONE.
WAY I SEE IT, AIN'T A DAMN THING COLD-BLOODED 'BOUT WHAT I DONE.
NOT ONE DAMN THING.

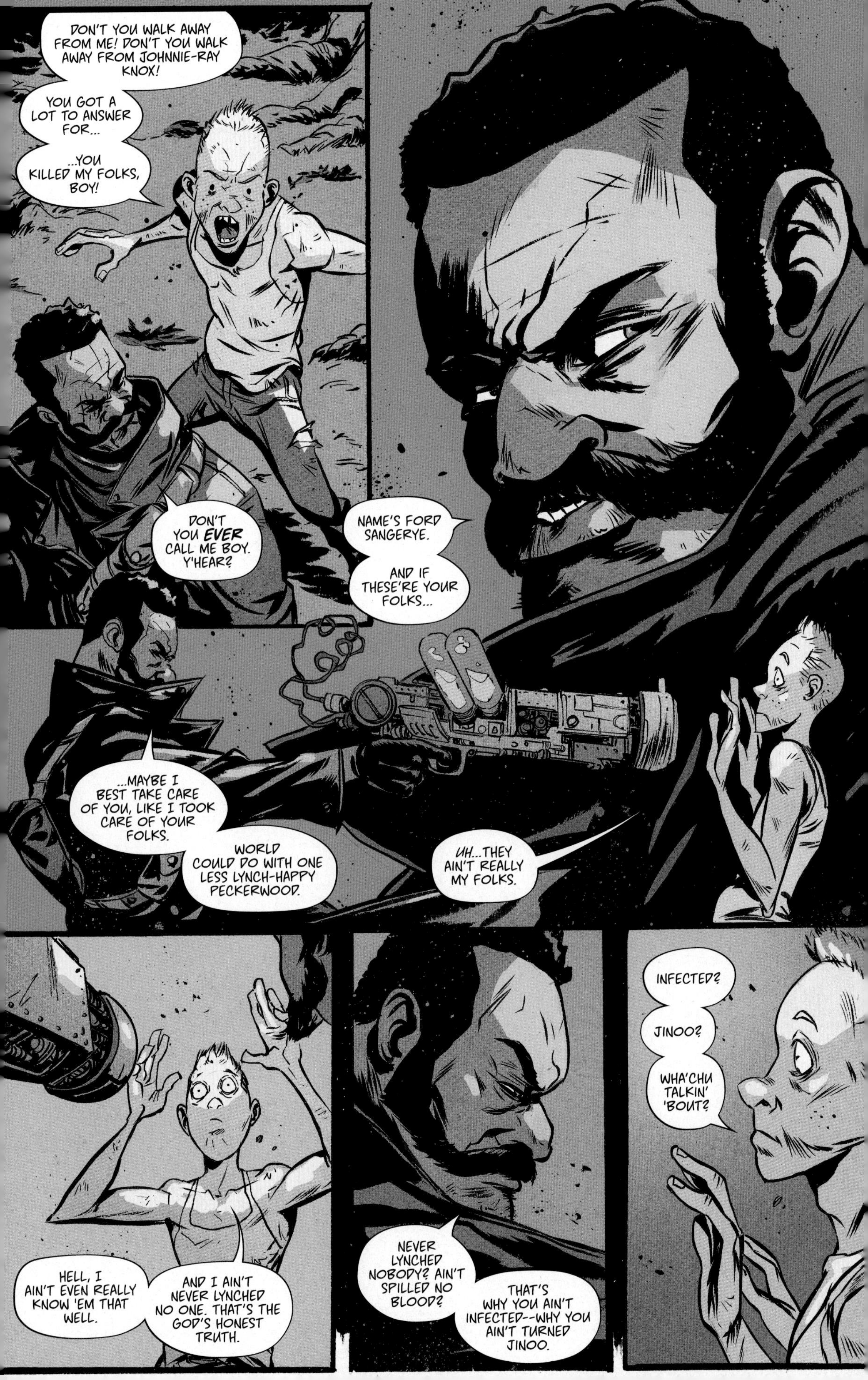
DON'T YOU WALK AWAY FROM ME! DON'T YOU WALK AWAY FROM JOHNNIE-RAY KNOX!
YOU GOT A LOT TO ANSWER FOR...
...YOU KILLED MY FOLKS, BOY!
DON'T YOU **EVER** CALL ME BOY. Y'HEAR?
NAME'S FORD SANGERYE.
AND IF THESE'RE YOUR FOLKS...
...MAYBE I BEST TAKE CARE OF YOU, LIKE I TOOK CARE OF YOUR FOLKS.
WORLD COULD DO WITH ONE LESS LYNCH-HAPPY PECKERWOOD.
UH...THEY AIN'T REALLY MY FOLKS.
HELL, I AIN'T EVEN REALLY KNOW 'EM THAT WELL.
AND I AIN'T NEVER LYNCHED NO ONE. THAT'S THE GOD'S HONEST TRUTH.
NEVER LYNCHED NOBODY? AIN'T SPILLED NO BLOOD?
THAT'S WHY YOU AIN'T INFECTED--WHY YOU AIN'T TURNED JINOO.
INFECTED?
JINOO?
WHA'CHU TALKIN' 'BOUT?

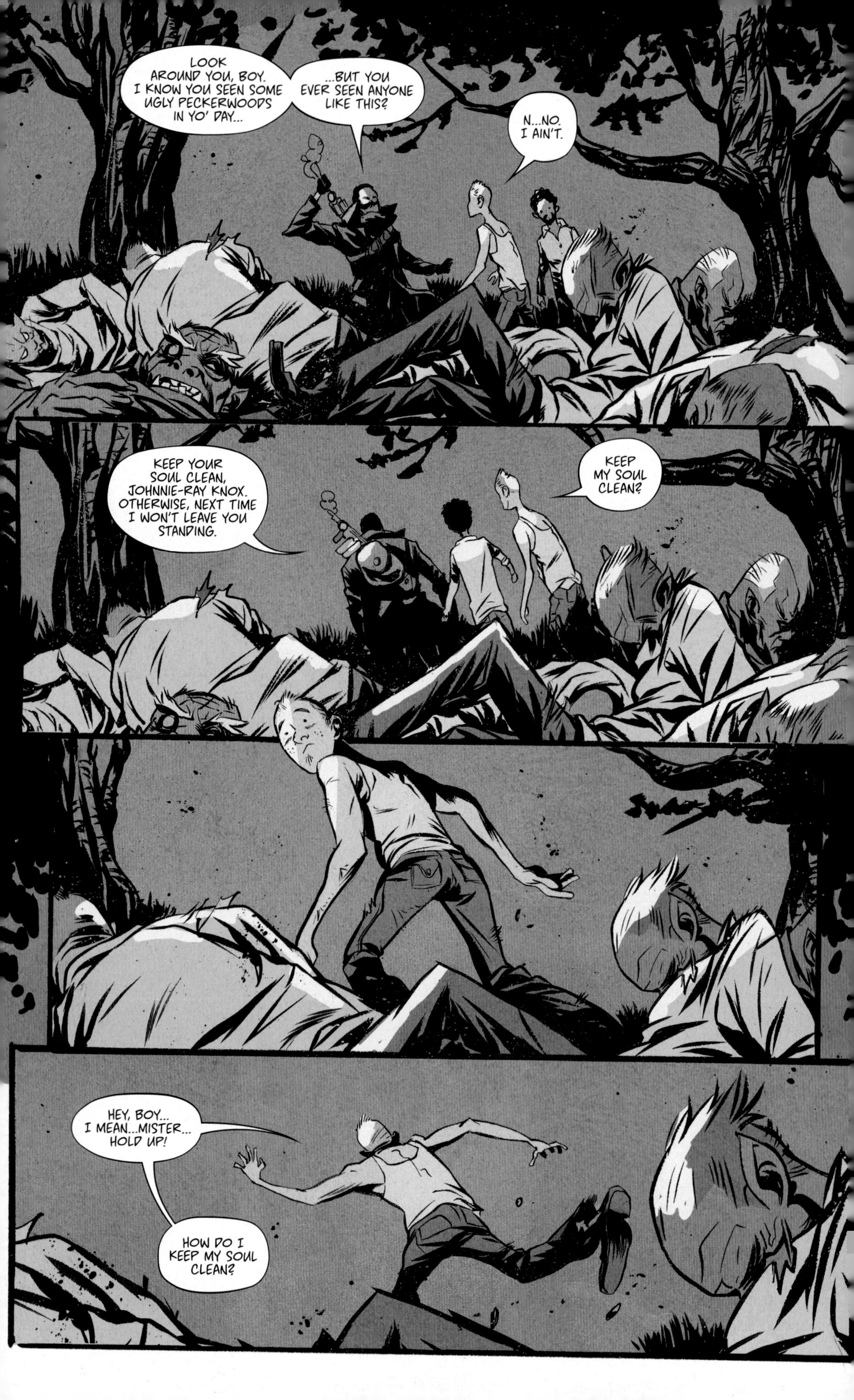
LOOK AROUND YOU, BOY. I KNOW YOU SEEN SOME UGLY PECKERWOODS IN YO' DAY...
...BUT YOU EVER SEEN ANYONE LIKE THIS?
N...NO. I AIN'T.
KEEP YOUR SOUL CLEAN, JOHNNIE-RAY KNOX. OTHERWISE, NEXT TIME I WON'T LEAVE YOU STANDING.
KEEP MY SOUL CLEAN?
HEY, BOY... I MEAN...MISTER... HOLD UP!
HOW DO I KEEP MY SOUL CLEAN?

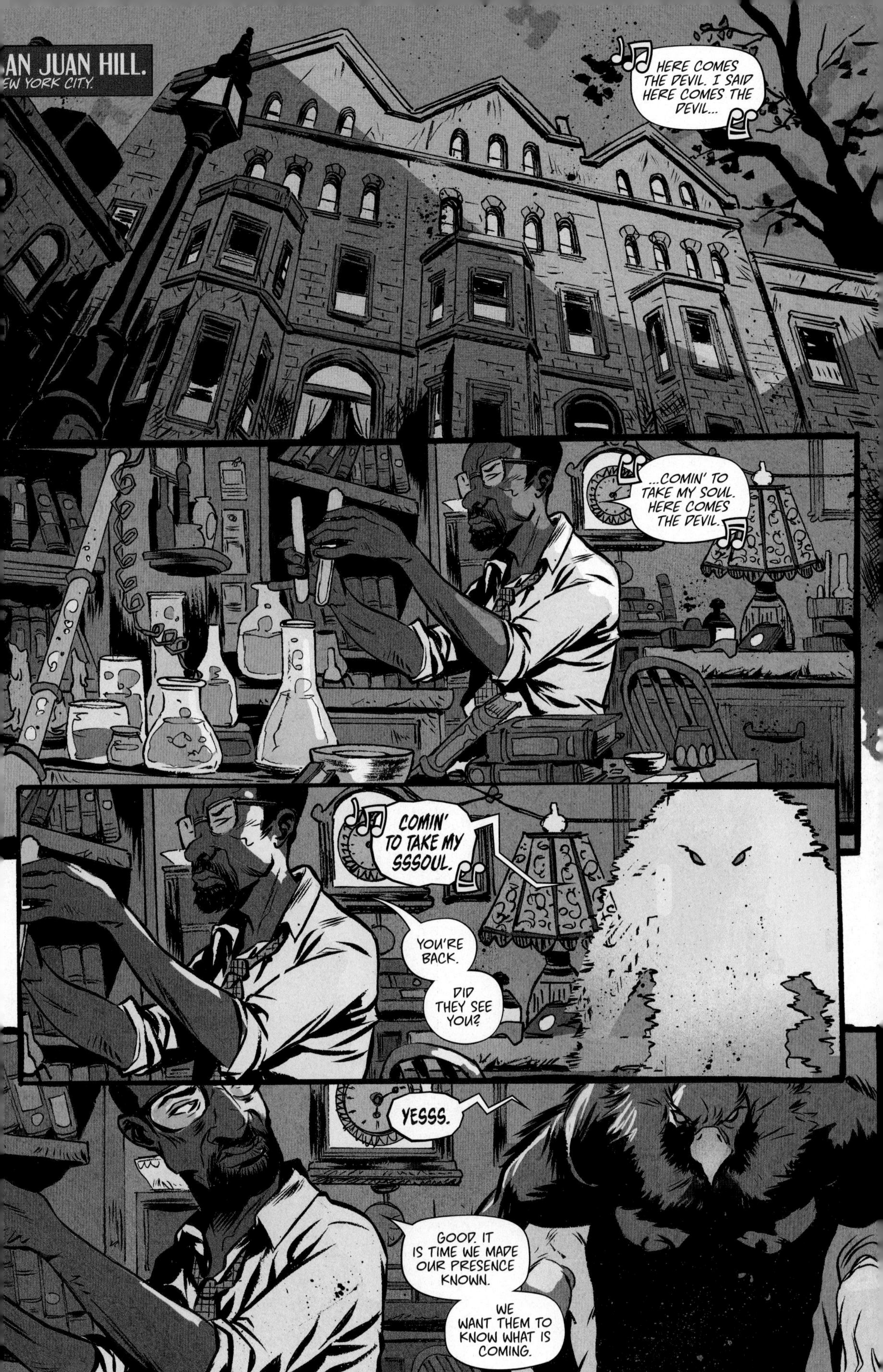
AN JUAN HILL.
EW YORK CITY.
HERE COMES THE DEVIL. I SAID HERE COMES THE DEVIL...
...COMIN' TO TAKE MY SOUL. HERE COMES THE DEVIL.
COMIN' TO TAKE MY SSSOUL.
YOU'RE BACK.
DID THEY SEE YOU?
YESSS.
GOOD. IT IS TIME WE MADE OUR PRESENCE KNOWN.
WE WANT THEM TO KNOW WHAT IS COMING.

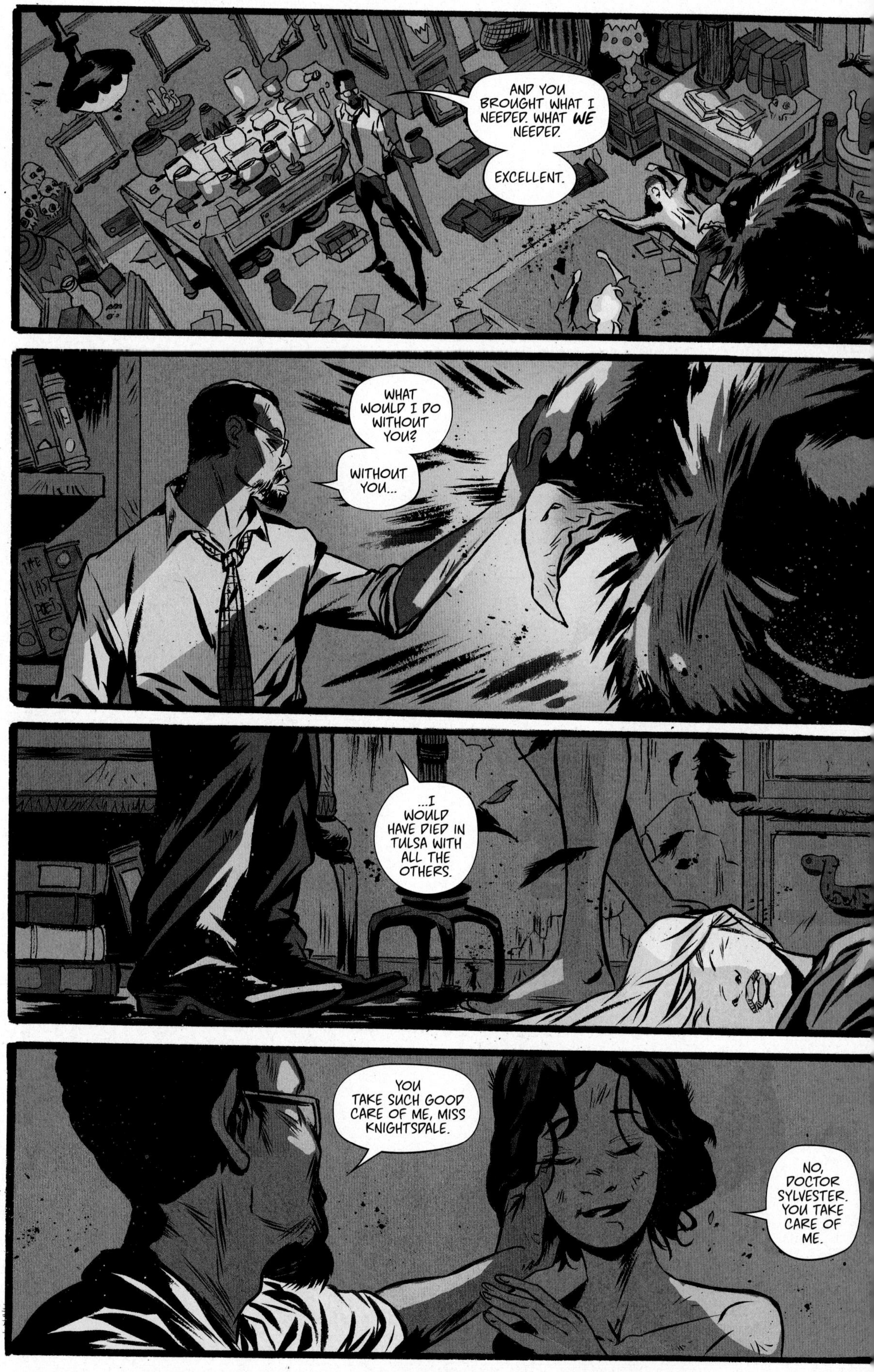
AND YOU BROUGHT WHAT I NEEDED. WHAT WE NEEDED.
EXCELLENT.
WHAT WOULD I DO WITHOUT YOU?
WITHOUT YOU...
...I WOULD HAVE DIED IN TULSA WITH ALL THE OTHERS.
YOU TAKE SUCH GOOD CARE OF ME, MISS KNIGHTSDALE.
NO, DOCTOR SYLVESTER. YOU TAKE CARE OF ME.

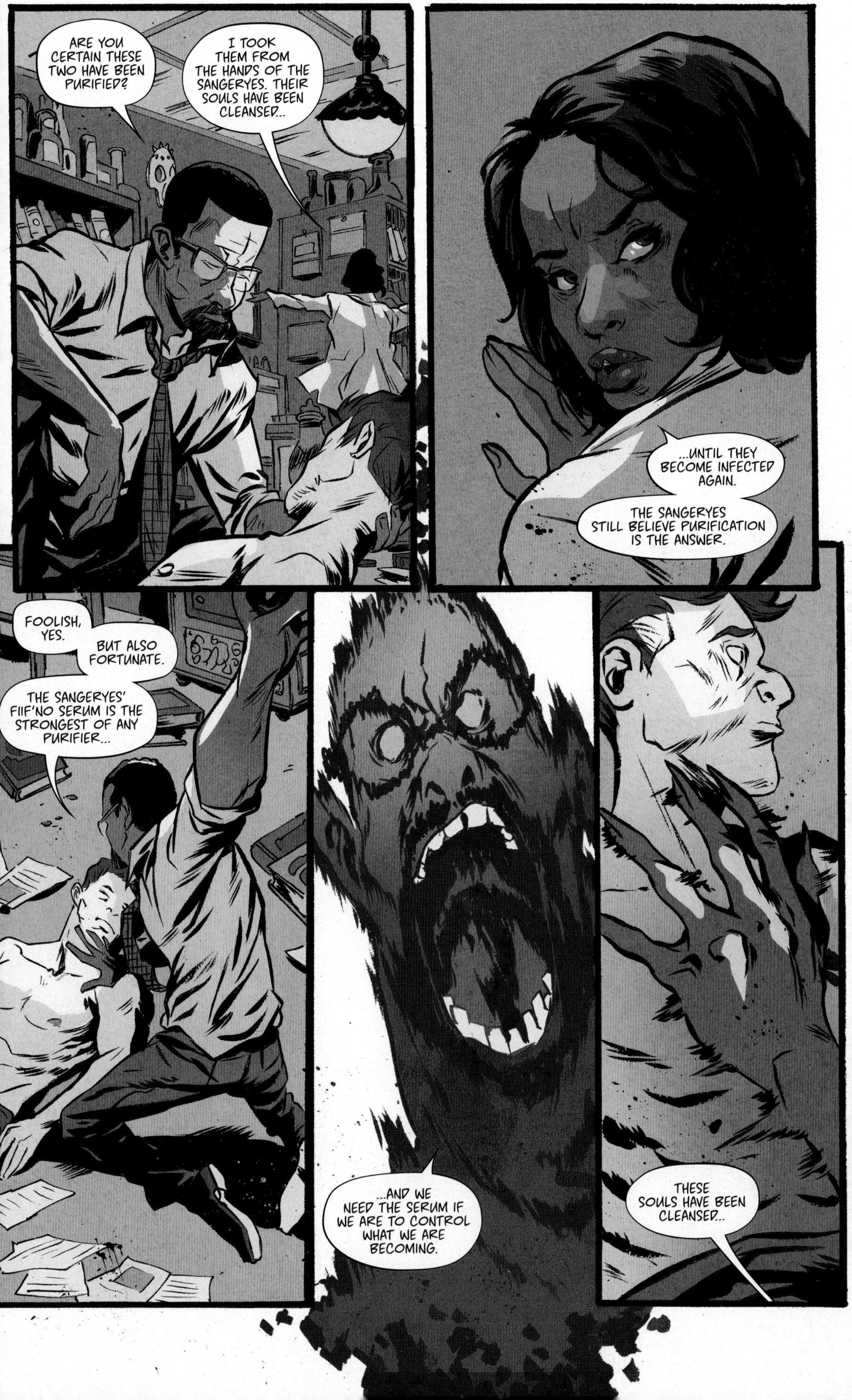
ARE YOU CERTAIN THESE TWO HAVE BEEN PURIFIED?
I TOOK THEM FROM THE HANDS OF THE SANGERYES. THEIR SOULS HAVE BEEN CLEANSED...
...UNTIL THEY BECOME INFECTED AGAIN.
THE SANGERYES STILL BELIEVE PURIFICATION IS THE ANSWER.
FOOLISH, YES.
BUT ALSO FORTUNATE.
THE SANGERYES' FIIF'NO SERUM IS THE STRONGEST OF ANY PURIFIER...
...AND WE NEED THE SERUM IF WE ARE TO CONTROL WHAT WE ARE BECOMING.
THESE SOULS HAVE BEEN CLEANSED...

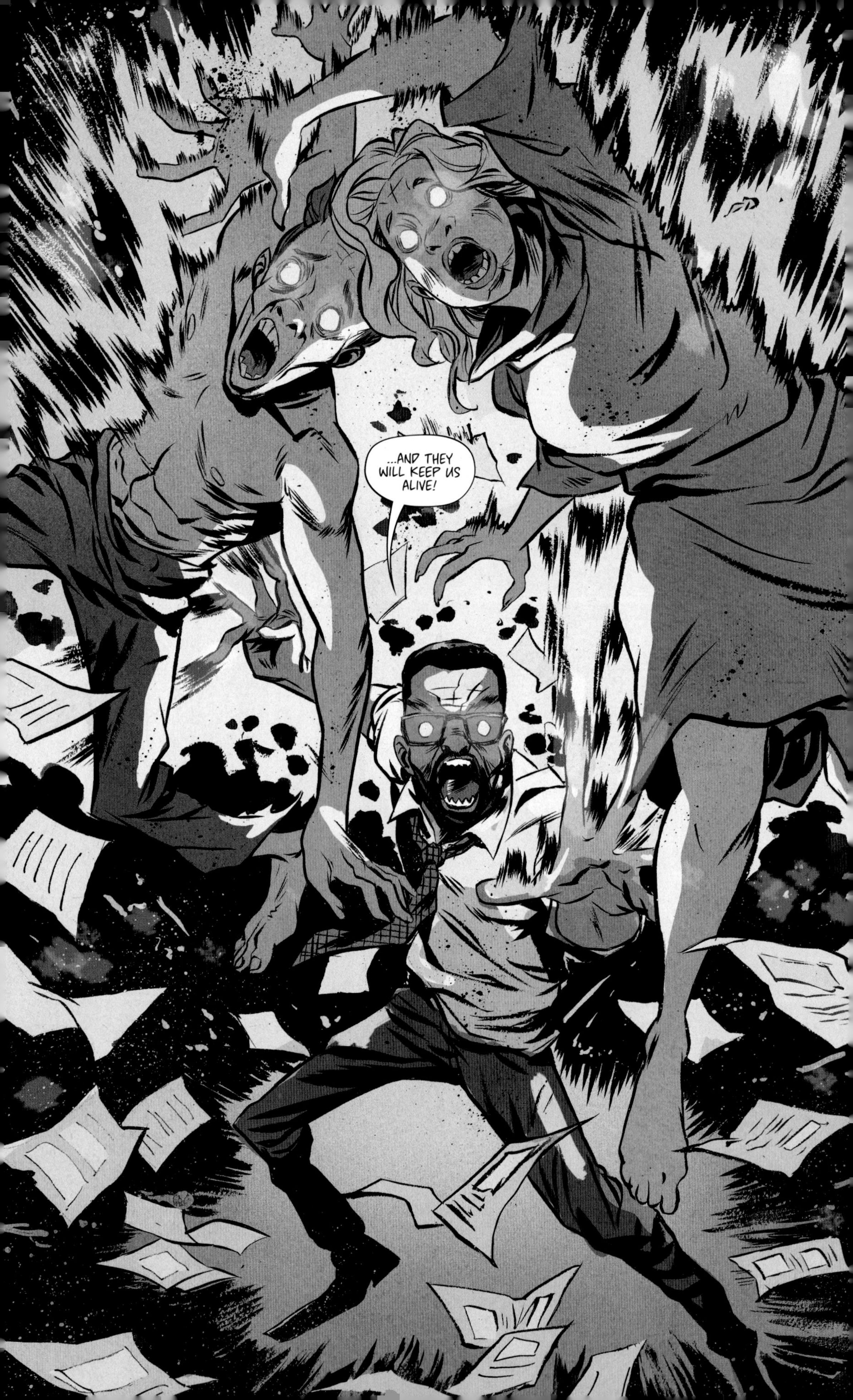
...AND THEY WILL KEEP US ALIVE!

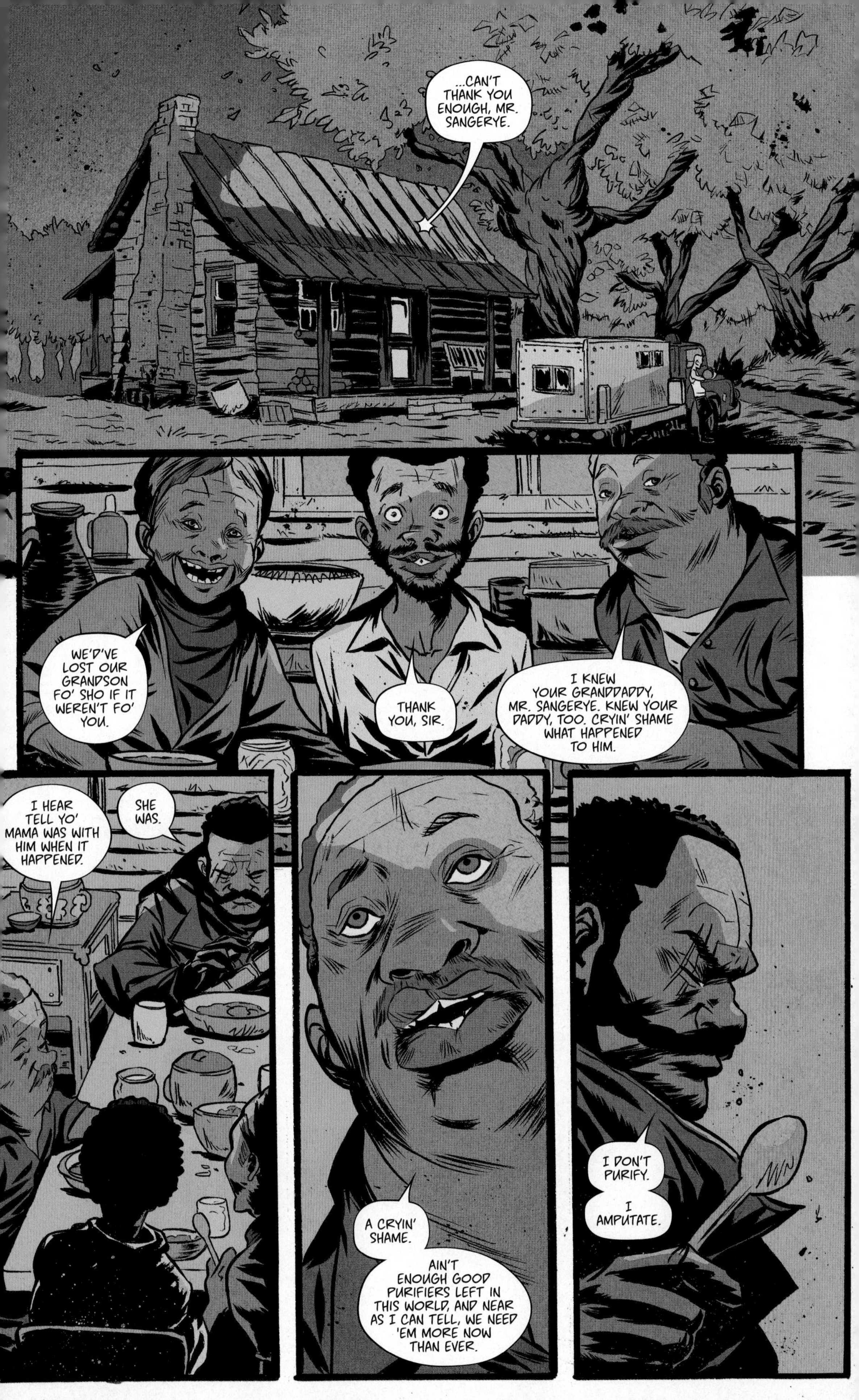
...CAN'T THANK YOU ENOUGH, MR. SANGERYE.
WE'D'VE LOST OUR GRANDSON FO' SHO IF IT WEREN'T FO' YOU.
THANK YOU, SIR.
I KNEW YOUR GRANDDADDY, MR. SANGERYE. KNEW YOUR DADDY, TOO. CRYIN' SHAME WHAT HAPPENED TO HIM.
I HEAR TELL YO' MAMA WAS WITH HIM WHEN IT HAPPENED.
SHE WAS.
A CRYIN' SHAME.
AIN'T ENOUGH GOOD PURIFIERS LEFT IN THIS WORLD, AND NEAR AS I CAN TELL, WE NEED 'EM MORE NOW THAN EVER.
I DON'T PURIFY.
I AMPUTATE.

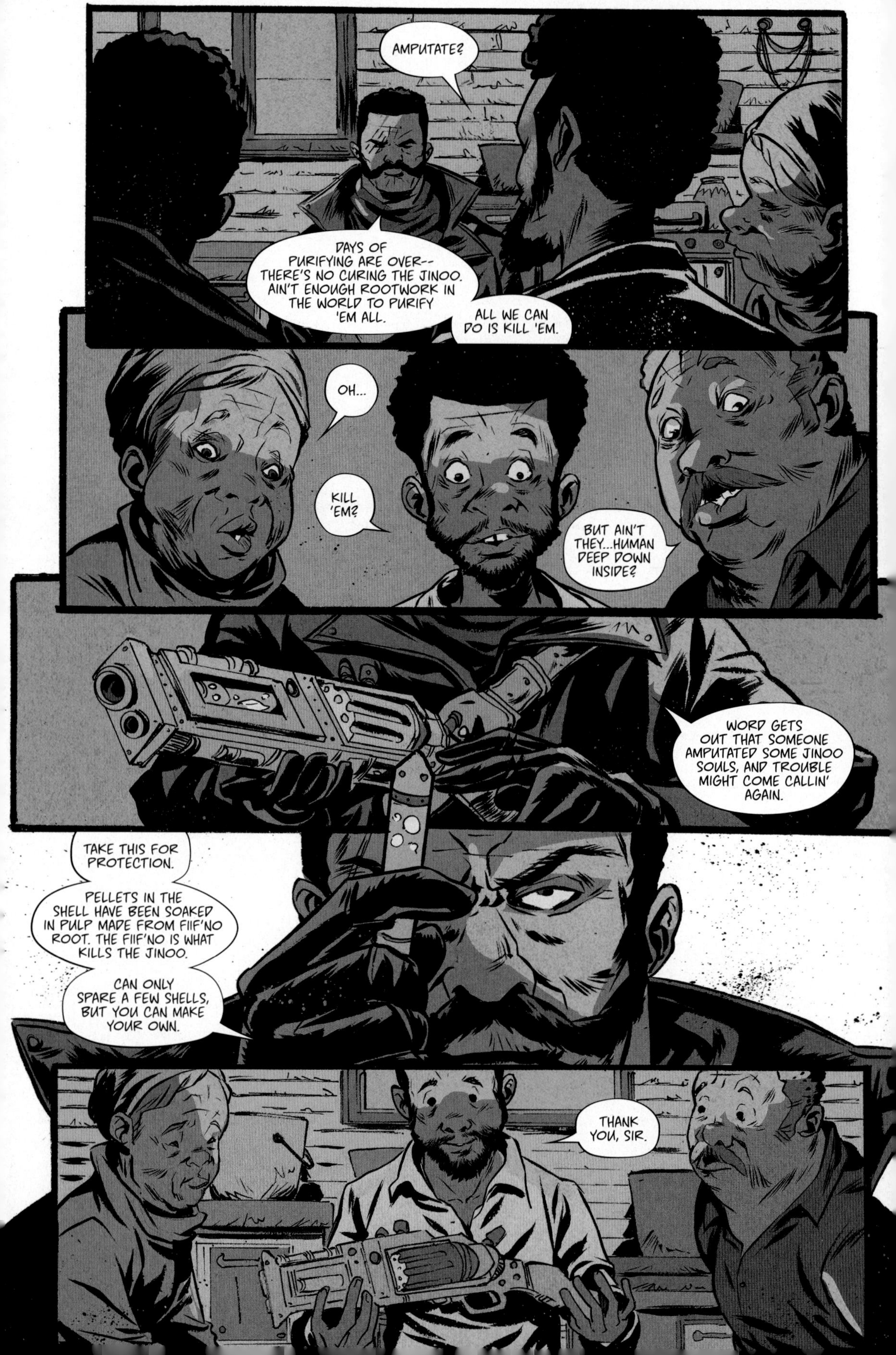
AMPUTATE?
DAYS OF PURIFYING ARE OVER-- THERE'S NO CURING THE JINOO. AIN'T ENOUGH ROOTWORK IN THE WORLD TO PURIFY 'EM ALL.
ALL WE CAN DO IS KILL 'EM.
OH...
KILL 'EM?
BUT AIN'T THEY...HUMAN DEEP DOWN INSIDE?
WORD GETS OUT THAT SOMEONE AMPUTATED SOME JINOO SOULS, AND TROUBLE MIGHT COME CALLIN' AGAIN.
TAKE THIS FOR PROTECTION.
PELLETS IN THE SHELL HAVE BEEN SOAKED IN PULP MADE FROM FIIF'NO ROOT. THE FIIF'NO IS WHAT KILLS THE JINOO.
CAN ONLY SPARE A FEW SHELLS, BUT YOU CAN MAKE YOUR OWN.
THANK YOU, SIR.

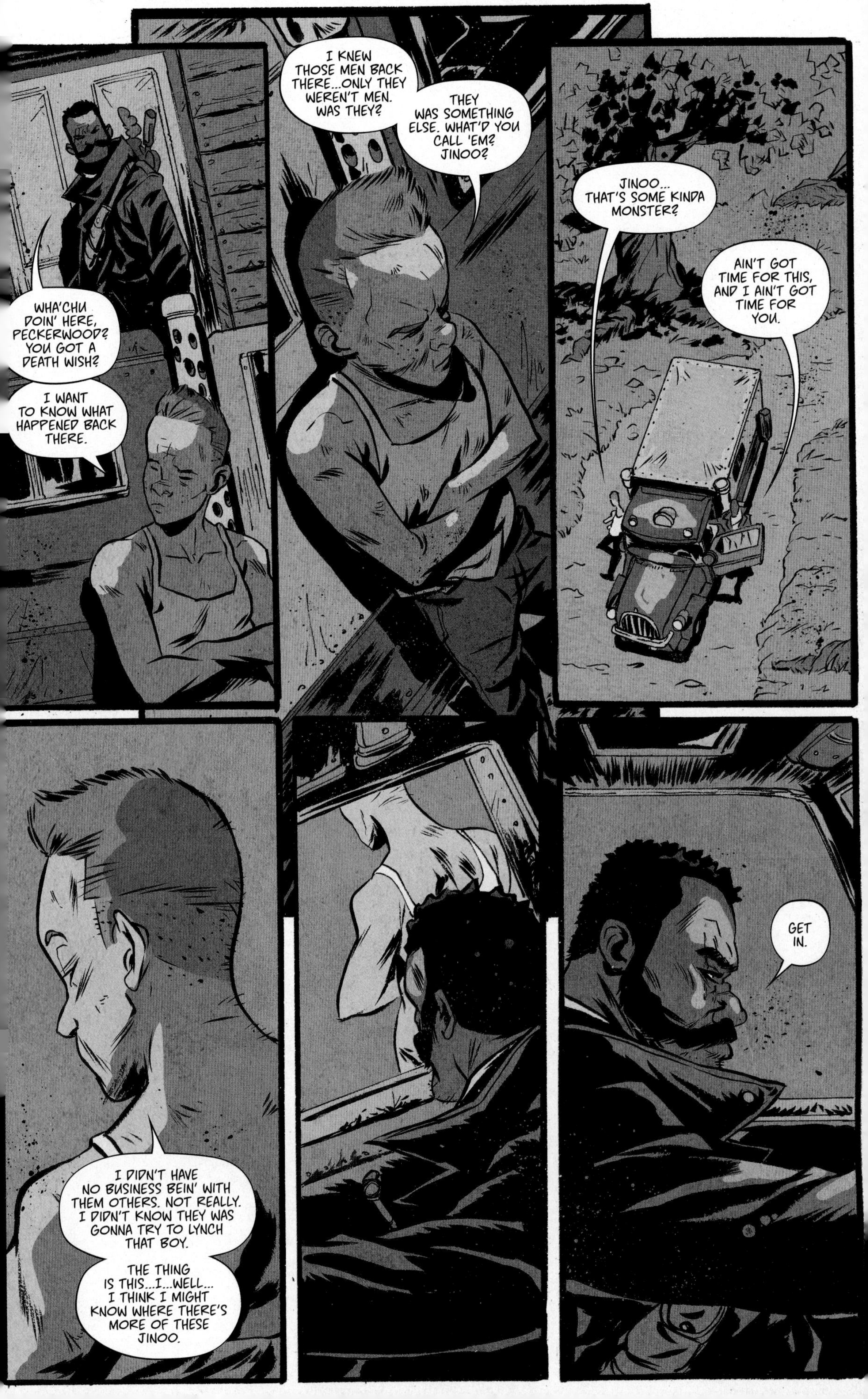
WHA'CHU DOIN' HERE, PECKERWOOD? YOU GOT A DEATH WISH?
I WANT TO KNOW WHAT HAPPENED BACK THERE.
I KNEW THOSE MEN BACK THERE...ONLY THEY WEREN'T MEN. WAS THEY?
THEY WAS SOMETHING ELSE. WHAT'D YOU CALL 'EM? JINOO?
JINOO... THAT'S SOME KINDA MONSTER?
AIN'T GOT TIME FOR THIS, AND I AIN'T GOT TIME FOR YOU.
I DIDN'T HAVE NO BUSINESS BEIN' WITH THEM OTHERS. NOT REALLY. I DIDN'T KNOW THEY WAS GONNA TRY TO LYNCH THAT BOY.
THE THING IS THIS...I...WELL... I THINK I MIGHT KNOW WHERE THERE'S MORE OF THESE JINOO.
GET IN.

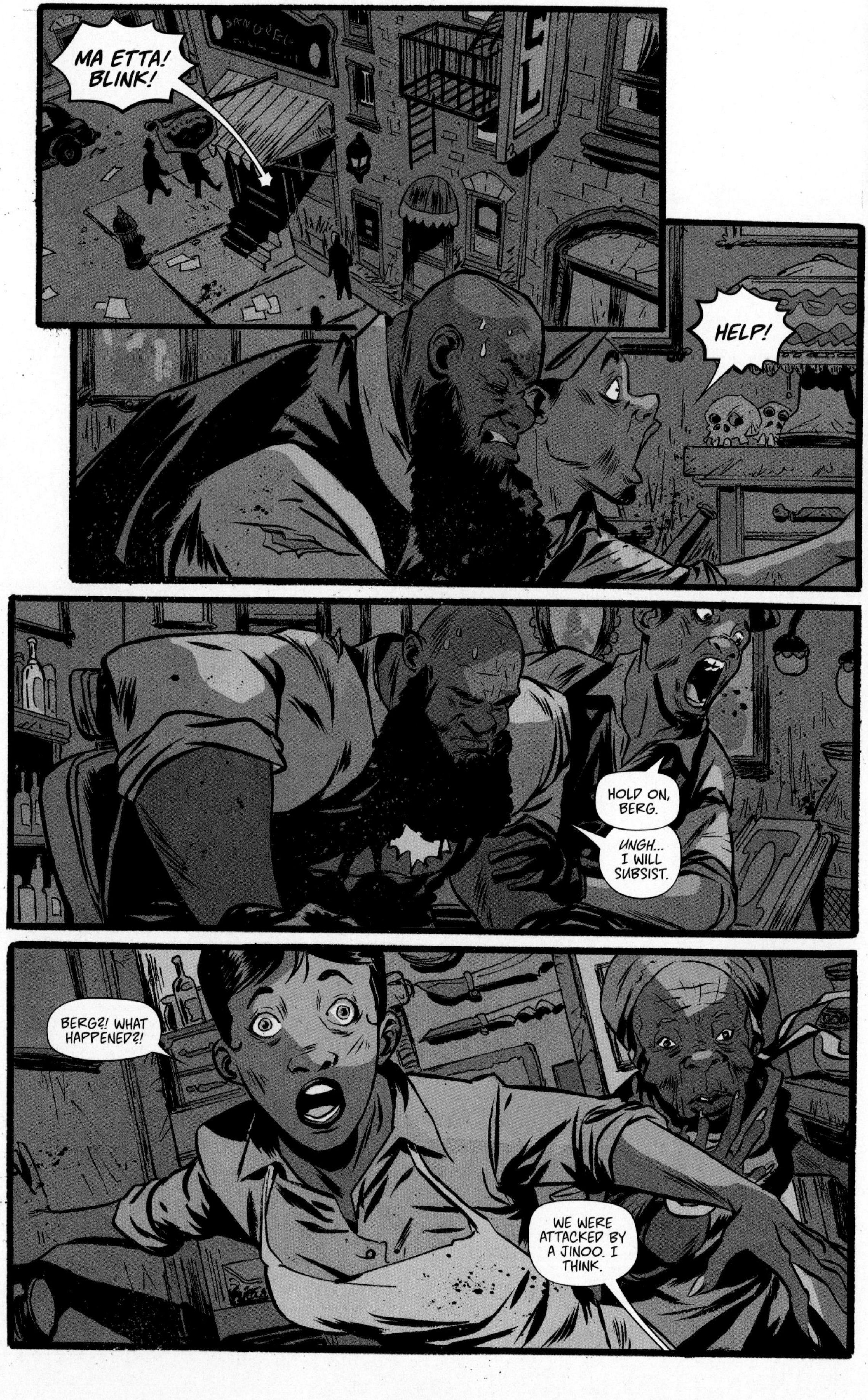
MA ETTA! BLINK!
HELP!
HOLD ON, BERG.
UNGH... I WILL SUBSIST.
BERG?! WHAT HAPPENED?!
WE WERE ATTACKED BY A JINOO. I THINK.

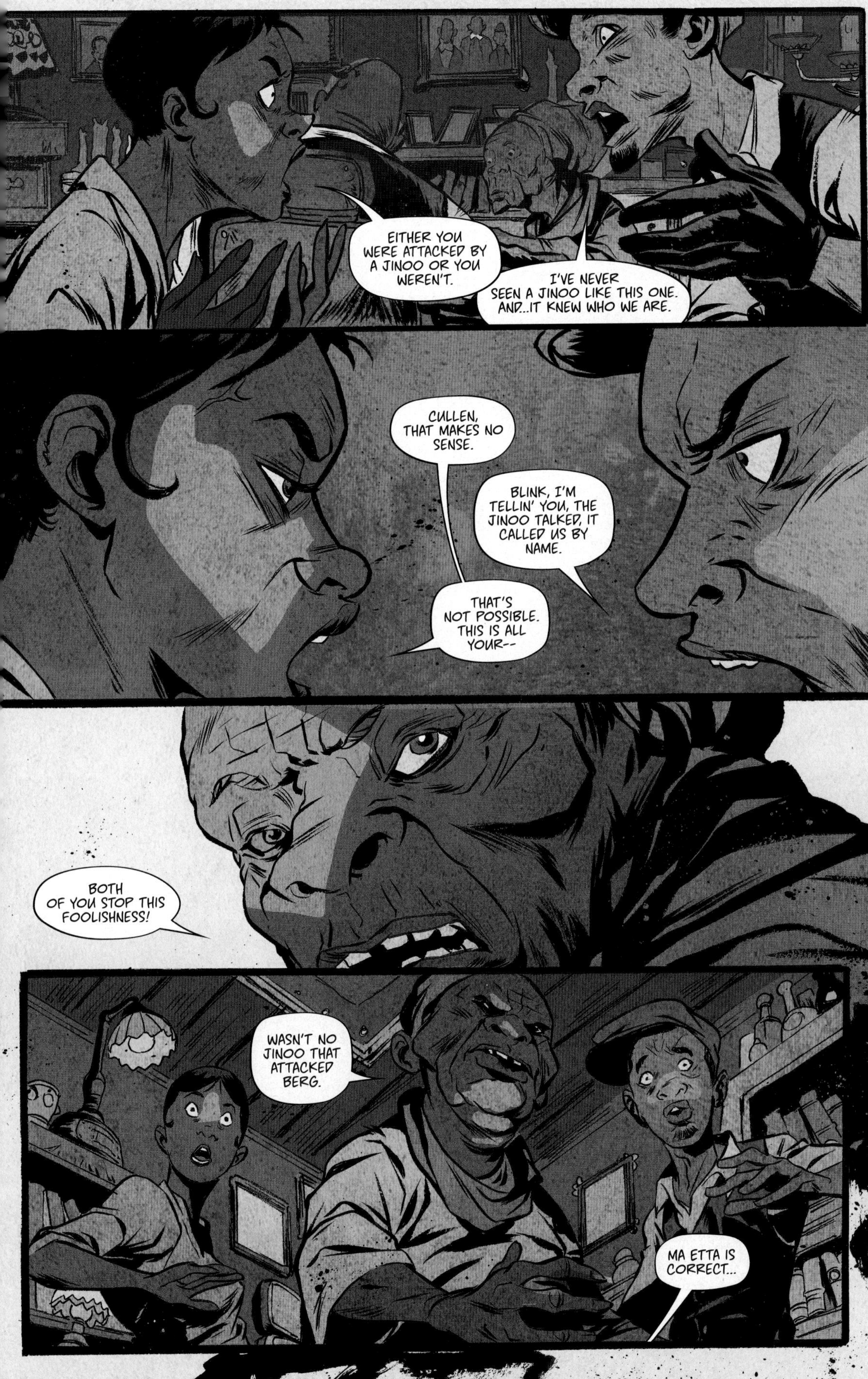
EITHER YOU WERE ATTACKED BY A JINOO OR YOU WEREN'T.
I'VE NEVER SEEN A JINOO LIKE THIS ONE. AND...IT KNEW WHO WE ARE.
CULLEN, THAT MAKES NO SENSE.
BLINK, I'M TELLIN' YOU, THE JINOO TALKED, IT CALLED US BY NAME.
THAT'S NOT POSSIBLE. THIS IS ALL YOUR--
BOTH OF YOU STOP THIS FOOLISHNESS!
WASN'T NO JINOO THAT ATTACKED BERG.
MA ETTA IS CORRECT...

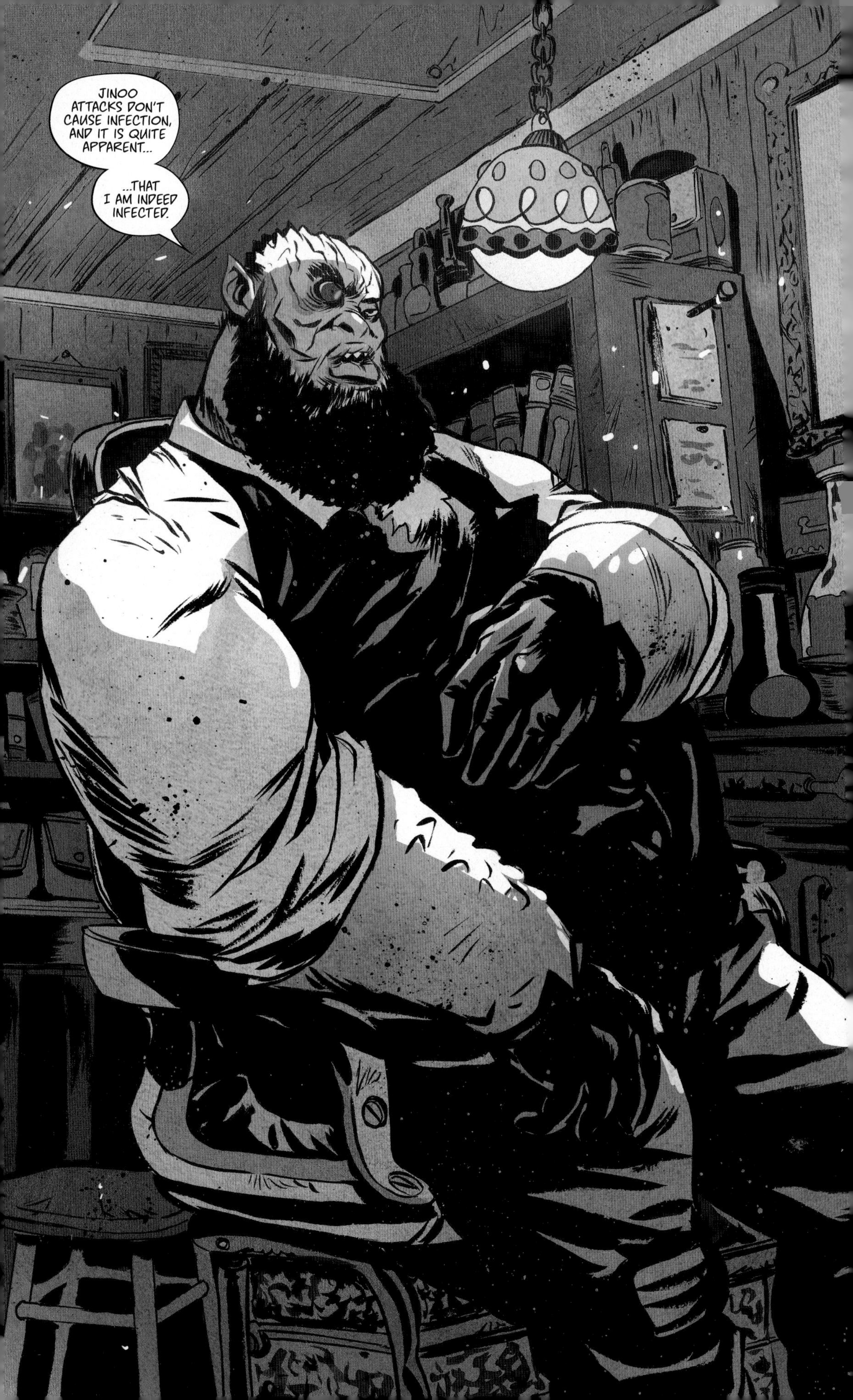
JINOO ATTACKS DON'T CAUSE INFECTION, AND IT IS QUITE APPARENT...
...THAT I AM INDEED INFECTED.

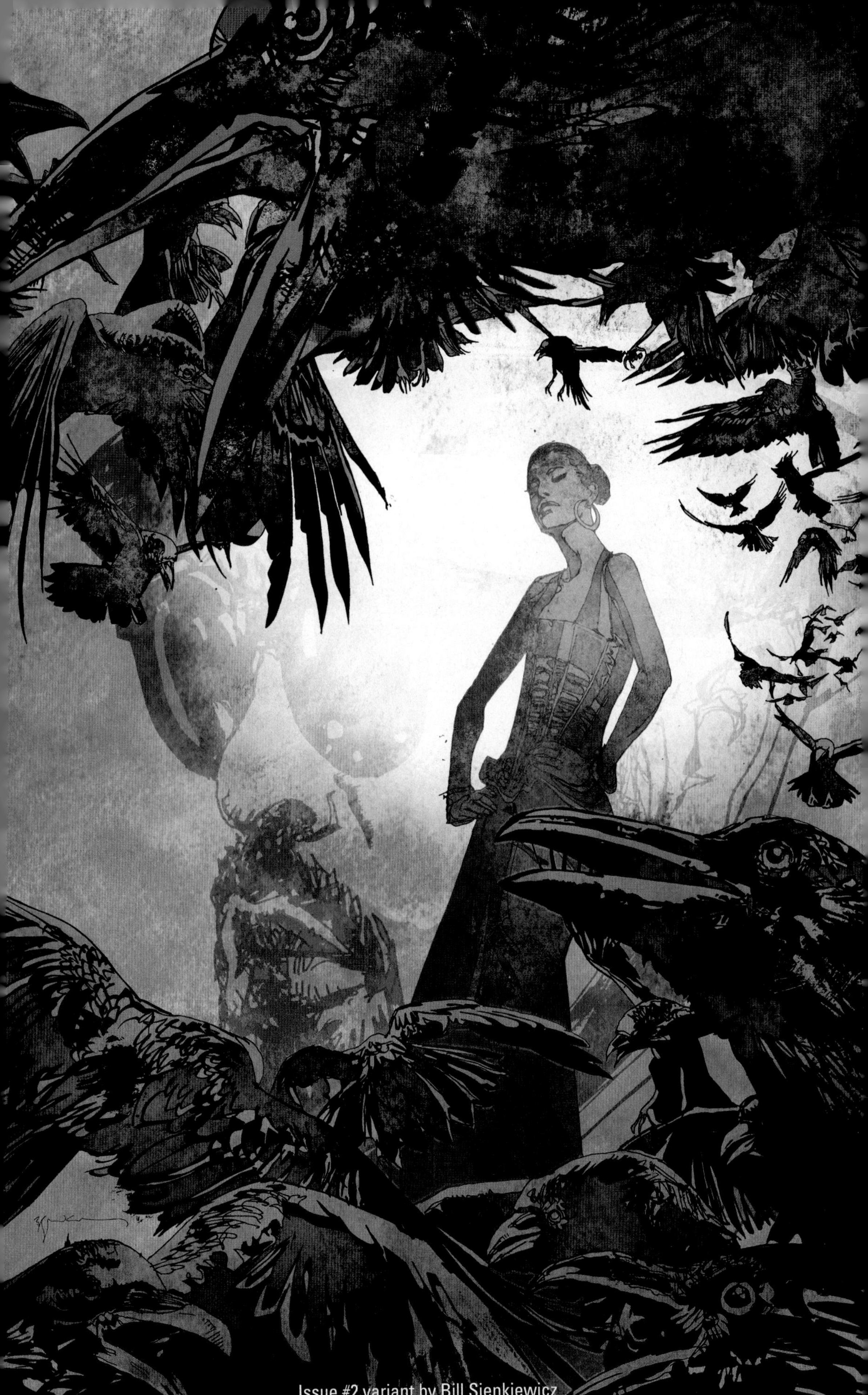

Issue #2 variant by Bill Sienkiewicz

CHAPTER THREE

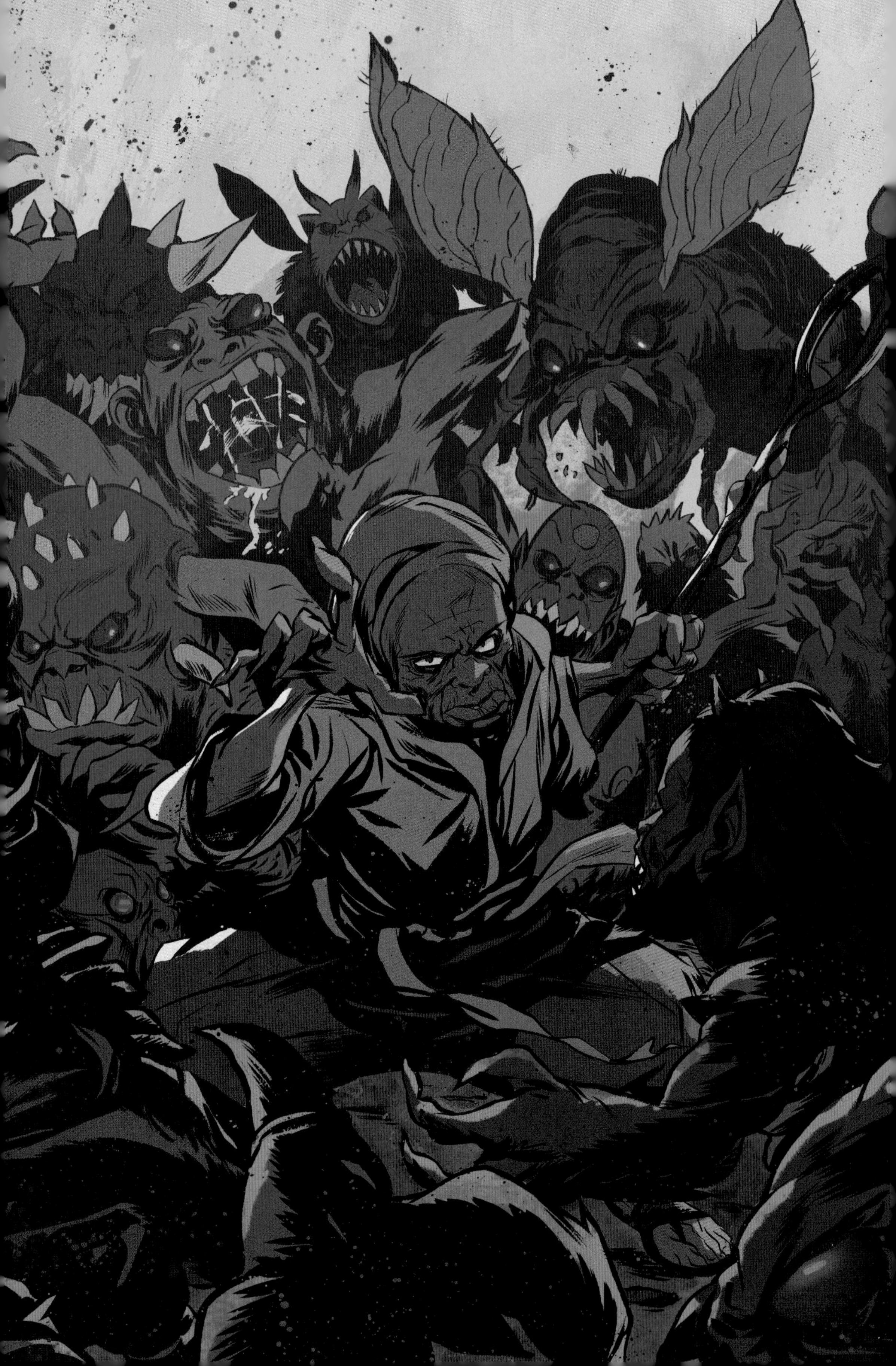

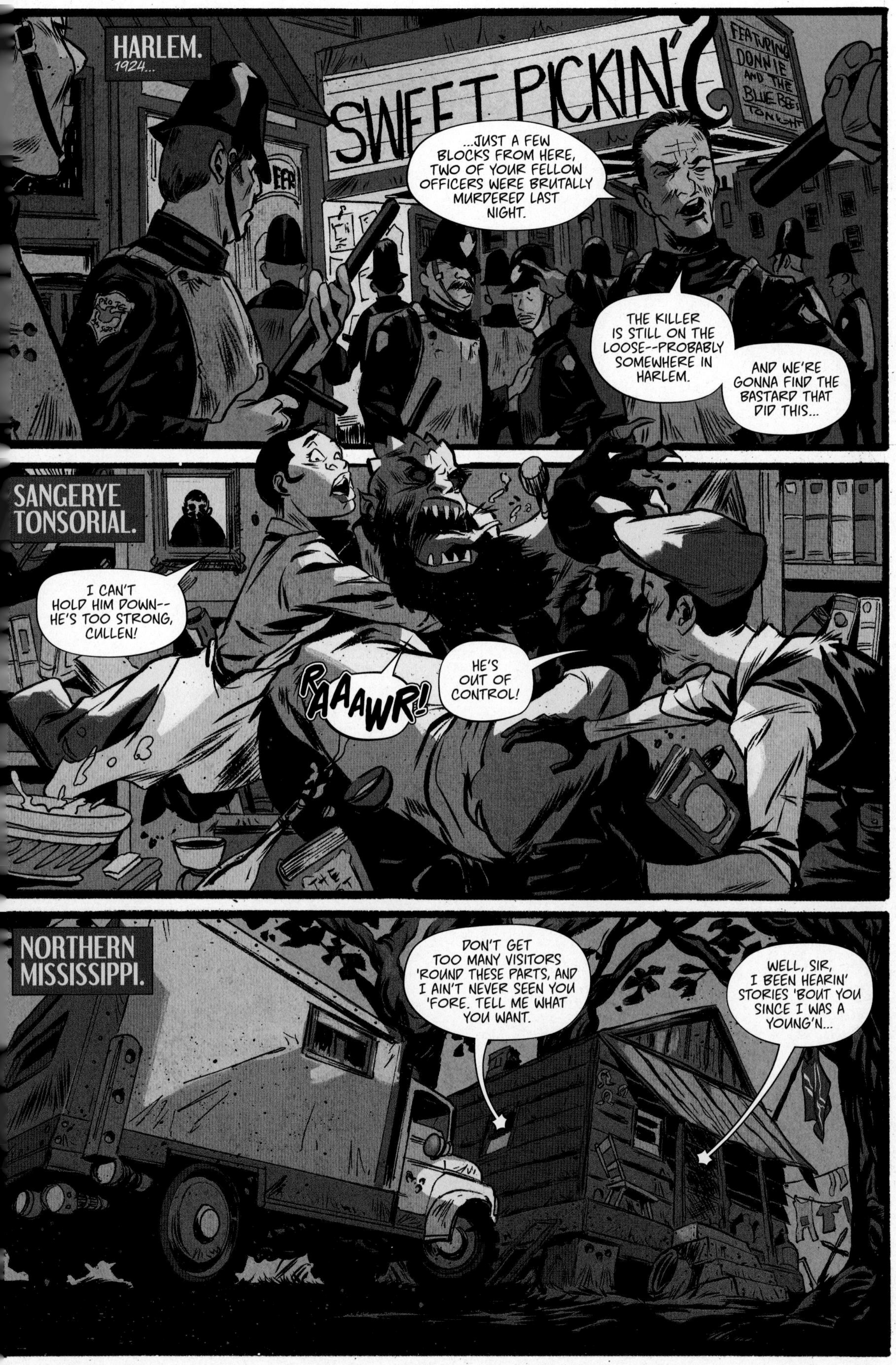
HARLEM.
1924...
SWEET PICKIN'S
FEATURING DONNIE AND THE BLUE BEES TONIGHT
...JUST A FEW BLOCKS FROM HERE, TWO OF YOUR FELLOW OFFICERS WERE BRUTALLY MURDERED LAST NIGHT.
THE KILLER IS STILL ON THE LOOSE--PROBABLY SOMEWHERE IN HARLEM.
AND WE'RE GONNA FIND THE BASTARD THAT DID THIS...
SANGERYE TONSORIAL.
I CAN'T HOLD HIM DOWN--HE'S TOO STRONG, CULLEN!
RAAAWR!
HE'S OUT OF CONTROL!
NORTHERN MISSISSIPPI.
DON'T GET TOO MANY VISITORS 'ROUND THESE PARTS, AND I AIN'T NEVER SEEN YOU 'FORE. TELL ME WHAT YOU WANT.
WELL, SIR, I BEEN HEARIN' STORIES 'BOUT YOU SINCE I WAS A YOUNG'N...

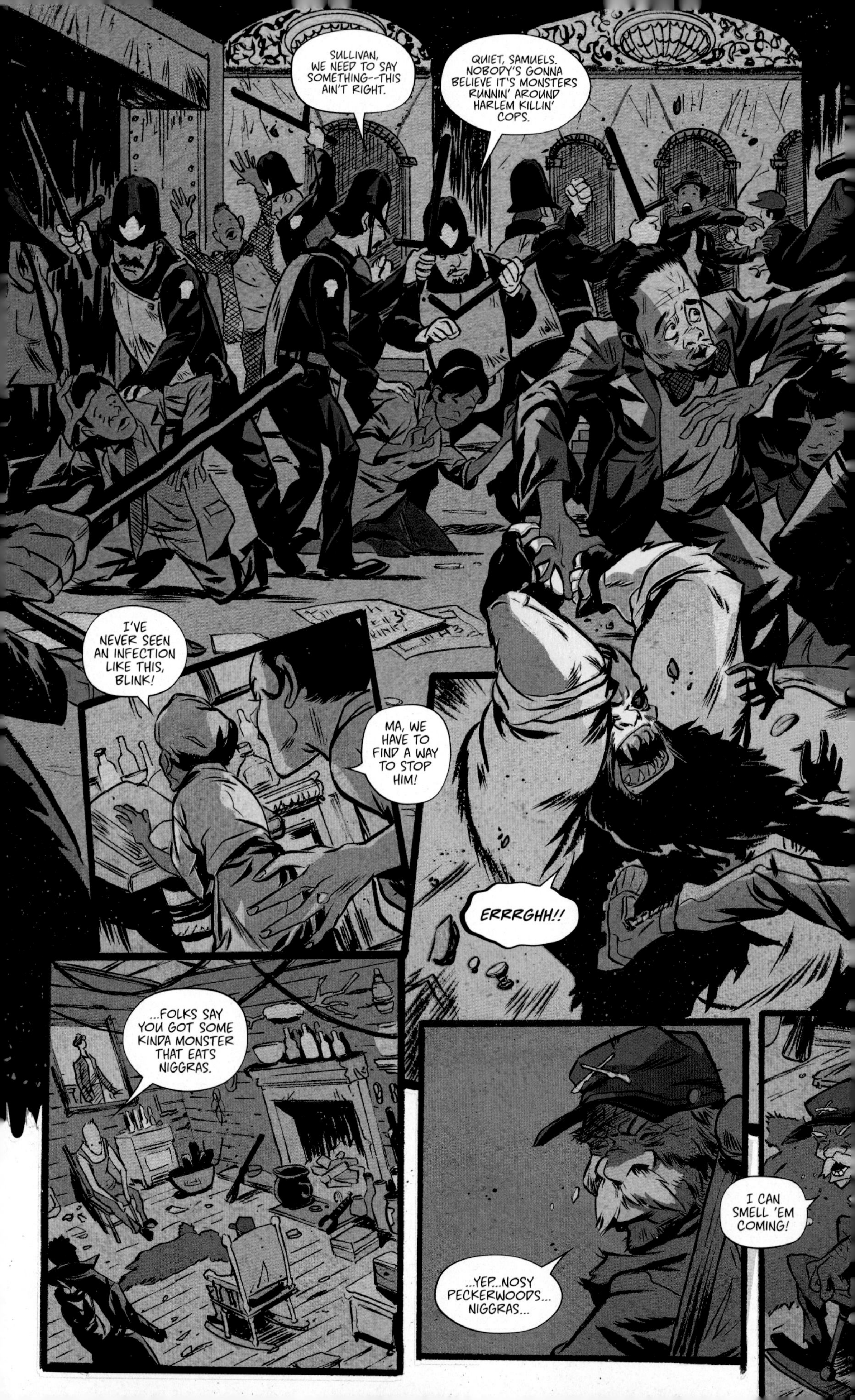
SULLIVAN, WE NEED TO SAY SOMETHING--THIS AIN'T RIGHT.
QUIET, SAMUELS. NOBODY'S GONNA BELIEVE IT'S MONSTERS RUNNIN' AROUND HARLEM KILLIN' COPS.
I'VE NEVER SEEN AN INFECTION LIKE THIS, BLINK!
MA, WE HAVE TO FIND A WAY TO STOP HIM!
ERRRGHH!!
...FOLKS SAY YOU GOT SOME KINDA MONSTER THAT EATS NIGGRAS.
...YEP...NOSY PECKERWOODS... NIGGRAS...
I CAN SMELL 'EM COMING!

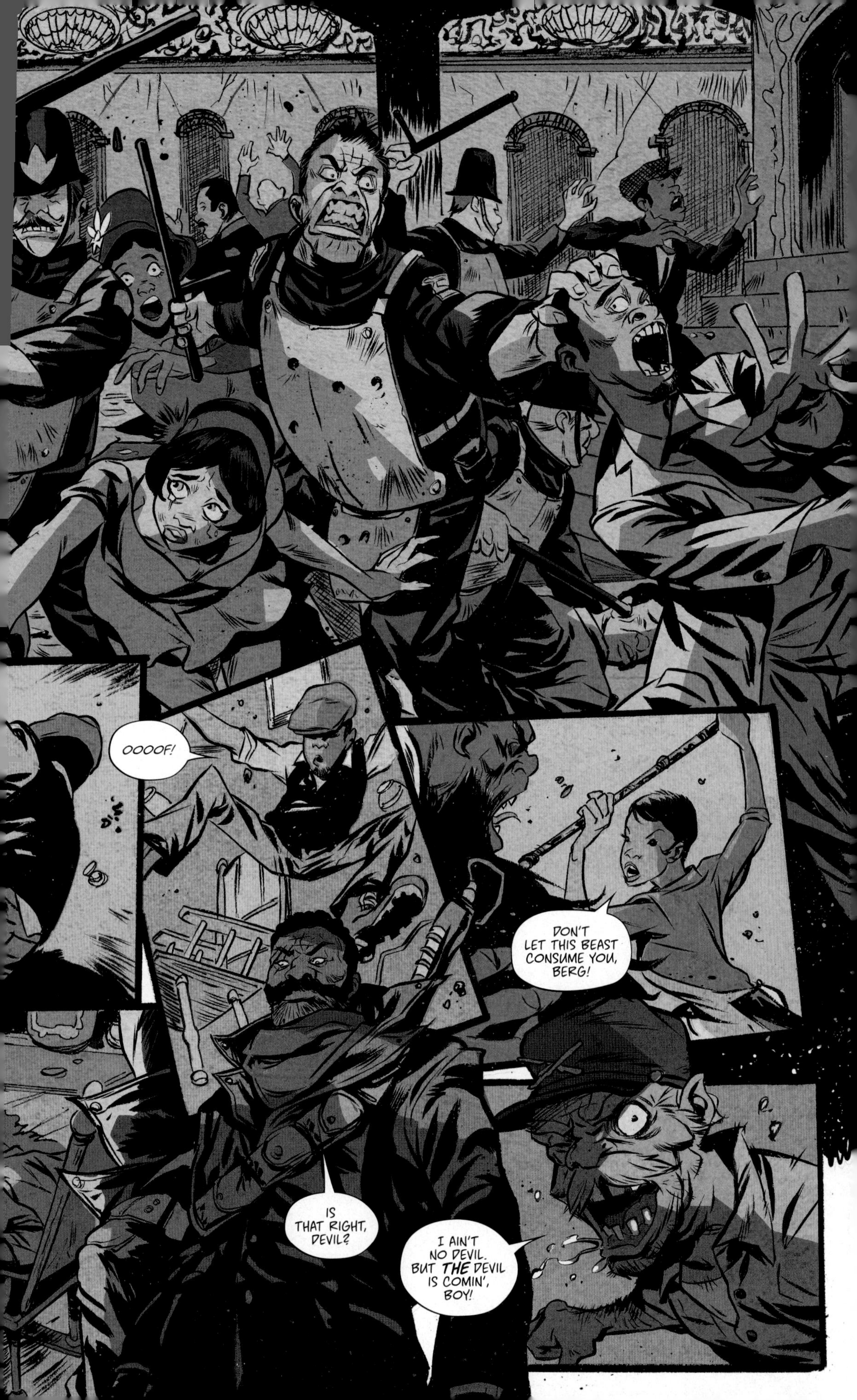
OOOOF!
DON'T LET THIS BEAST CONSUME YOU, BERG!
IS THAT RIGHT, DEVIL?
I AIN'T NO DEVIL. BUT THE DEVIL IS COMIN', BOY!

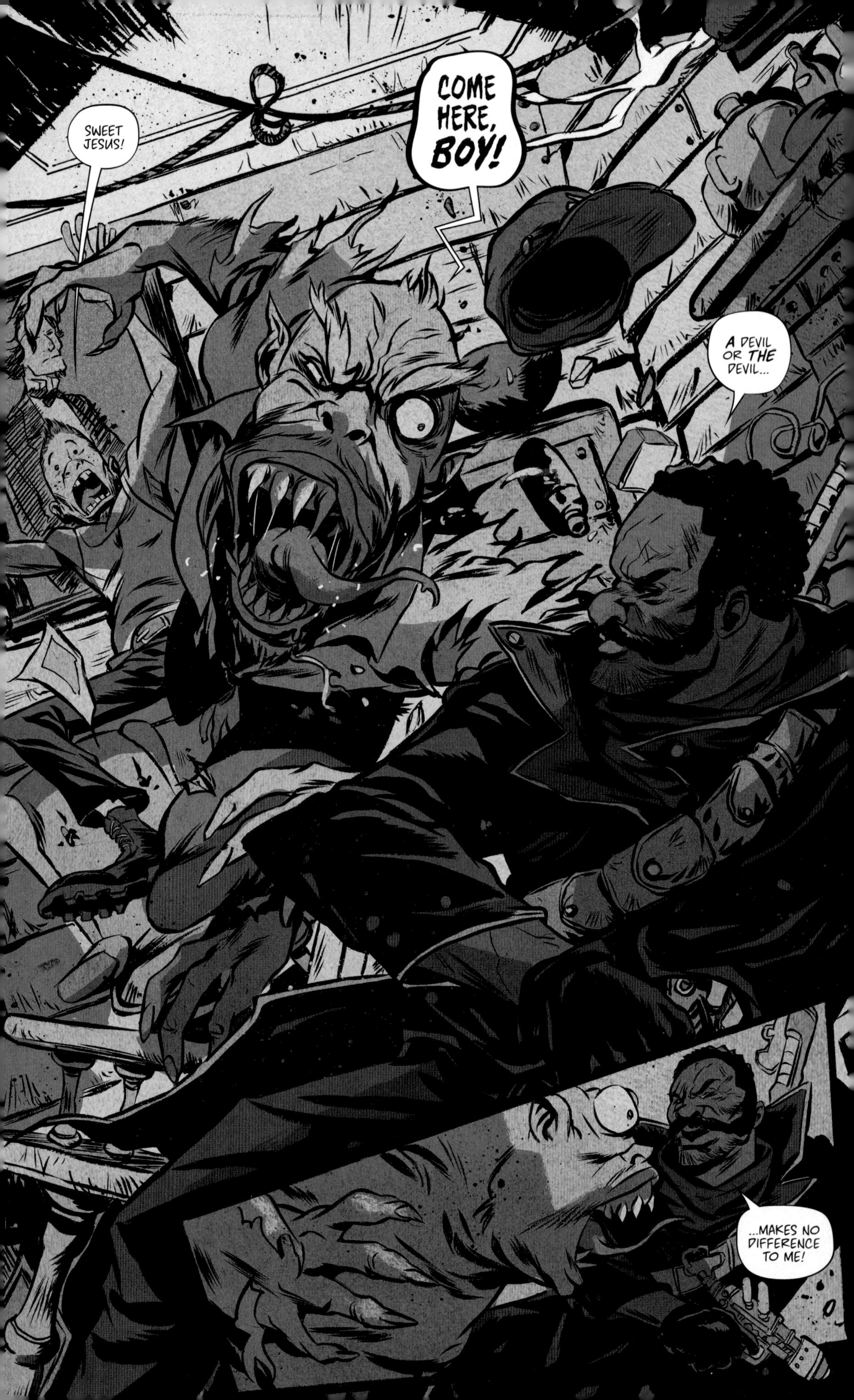
SWEET JESUS!
COME HERE, BOY!
A DEVIL OR THE DEVIL...
...MAKES NO DIFFERENCE TO ME!

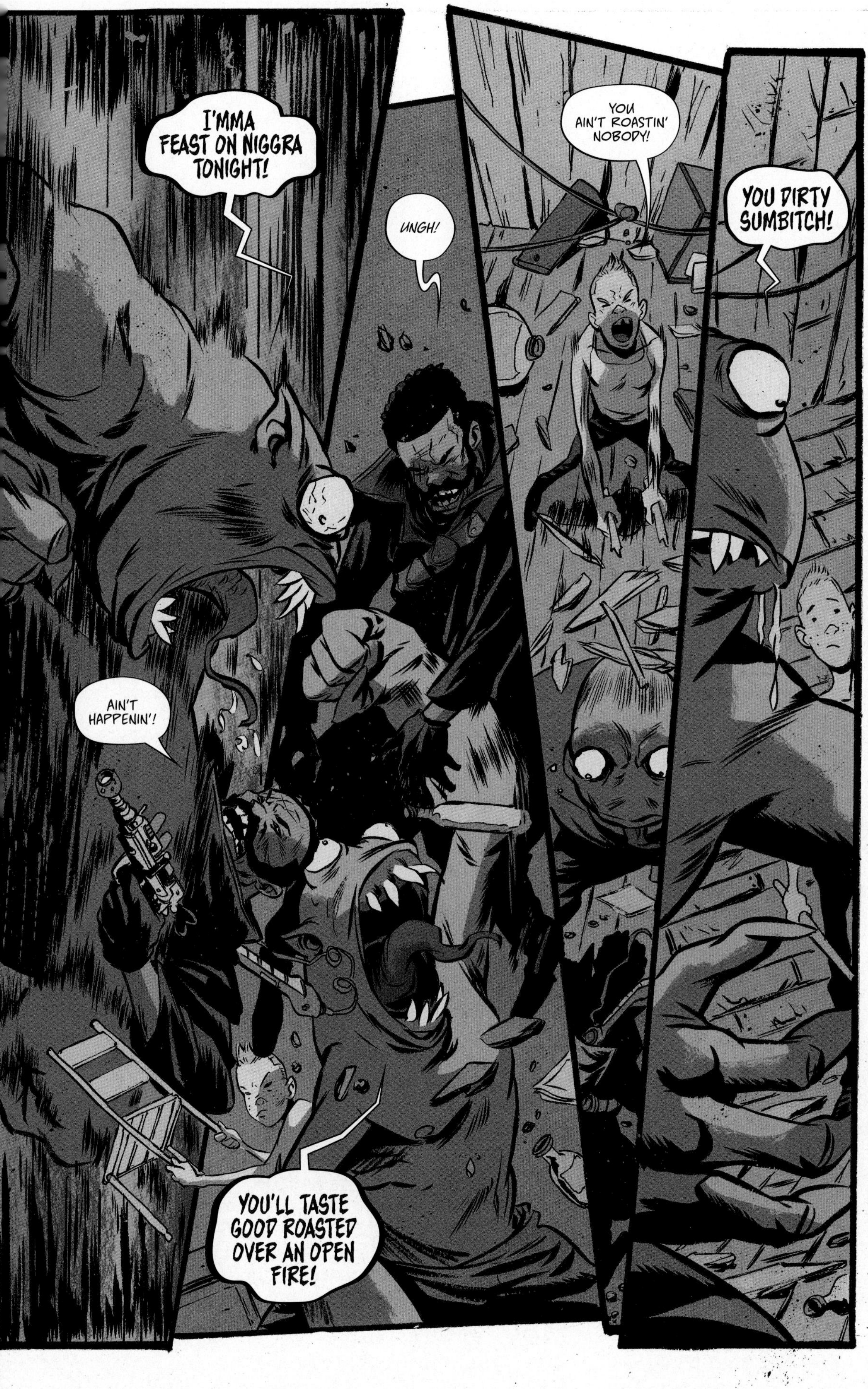
I'MMA FEAST ON NIGGRA TONIGHT!
AIN'T HAPPENIN'!
UNGH!
YOU'LL TASTE GOOD ROASTED OVER AN OPEN FIRE!
YOU AIN'T ROASTIN' NOBODY!
YOU DIRTY SUMBITCH!

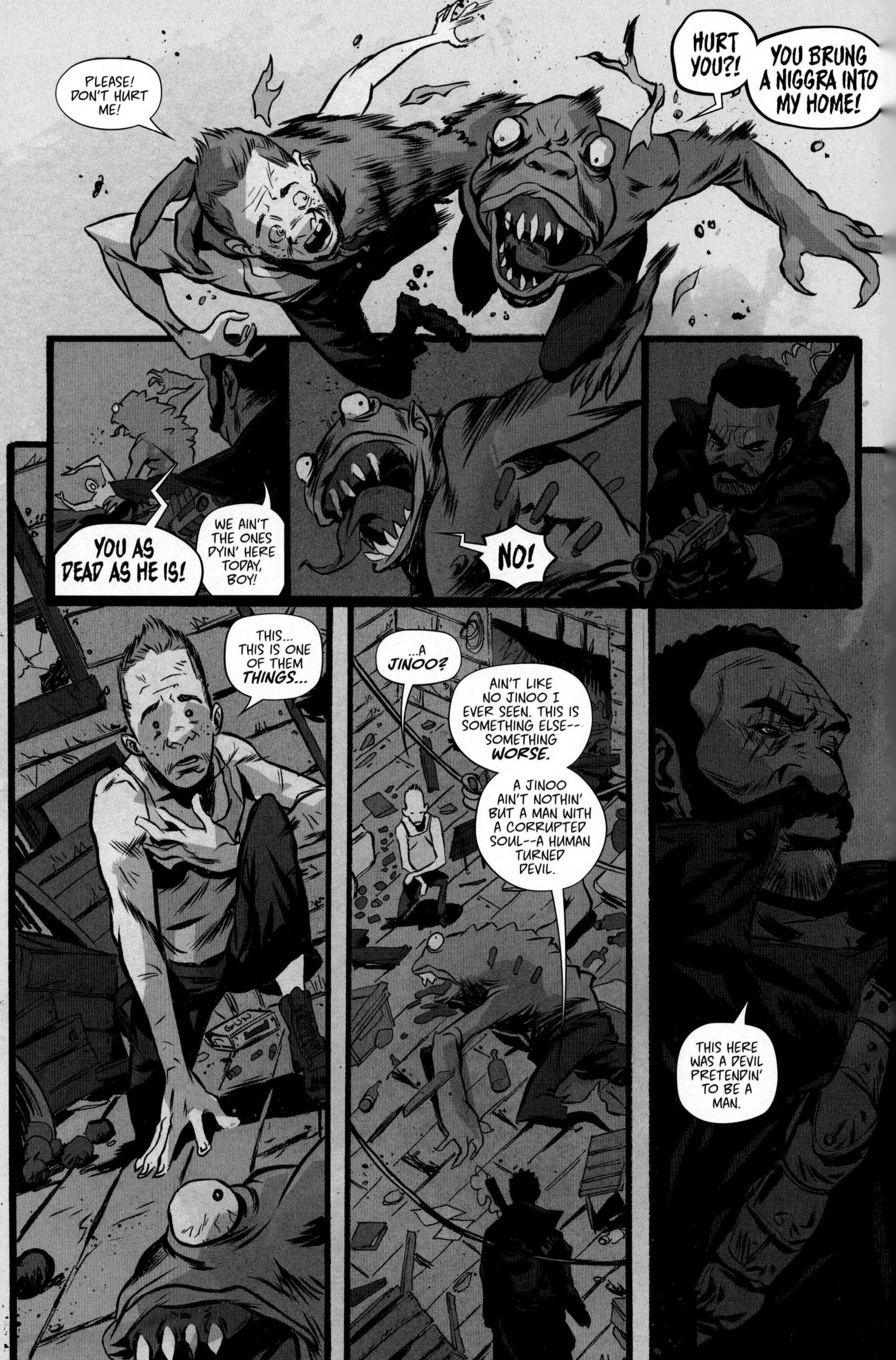
PLEASE! DON'T HURT ME!
HURT YOU?!
YOU BRUNG A NIGGRA INTO MY HOME!
YOU AS DEAD AS HE IS!
WE AIN'T THE ONES DYIN' HERE TODAY, BOY!
NO!
THIS... THIS IS ONE OF THEM THINGS...
...A JINOO?
AIN'T LIKE NO JINOO I EVER SEEN. THIS IS SOMETHING ELSE-- SOMETHING WORSE.
A JINOO AIN'T NOTHIN' BUT A MAN WITH A CORRUPTED SOUL--A HUMAN TURNED DEVIL.
THIS HERE WAS A DEVIL PRETENDIN' TO BE A MAN.

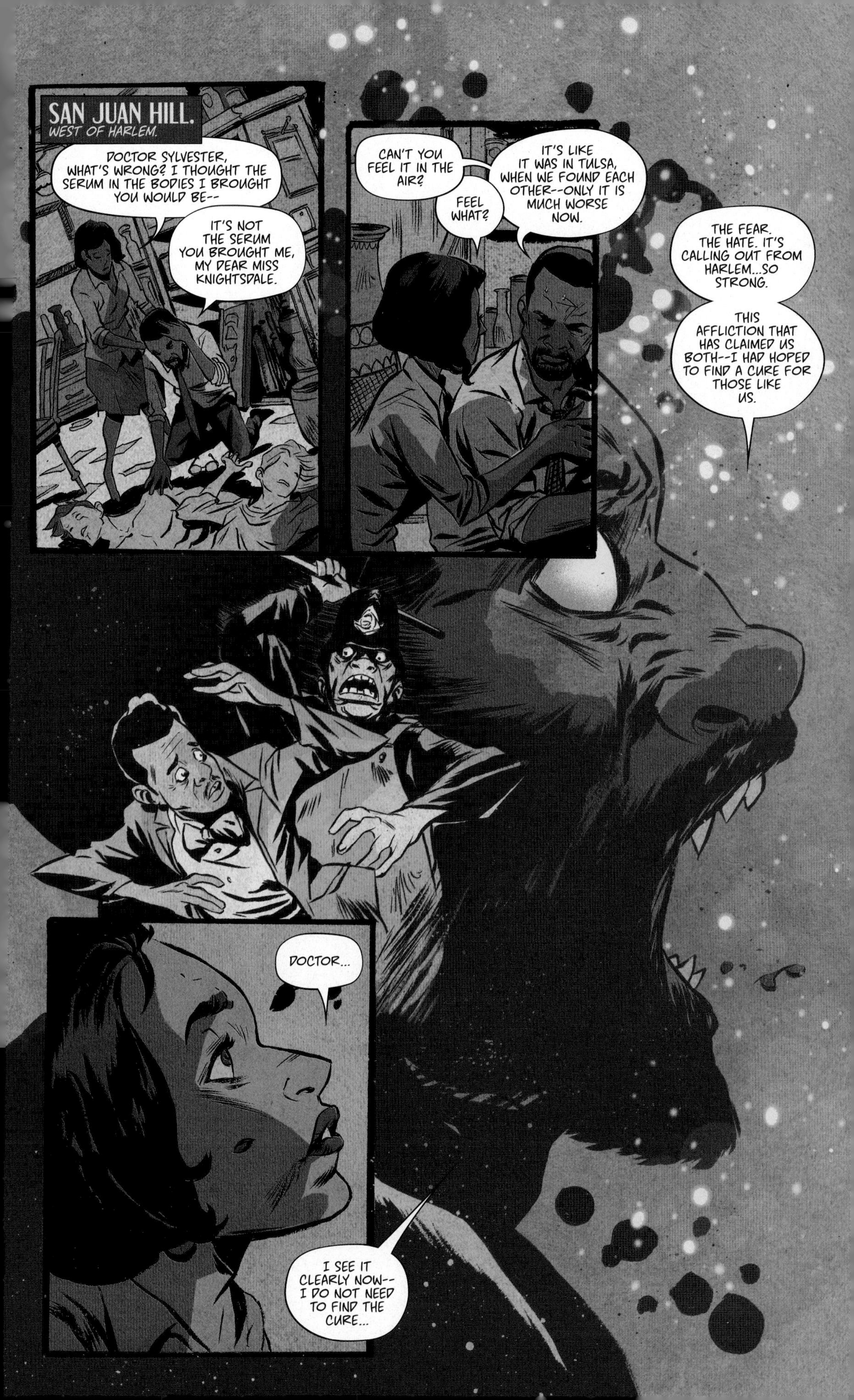
SAN JUAN HILL.
WEST OF HARLEM.
DOCTOR SYLVESTER, WHAT'S WRONG? I THOUGHT THE SERUM IN THE BODIES I BROUGHT YOU WOULD BE--
IT'S NOT THE SERUM YOU BROUGHT ME, MY DEAR MISS KNIGHTSDALE.
CAN'T YOU FEEL IT IN THE AIR?
FEEL WHAT?
IT'S LIKE IT WAS IN TULSA, WHEN WE FOUND EACH OTHER--ONLY IT IS MUCH WORSE NOW.
THE FEAR. THE HATE. IT'S CALLING OUT FROM HARLEM...SO STRONG.
THIS AFFLICTION THAT HAS CLAIMED US BOTH--I HAD HOPED TO FIND A CURE FOR THOSE LIKE US.
DOCTOR...
I SEE IT CLEARLY NOW--I DO NOT NEED TO FIND THE CURE...

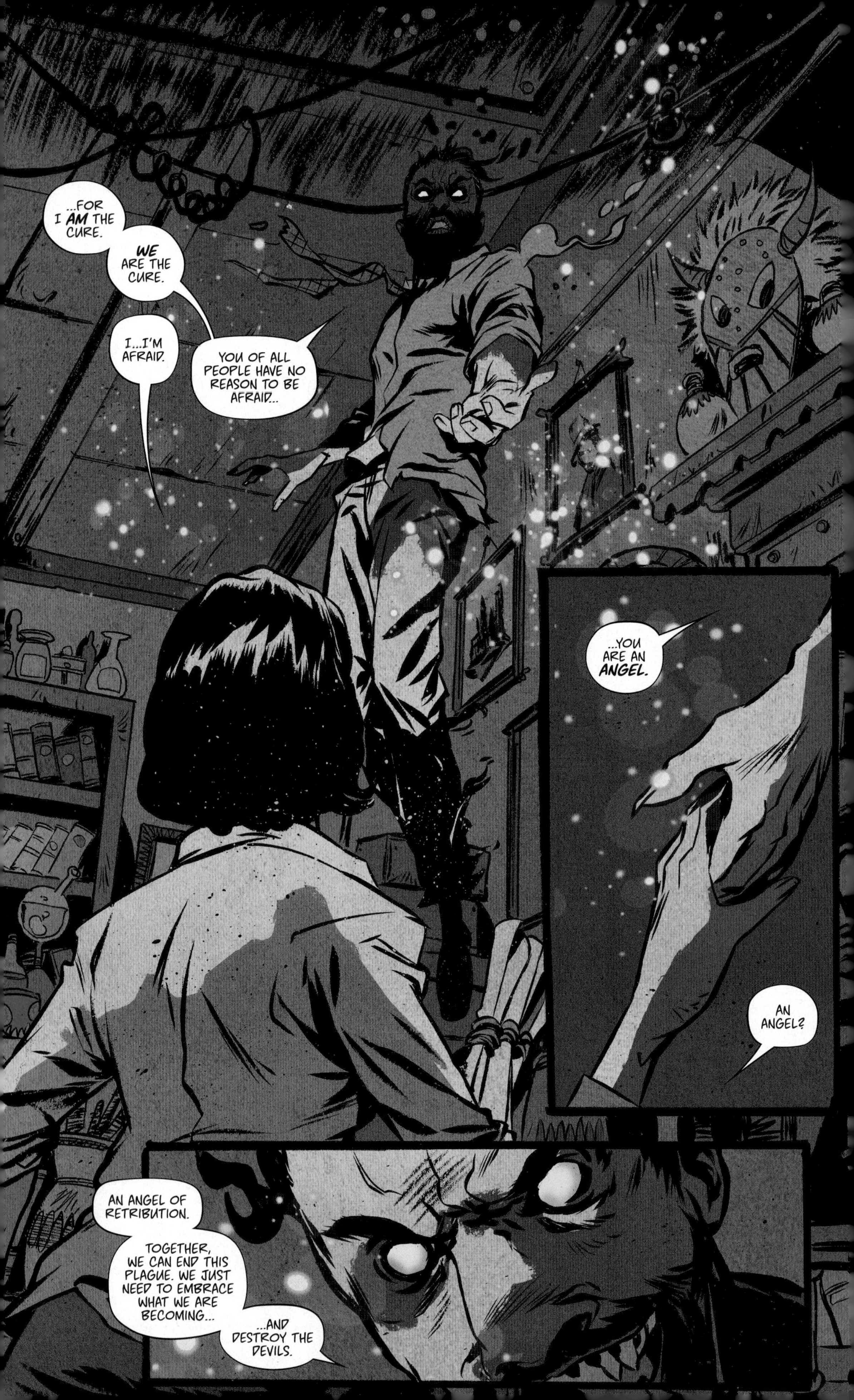
...FOR I AM THE CURE.
WE ARE THE CURE.
I...I'M AFRAID.
YOU OF ALL PEOPLE HAVE NO REASON TO BE AFRAID...
...YOU ARE AN ANGEL.
AN ANGEL?
AN ANGEL OF RETRIBUTION.
TOGETHER, WE CAN END THIS PLAGUE. WE JUST NEED TO EMBRACE WHAT WE ARE BECOMING...
...AND DESTROY THE DEVILS.

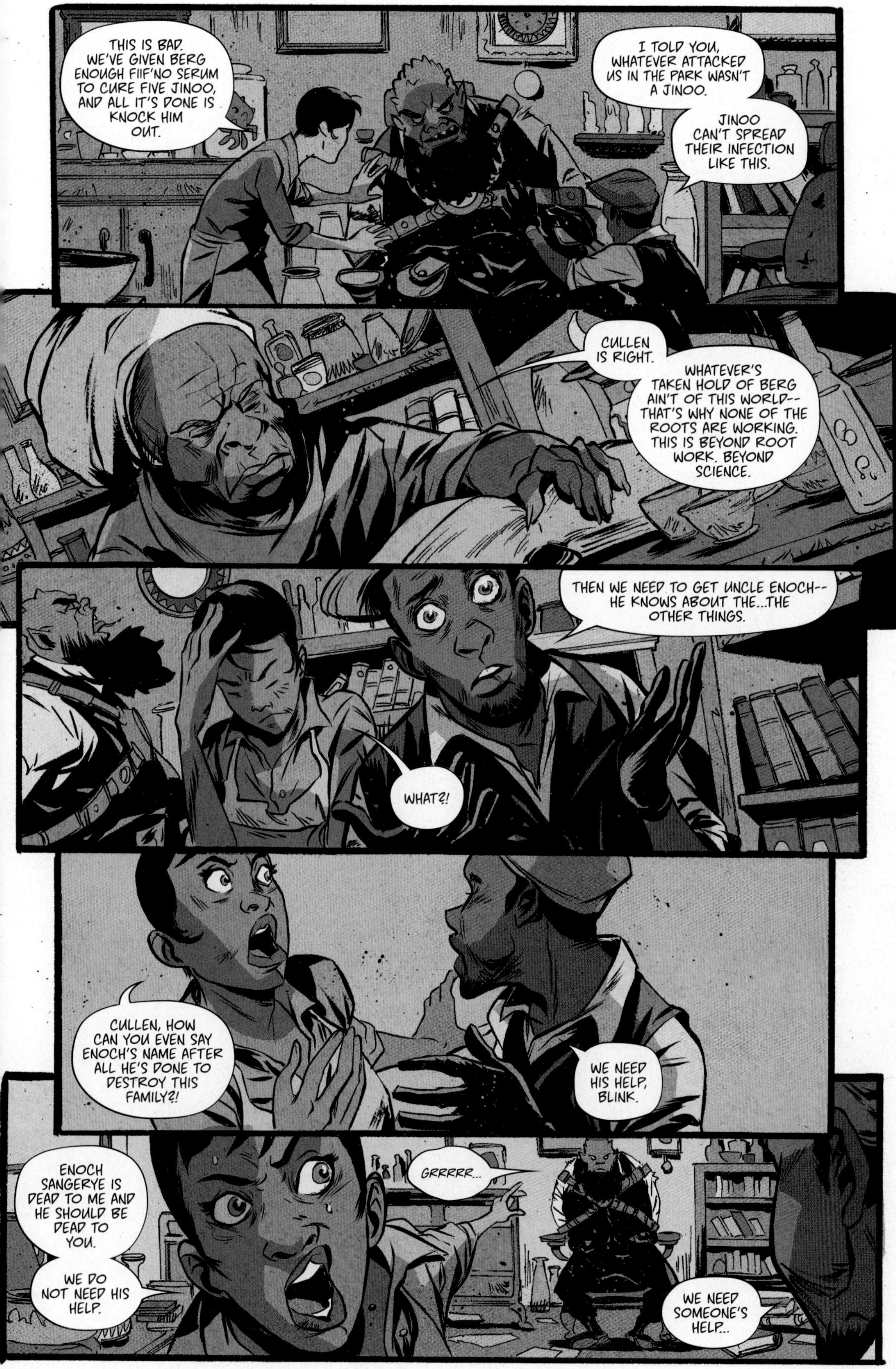
THIS IS BAD. WE'VE GIVEN BERG ENOUGH FIIF'NO SERUM TO CURE FIVE JINOO, AND ALL IT'S DONE IS KNOCK HIM OUT.
I TOLD YOU, WHATEVER ATTACKED US IN THE PARK WASN'T A JINOO.
JINOO CAN'T SPREAD THEIR INFECTION LIKE THIS.
CULLEN IS RIGHT.
WHATEVER'S TAKEN HOLD OF BERG AIN'T OF THIS WORLD--THAT'S WHY NONE OF THE ROOTS ARE WORKING. THIS IS BEYOND ROOT WORK. BEYOND SCIENCE.
THEN WE NEED TO GET UNCLE ENOCH--HE KNOWS ABOUT THE...THE OTHER THINGS.
WHAT?!
CULLEN, HOW CAN YOU EVEN SAY ENOCH'S NAME AFTER ALL HE'S DONE TO DESTROY THIS FAMILY?!
WE NEED HIS HELP, BLINK.
ENOCH SANGERYE IS DEAD TO ME AND HE SHOULD BE DEAD TO YOU.
WE DO NOT NEED HIS HELP.
GRRRRR...
WE NEED SOMEONE'S HELP...

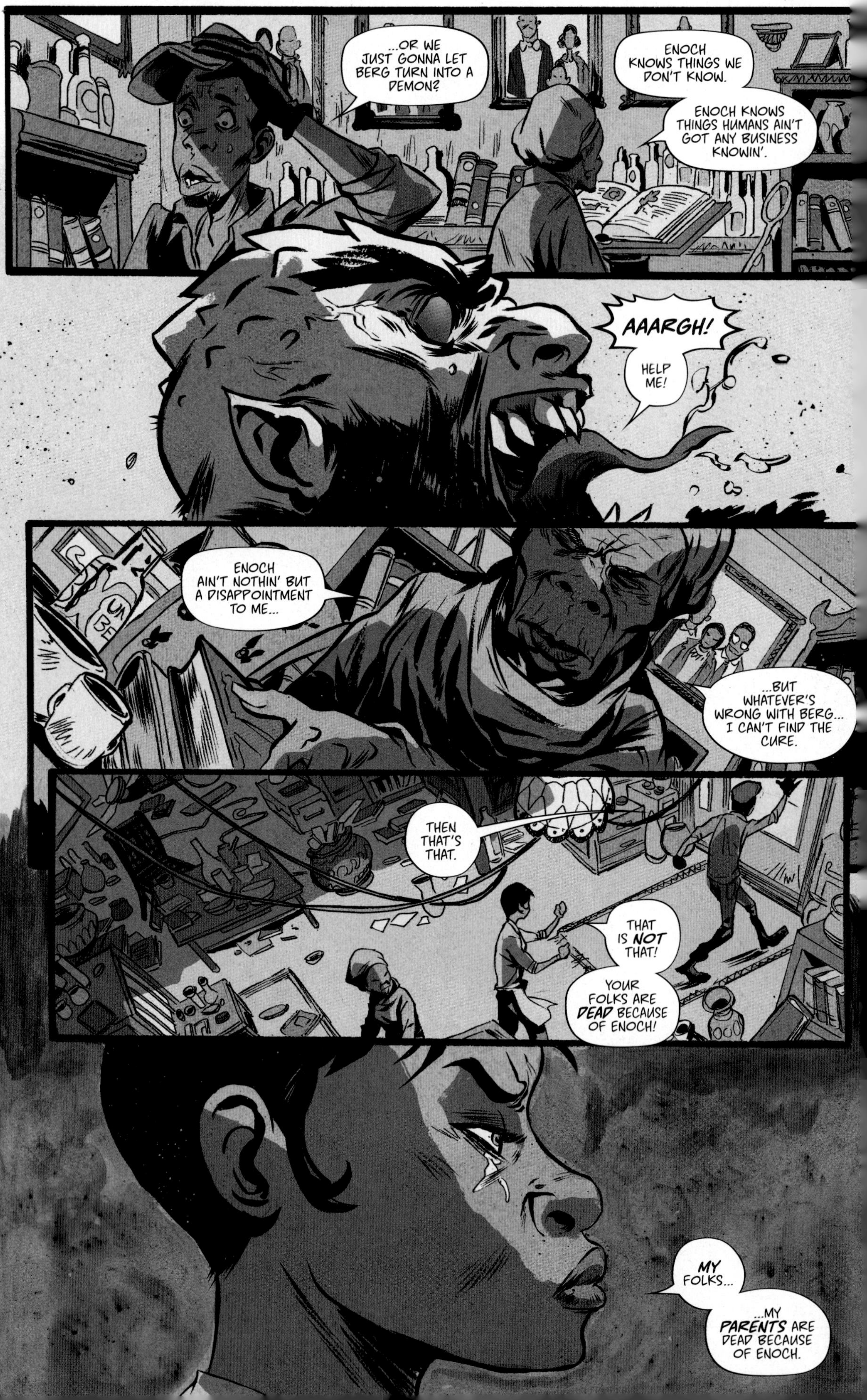
...OR WE JUST GONNA LET BERG TURN INTO A DEMON?
ENOCH KNOWS THINGS WE DON'T KNOW.
ENOCH KNOWS THINGS HUMANS AIN'T GOT ANY BUSINESS KNOWIN'.
AAARGH!
HELP ME!
ENOCH AIN'T NOTHIN' BUT A DISAPPOINTMENT TO ME...
...BUT WHATEVER'S WRONG WITH BERG... I CAN'T FIND THE CURE.
THEN THAT'S THAT.
THAT IS NOT THAT!
YOUR FOLKS ARE DEAD BECAUSE OF ENOCH!
MY FOLKS...
...MY PARENTS ARE DEAD BECAUSE OF ENOCH.

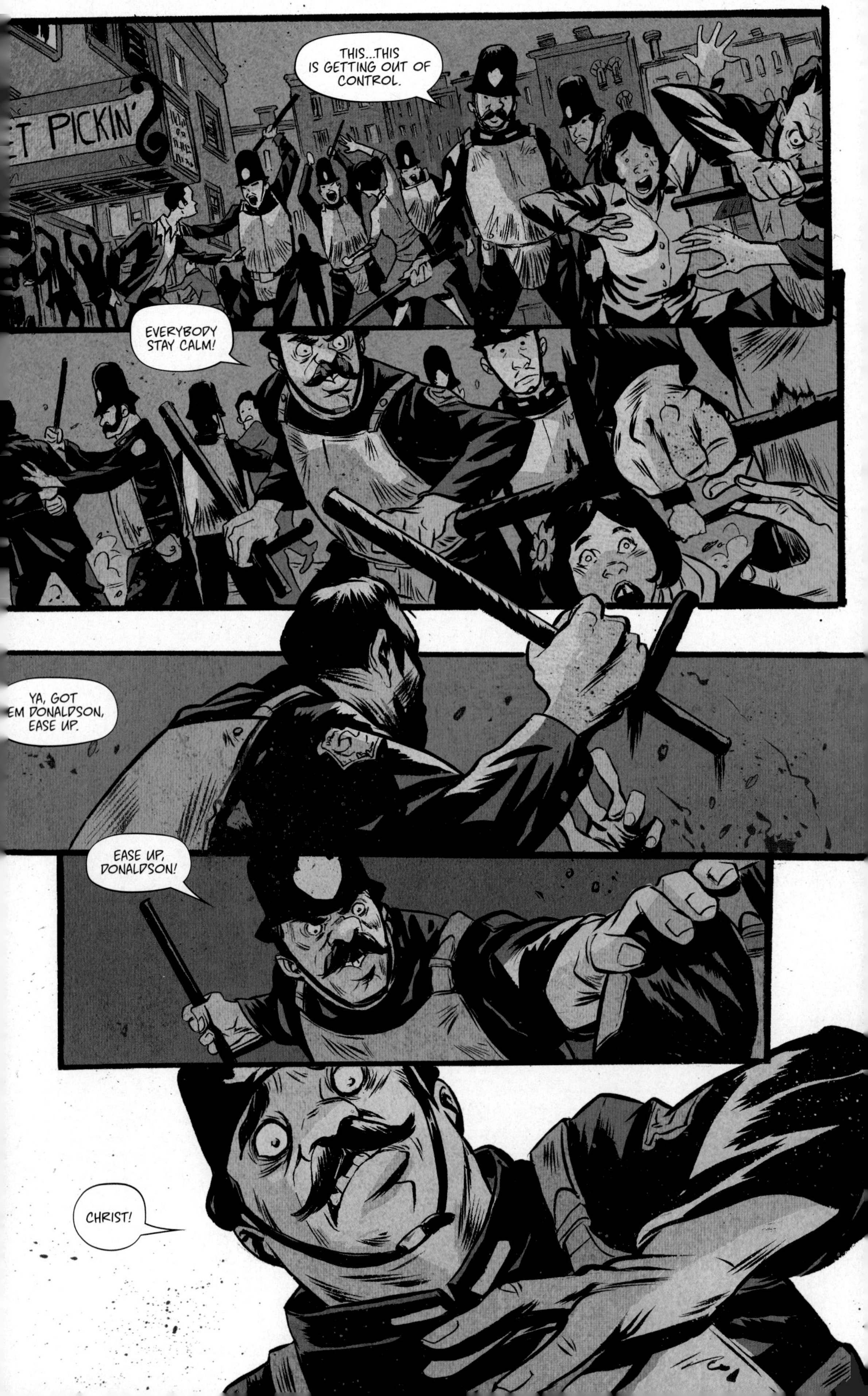
ET PICKIN'
THIS...THIS IS GETTING OUT OF CONTROL.
EVERYBODY STAY CALM!
YA, GOT 'EM DONALDSON, EASE UP.
EASE UP, DONALDSON!
CHRIST!

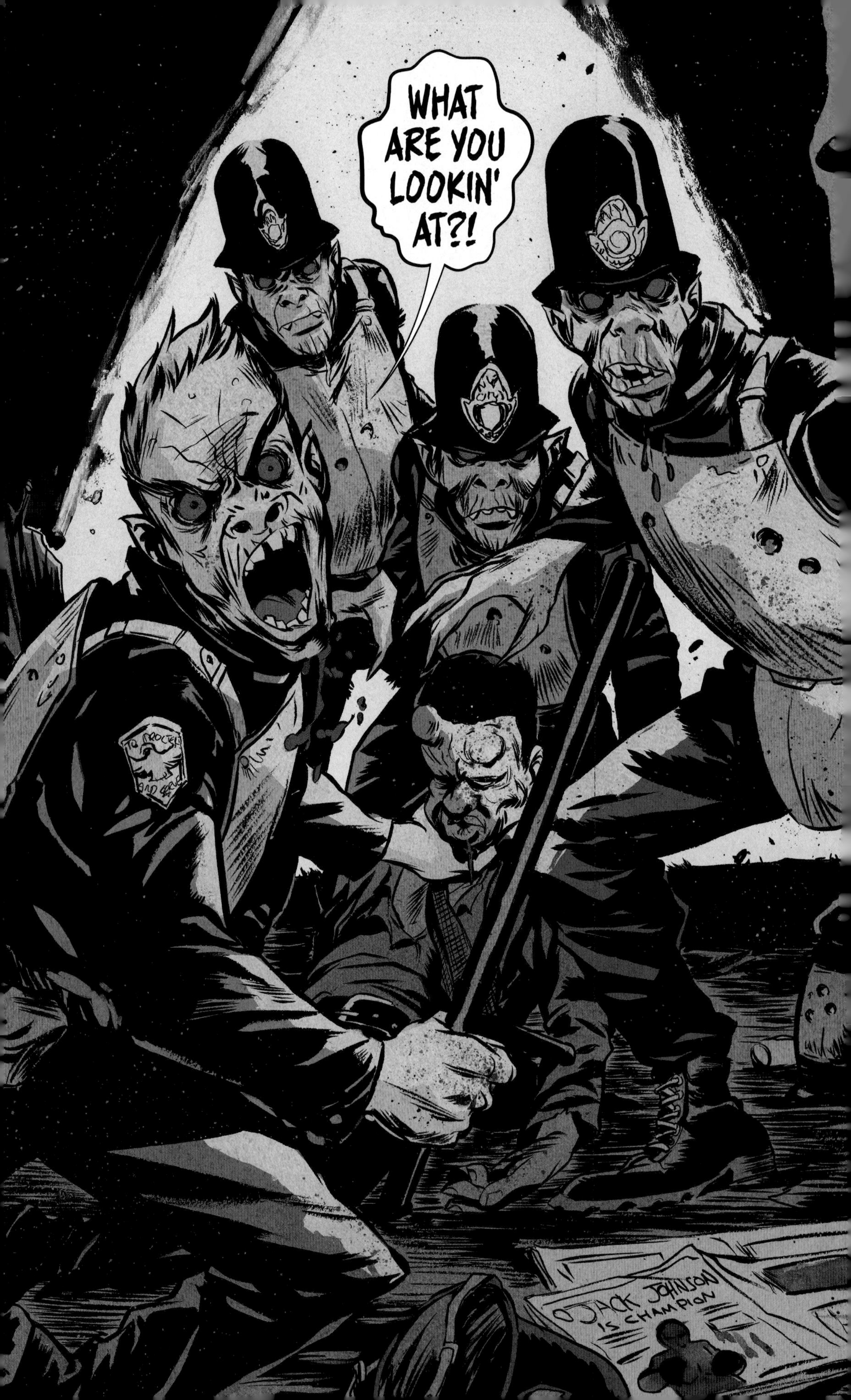
WHAT ARE YOU LOOKIN' AT?!
JACK JOHNSON IS CHAMPION

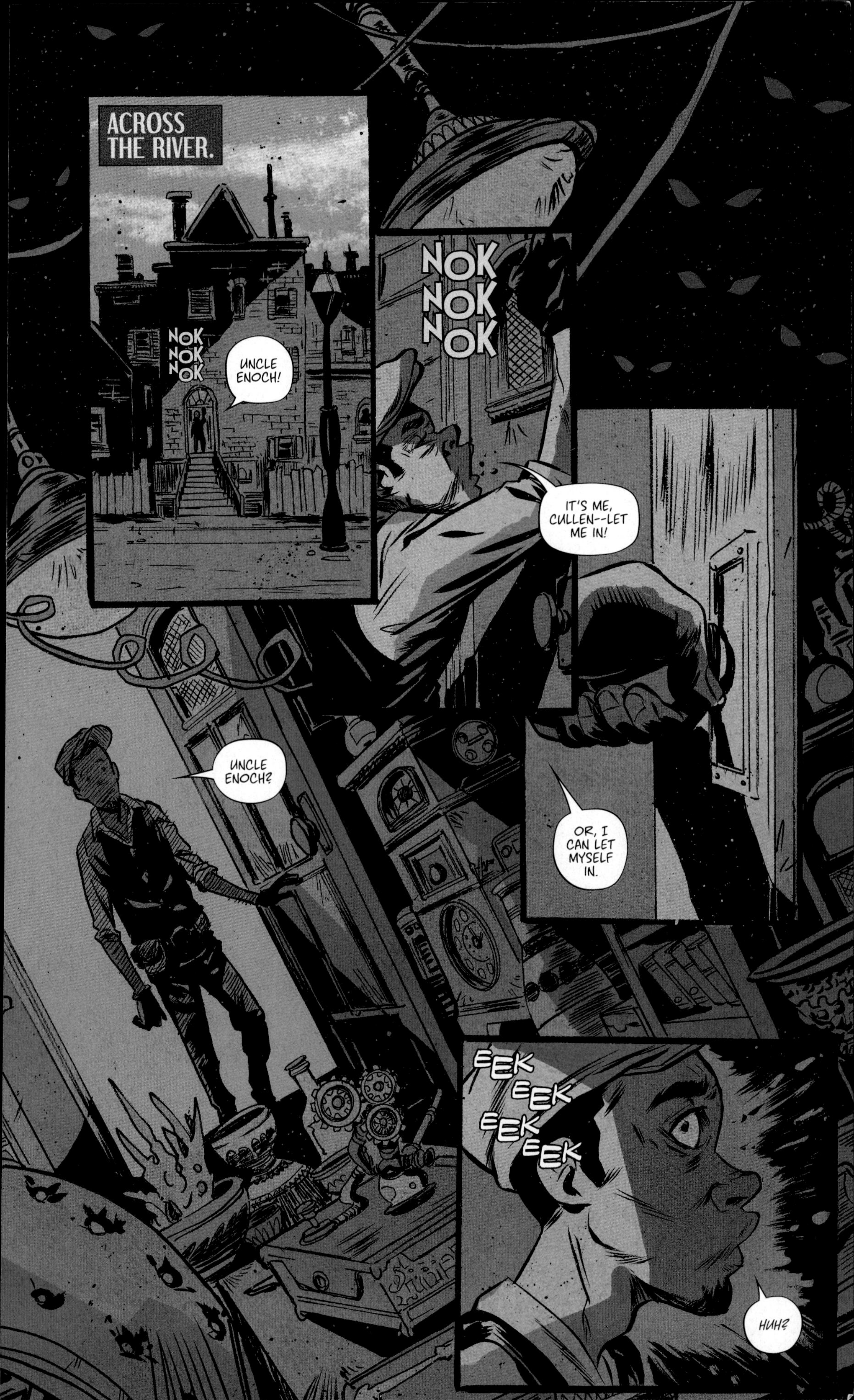
ACROSS THE RIVER.
NOK NOK NOK
UNCLE ENOCH!
NOK NOK NOK
IT'S ME, CULLEN--LET ME IN!
OR, I CAN LET MYSELF IN.
UNCLE ENOCH?
EEK EEK EEK EEK
HUH?

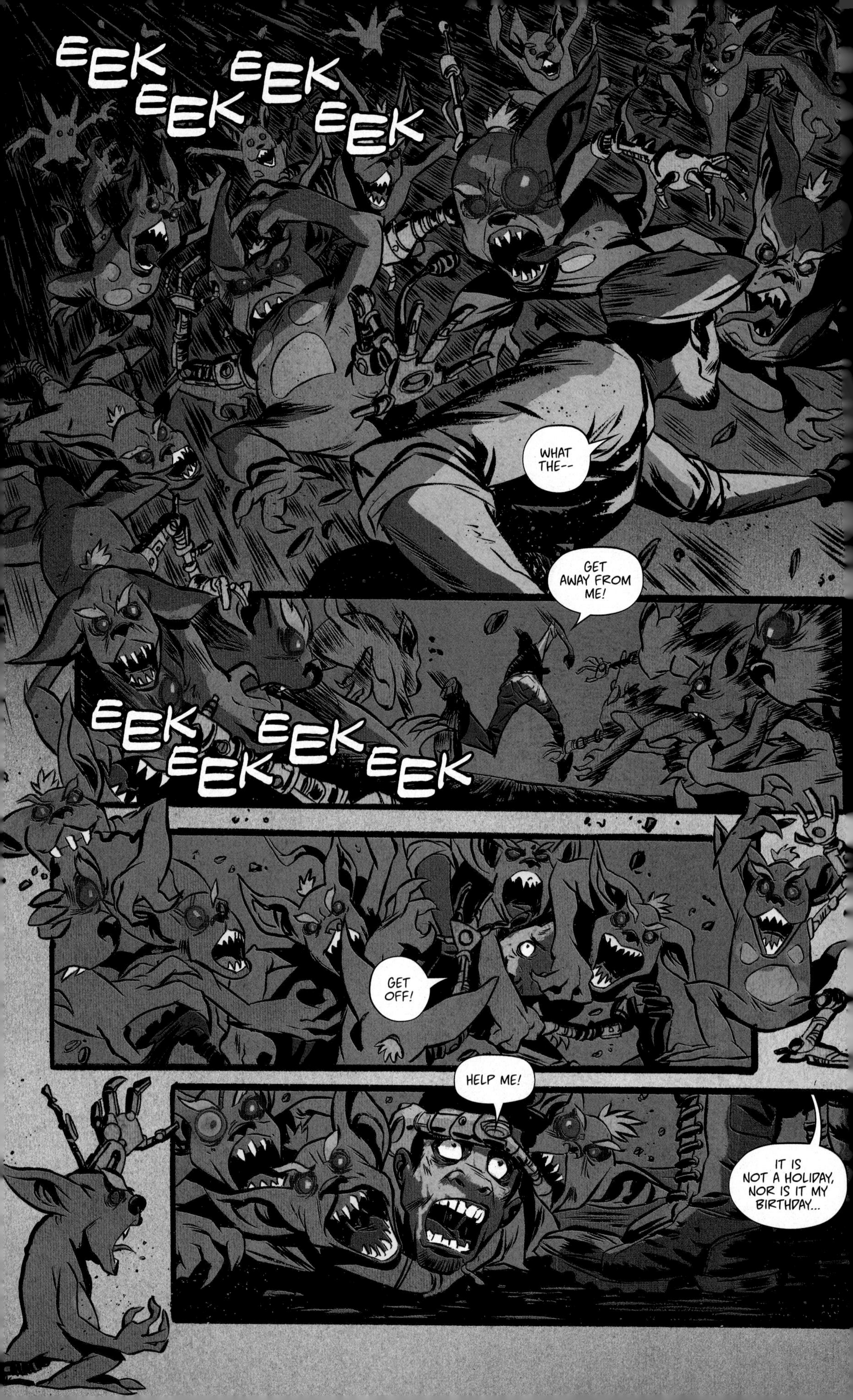
EEK EEK EEK EEK
WHAT THE--
GET AWAY FROM ME!
EEK EEK EEK EEK
GET OFF!
HELP ME!
IT IS NOT A HOLIDAY, NOR IS IT MY BIRTHDAY...

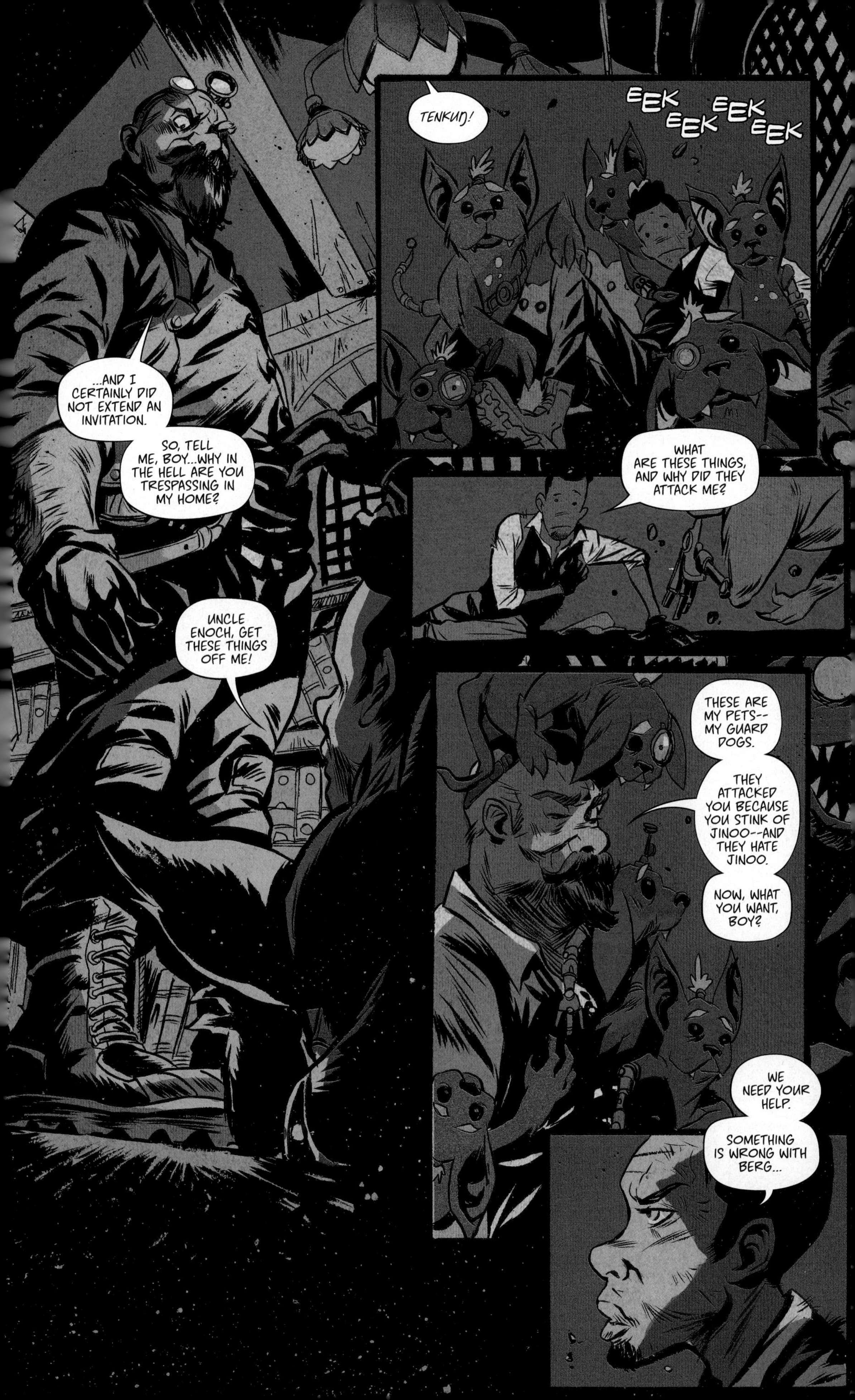
TENKUN!
EEK EEK EEK EEK EEK
...AND I CERTAINLY DID NOT EXTEND AN INVITATION.
SO, TELL ME, BOY...WHY IN THE HELL ARE YOU TRESPASSING IN MY HOME?
UNCLE ENOCH, GET THESE THINGS OFF ME!
WHAT ARE THESE THINGS, AND WHY DID THEY ATTACK ME?
THESE ARE MY PETS--MY GUARD DOGS.
THEY ATTACKED YOU BECAUSE YOU STINK OF JINOO--AND THEY HATE JINOO.
NOW, WHAT YOU WANT, BOY?
WE NEED YOUR HELP.
SOMETHING IS WRONG WITH BERG...

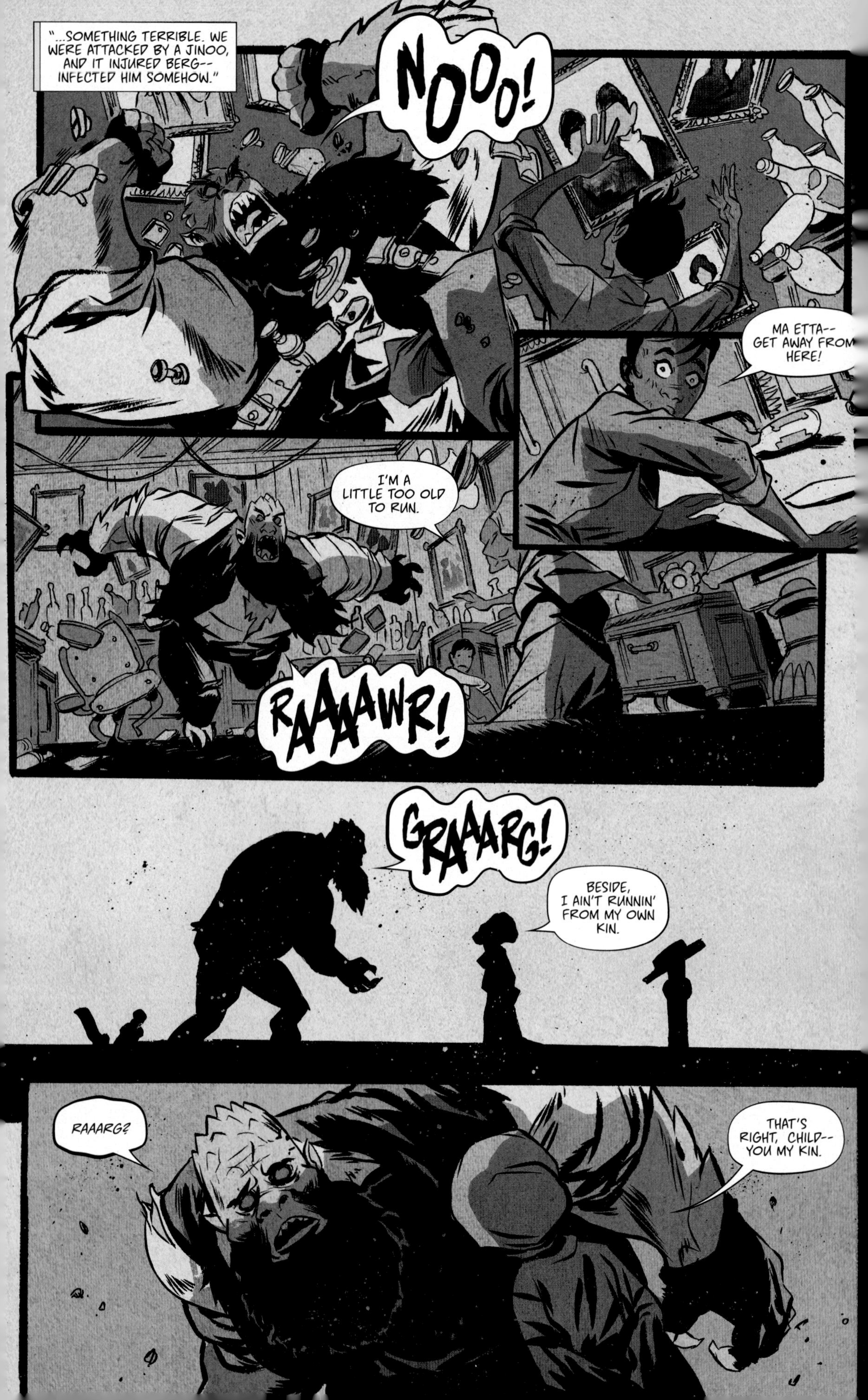
"...SOMETHING TERRIBLE. WE WERE ATTACKED BY A JINOO, AND IT INJURED BERG-- INFECTED HIM SOMEHOW."
NOOO!
MA ETTA-- GET AWAY FROM HERE!
I'M A LITTLE TOO OLD TO RUN.
RAAAAWR!
GRAAARG!
BESIDE, I AIN'T RUNNIN' FROM MY OWN KIN.
RAAARG?
THAT'S RIGHT, CHILD-- YOU MY KIN.

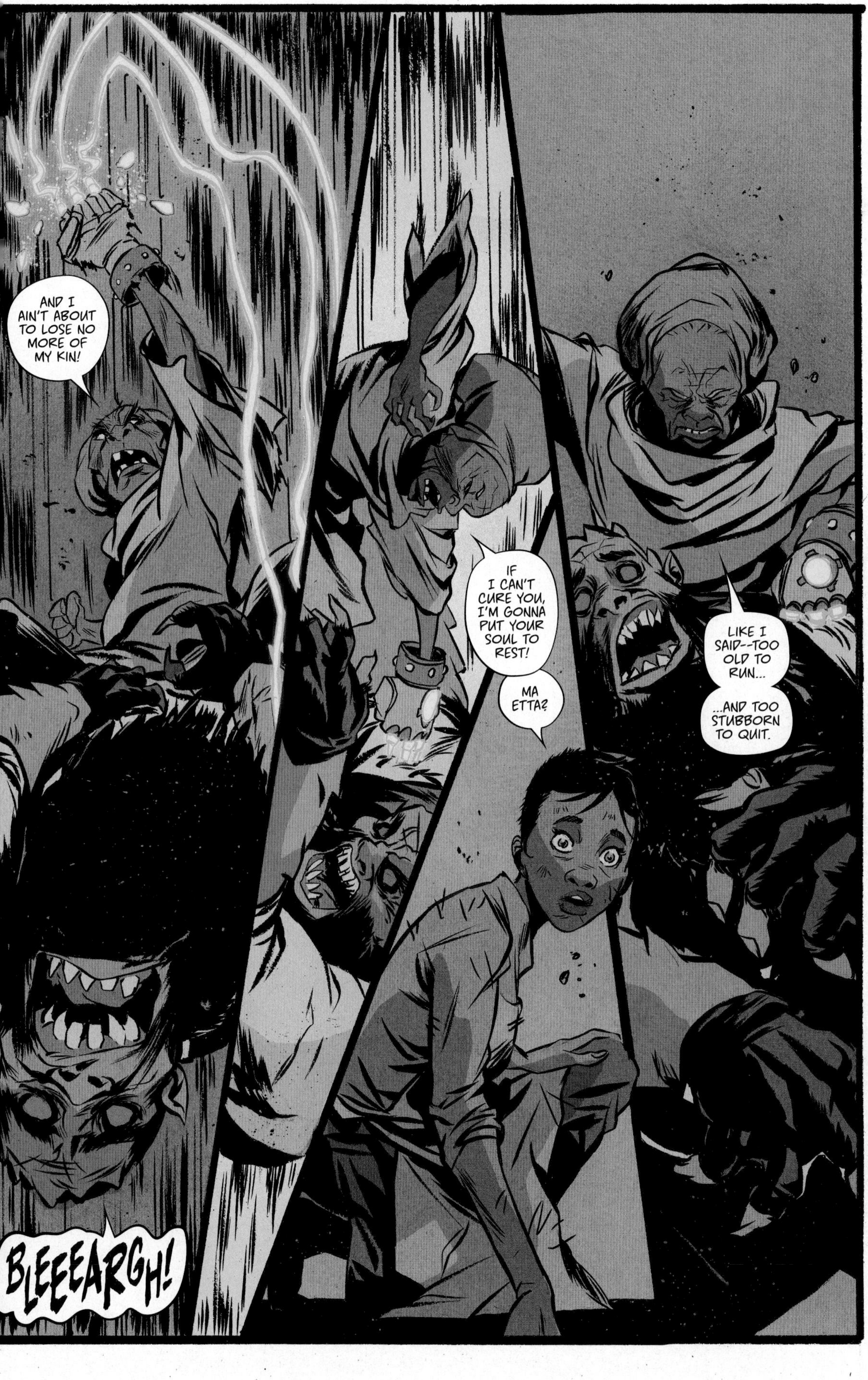
AND I AIN'T ABOUT TO LOSE NO MORE OF MY KIN!
IF I CAN'T CURE YOU, I'M GONNA PUT YOUR SOUL TO REST!
MA ETTA?
LIKE I SAID--TOO OLD TO RUN...
...AND TOO STUBBORN TO QUIT.
BLEEEARGH!

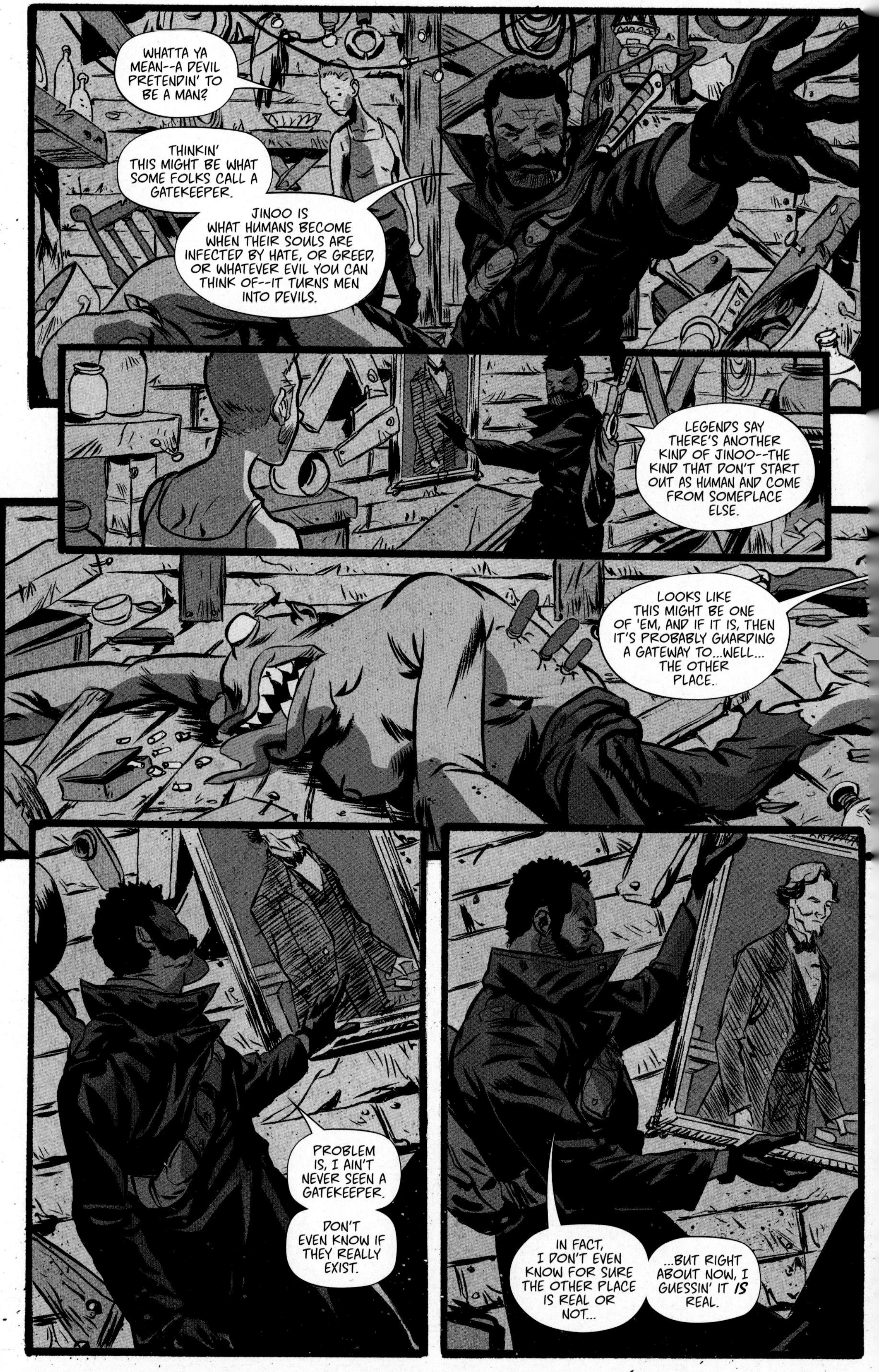
WHATTA YA MEAN--A DEVIL PRETENDIN' TO BE A MAN?
THINKIN' THIS MIGHT BE WHAT SOME FOLKS CALL A GATEKEEPER.
JINOO IS WHAT HUMANS BECOME WHEN THEIR SOULS ARE INFECTED BY HATE, OR GREED, OR WHATEVER EVIL YOU CAN THINK OF--IT TURNS MEN INTO DEVILS.
LEGENDS SAY THERE'S ANOTHER KIND OF JINOO--THE KIND THAT DON'T START OUT AS HUMAN AND COME FROM SOMEPLACE ELSE.
LOOKS LIKE THIS MIGHT BE ONE OF 'EM, AND IF IT IS, THEN IT'S PROBABLY GUARDING A GATEWAY TO...WELL... THE OTHER PLACE.
PROBLEM IS, I AIN'T NEVER SEEN A GATEKEEPER.
DON'T EVEN KNOW IF THEY REALLY EXIST.
IN FACT, I DON'T EVEN KNOW FOR SURE THE OTHER PLACE IS REAL OR NOT...
...BUT RIGHT ABOUT NOW, I GUESSIN' IT *IS* REAL.

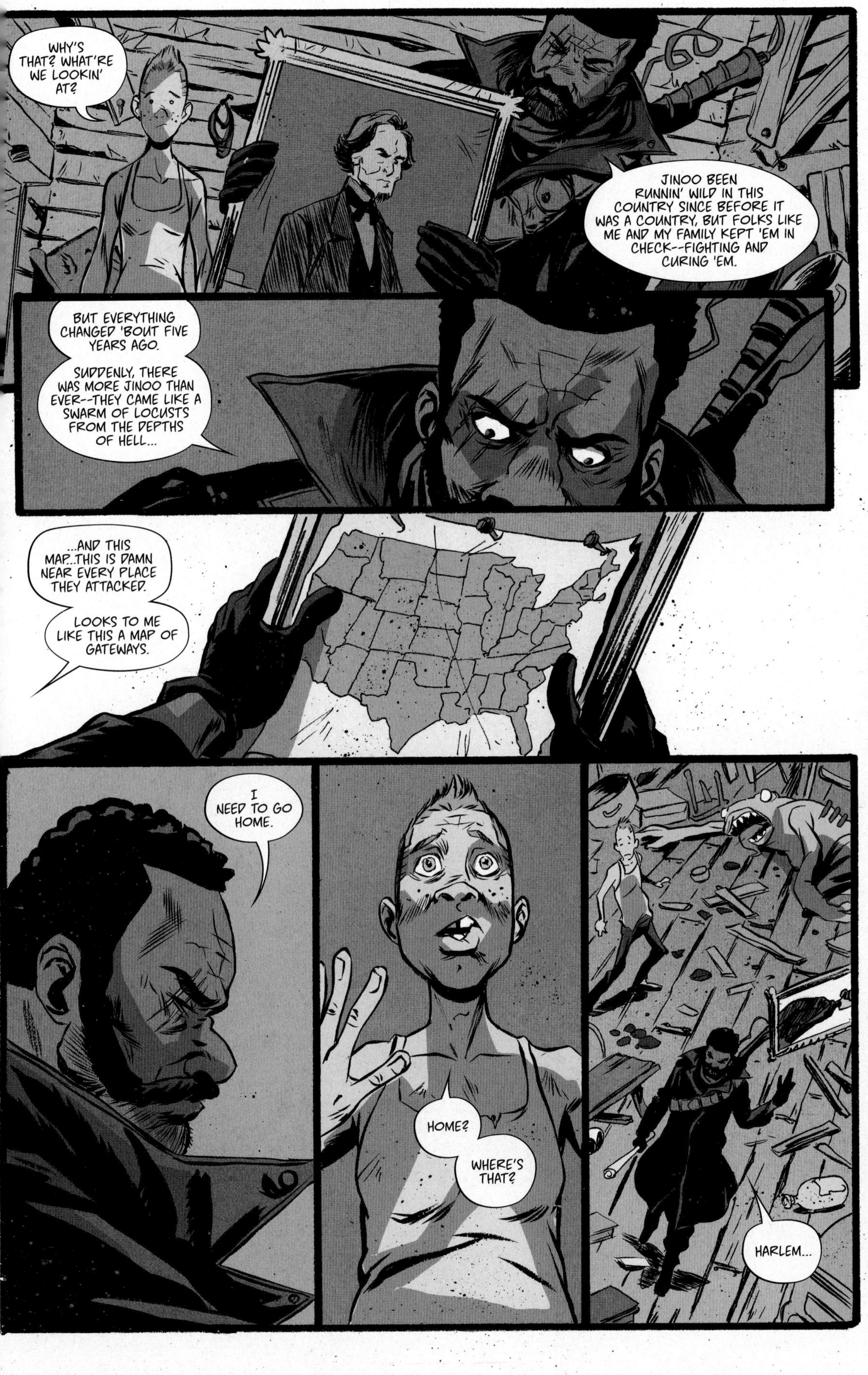
WHY'S THAT? WHAT'RE WE LOOKIN' AT?
JINOO BEEN RUNNIN' WILD IN THIS COUNTRY SINCE BEFORE IT WAS A COUNTRY, BUT FOLKS LIKE ME AND MY FAMILY KEPT 'EM IN CHECK--FIGHTING AND CURING 'EM.
BUT EVERYTHING CHANGED 'BOUT FIVE YEARS AGO.
SUDDENLY, THERE WAS MORE JINOO THAN EVER--THEY CAME LIKE A SWARM OF LOCUSTS FROM THE DEPTHS OF HELL...
...AND THIS MAP...THIS IS DAMN NEAR EVERY PLACE THEY ATTACKED.
LOOKS TO ME LIKE THIS A MAP OF GATEWAYS.
I NEED TO GO HOME.
HOME?
WHERE'S THAT?
HARLEM...

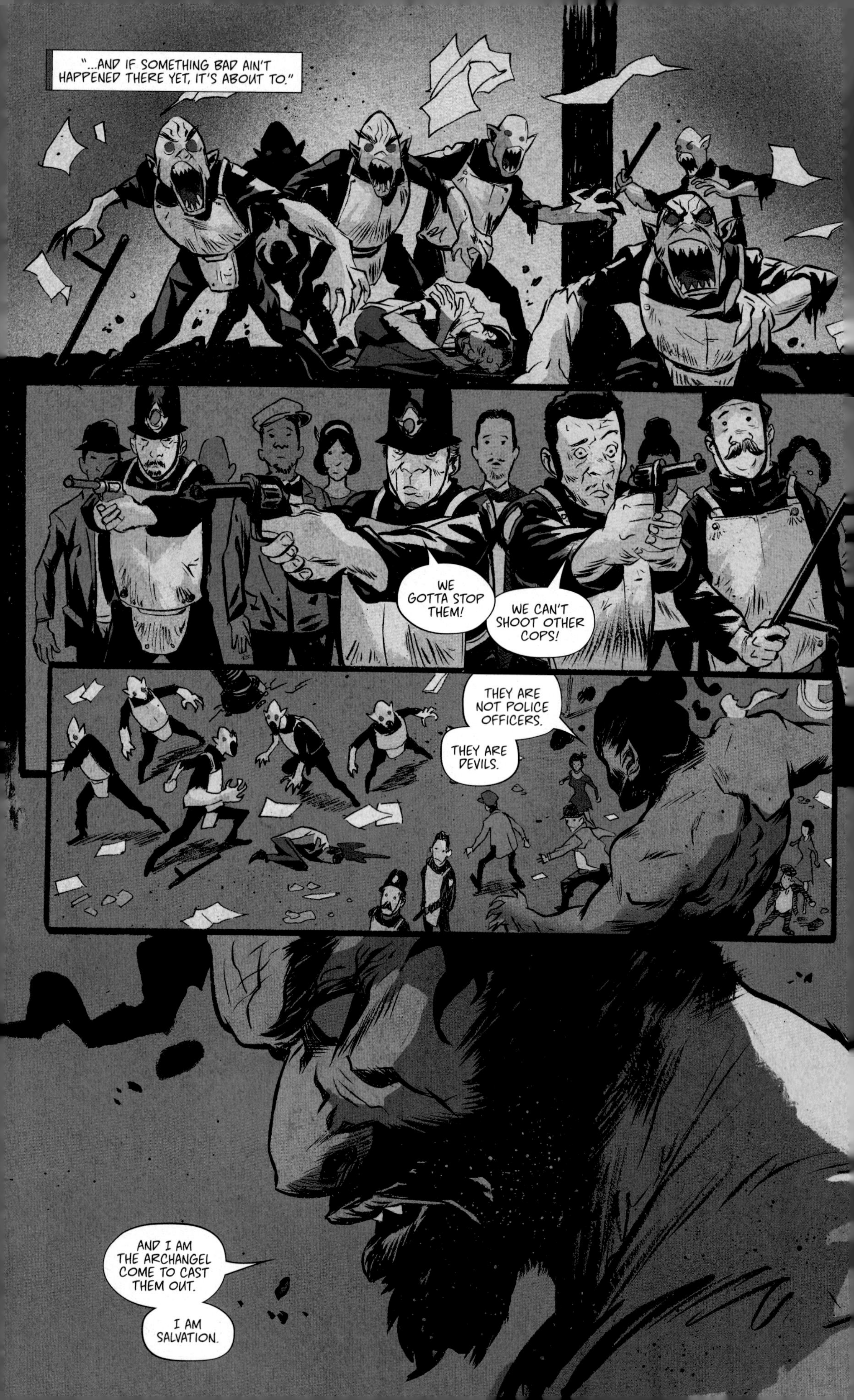
"...AND IF SOMETHING BAD AIN'T HAPPENED THERE YET, IT'S ABOUT TO."
WE GOTTA STOP THEM!
WE CAN'T SHOOT OTHER COPS!
THEY ARE NOT POLICE OFFICERS.
THEY ARE DEVILS.
AND I AM THE ARCHANGEL COME TO CAST THEM OUT.
I AM SALVATION.

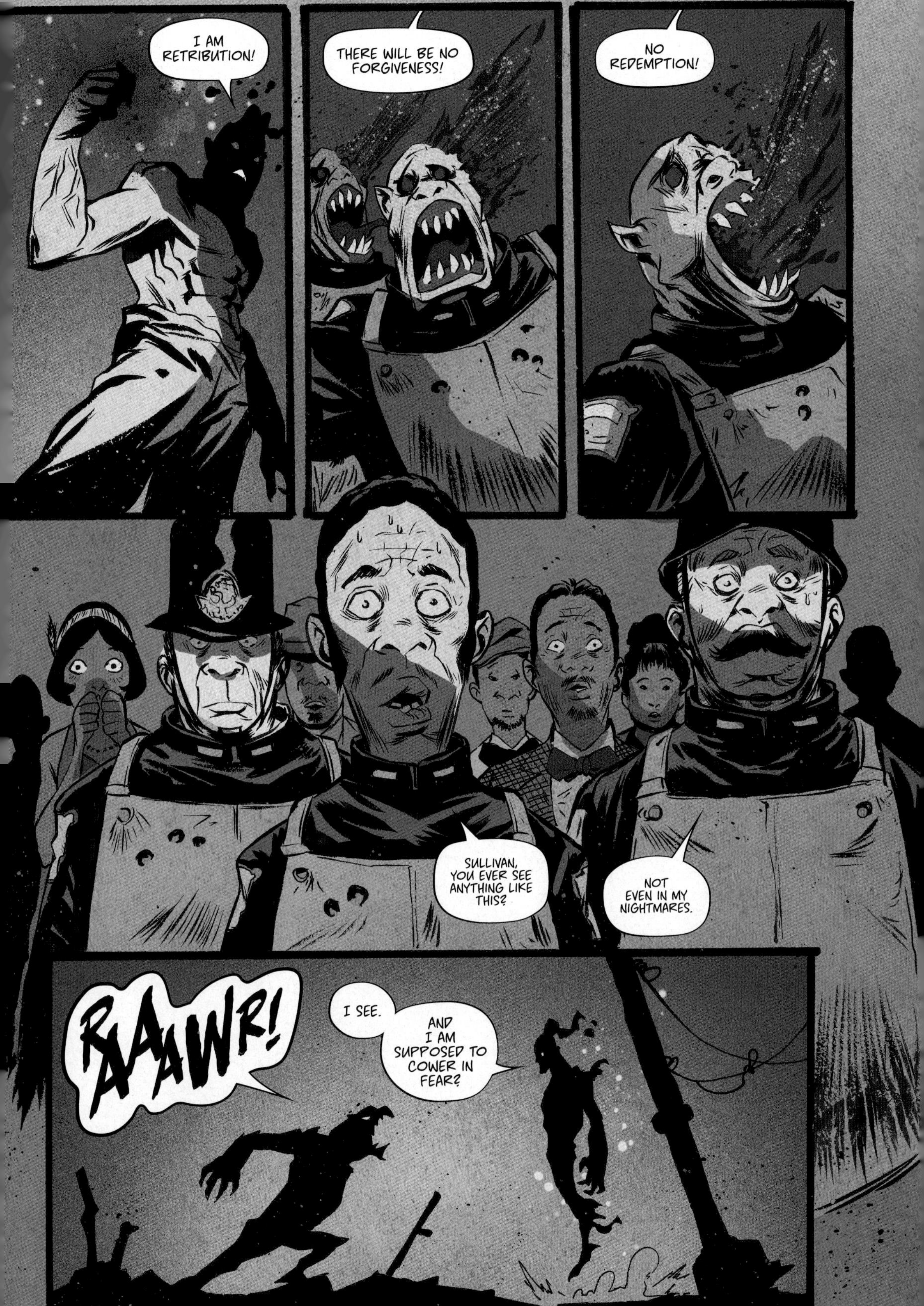
I AM RETRIBUTION!
THERE WILL BE NO FORGIVENESS!
NO REDEMPTION!
SULLIVAN, YOU EVER SEE ANYTHING LIKE THIS?
NOT EVEN IN MY NIGHTMARES.
RAAAWR!
I SEE.
AND I AM SUPPOSED TO COWER IN FEAR?

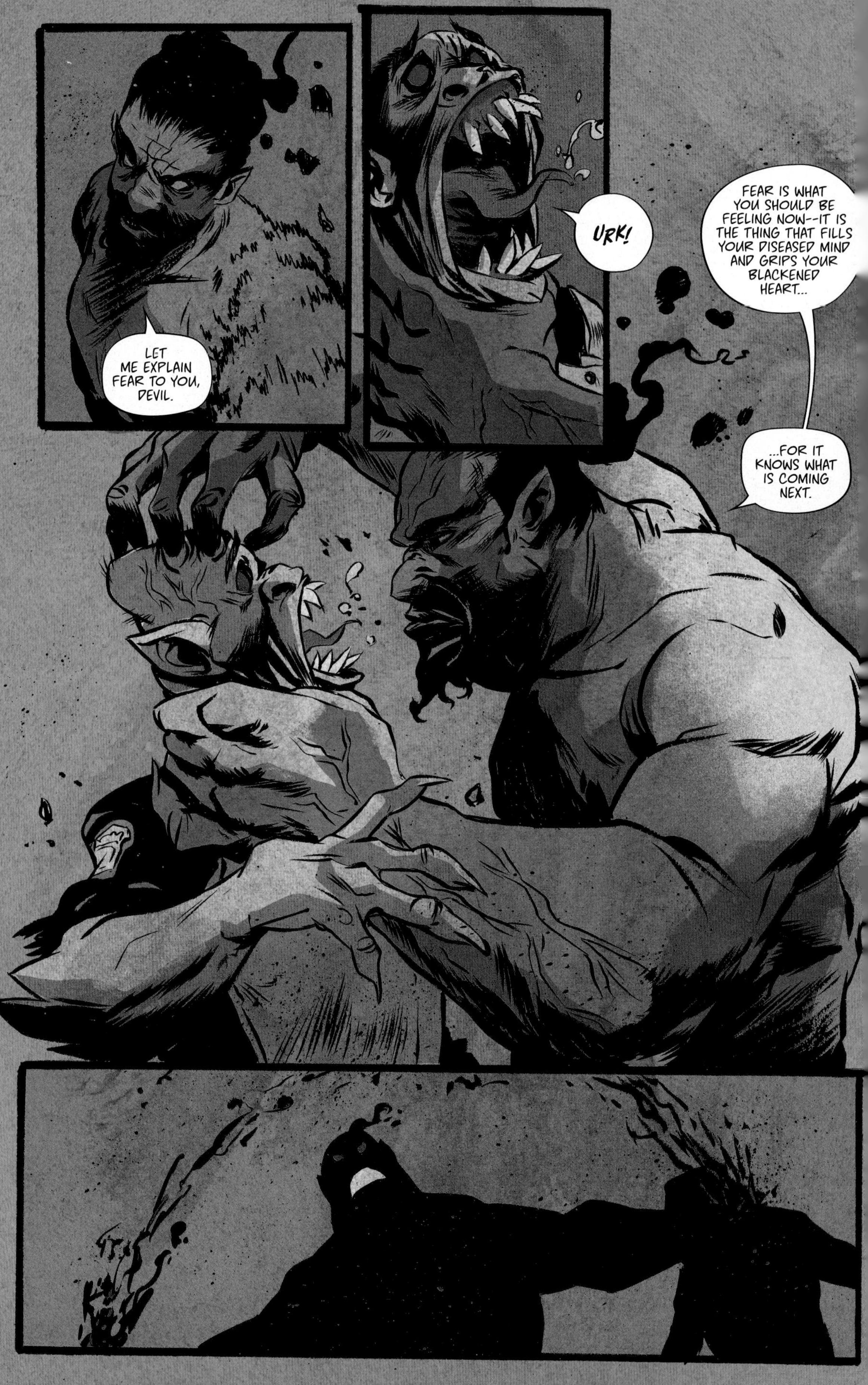
LET ME EXPLAIN FEAR TO YOU, DEVIL.
URK!
FEAR IS WHAT YOU SHOULD BE FEELING NOW--IT IS THE THING THAT FILLS YOUR DISEASED MIND AND GRIPS YOUR BLACKENED HEART...
...FOR IT KNOWS WHAT IS COMING NEXT.

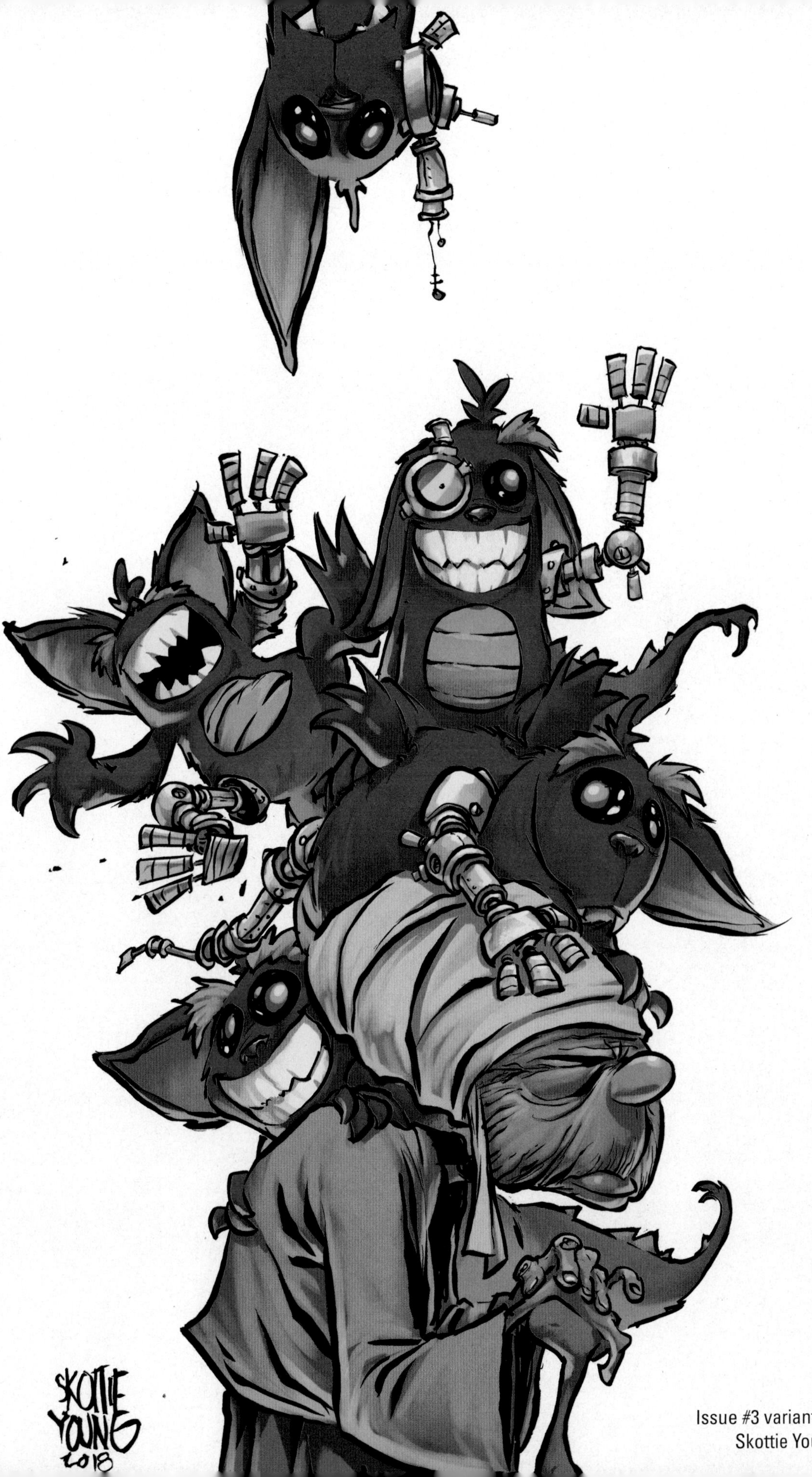
SKOTTIE YOUNG 2018

Issue #3 variant by
Skottie Young

CHAPTER FOUR

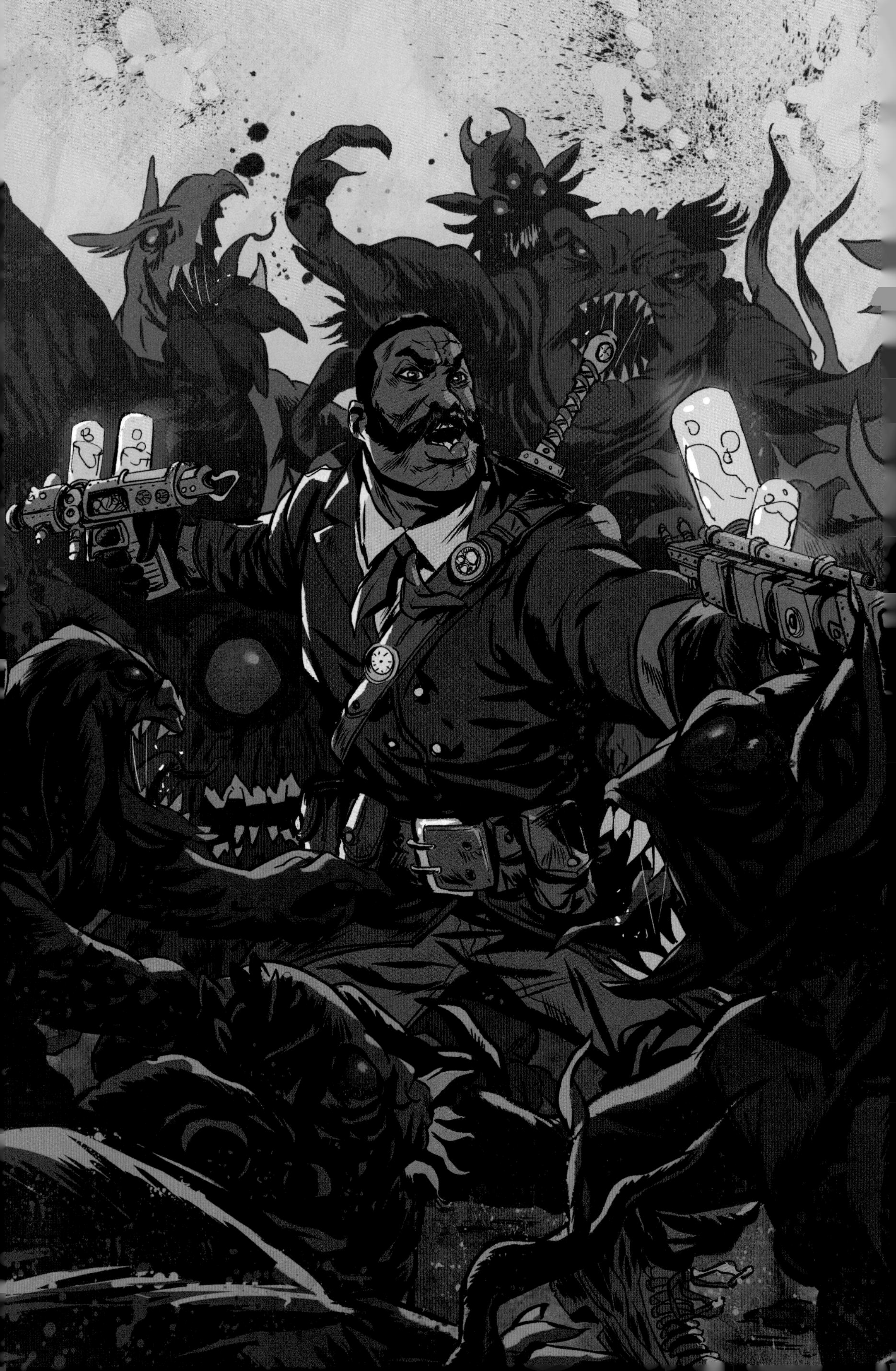

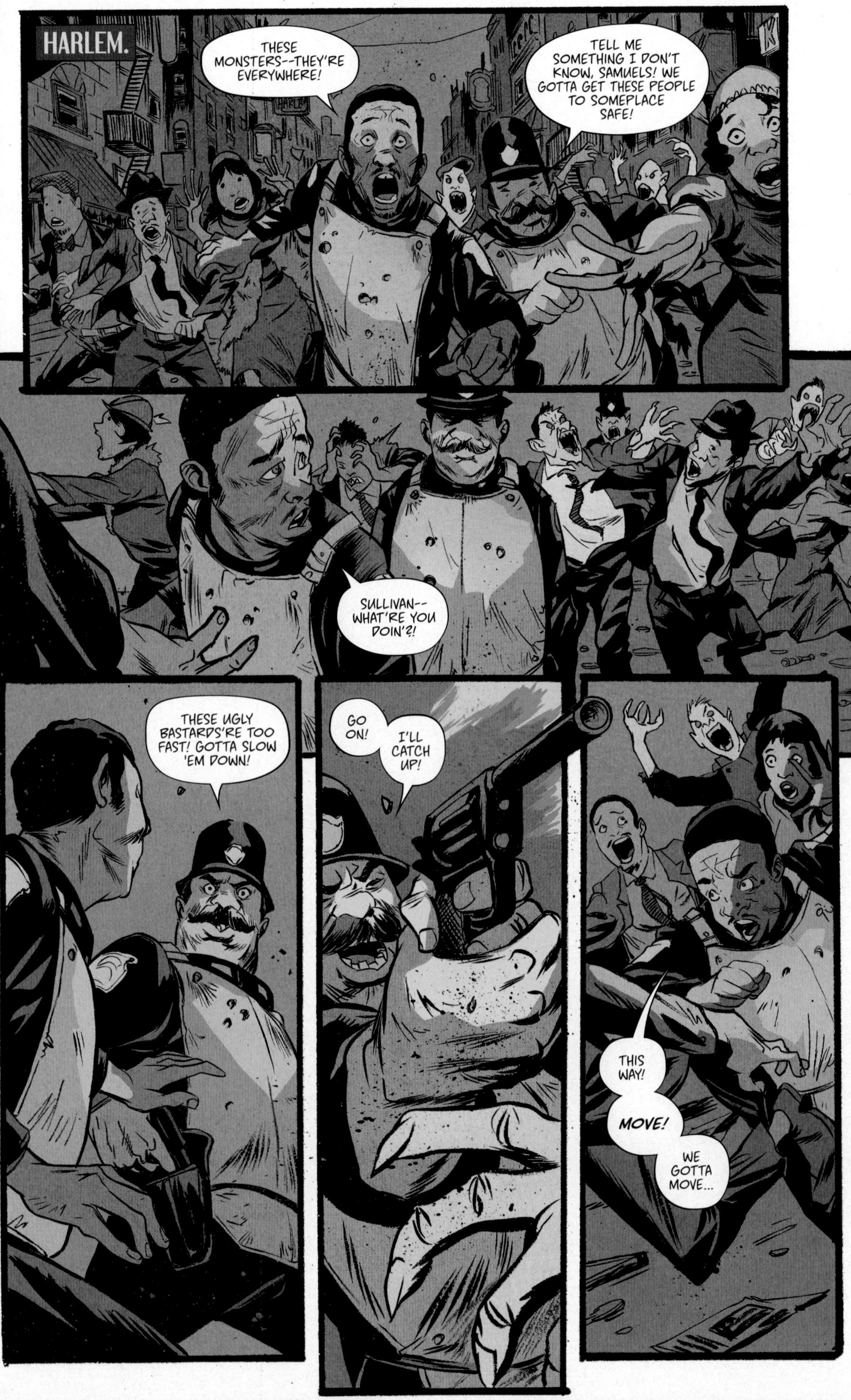
HARLEM.
THESE MONSTERS--THEY'RE EVERYWHERE!
TELL ME SOMETHING I DON'T KNOW, SAMUELS! WE GOTTA GET THESE PEOPLE TO SOMEPLACE SAFE!
SULLIVAN--WHAT'RE YOU DOIN'?!
THESE UGLY BASTARDS'RE TOO FAST! GOTTA SLOW 'EM DOWN!
GO ON!
I'LL CATCH UP!
THIS WAY!
MOVE!
WE GOTTA MOVE...

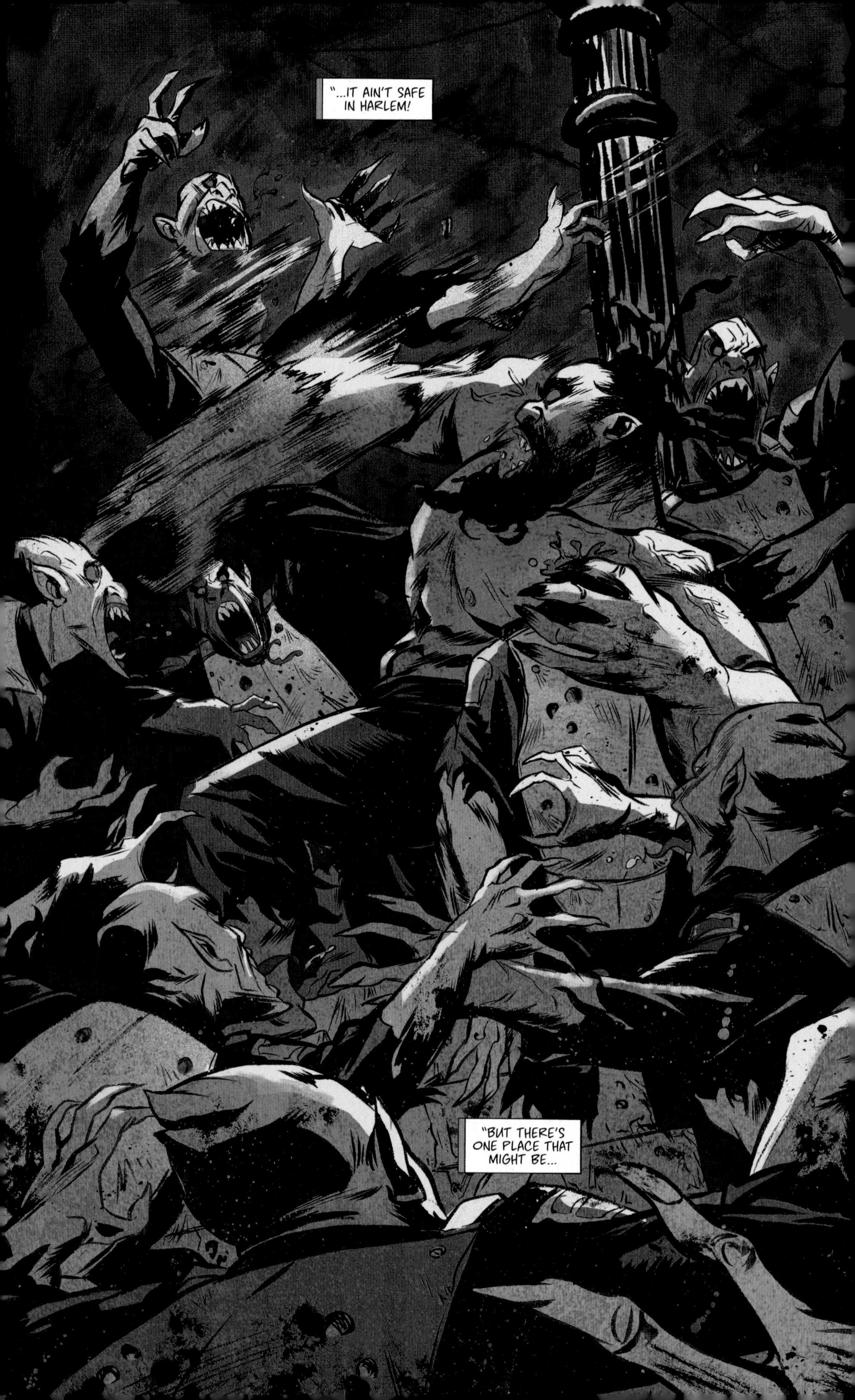
"...IT AIN'T SAFE IN HARLEM!
"BUT THERE'S ONE PLACE THAT MIGHT BE...

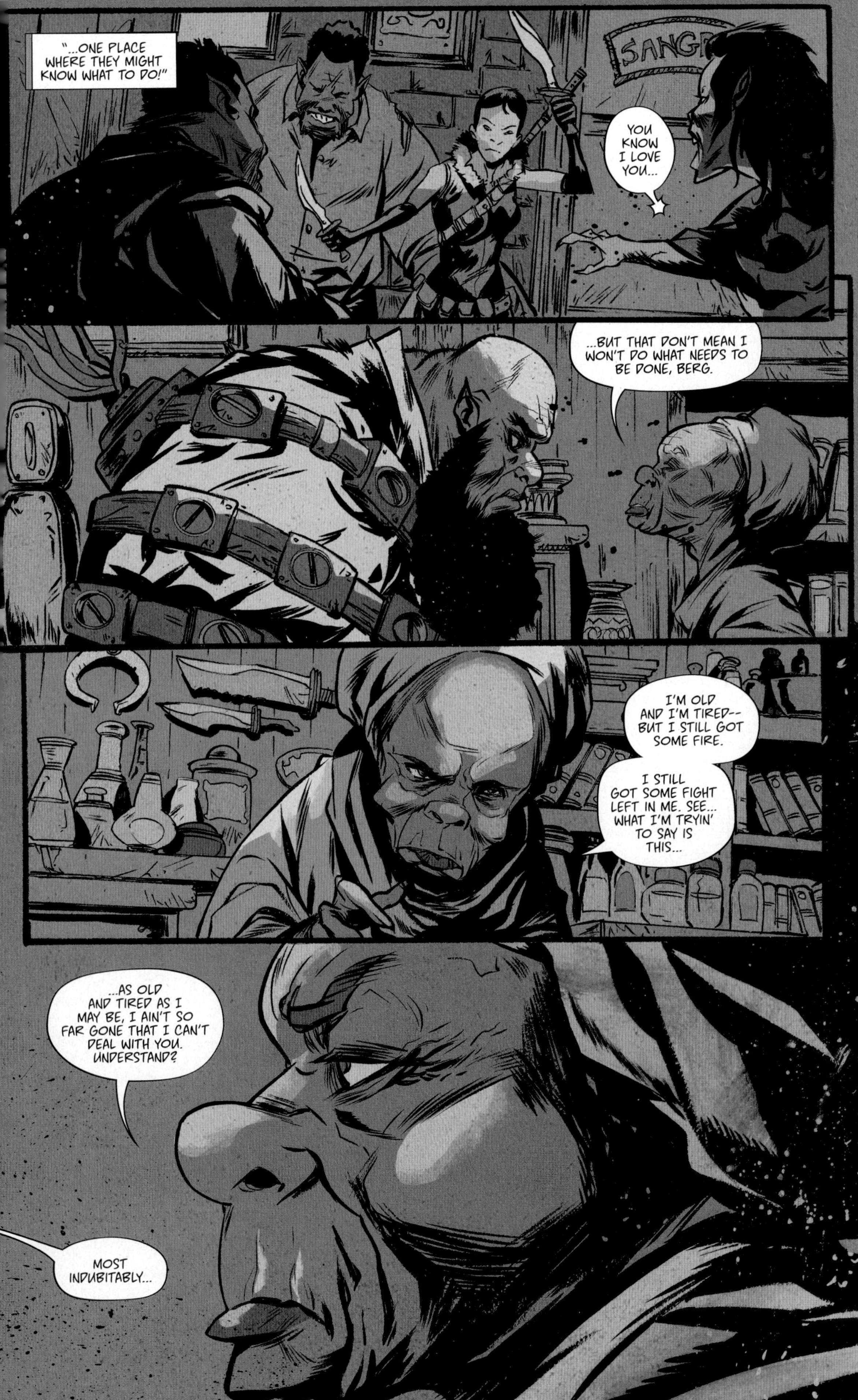
"...ONE PLACE WHERE THEY MIGHT KNOW WHAT TO DO!"
YOU KNOW I LOVE YOU...
...BUT THAT DON'T MEAN I WON'T DO WHAT NEEDS TO BE DONE, BERG.
SANGR
I'M OLD AND I'M TIRED-- BUT I STILL GOT SOME FIRE.
I STILL GOT SOME FIGHT LEFT IN ME. SEE... WHAT I'M TRYIN' TO SAY IS THIS...
...AS OLD AND TIRED AS I MAY BE, I AIN'T SO FAR GONE THAT I CAN'T DEAL WITH YOU. UNDERSTAND?
MOST INDUBITABLY...

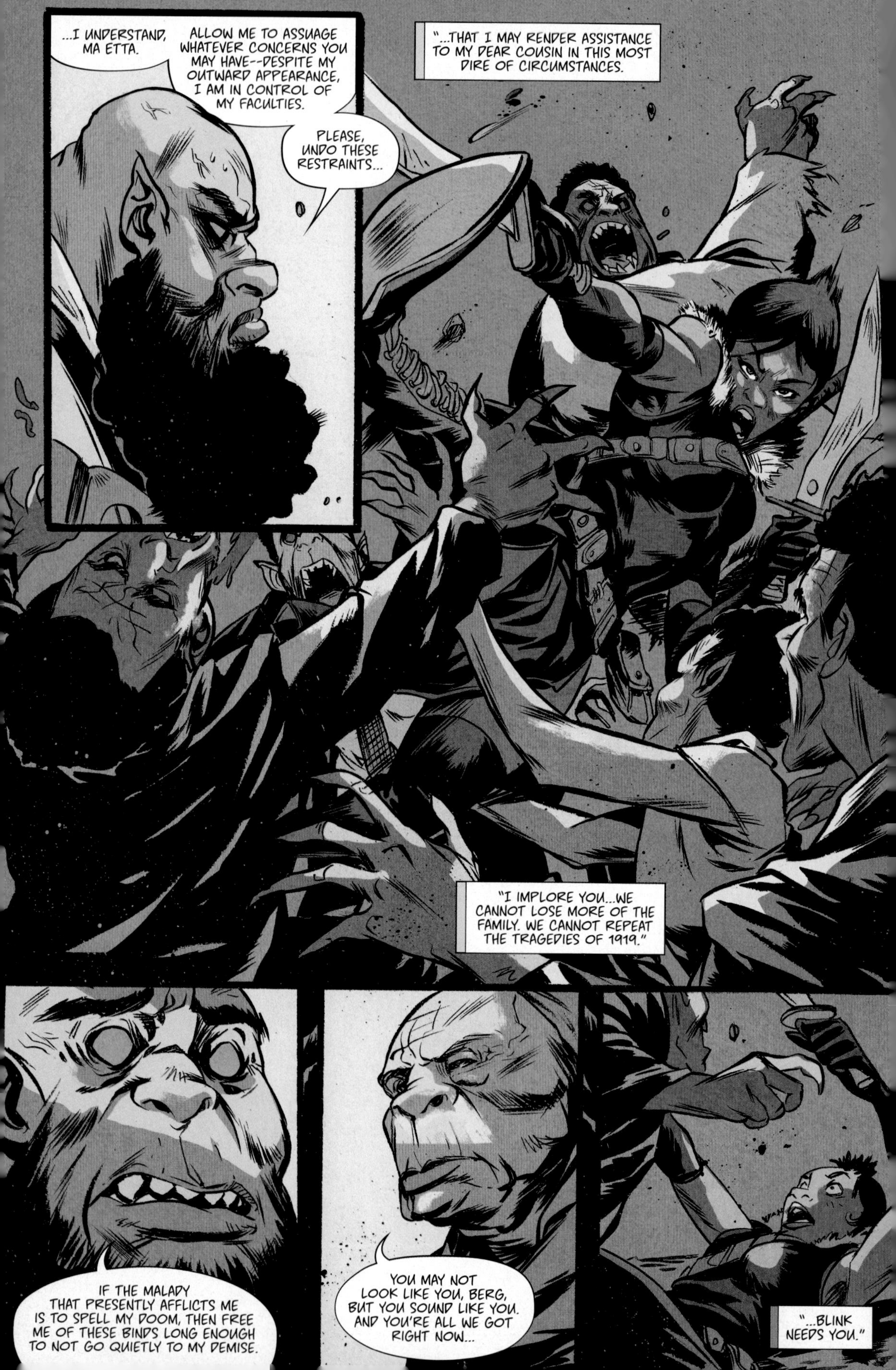
...I UNDERSTAND, MA ETTA.
ALLOW ME TO ASSUAGE WHATEVER CONCERNS YOU MAY HAVE--DESPITE MY OUTWARD APPEARANCE, I AM IN CONTROL OF MY FACULTIES.
PLEASE, UNDO THESE RESTRAINTS...
"...THAT I MAY RENDER ASSISTANCE TO MY DEAR COUSIN IN THIS MOST DIRE OF CIRCUMSTANCES.
"I IMPLORE YOU...WE CANNOT LOSE MORE OF THE FAMILY. WE CANNOT REPEAT THE TRAGEDIES OF 1919."
IF THE MALADY THAT PRESENTLY AFFLICTS ME IS TO SPELL MY DOOM, THEN FREE ME OF THESE BINDS LONG ENOUGH TO NOT GO QUIETLY TO MY DEMISE.
YOU MAY NOT LOOK LIKE YOU, BERG, BUT YOU SOUND LIKE YOU. AND YOU'RE ALL WE GOT RIGHT NOW...
"...BLINK NEEDS YOU."

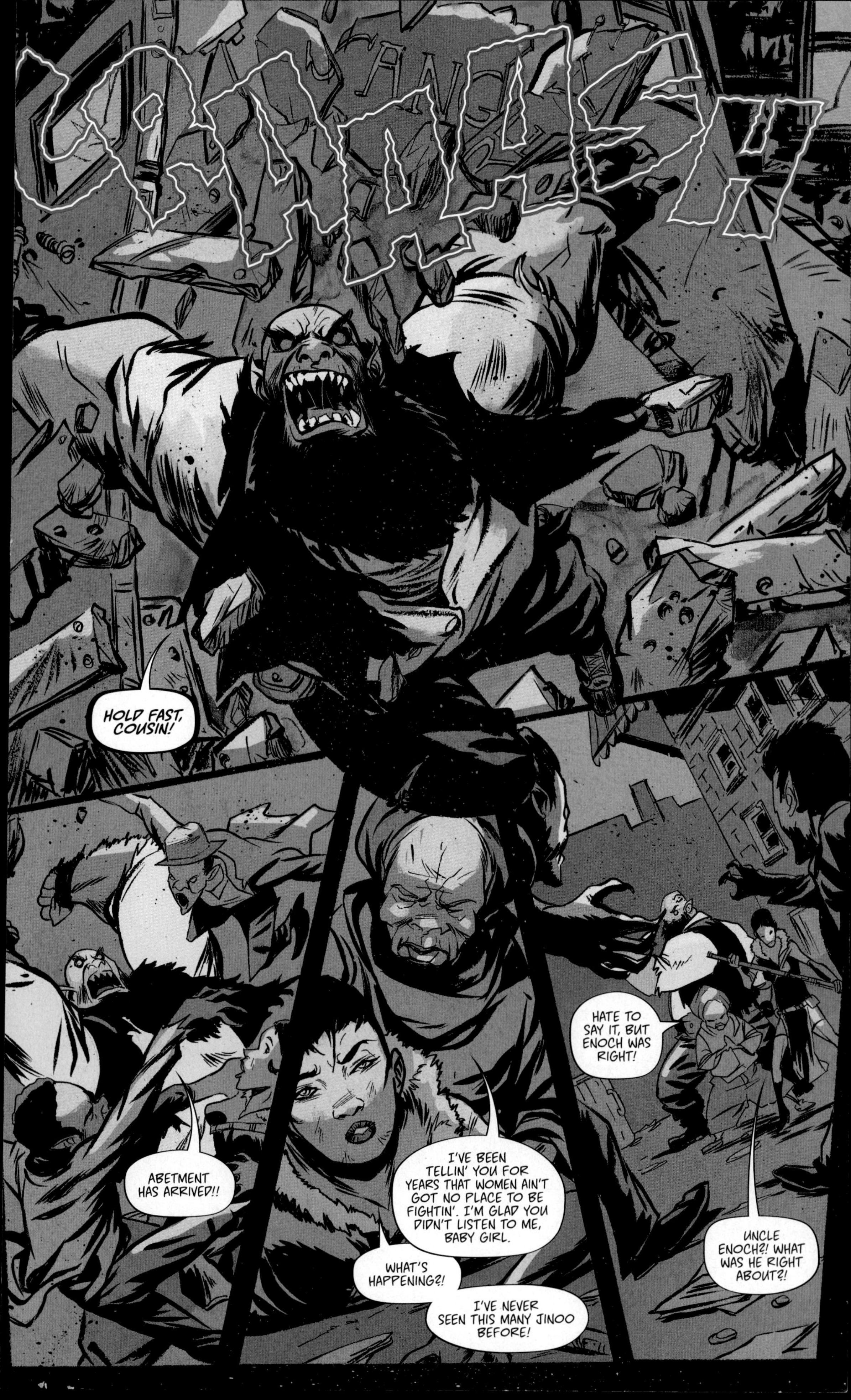
SMASH!!
HOLD FAST, COUSIN!
ABETMENT HAS ARRIVED!!
I'VE BEEN TELLIN' YOU FOR YEARS THAT WOMEN AIN'T GOT NO PLACE TO BE FIGHTIN'. I'M GLAD YOU DIDN'T LISTEN TO ME, BABY GIRL.
WHAT'S HAPPENING?!
I'VE NEVER SEEN THIS MANY JINOO BEFORE!
HATE TO SAY IT, BUT ENOCH WAS RIGHT!
UNCLE ENOCH?! WHAT WAS HE RIGHT ABOUT?!

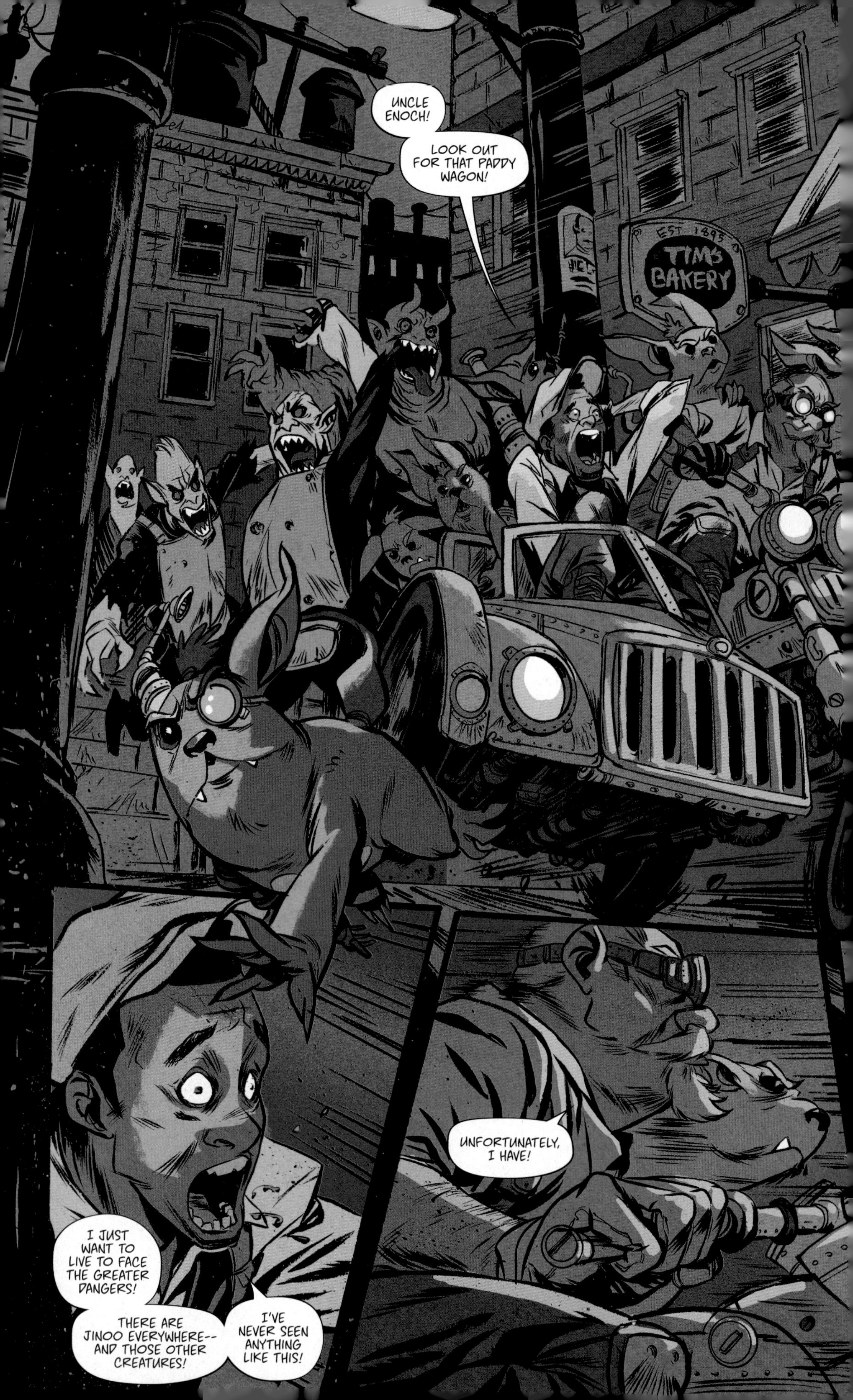
UNCLE ENOCH!
LOOK OUT FOR THAT PADDY WAGON!
EST 1895
TIM'S BAKERY
I JUST WANT TO LIVE TO FACE THE GREATER DANGERS!
THERE ARE JINOO EVERYWHERE-- AND THOSE OTHER CREATURES!
I'VE NEVER SEEN ANYTHING LIKE THIS!
UNFORTUNATELY, I HAVE!

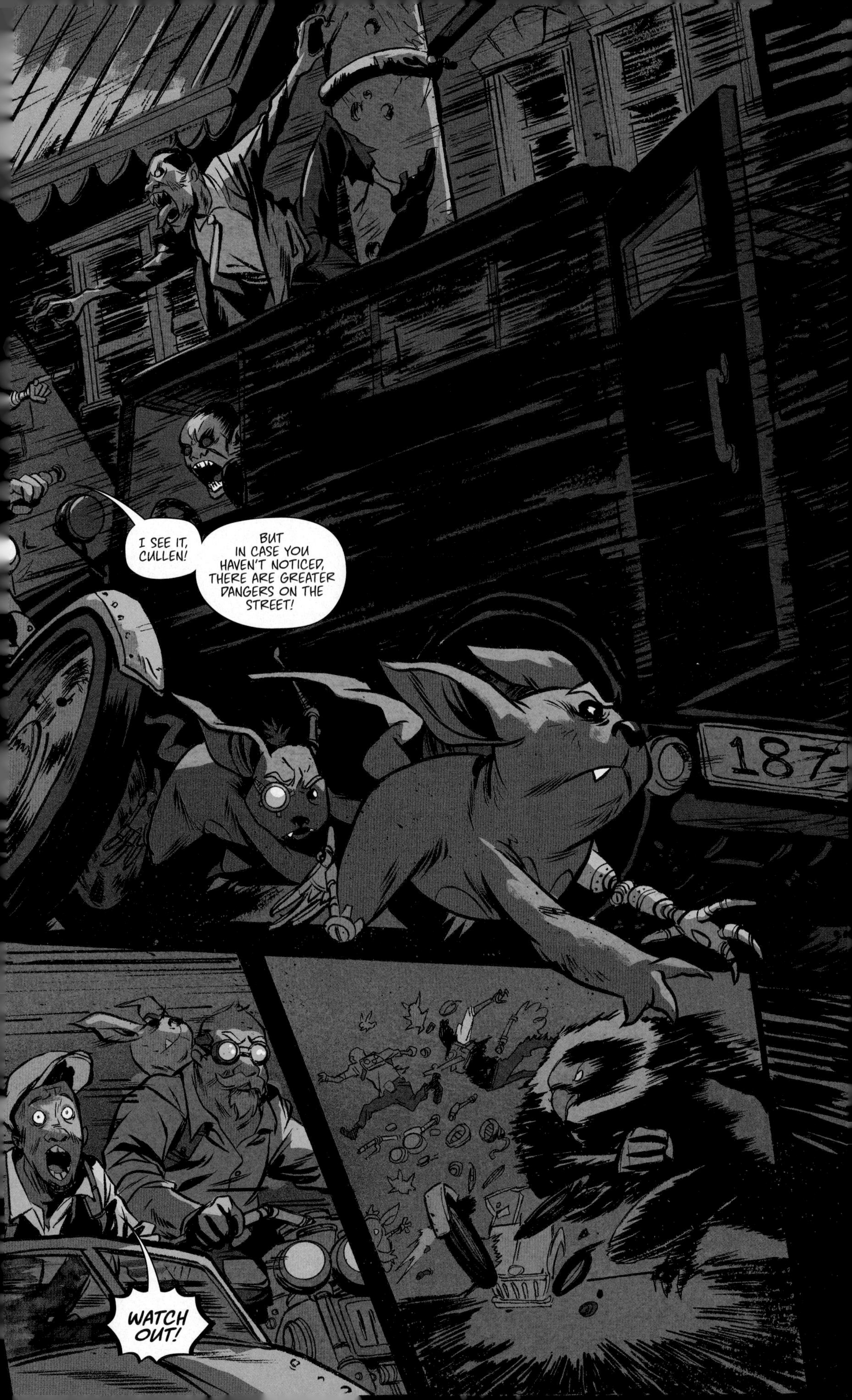
I SEE IT, CULLEN!
BUT IN CASE YOU HAVEN'T NOTICED, THERE ARE GREATER DANGERS ON THE STREET!
187
WATCH OUT!

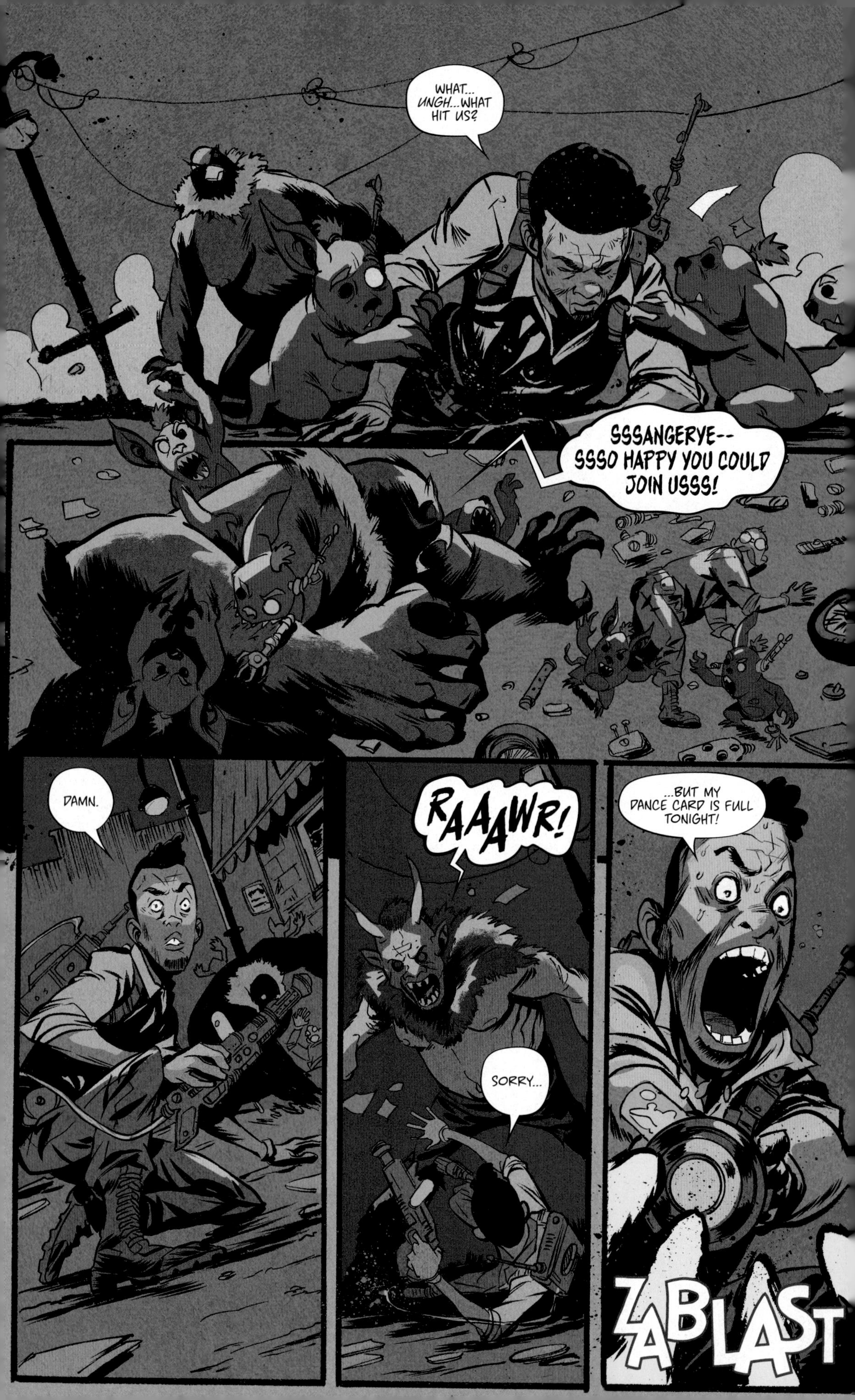
WHAT... UNGH...WHAT HIT US?
SSSANGERYE-- SSSO HAPPY YOU COULD JOIN USSS!
DAMN.
RAAAWR!
SORRY...
...BUT MY DANCE CARD IS FULL TONIGHT!
ZABLAST

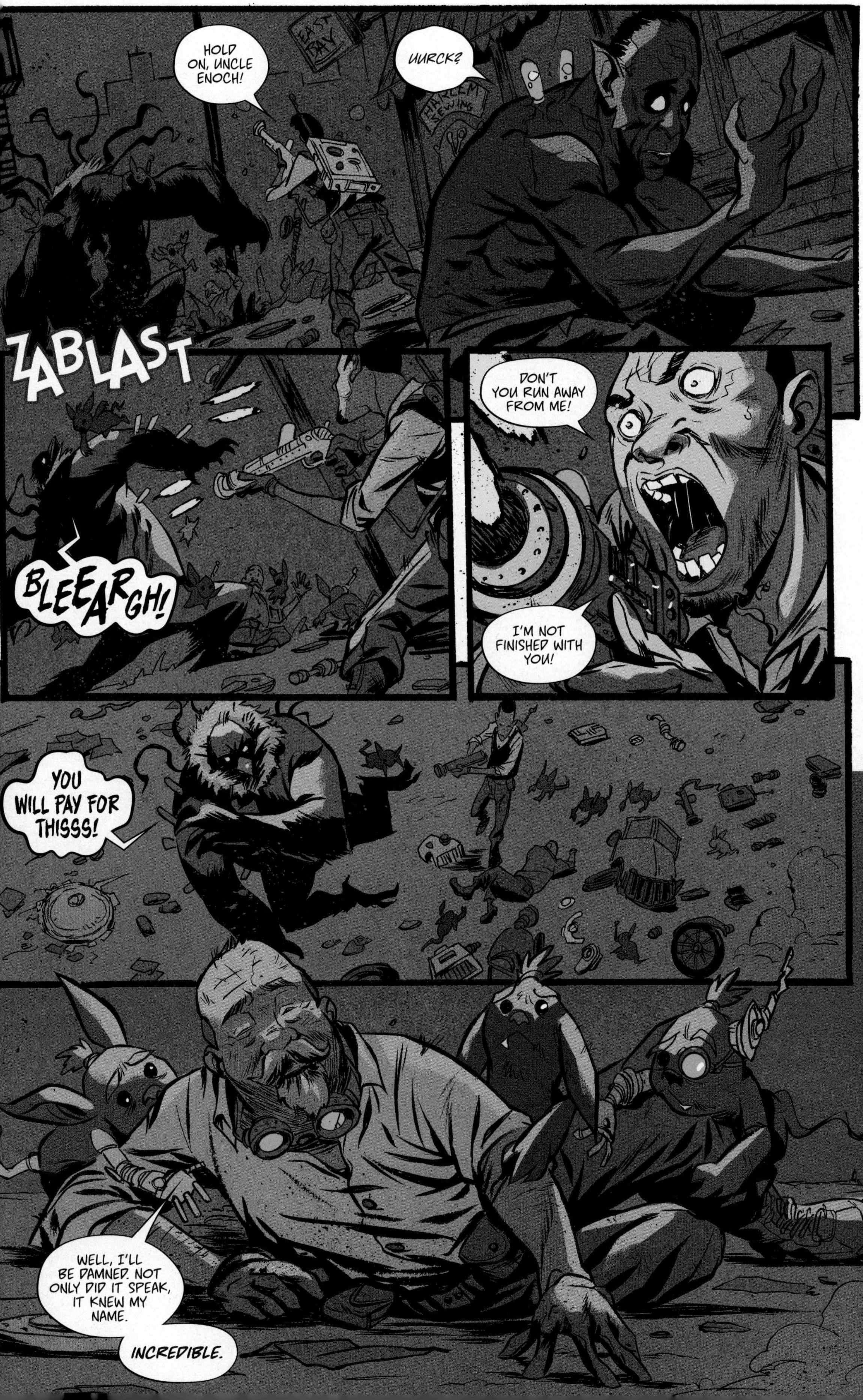

HOLD ON, UNCLE ENOCH!
UURCK?
ZABLAST
BLEEARGH!
DON'T YOU RUN AWAY FROM ME!
I'M NOT FINISHED WITH YOU!
YOU WILL PAY FOR THISSS!
WELL, I'LL BE DAMNED. NOT ONLY DID IT SPEAK, IT KNEW MY NAME.
INCREDIBLE.

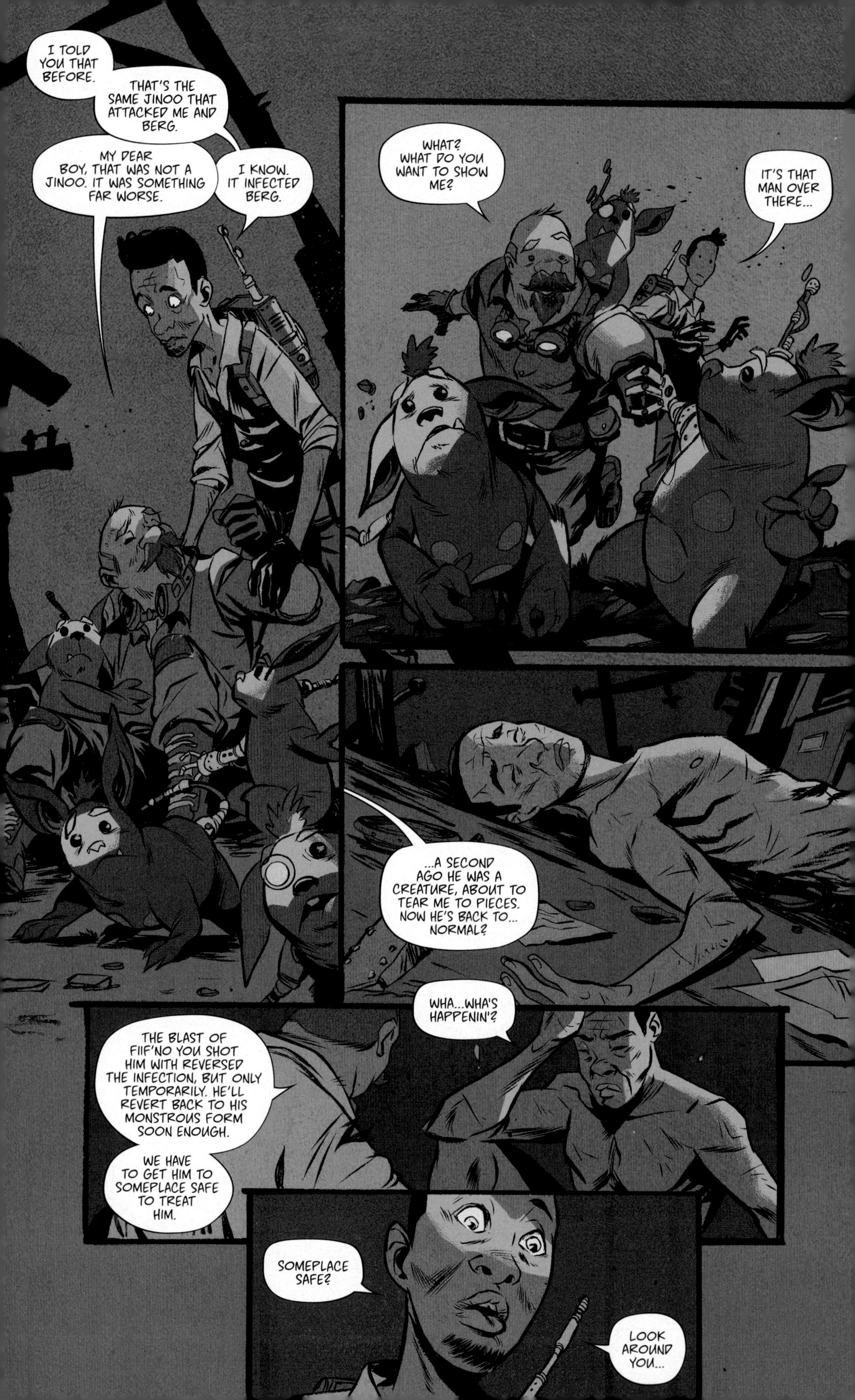
I TOLD YOU THAT BEFORE.
THAT'S THE SAME JINOO THAT ATTACKED ME AND BERG.
MY DEAR BOY, THAT WAS NOT A JINOO. IT WAS SOMETHING FAR WORSE.
I KNOW. IT INFECTED BERG.
WHAT? WHAT DO YOU WANT TO SHOW ME?
IT'S THAT MAN OVER THERE...
...A SECOND AGO HE WAS A CREATURE, ABOUT TO TEAR ME TO PIECES. NOW HE'S BACK TO... NORMAL?
WHA...WHA'S HAPPENIN'?
THE BLAST OF FIIF'NO YOU SHOT HIM WITH REVERSED THE INFECTION, BUT ONLY TEMPORARILY. HE'LL REVERT BACK TO HIS MONSTROUS FORM SOON ENOUGH.
WE HAVE TO GET HIM TO SOMEPLACE SAFE TO TREAT HIM.
SOMEPLACE SAFE?
LOOK AROUND YOU...

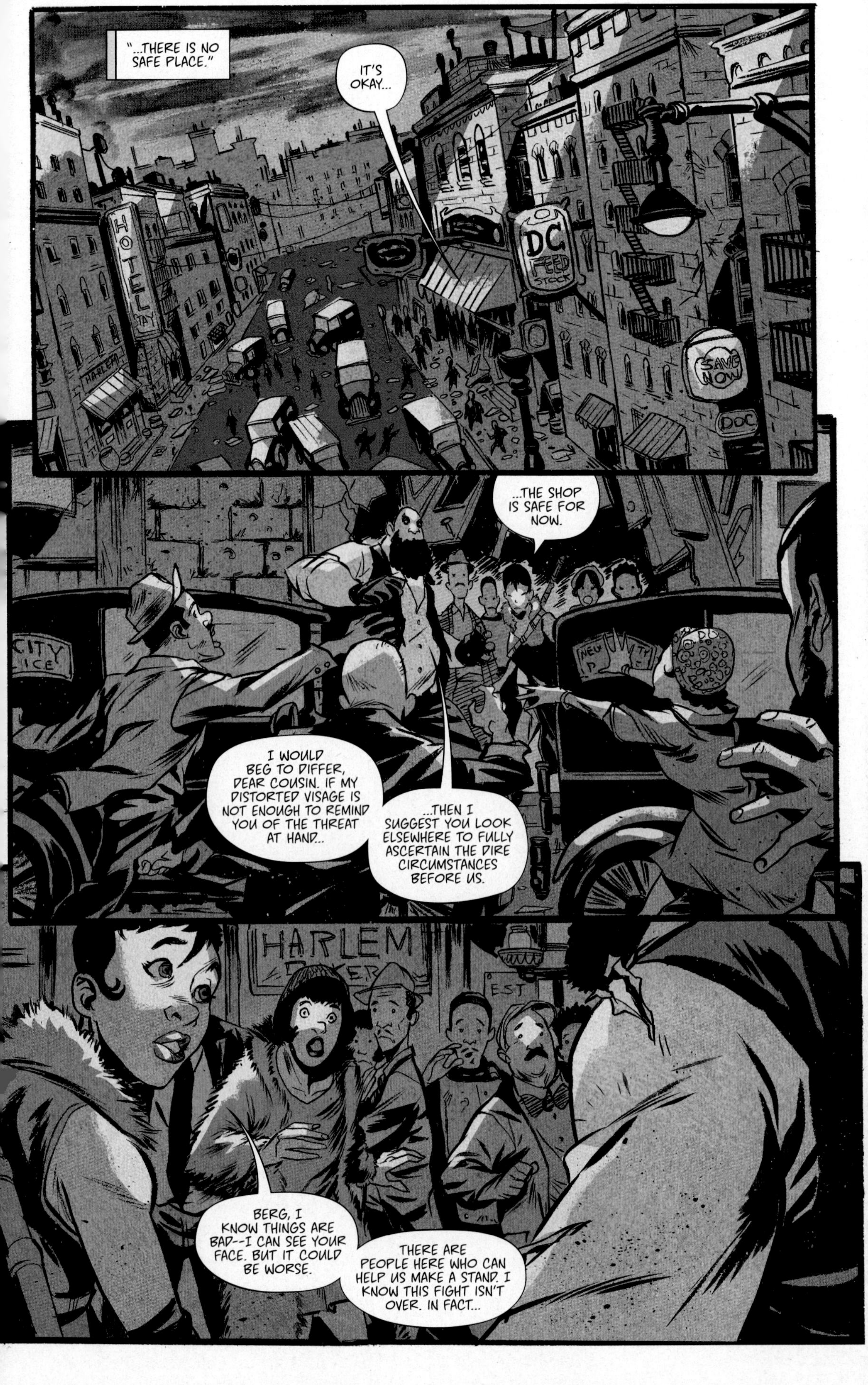
"...THERE IS NO SAFE PLACE."
IT'S OKAY...
HOTEL
HARLEM
DC FEED STOCK
SAVE NOW
DOC
...THE SHOP IS SAFE FOR NOW.
I WOULD BEG TO DIFFER, DEAR COUSIN. IF MY DISTORTED VISAGE IS NOT ENOUGH TO REMIND YOU OF THE THREAT AT HAND...
...THEN I SUGGEST YOU LOOK ELSEWHERE TO FULLY ASCERTAIN THE DIRE CIRCUMSTANCES BEFORE US.
HARLEM
BERG, I KNOW THINGS ARE BAD--I CAN SEE YOUR FACE. BUT IT COULD BE WORSE.
THERE ARE PEOPLE HERE WHO CAN HELP US MAKE A STAND. I KNOW THIS FIGHT ISN'T OVER. IN FACT...

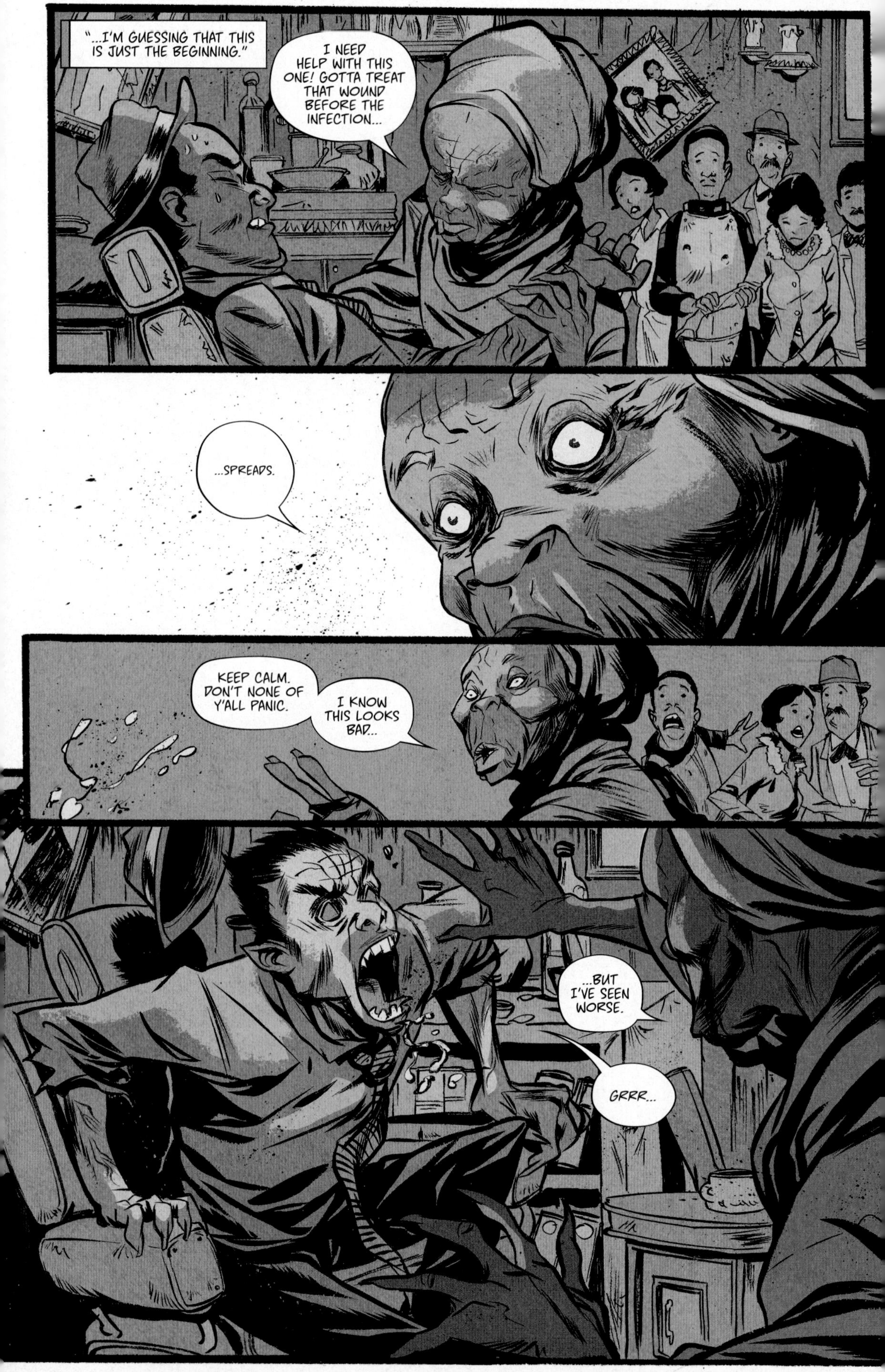
"...I'M GUESSING THAT THIS IS JUST THE BEGINNING."
I NEED HELP WITH THIS ONE! GOTTA TREAT THAT WOUND BEFORE THE INFECTION...
...SPREADS.
KEEP CALM. DON'T NONE OF Y'ALL PANIC.
I KNOW THIS LOOKS BAD...
...BUT I'VE SEEN WORSE.
GRRR...

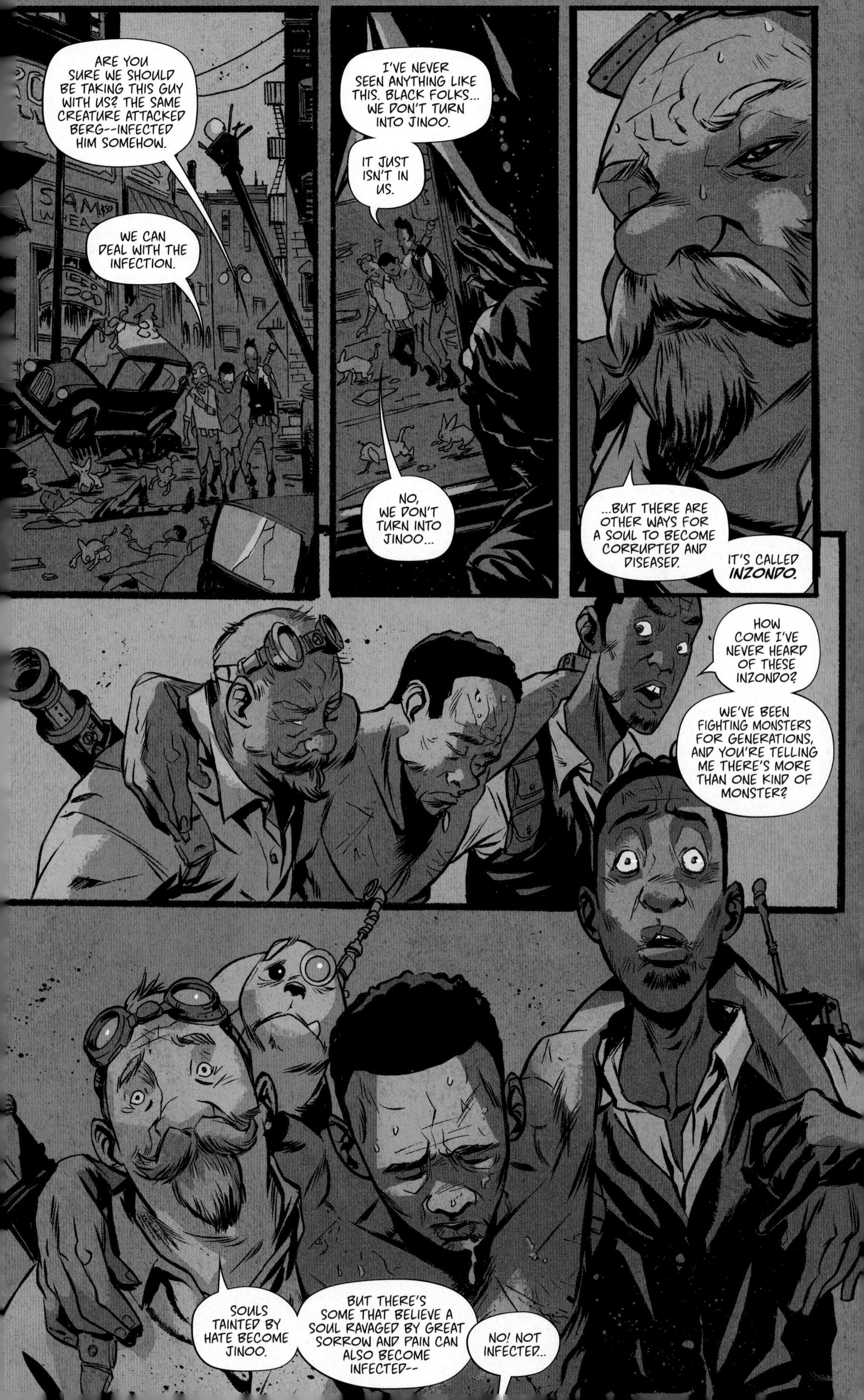
ARE YOU SURE WE SHOULD BE TAKING THIS GUY WITH US? THE SAME CREATURE ATTACKED BERG--INFECTED HIM SOMEHOW.
WE CAN DEAL WITH THE INFECTION.
I'VE NEVER SEEN ANYTHING LIKE THIS. BLACK FOLKS... WE DON'T TURN INTO JINOO.
IT JUST ISN'T IN US.
NO, WE DON'T TURN INTO JINOO...
...BUT THERE ARE OTHER WAYS FOR A SOUL TO BECOME CORRUPTED AND DISEASED.
IT'S CALLED ***INZONDO.***
HOW COME I'VE NEVER HEARD OF THESE INZONDO?
WE'VE BEEN FIGHTING MONSTERS FOR GENERATIONS, AND YOU'RE TELLING ME THERE'S MORE THAN ONE KIND OF MONSTER?
SOULS TAINTED BY HATE BECOME JINOO.
BUT THERE'S SOME THAT BELIEVE A SOUL RAVAGED BY GREAT SORROW AND PAIN CAN ALSO BECOME INFECTED--
NO! NOT INFECTED...

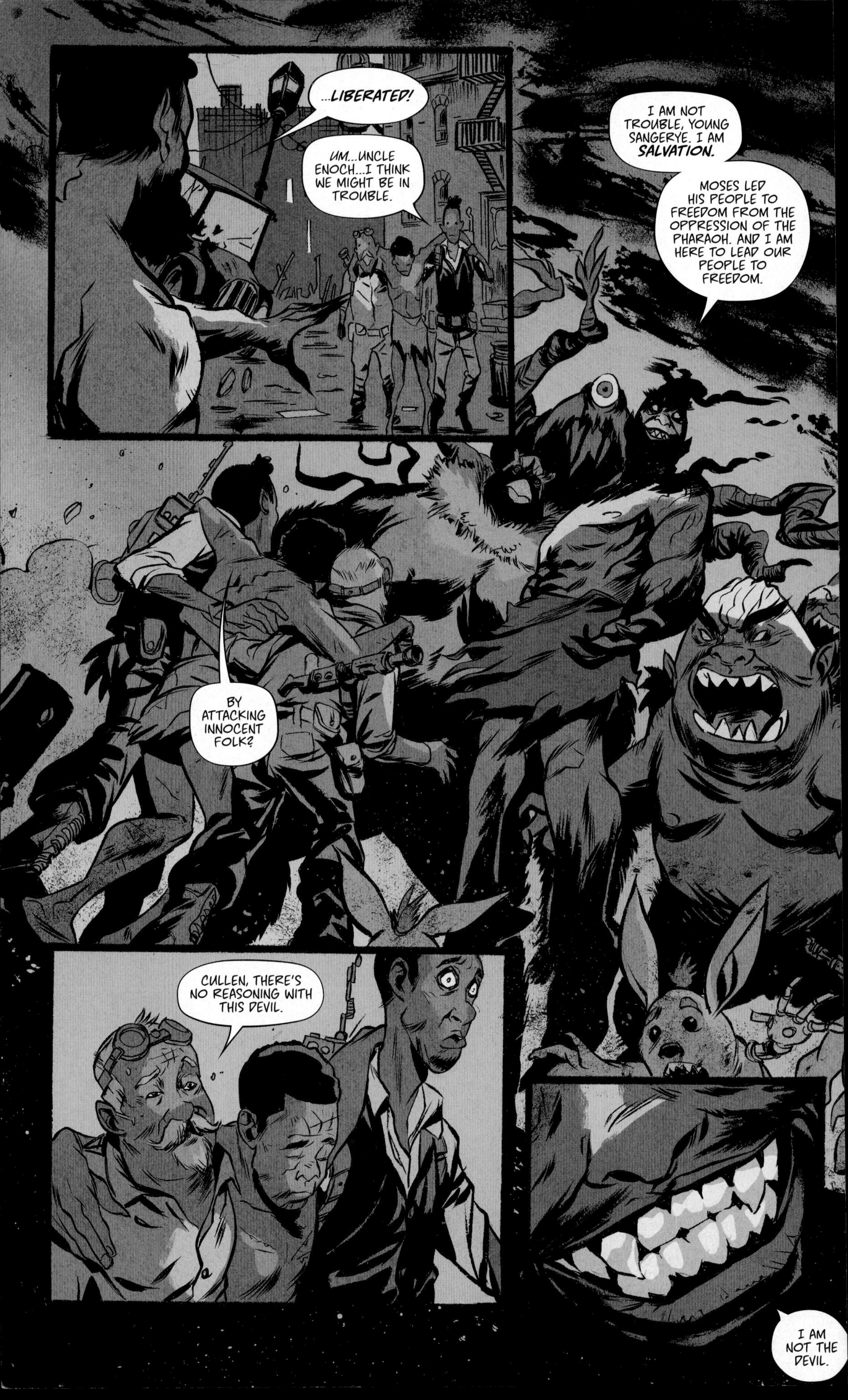
...LIBERATED!
UM...UNCLE ENOCH...I THINK WE MIGHT BE IN TROUBLE.
I AM NOT TROUBLE, YOUNG SANGERYE. I AM SALVATION.
MOSES LED HIS PEOPLE TO FREEDOM FROM THE OPPRESSION OF THE PHARAOH. AND I AM HERE TO LEAD OUR PEOPLE TO FREEDOM.
BY ATTACKING INNOCENT FOLK?
CULLEN, THERE'S NO REASONING WITH THIS DEVIL.
I AM NOT THE DEVIL.

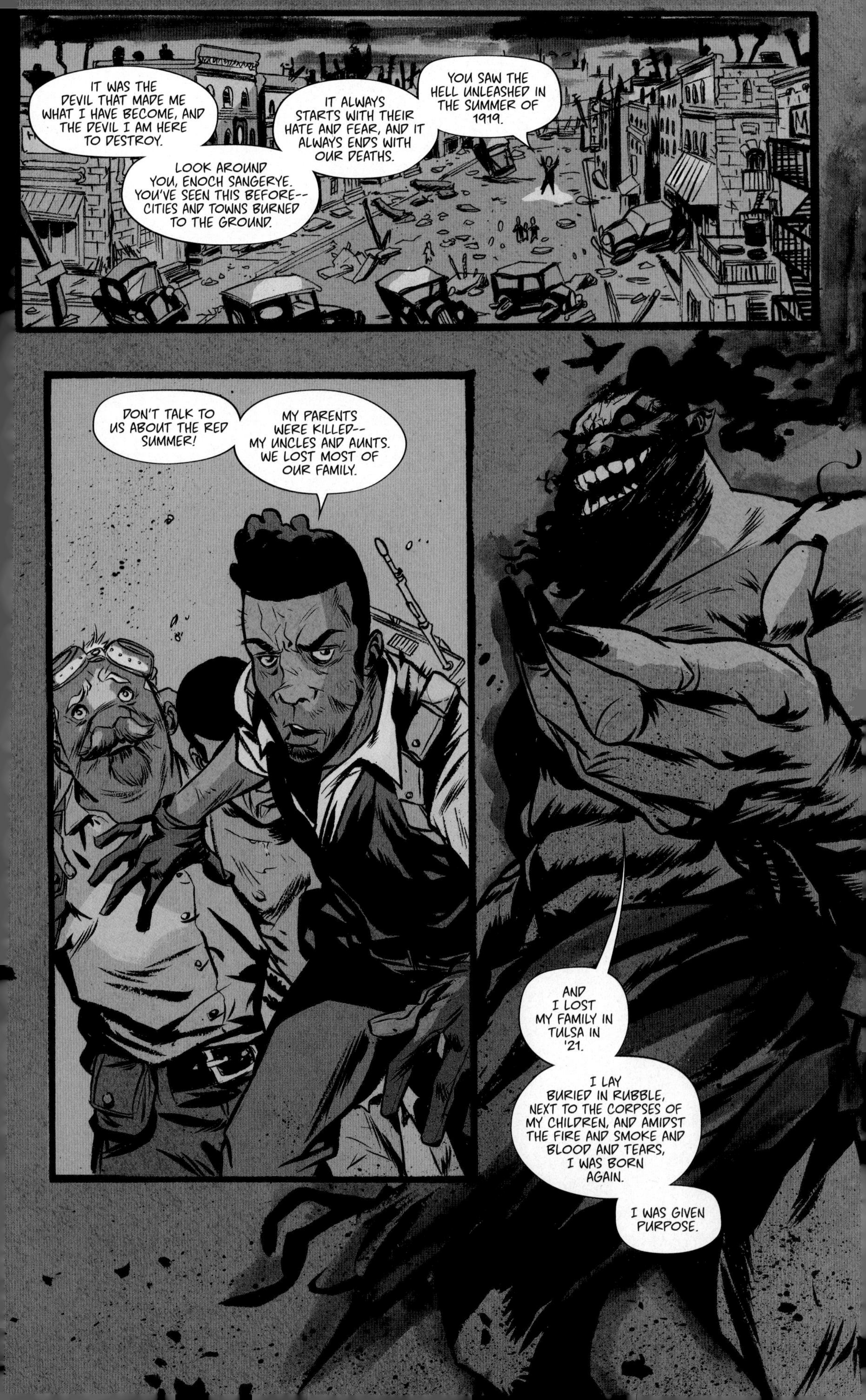
IT WAS THE DEVIL THAT MADE ME WHAT I HAVE BECOME, AND THE DEVIL I AM HERE TO DESTROY.
LOOK AROUND YOU, ENOCH SANGERYE. YOU'VE SEEN THIS BEFORE--CITIES AND TOWNS BURNED TO THE GROUND.
IT ALWAYS STARTS WITH THEIR HATE AND FEAR, AND IT ALWAYS ENDS WITH OUR DEATHS.
YOU SAW THE HELL UNLEASHED IN THE SUMMER OF 1919.
DON'T TALK TO US ABOUT THE RED SUMMER!
MY PARENTS WERE KILLED--MY UNCLES AND AUNTS. WE LOST MOST OF OUR FAMILY.
AND I LOST MY FAMILY IN TULSA IN '21.
I LAY BURIED IN RUBBLE, NEXT TO THE CORPSES OF MY CHILDREN, AND AMIDST THE FIRE AND SMOKE AND BLOOD AND TEARS, I WAS BORN AGAIN.
I WAS GIVEN PURPOSE.

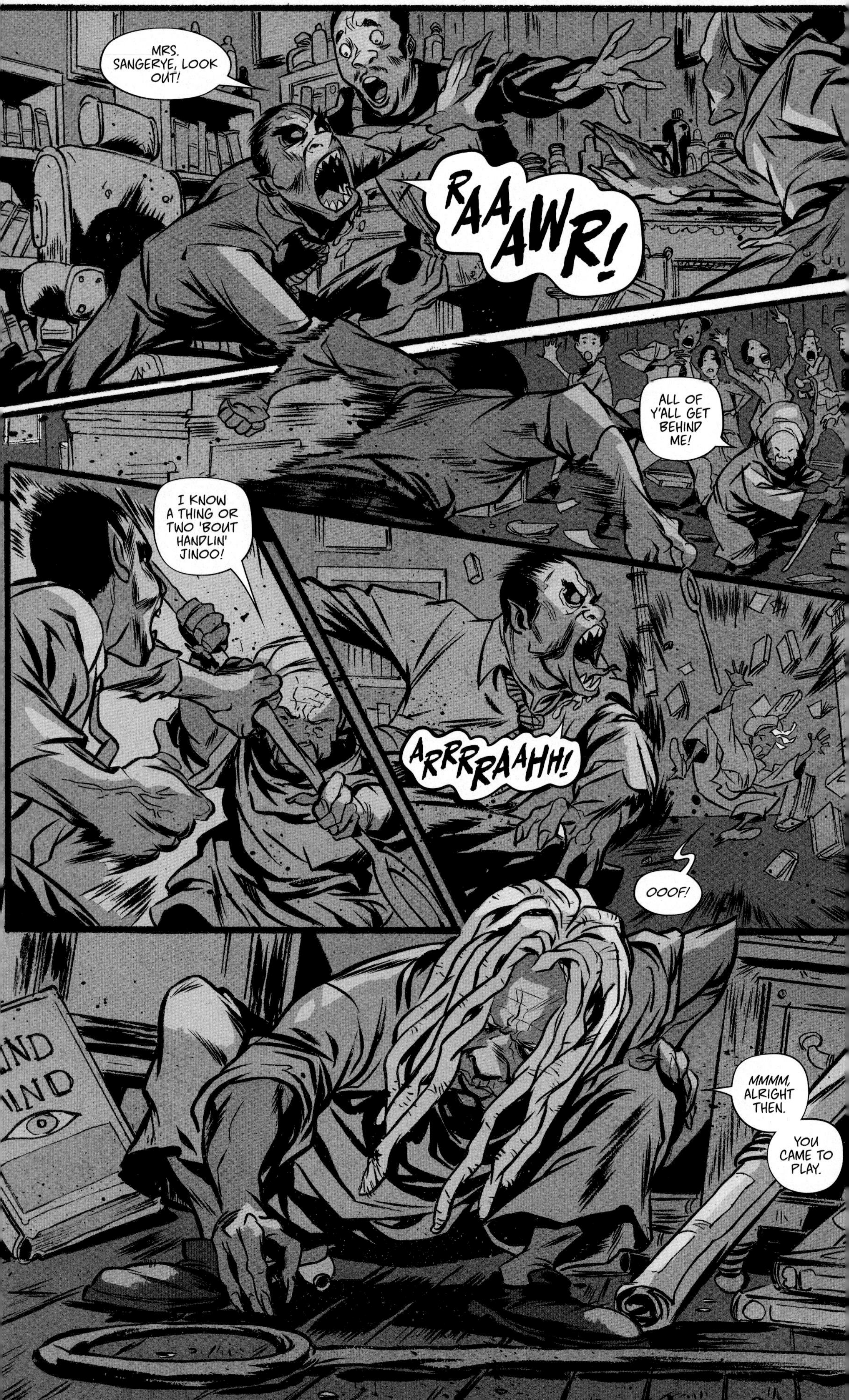
MRS. SANGERYE, LOOK OUT!
RAAAWR!
ALL OF Y'ALL GET BEHIND ME!
I KNOW A THING OR TWO 'BOUT HANDLIN' JINOO!
ARRRRAAHH!
OOOF!
MMMM, ALRIGHT THEN.
YOU CAME TO PLAY.

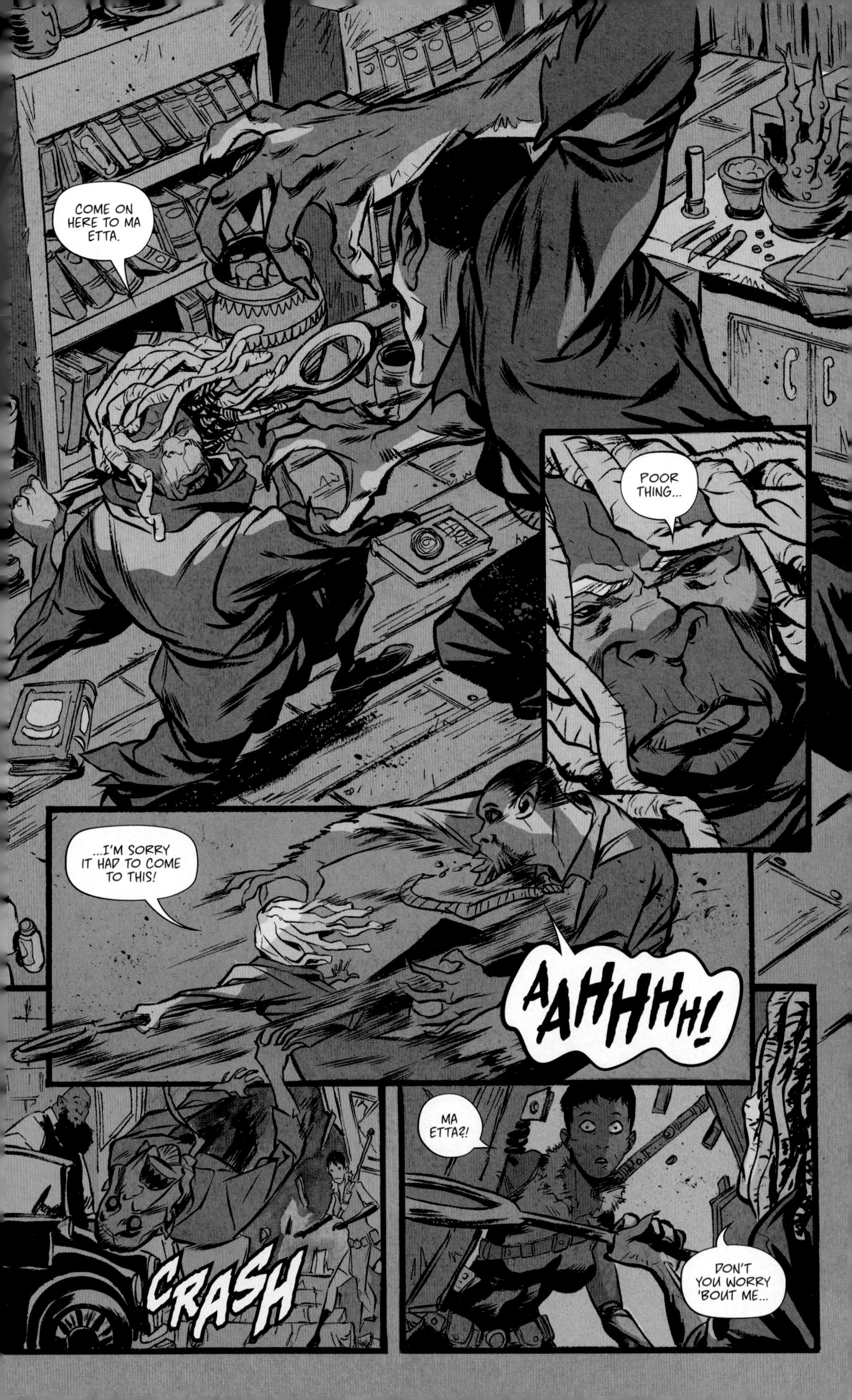
COME ON HERE TO MA ETTA.
POOR THING...
...I'M SORRY IT HAD TO COME TO THIS!
AAHHHH!
CRASH
MA ETTA?!
DON'T YOU WORRY 'BOUT ME...

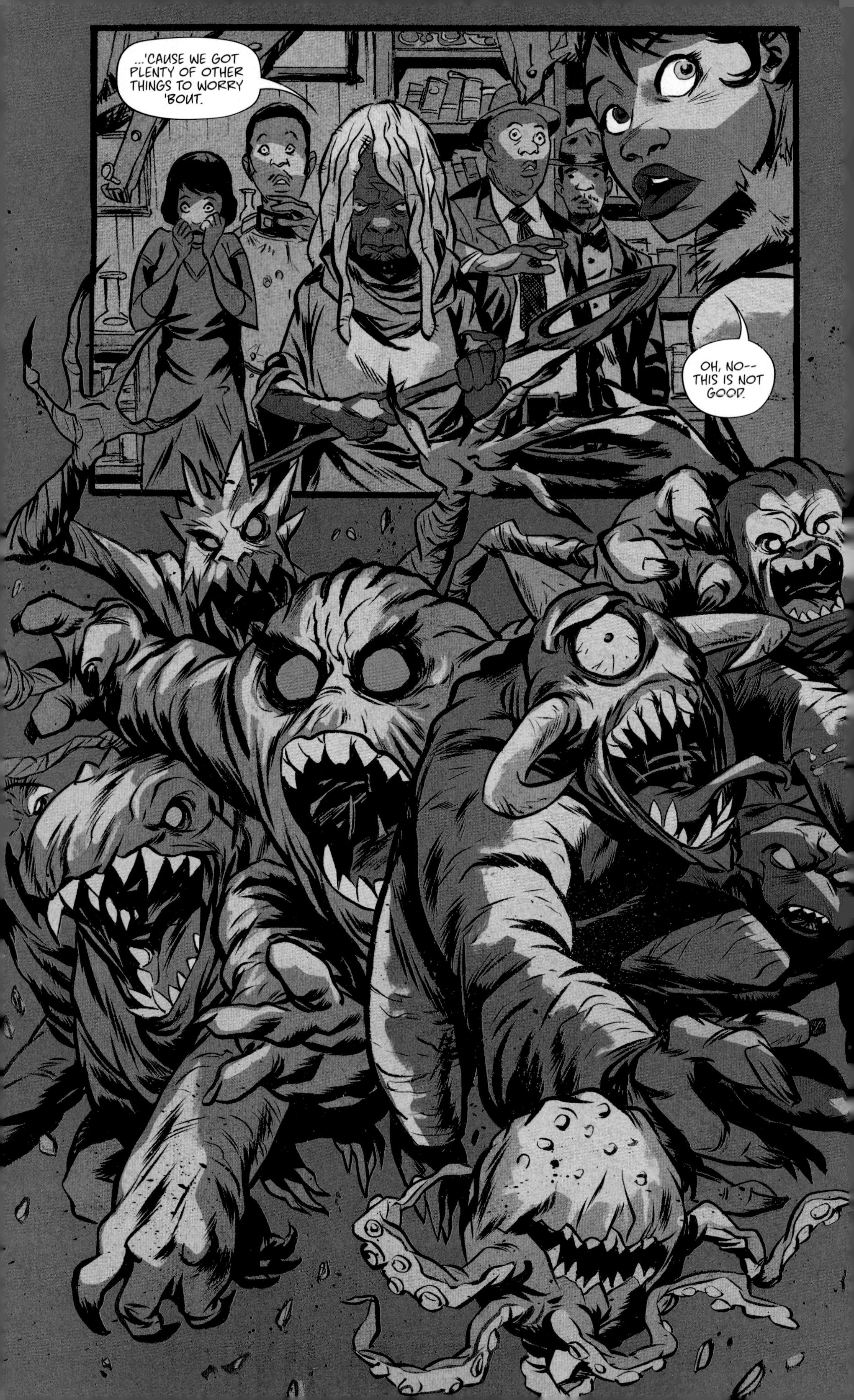
...'CAUSE WE GOT PLENTY OF OTHER THINGS TO WORRY 'BOUT.
OH, NO-- THIS IS NOT GOOD.

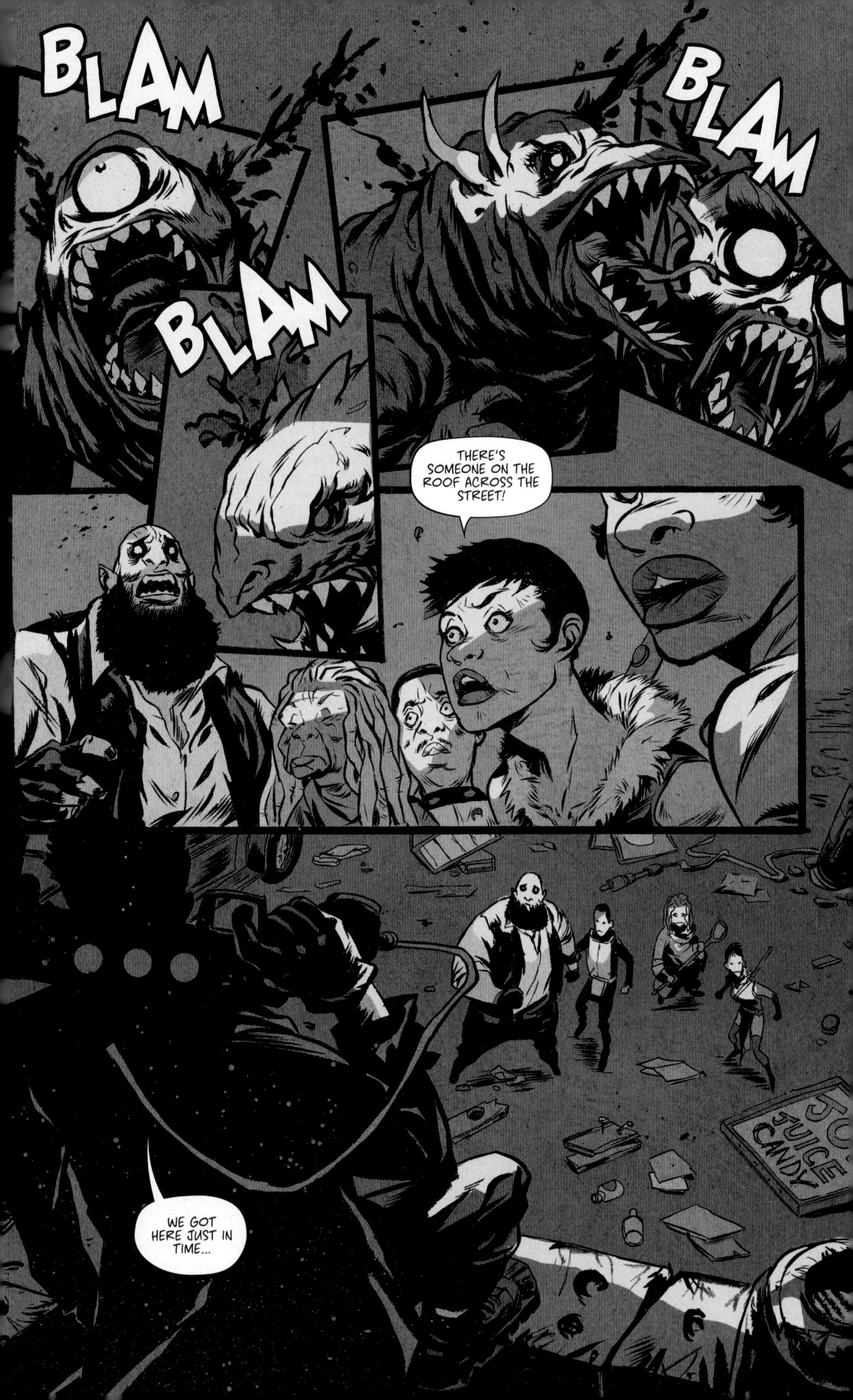
BLAM
BLAM
BLAM
THERE'S SOMEONE ON THE ROOF ACROSS THE STREET!
WE GOT HERE JUST IN TIME...
JUICE CANDY

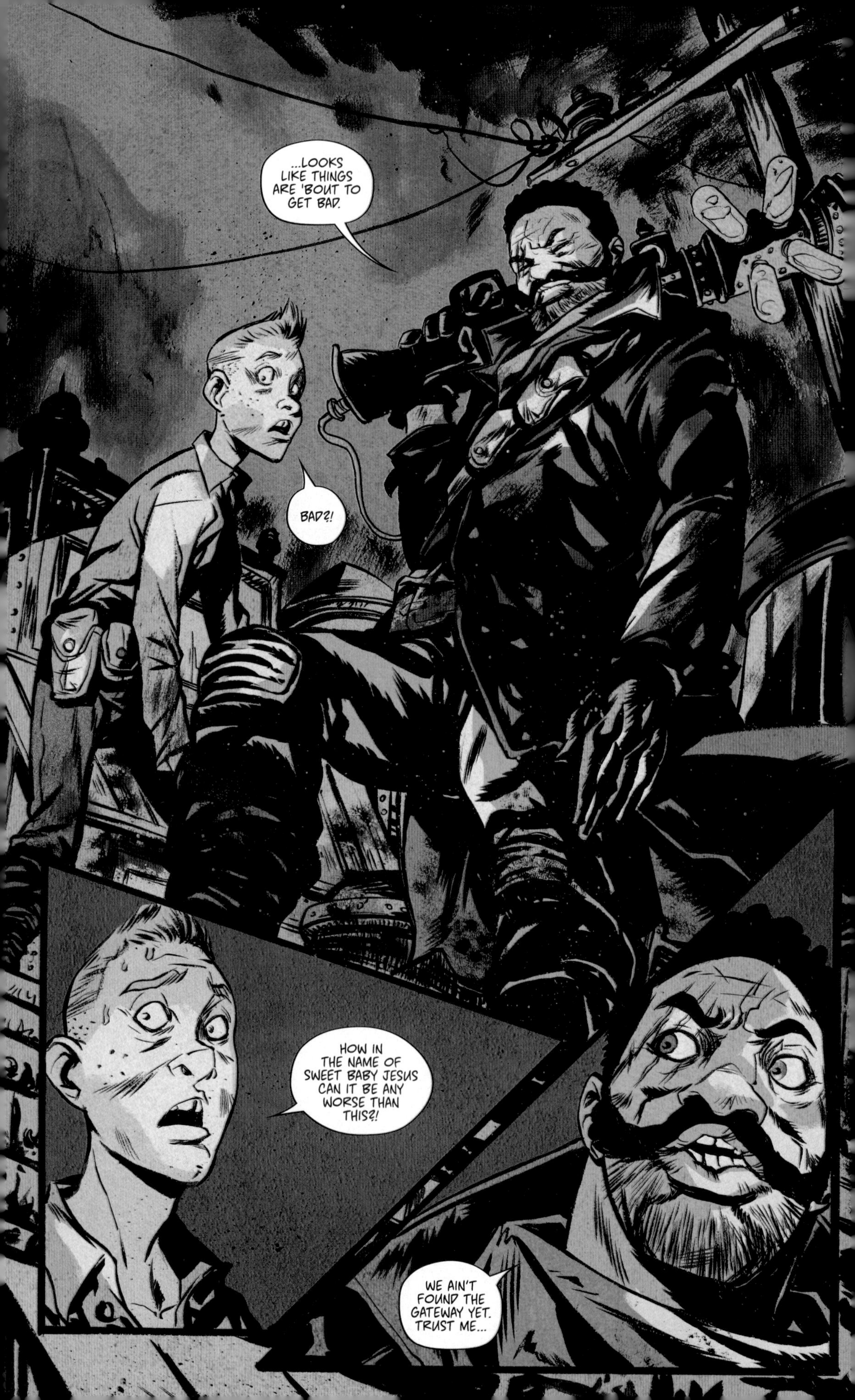
...LOOKS LIKE THINGS ARE 'BOUT TO GET BAD.
BAD?!
HOW IN THE NAME OF SWEET BABY JESUS CAN IT BE ANY WORSE THAN THIS?!
WE AIN'T FOUND THE GATEWAY YET. TRUST ME...

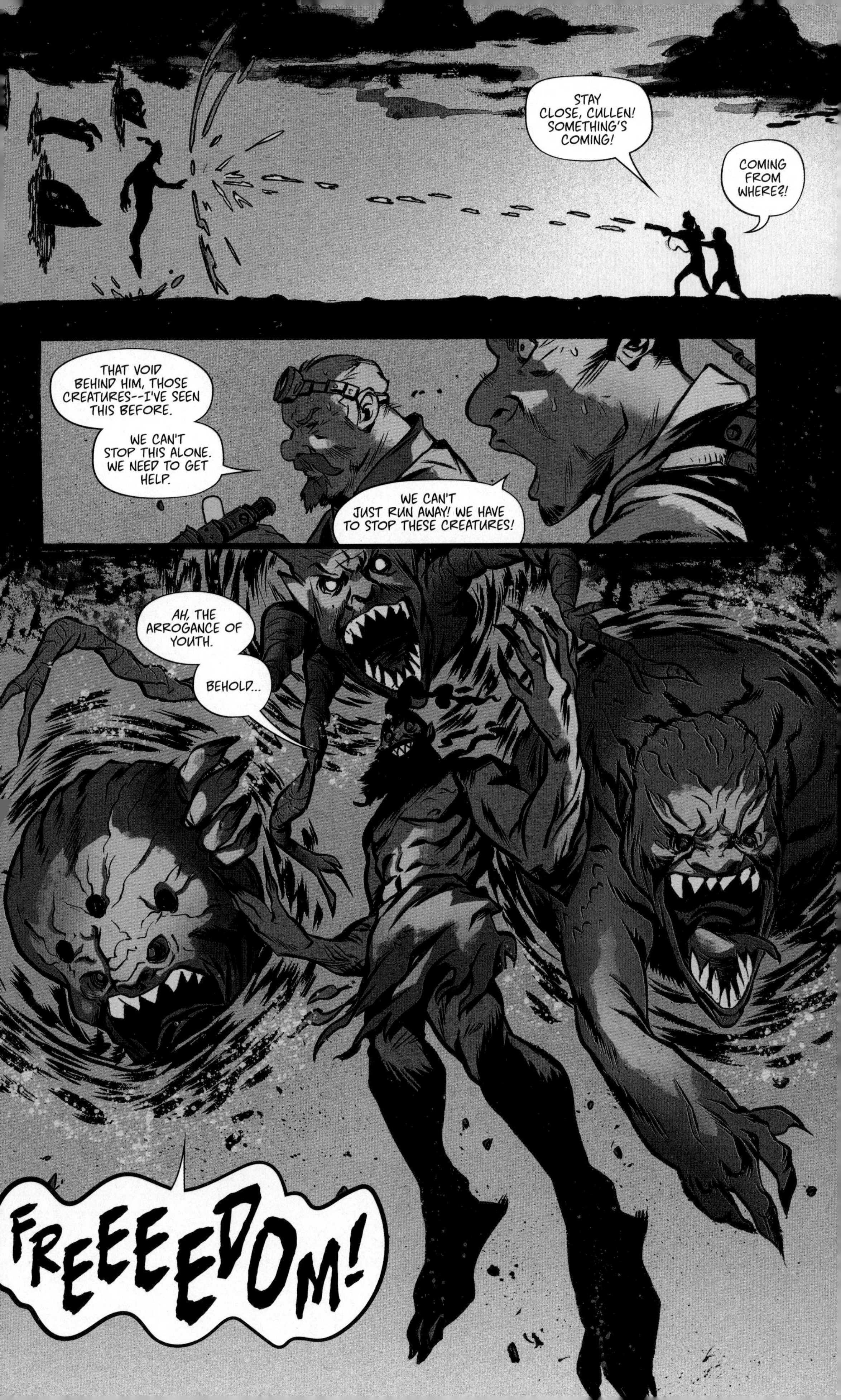
STAY CLOSE, CULLEN! SOMETHING'S COMING!
COMING FROM WHERE?!
THAT VOID BEHIND HIM, THOSE CREATURES--I'VE SEEN THIS BEFORE.
WE CAN'T STOP THIS ALONE. WE NEED TO GET HELP.
WE CAN'T JUST RUN AWAY! WE HAVE TO STOP THESE CREATURES!
AH, THE ARROGANCE OF YOUTH.
BEHOLD...
FREEEEDOM!

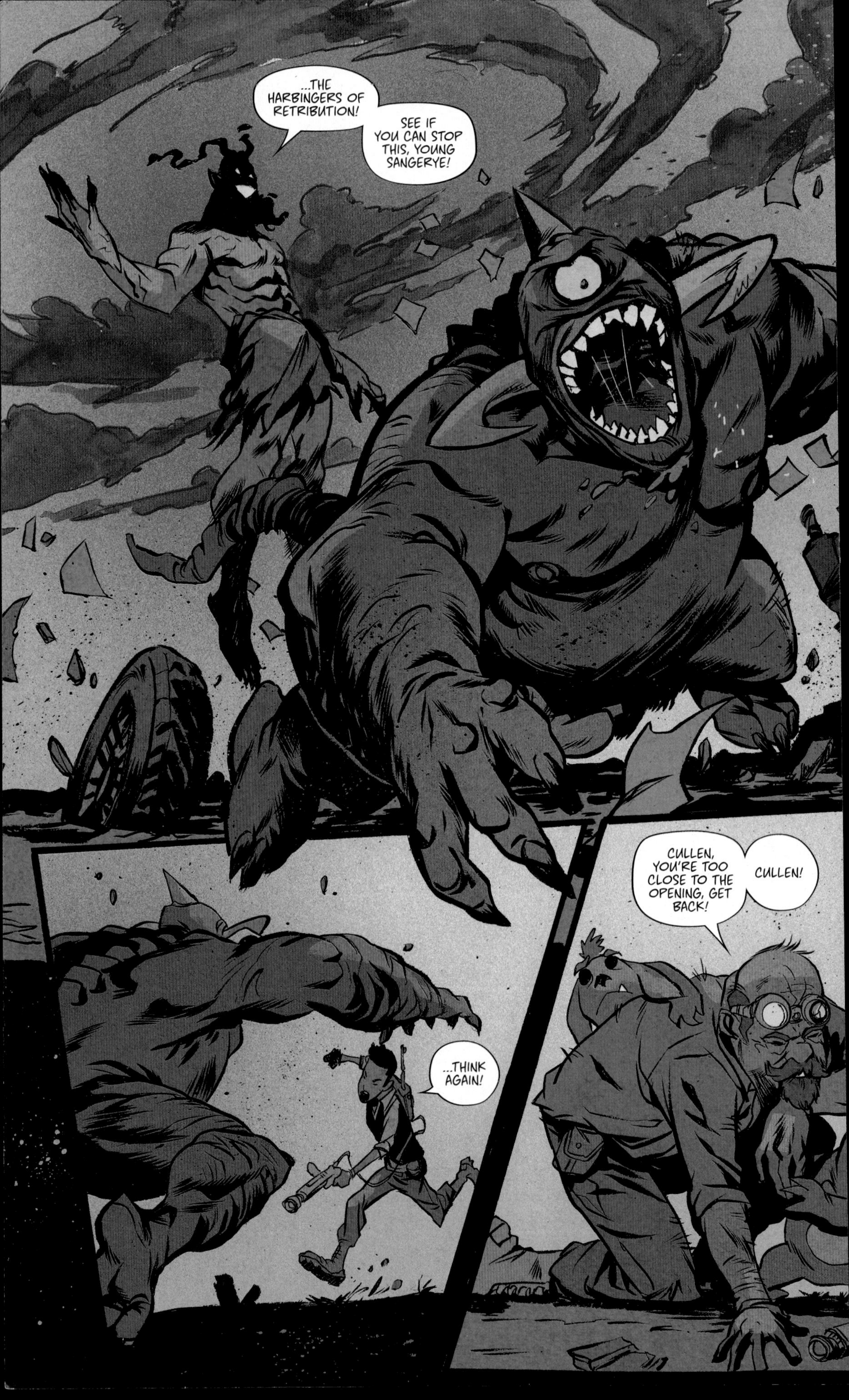
...THE HARBINGERS OF RETRIBUTION!
SEE IF YOU CAN STOP THIS, YOUNG SANGERYE!
...THINK AGAIN!
CULLEN, YOU'RE TOO CLOSE TO THE OPENING, GET BACK!
CULLEN!

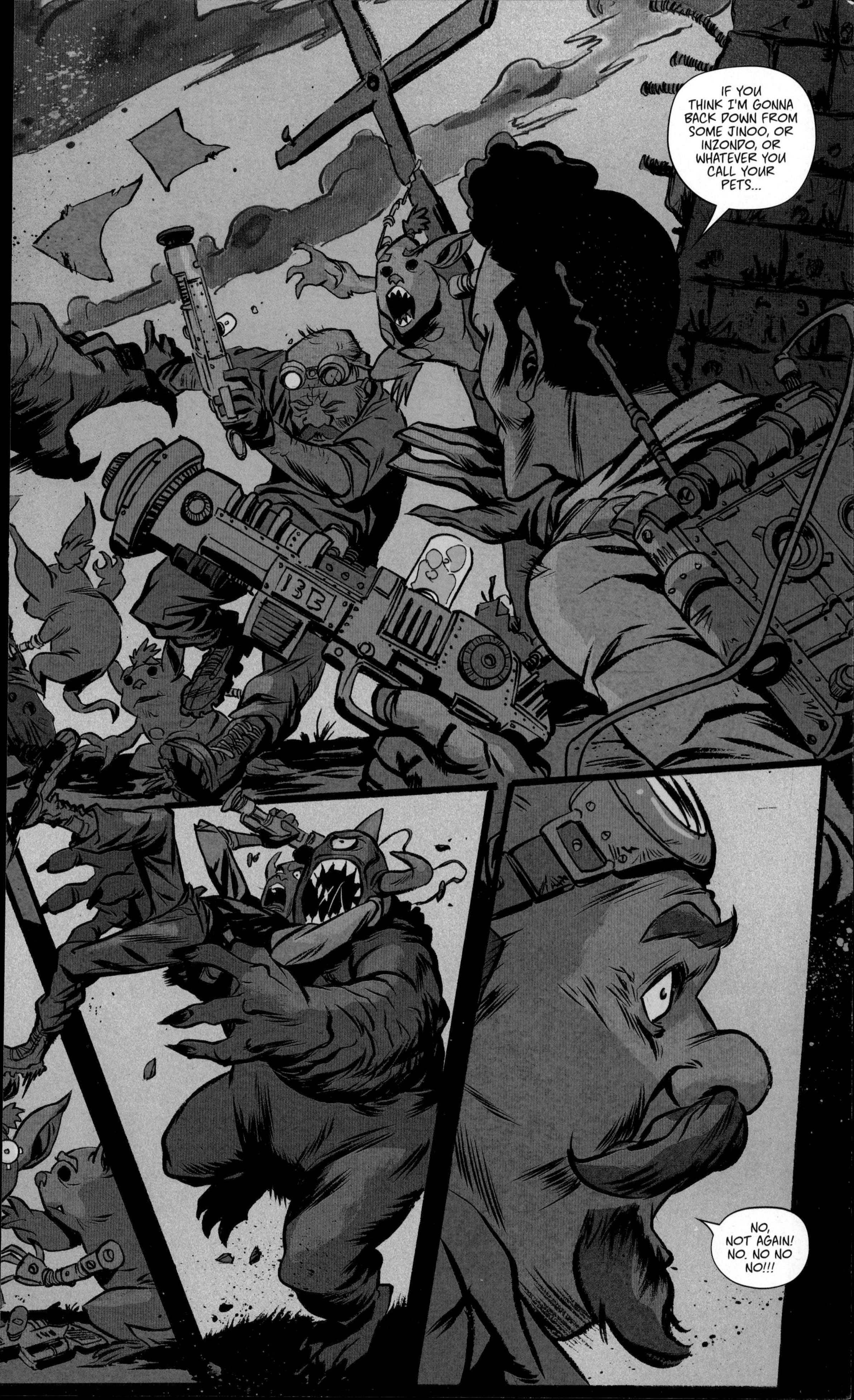
IF YOU THINK I'M GONNA BACK DOWN FROM SOME JINOO, OR INZONDO, OR WHATEVER YOU CALL YOUR PETS...
NO, NOT AGAIN! NO. NO NO NO!!!

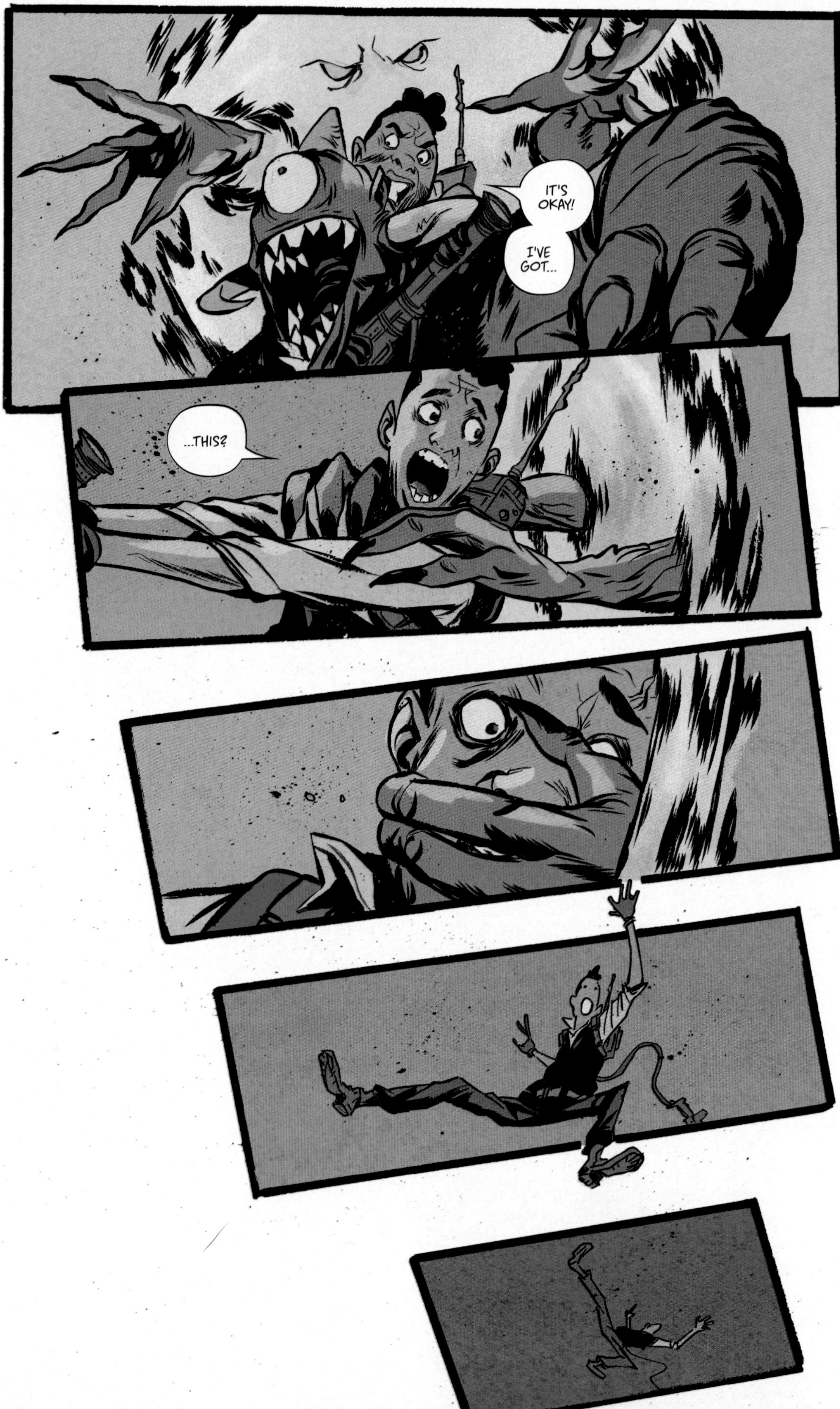
IT'S OKAY!
I'VE GOT...
...THIS?

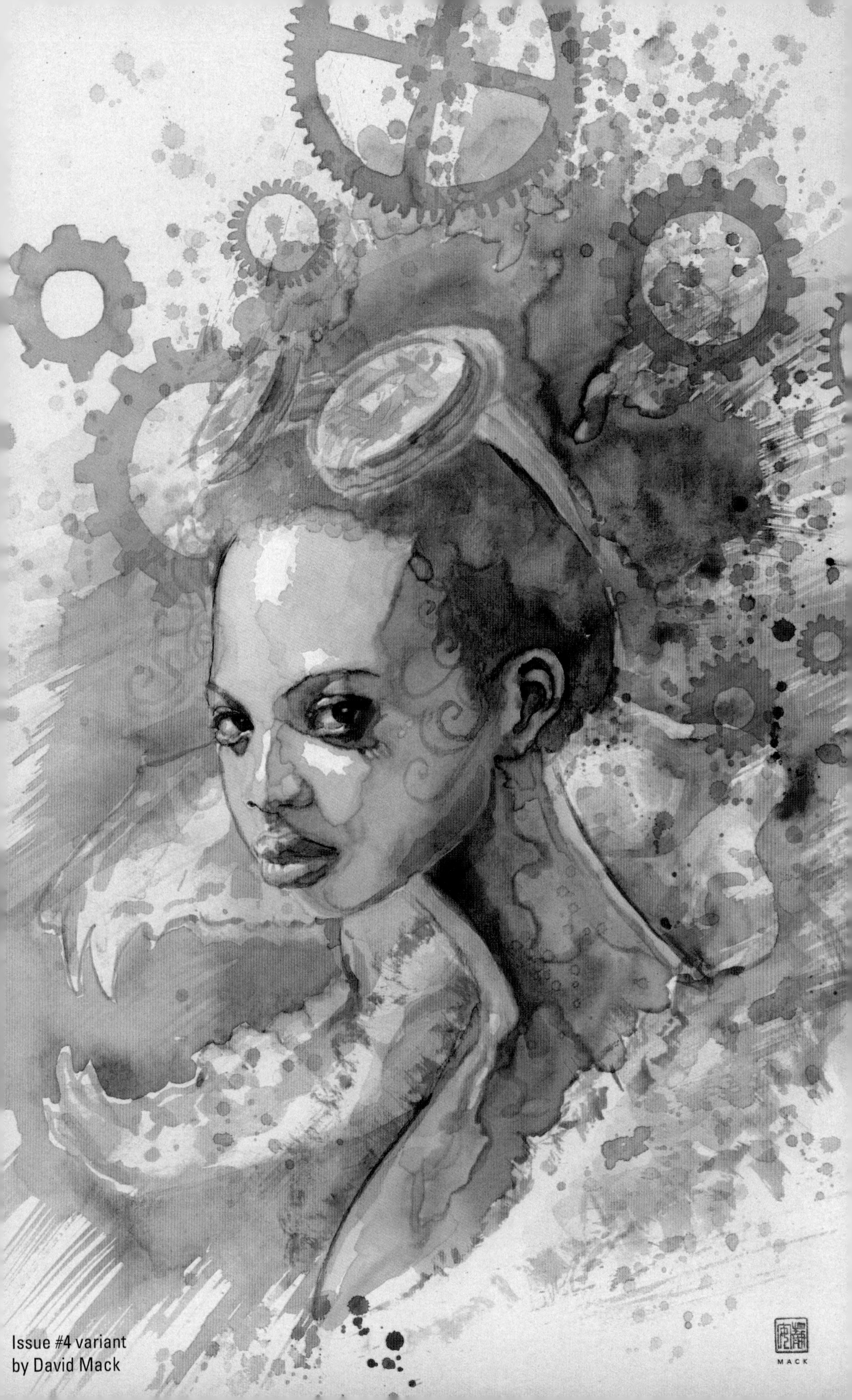

Issue #4 variant
by David Mack

CHAPTER FIVE

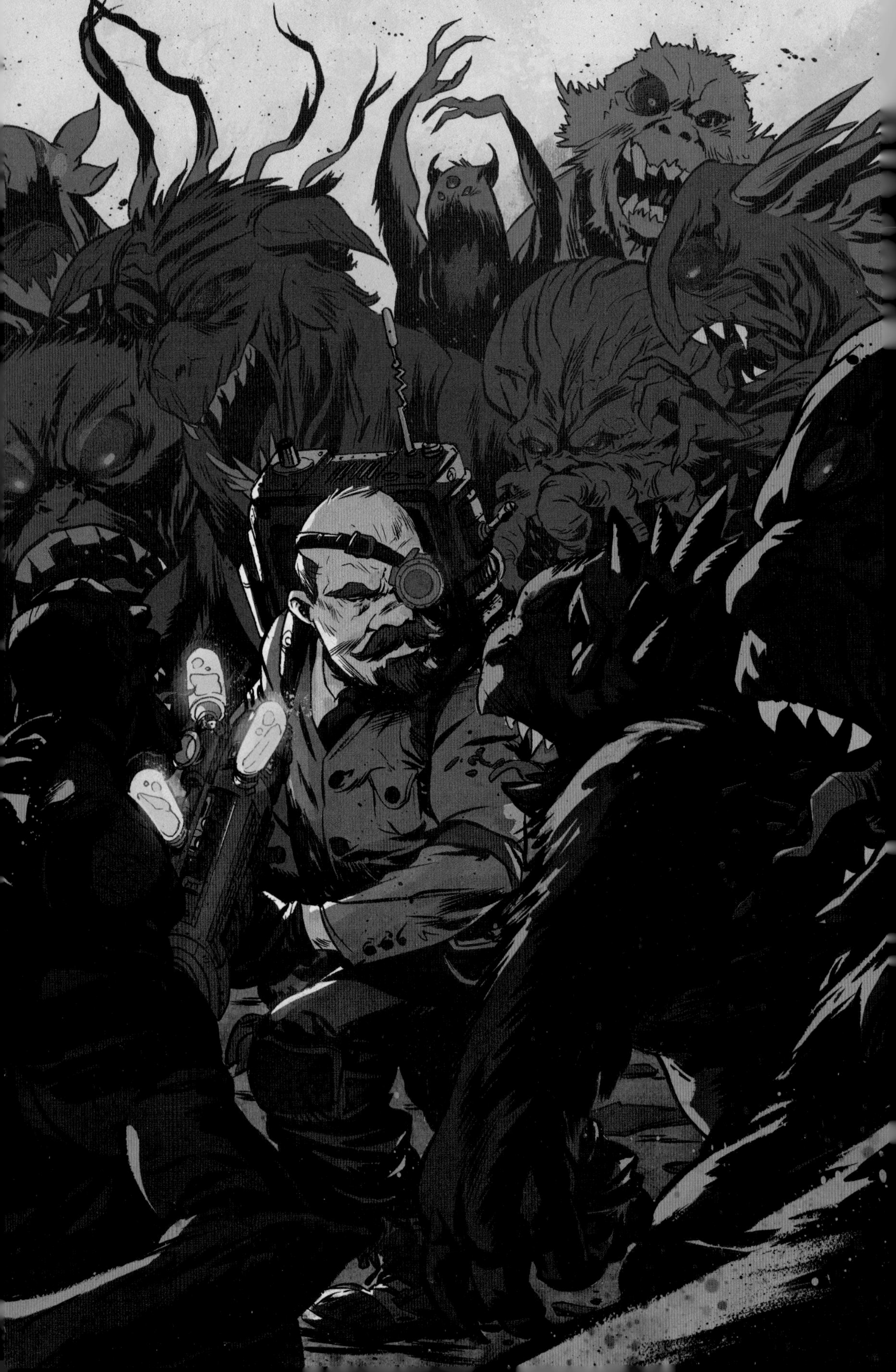

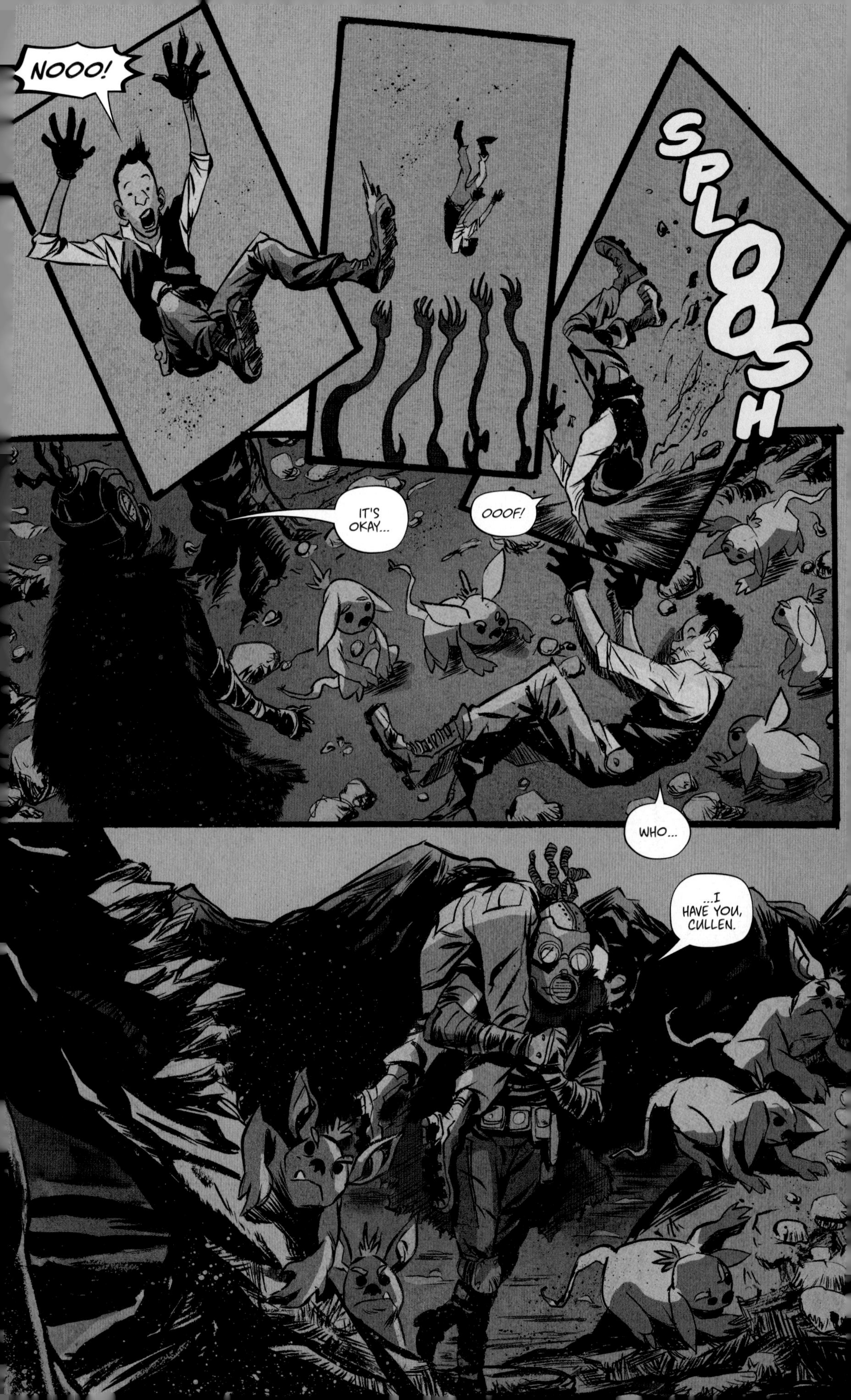
NOOO!
SPLOOSH
IT'S OKAY...
OOOF!
WHO...
...I HAVE YOU, CULLEN.

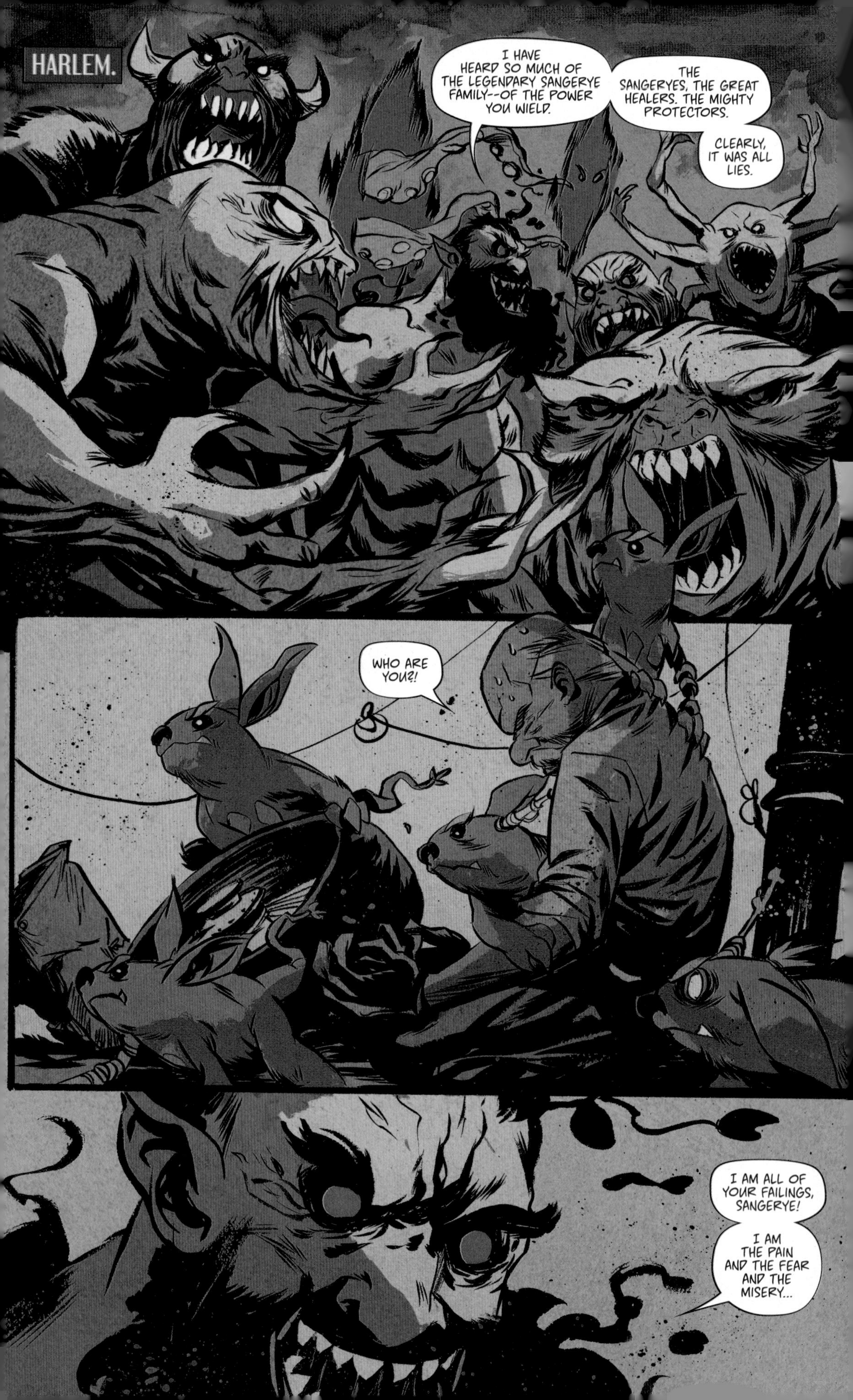

HARLEM.
I HAVE HEARD SO MUCH OF THE LEGENDARY SANGERYE FAMILY--OF THE POWER YOU WIELD.
THE SANGERYES, THE GREAT HEALERS. THE MIGHTY PROTECTORS.
CLEARLY, IT WAS ALL LIES.
WHO ARE YOU?!
I AM ALL OF YOUR FAILINGS, SANGERYE!
I AM THE PAIN AND THE FEAR AND THE MISERY...

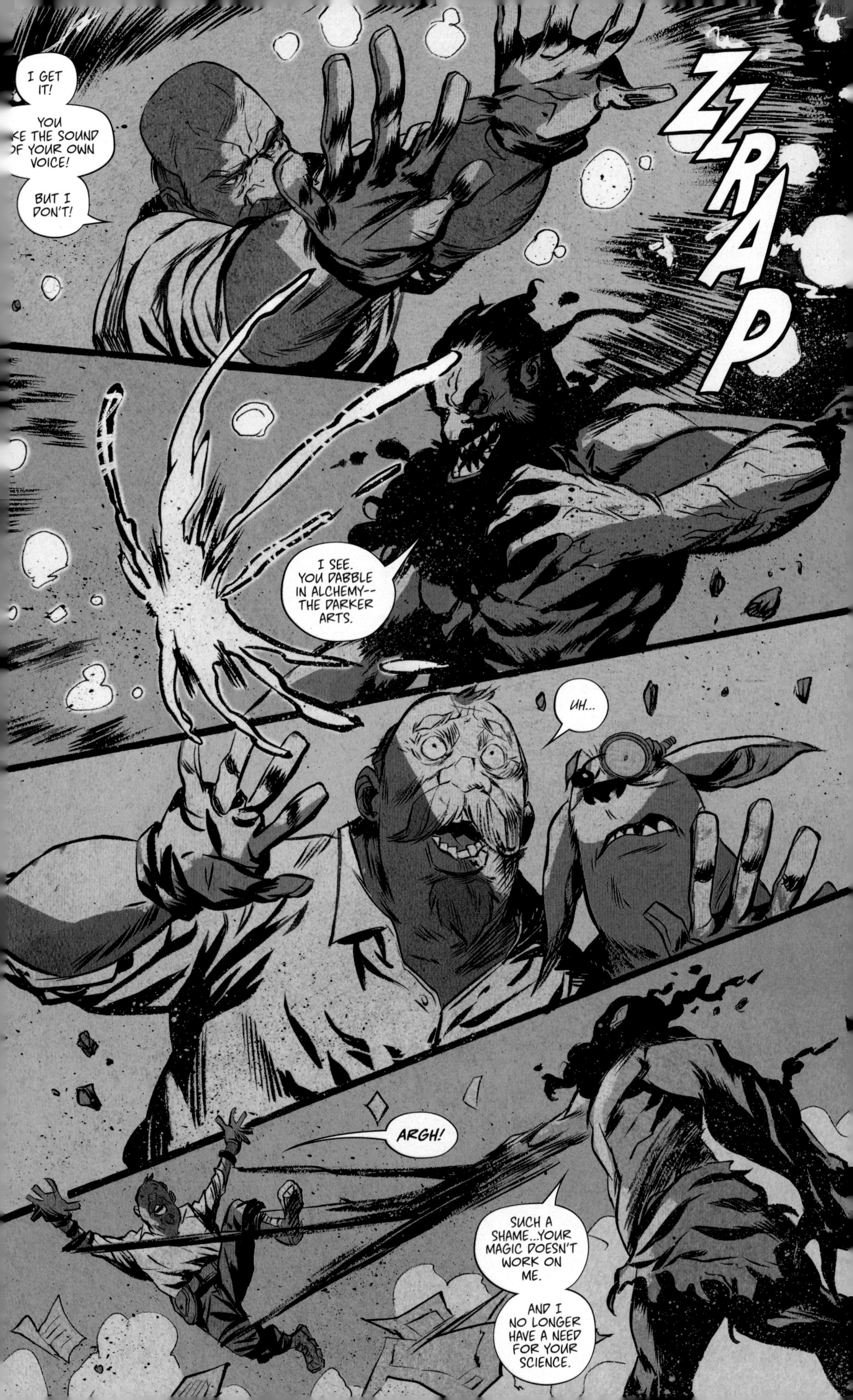

I GET IT!
YOU KE THE SOUND OF YOUR OWN VOICE!
BUT I DON'T!
ZZRAP
I SEE. YOU DABBLE IN ALCHEMY-- THE DARKER ARTS.
UH...
ARGH!
SUCH A SHAME...YOUR MAGIC DOESN'T WORK ON ME.
AND I NO LONGER HAVE A NEED FOR YOUR SCIENCE.

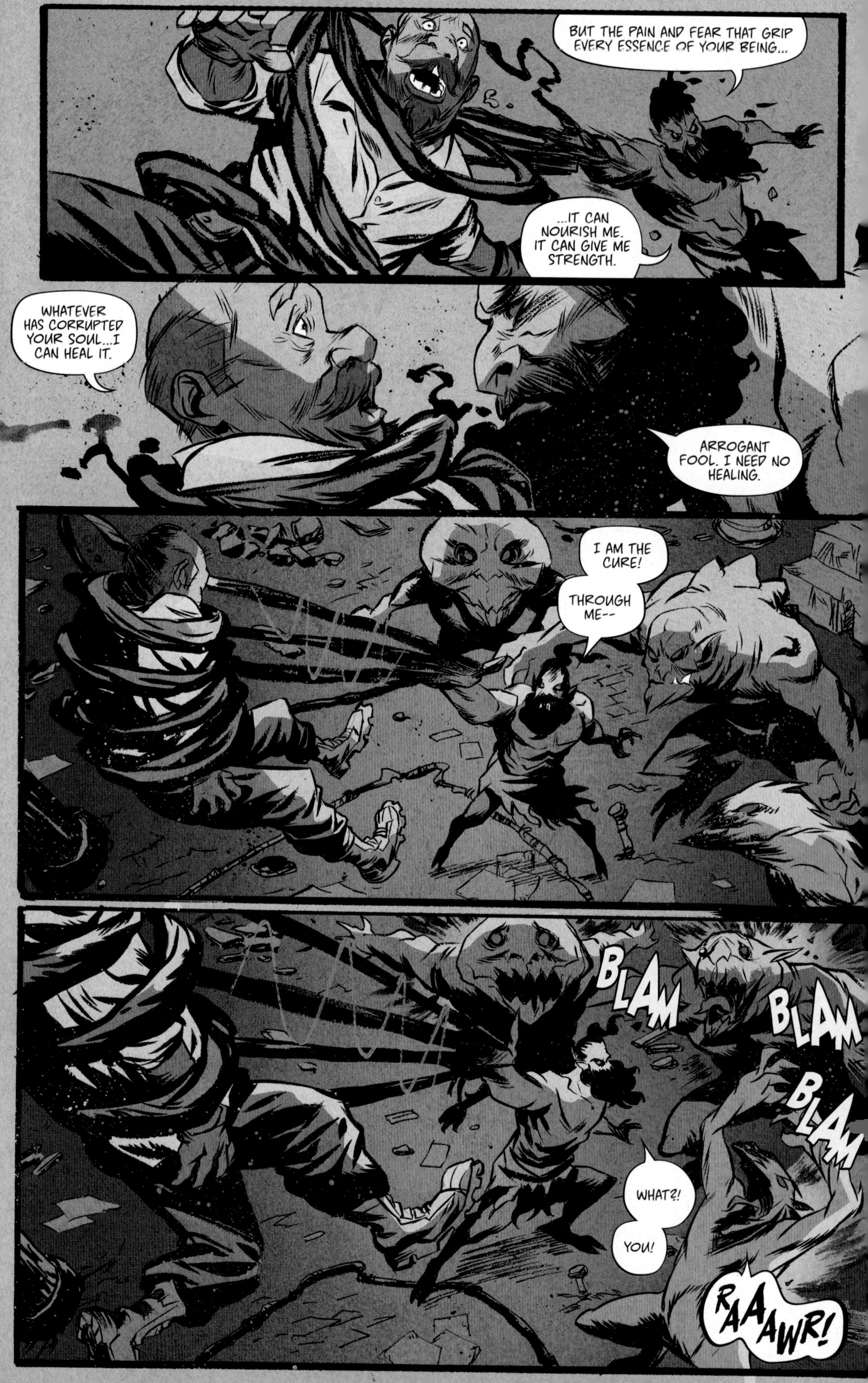

BUT THE PAIN AND FEAR THAT GRIP EVERY ESSENCE OF YOUR BEING...
...IT CAN NOURISH ME. IT CAN GIVE ME STRENGTH.
WHATEVER HAS CORRUPTED YOUR SOUL...I CAN HEAL IT.
ARROGANT FOOL. I NEED NO HEALING.
I AM THE CURE!
THROUGH ME--
BLAM
BLAM
BLAM
WHAT?!
YOU!
RAAAWR!

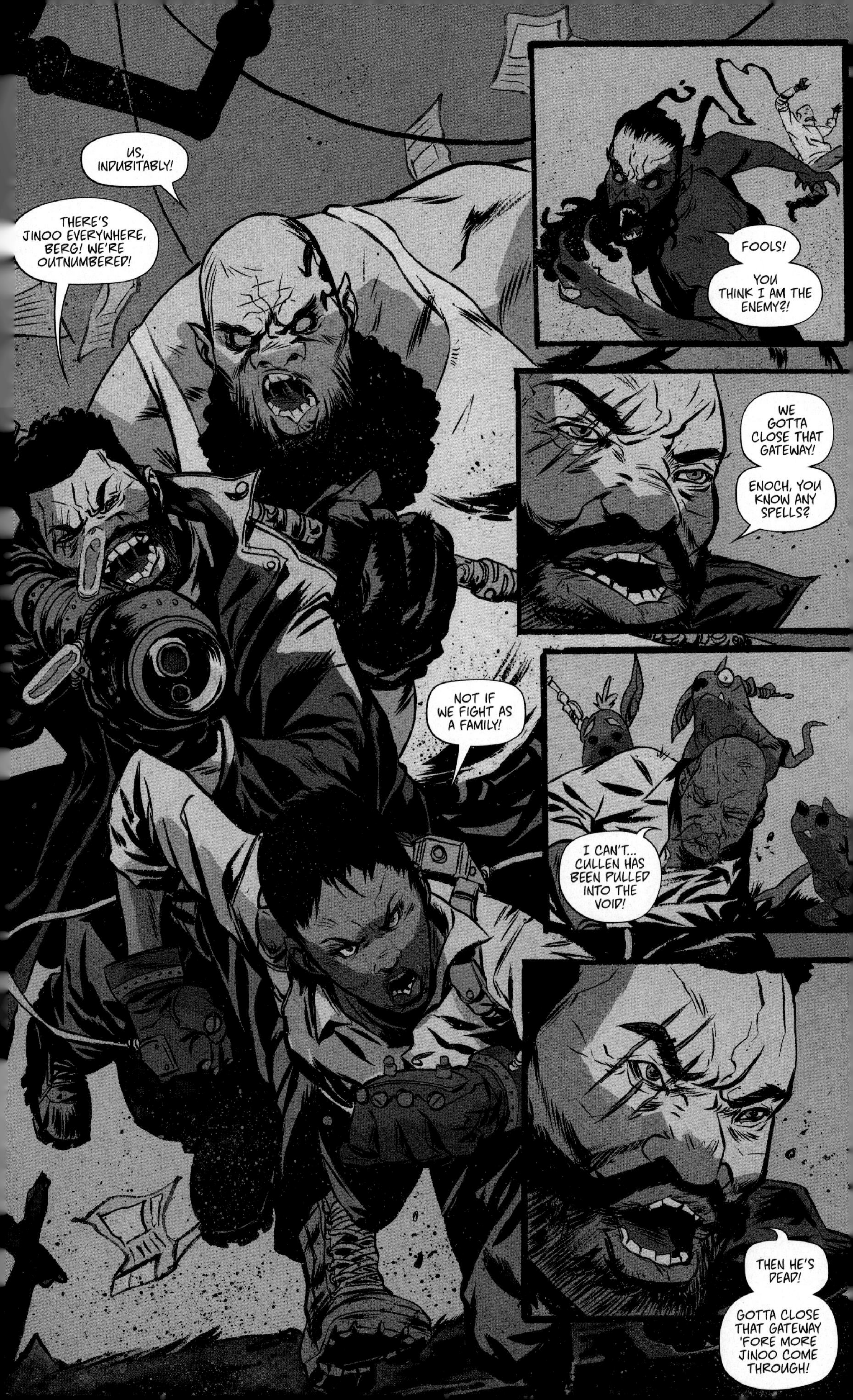
US, INDUBITABLY!
THERE'S JINOO EVERYWHERE, BERG! WE'RE OUTNUMBERED!
FOOLS!
YOU THINK I AM THE ENEMY?!
WE GOTTA CLOSE THAT GATEWAY!
ENOCH, YOU KNOW ANY SPELLS?
NOT IF WE FIGHT AS A FAMILY!
I CAN'T... CULLEN HAS BEEN PULLED INTO THE VOID!
THEN HE'S DEAD!
GOTTA CLOSE THAT GATEWAY 'FORE MORE JINOO COME THROUGH!

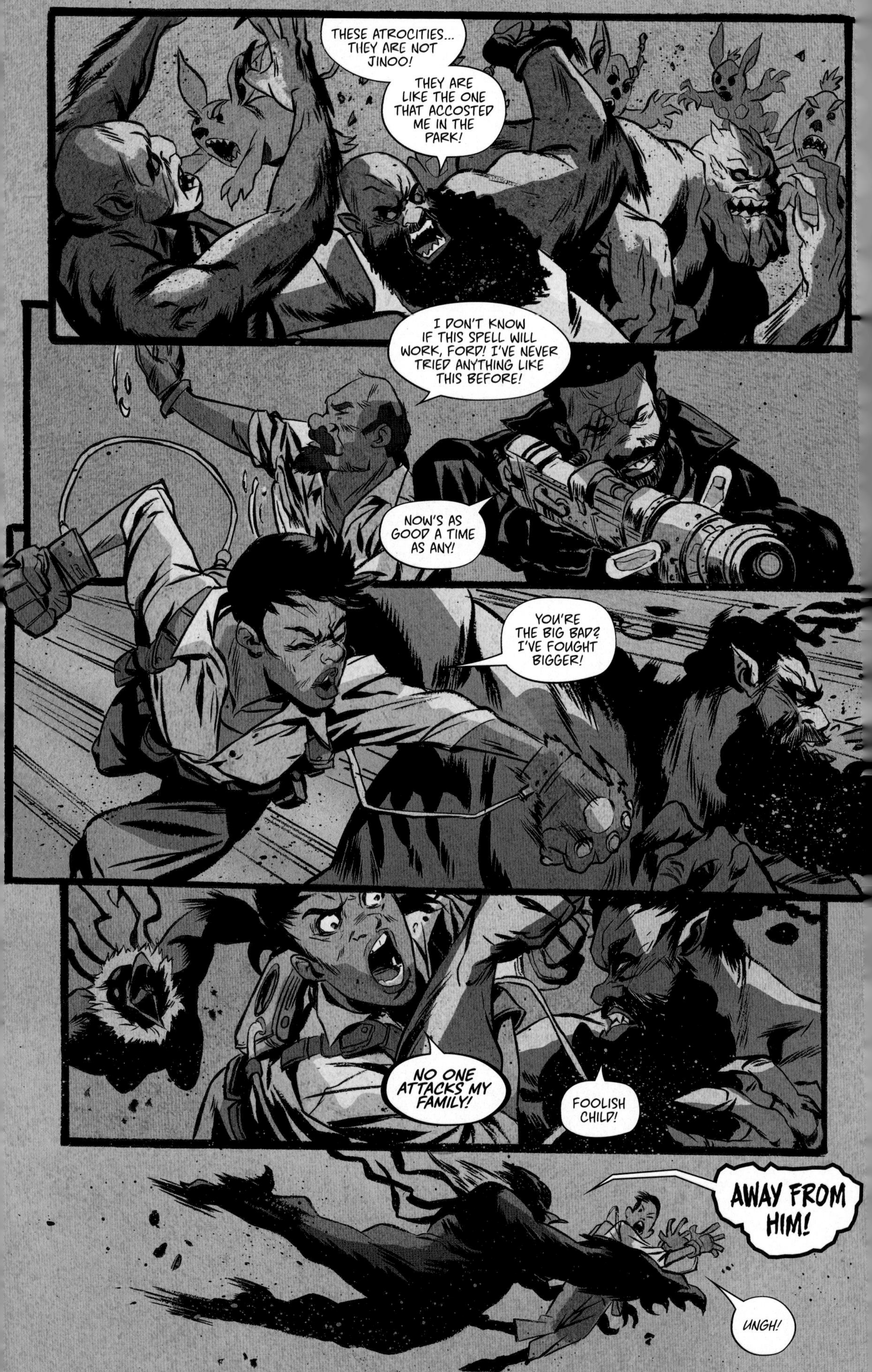
THESE ATROCITIES... THEY ARE NOT JINOO!
THEY ARE LIKE THE ONE THAT ACCOSTED ME IN THE PARK!
I DON'T KNOW IF THIS SPELL WILL WORK, FORD! I'VE NEVER TRIED ANYTHING LIKE THIS BEFORE!
NOW'S AS GOOD A TIME AS ANY!
YOU'RE THE BIG BAD? I'VE FOUGHT BIGGER!
NO ONE ATTACKS MY FAMILY!
FOOLISH CHILD!
AWAY FROM HIM!
UNGH!

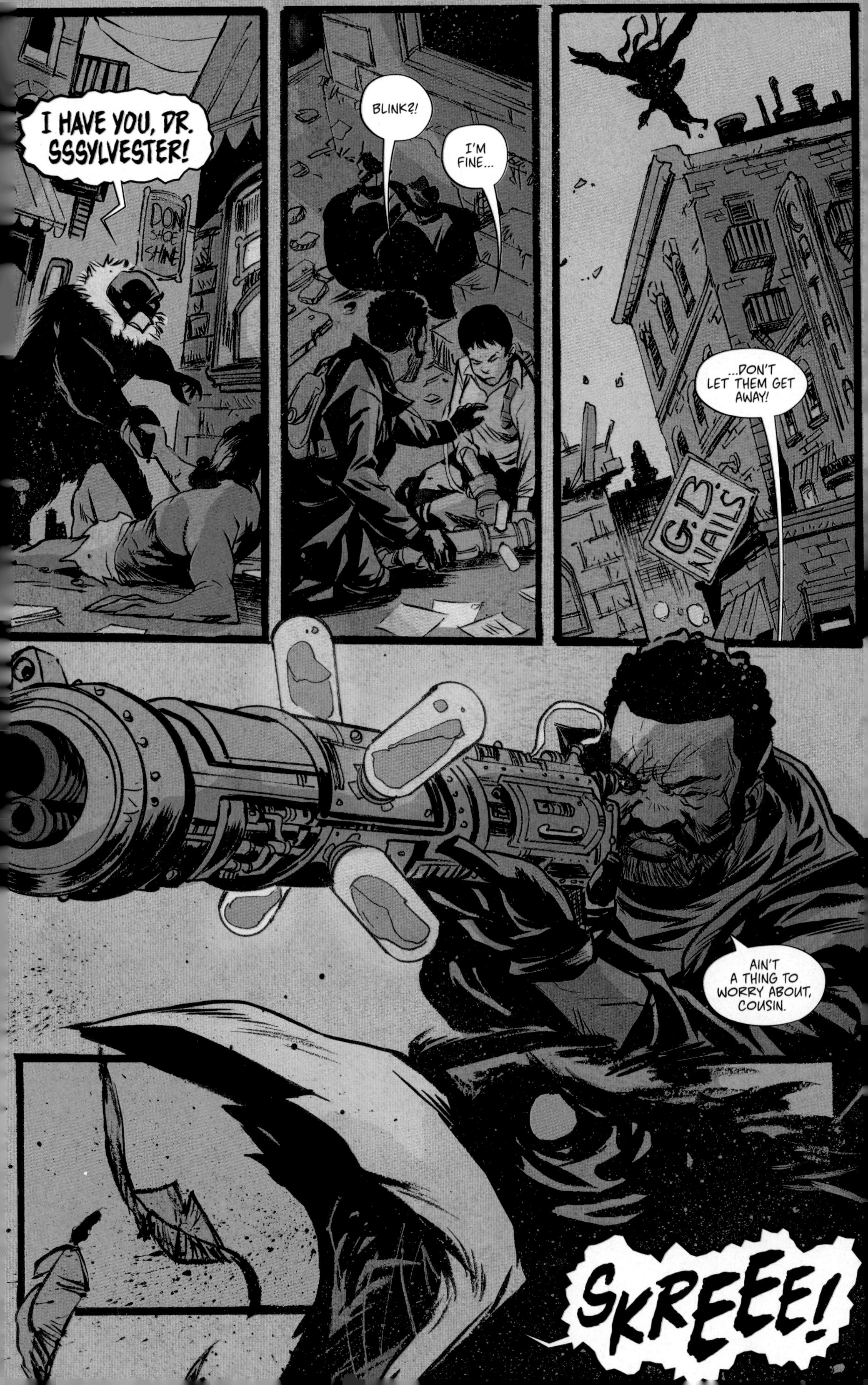
I HAVE YOU, DR. SSSYLVESTER!
DON SHOE SHINE
BLINK?!
I'M FINE...
...DON'T LET THEM GET AWAY!
G.B.'S NAILS
AIN'T A THING TO WORRY ABOUT, COUSIN.
SKREEEE!

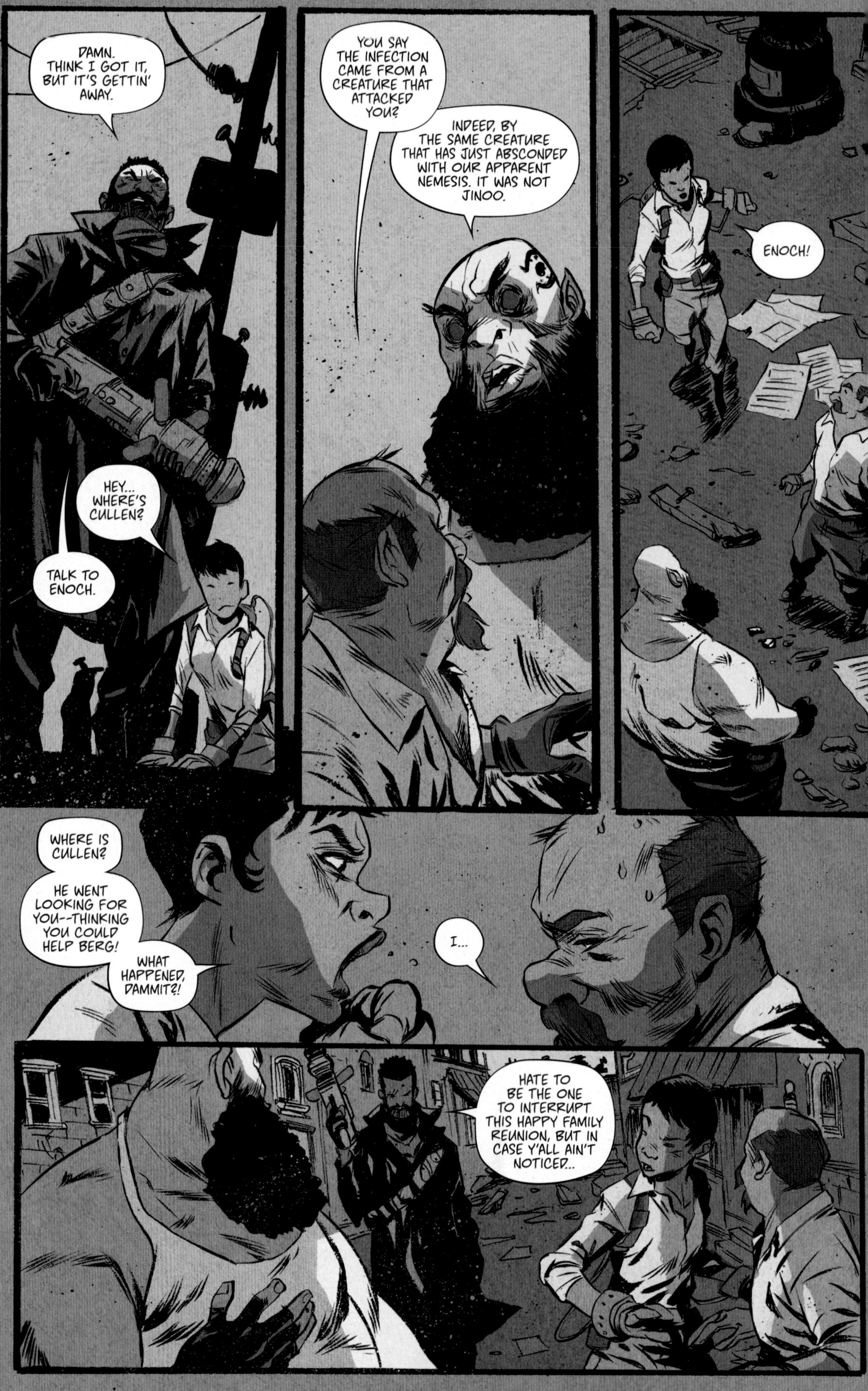
DAMN. THINK I GOT IT, BUT IT'S GETTIN' AWAY.
HEY... WHERE'S CULLEN?
TALK TO ENOCH.
YOU SAY THE INFECTION CAME FROM A CREATURE THAT ATTACKED YOU?
INDEED, BY THE SAME CREATURE THAT HAS JUST ABSCONDED WITH OUR APPARENT NEMESIS. IT WAS NOT JINOO.
ENOCH!
WHERE IS CULLEN?
HE WENT LOOKING FOR YOU--THINKING YOU COULD HELP BERG!
WHAT HAPPENED, DAMMIT?!
I...
HATE TO BE THE ONE TO INTERRUPT THIS HAPPY FAMILY REUNION, BUT IN CASE Y'ALL AIN'T NOTICED...

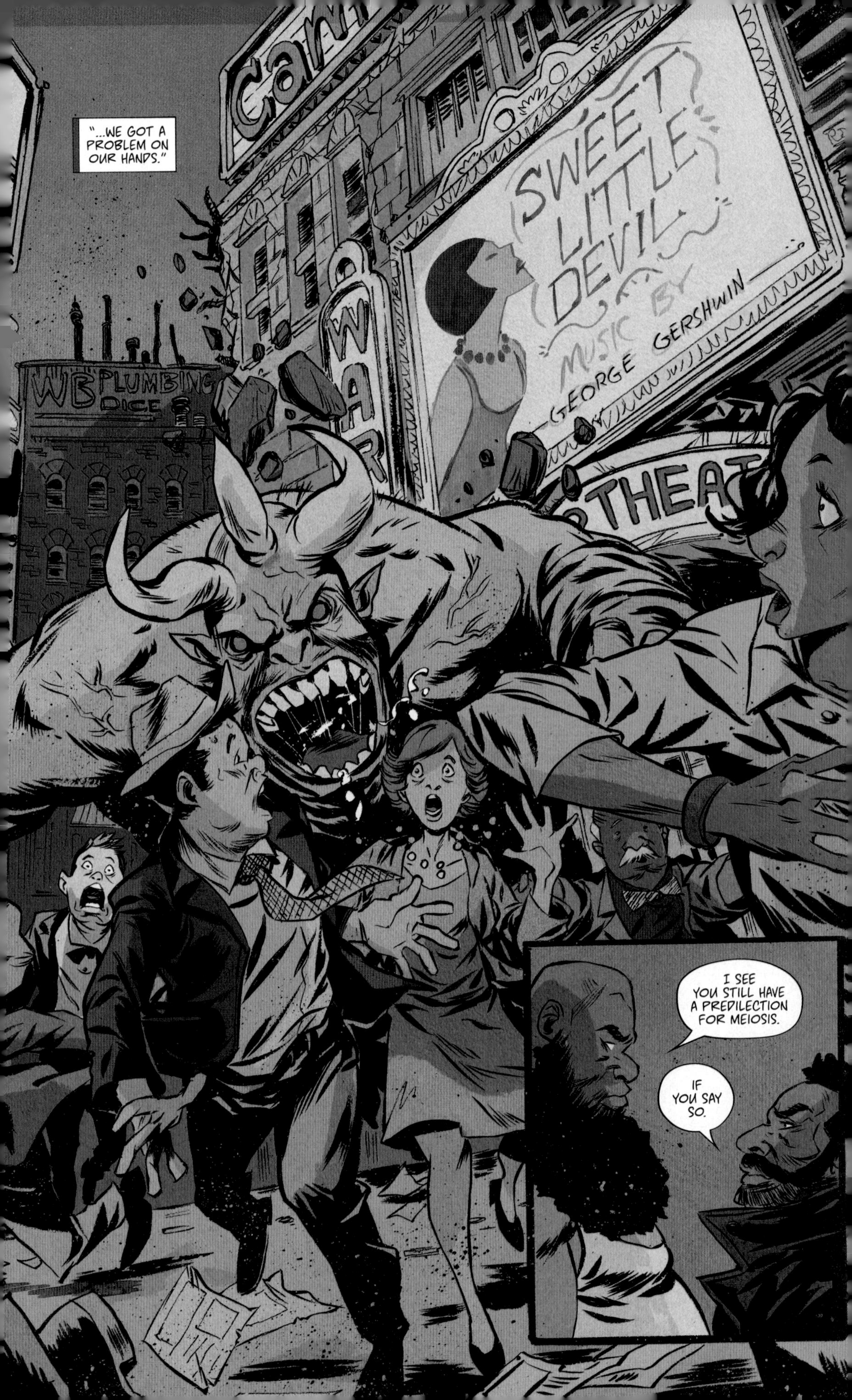
"...WE GOT A PROBLEM ON OUR HANDS."
SWEET LITTLE DEVIL
MUSIC BY GEORGE GERSHWIN
WB PLUMBING
THEAT
I SEE YOU STILL HAVE A PREDILECTION FOR MEIOSIS.
IF YOU SAY SO.

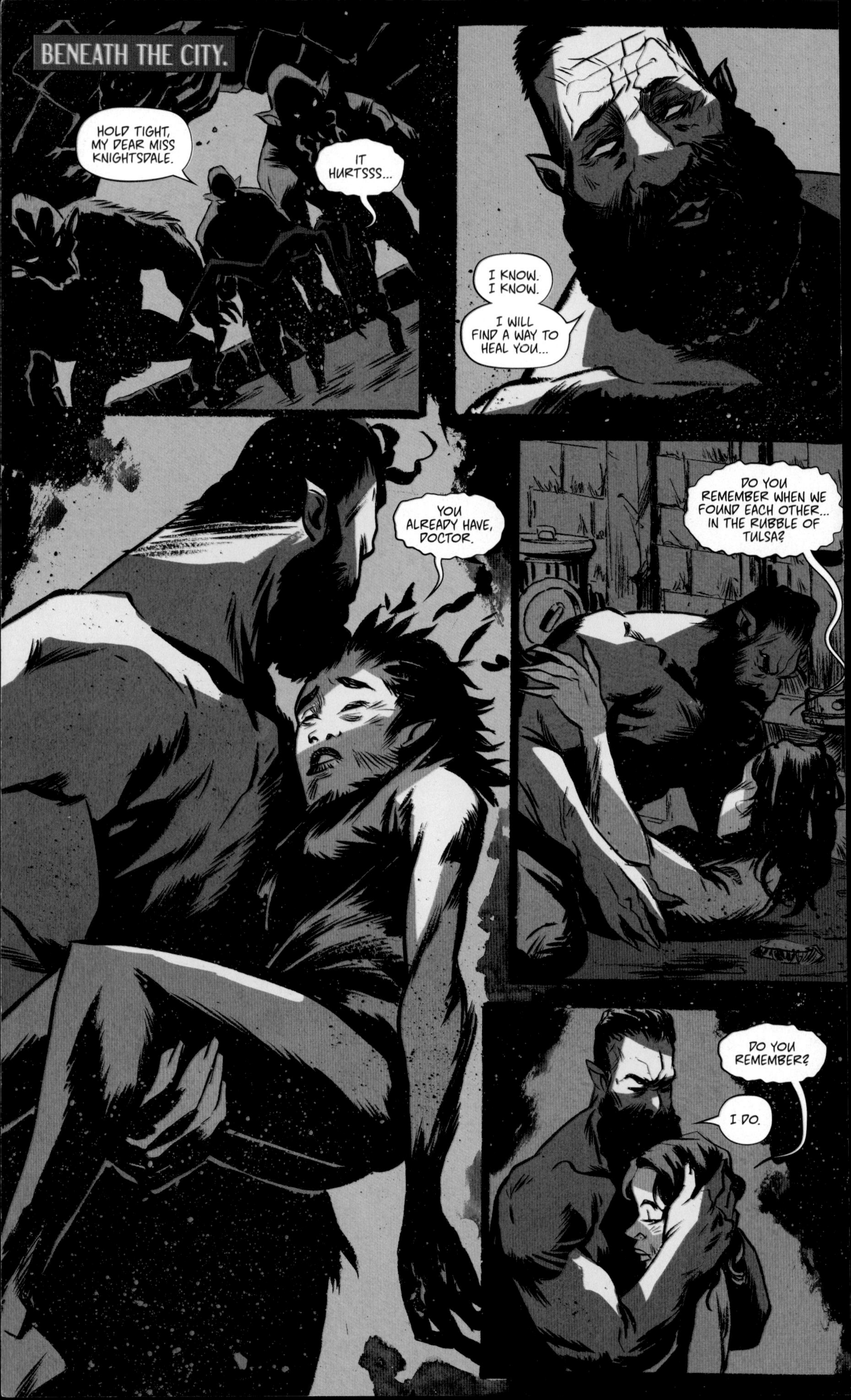
BENEATH THE CITY.
HOLD TIGHT, MY DEAR MISS KNIGHTSDALE.
IT HURTSSS...
I KNOW. I KNOW.
I WILL FIND A WAY TO HEAL YOU...
YOU ALREADY HAVE, DOCTOR.
DO YOU REMEMBER WHEN WE FOUND EACH OTHER... IN THE RUBBLE OF TULSA?
DO YOU REMEMBER?
I DO.

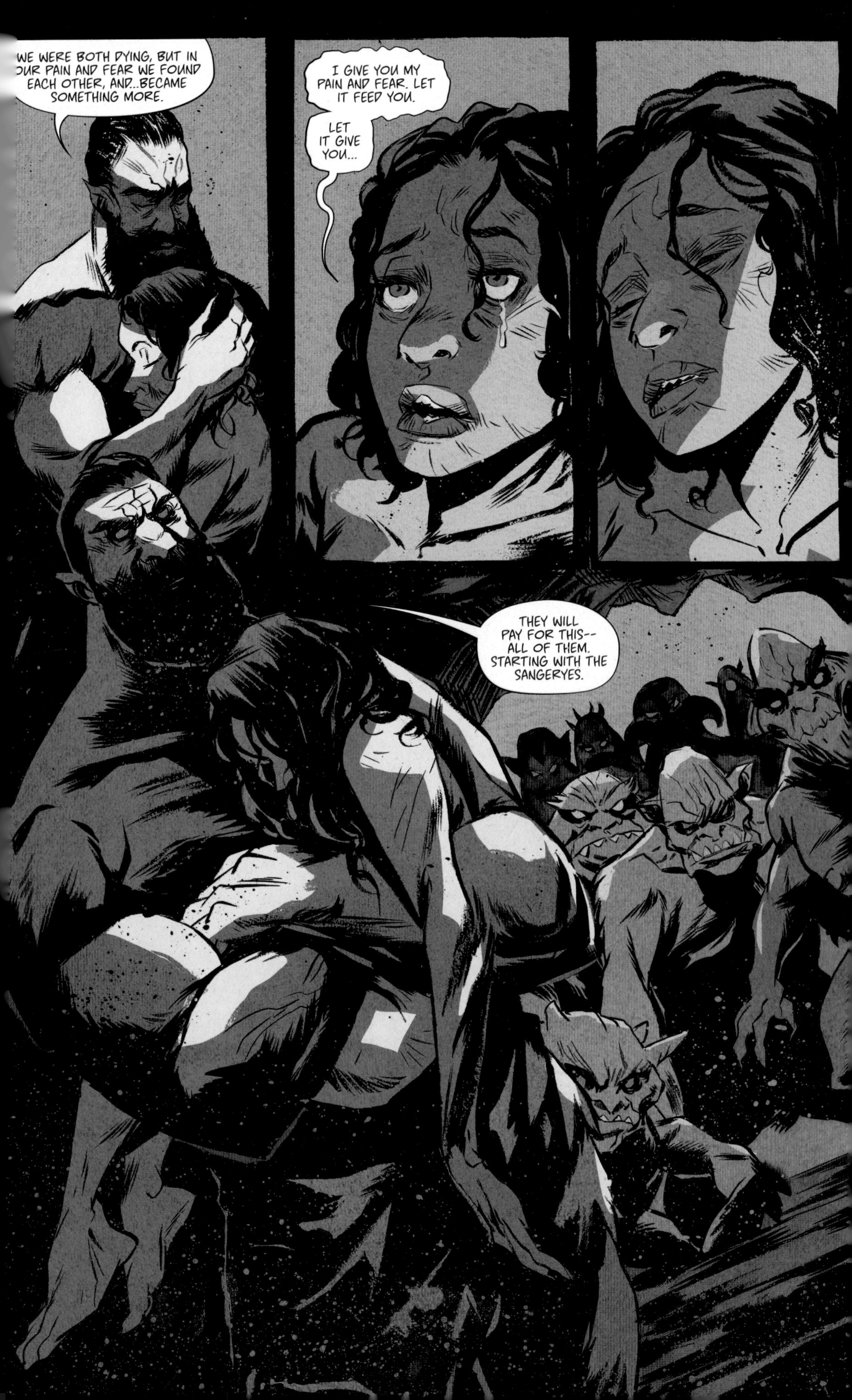
WE WERE BOTH DYING, BUT IN OUR PAIN AND FEAR WE FOUND EACH OTHER, AND...BECAME SOMETHING MORE.
I GIVE YOU MY PAIN AND FEAR. LET IT FEED YOU.
LET IT GIVE YOU...
THEY WILL PAY FOR THIS-- ALL OF THEM. STARTING WITH THE SANGERYES.

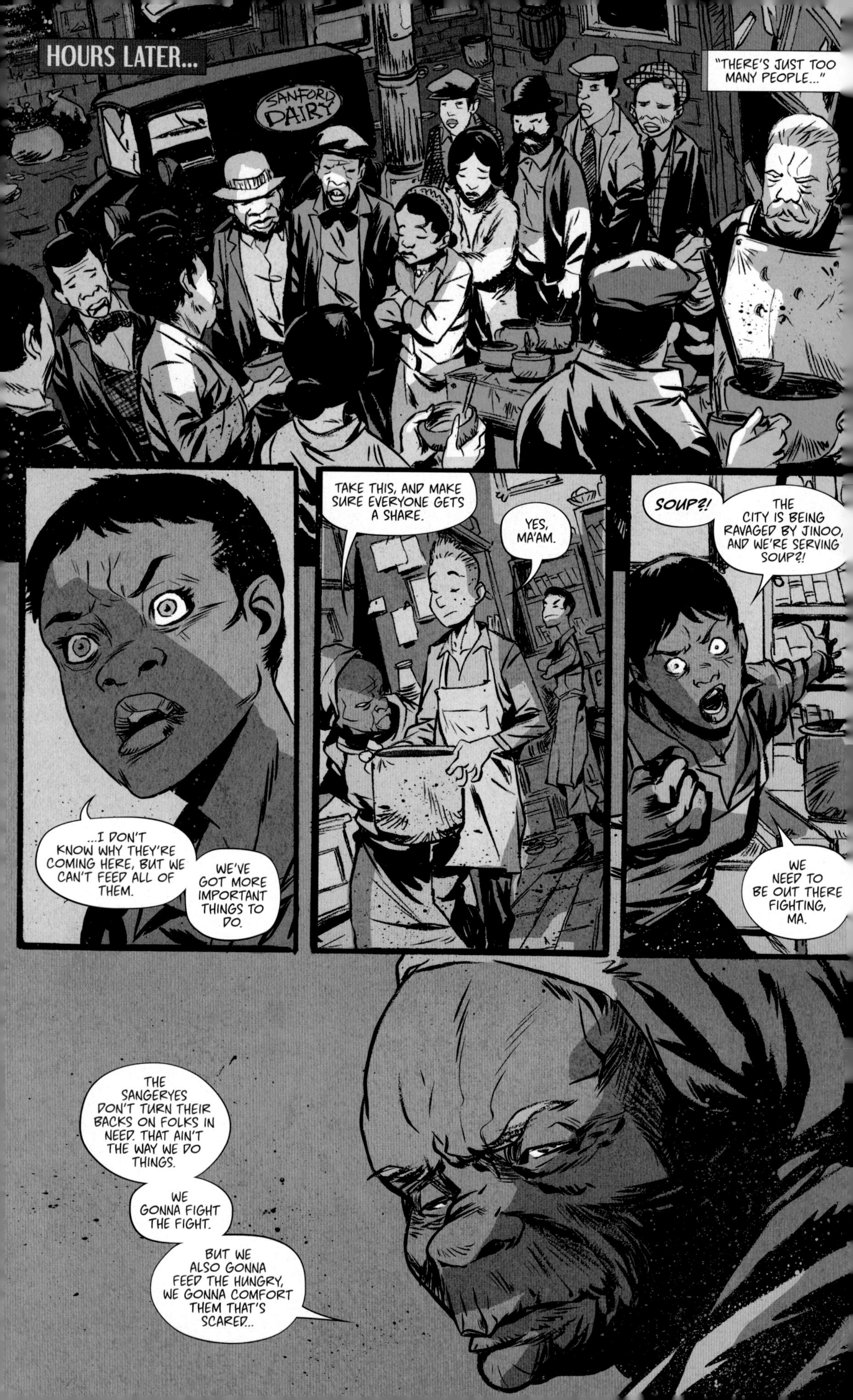
HOURS LATER...
SANFORD DAIRY
"THERE'S JUST TOO MANY PEOPLE..."
...I DON'T KNOW WHY THEY'RE COMING HERE, BUT WE CAN'T FEED ALL OF THEM.
WE'VE GOT MORE IMPORTANT THINGS TO DO.
TAKE THIS, AND MAKE SURE EVERYONE GETS A SHARE.
YES, MA'AM.
SOUP?!
THE CITY IS BEING RAVAGED BY JINOO, AND WE'RE SERVING SOUP?!
WE NEED TO BE OUT THERE FIGHTING, MA.
THE SANGERYES DON'T TURN THEIR BACKS ON FOLKS IN NEED. THAT AIN'T THE WAY WE DO THINGS.
WE GONNA FIGHT THE FIGHT.
BUT WE ALSO GONNA FEED THE HUNGRY, WE GONNA COMFORT THEM THAT'S SCARED...

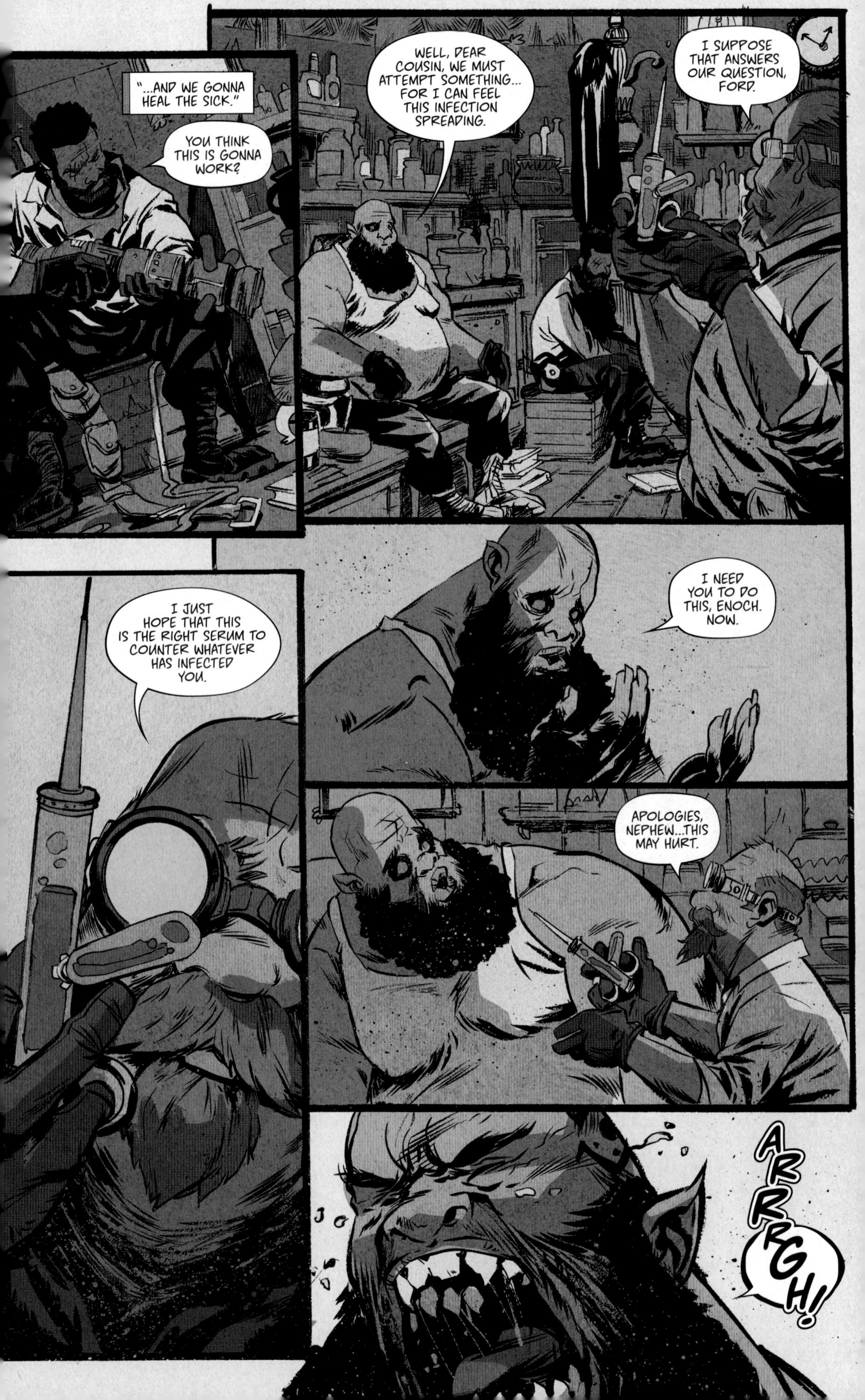
"...AND WE GONNA HEAL THE SICK."
YOU THINK THIS IS GONNA WORK?
WELL, DEAR COUSIN, WE MUST ATTEMPT SOMETHING... FOR I CAN FEEL THIS INFECTION SPREADING.
I SUPPOSE THAT ANSWERS OUR QUESTION, FORD.
I NEED YOU TO DO THIS, ENOCH. NOW.
I JUST HOPE THAT THIS IS THE RIGHT SERUM TO COUNTER WHATEVER HAS INFECTED YOU.
APOLOGIES, NEPHEW...THIS MAY HURT.
ARRRGH!

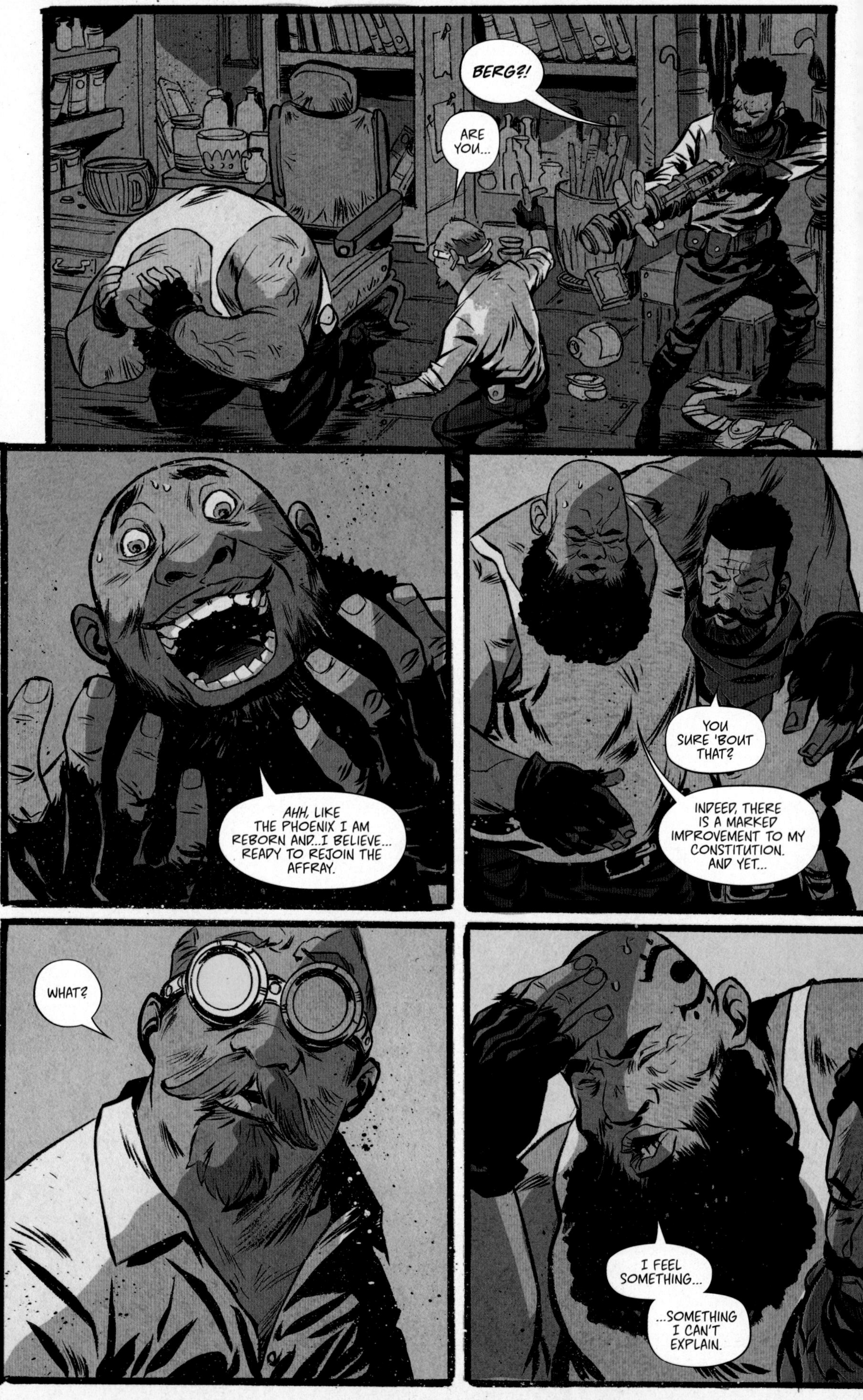

BERG?!
ARE YOU...
AHH, LIKE THE PHOENIX I AM REBORN AND...I BELIEVE... READY TO REJOIN THE AFFRAY.
YOU SURE 'BOUT THAT?
INDEED, THERE IS A MARKED IMPROVEMENT TO MY CONSTITUTION. AND YET...
WHAT?
I FEEL SOMETHING...
...SOMETHING I CAN'T EXPLAIN.

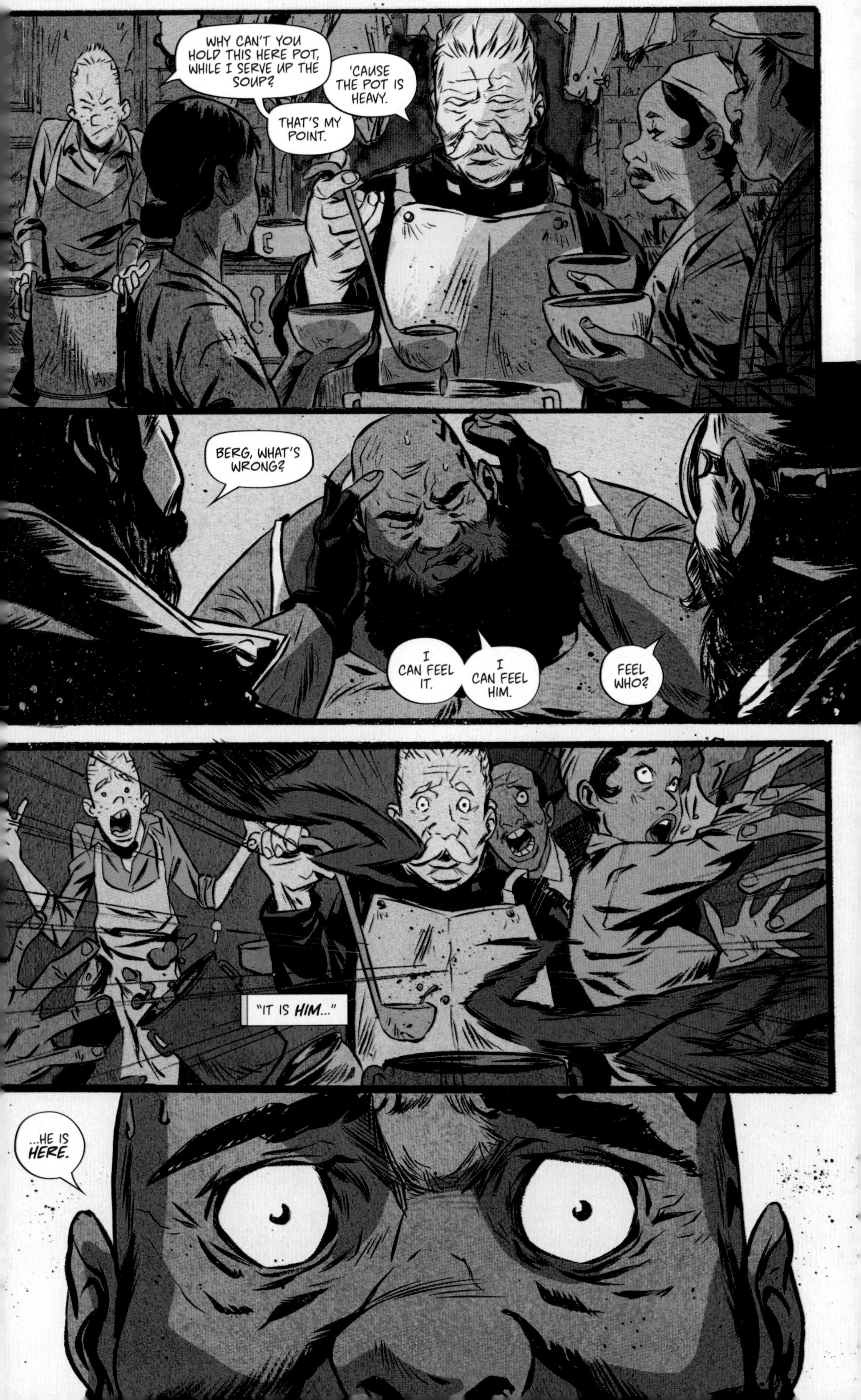

WHY CAN'T YOU HOLD THIS HERE POT, WHILE I SERVE UP THE SOUP?
'CAUSE THE POT IS HEAVY.
THAT'S MY POINT.
BERG, WHAT'S WRONG?
I CAN FEEL IT.
I CAN FEEL HIM.
FEEL WHO?
"IT IS HIM..."
...HE IS HERE.

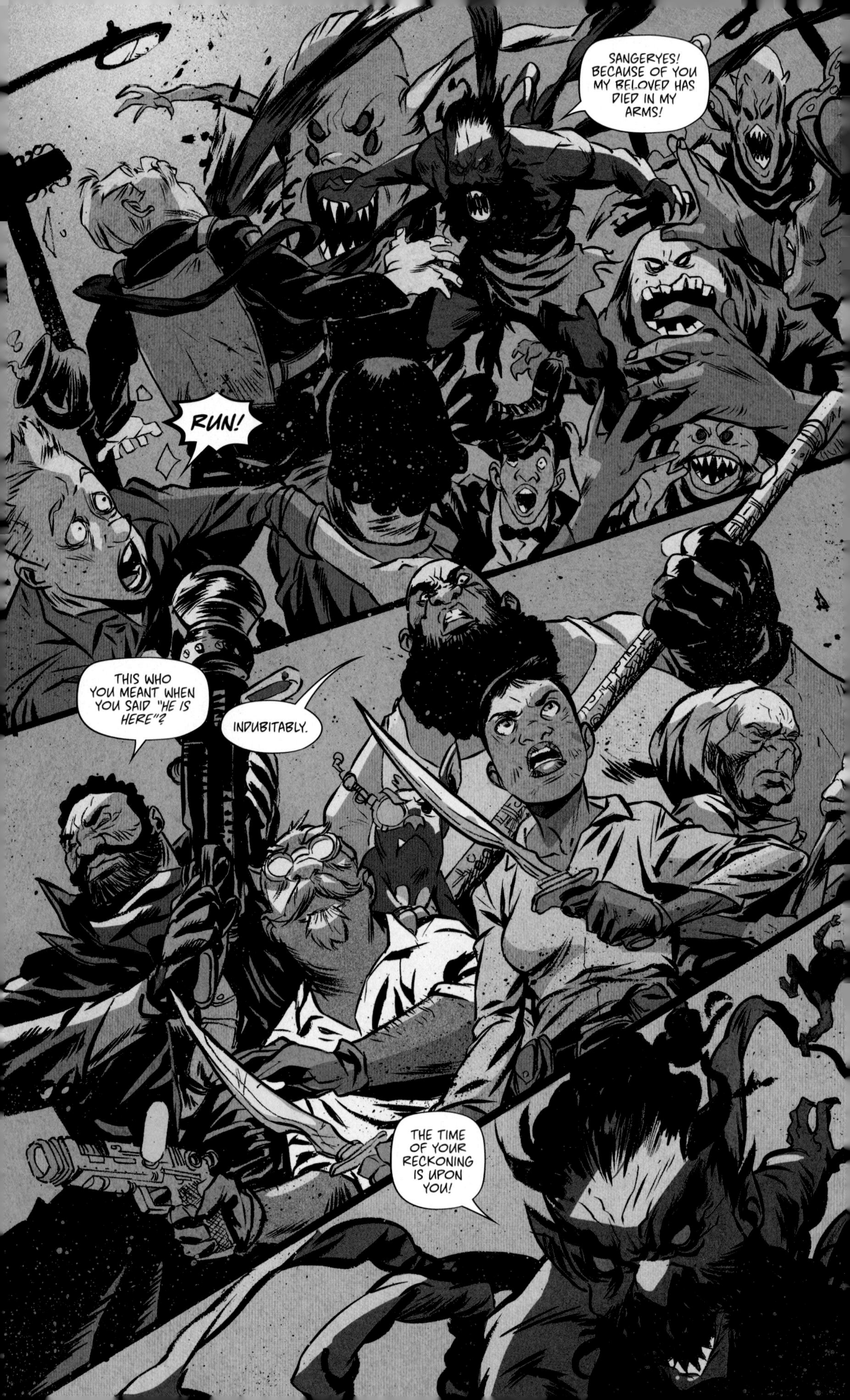
SANGERYES! BECAUSE OF YOU MY BELOVED HAS DIED IN MY ARMS!
RUN!
THIS WHO YOU MEANT WHEN YOU SAID "HE IS HERE"?
INDUBITABLY.
THE TIME OF YOUR RECKONING IS UPON YOU!

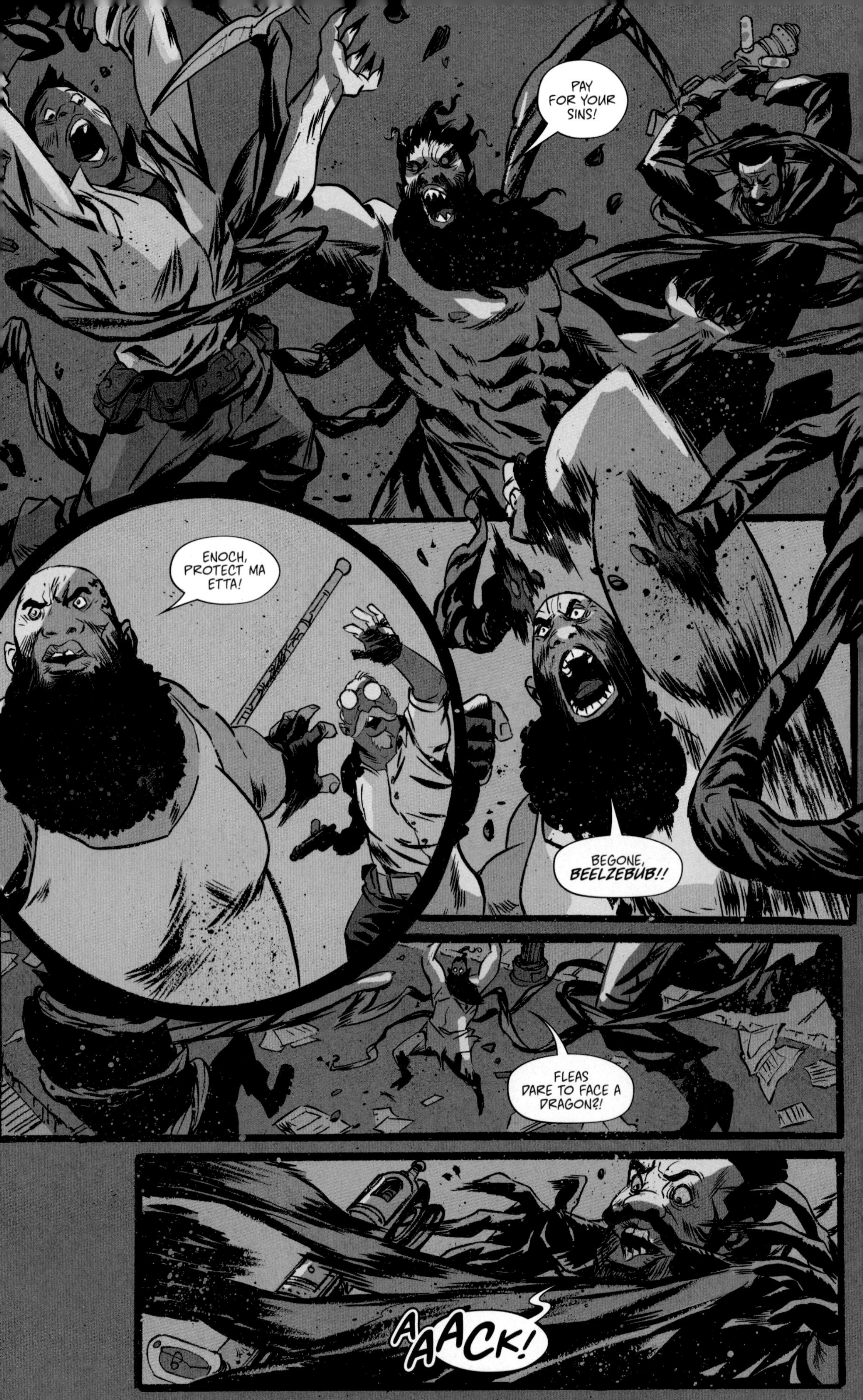
PAY FOR YOUR SINS!
ENOCH, PROTECT MA ETTA!
BEGONE, BEELZEBUB!!
FLEAS DARE TO FACE A DRAGON?!
AAACK!

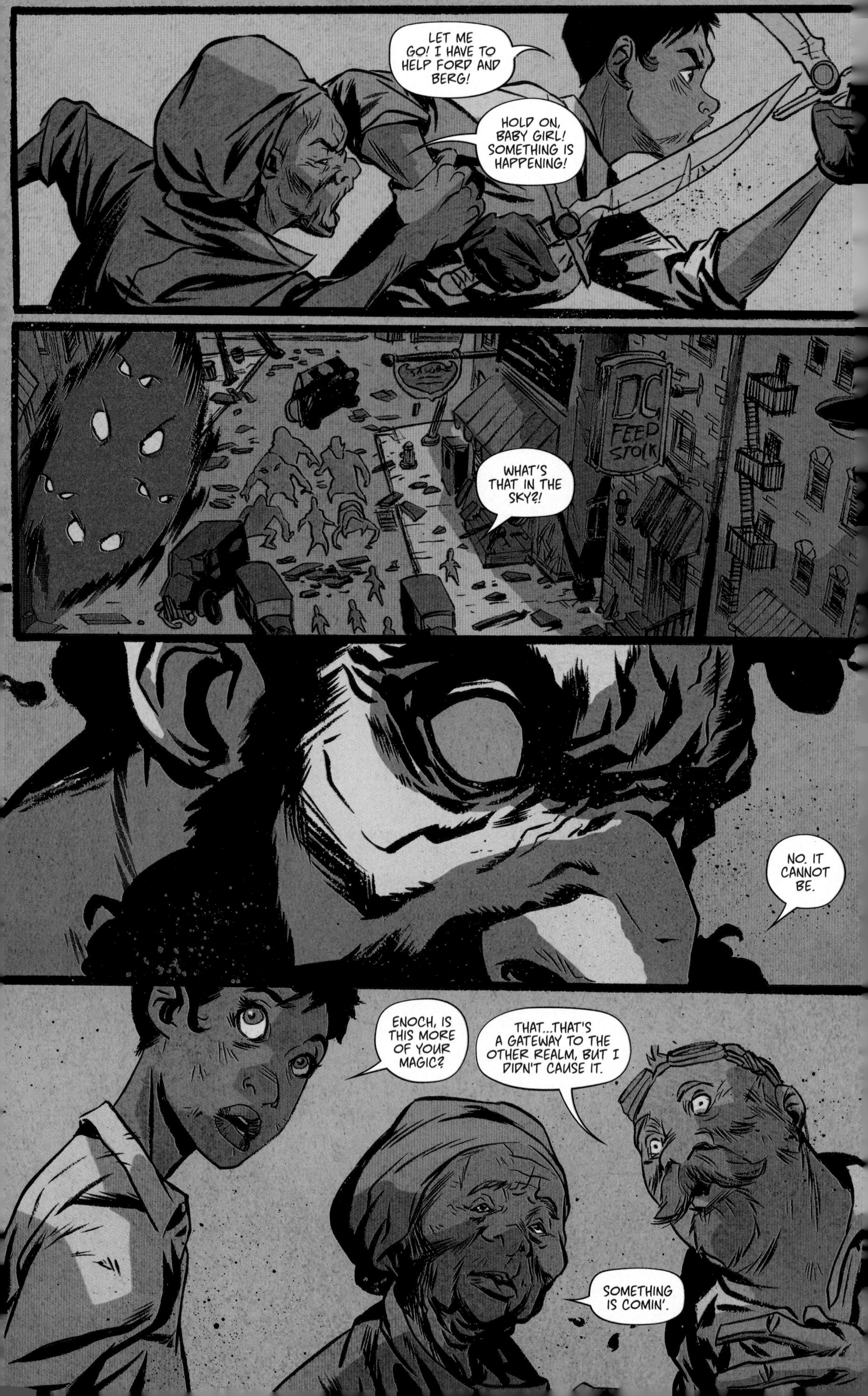
LET ME GO! I HAVE TO HELP FORD AND BERG!
HOLD ON, BABY GIRL! SOMETHING IS HAPPENING!
DC FEED STOCK
WHAT'S THAT IN THE SKY?!
NO. IT CANNOT BE.
ENOCH, IS THIS MORE OF YOUR MAGIC?
THAT...THAT'S A GATEWAY TO THE OTHER REALM, BUT I DIDN'T CAUSE IT.
SOMETHING IS COMIN'.

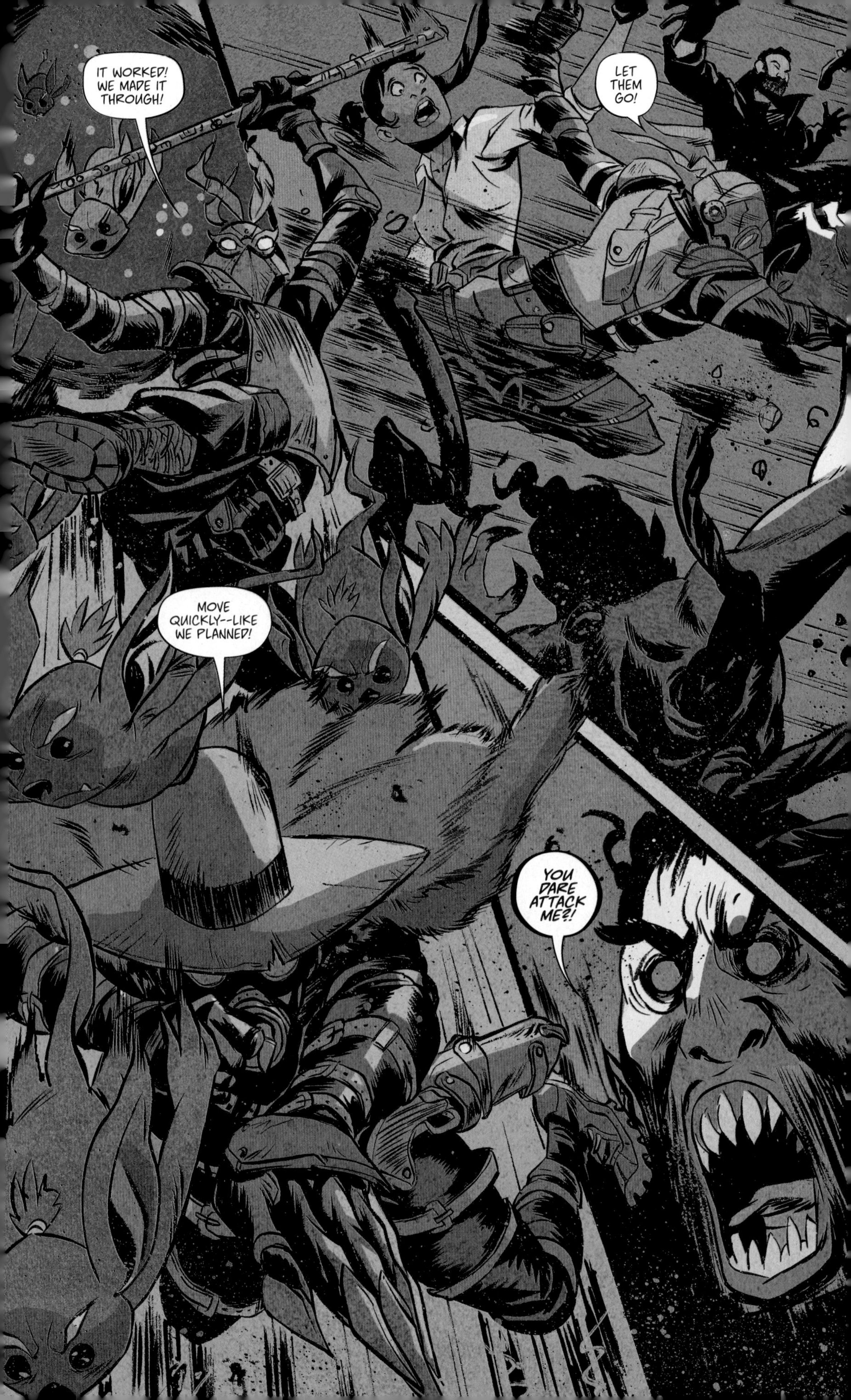
IT WORKED! WE MADE IT THROUGH!
LET THEM GO!
MOVE QUICKLY--LIKE WE PLANNED!
YOU DARE ATTACK ME?!

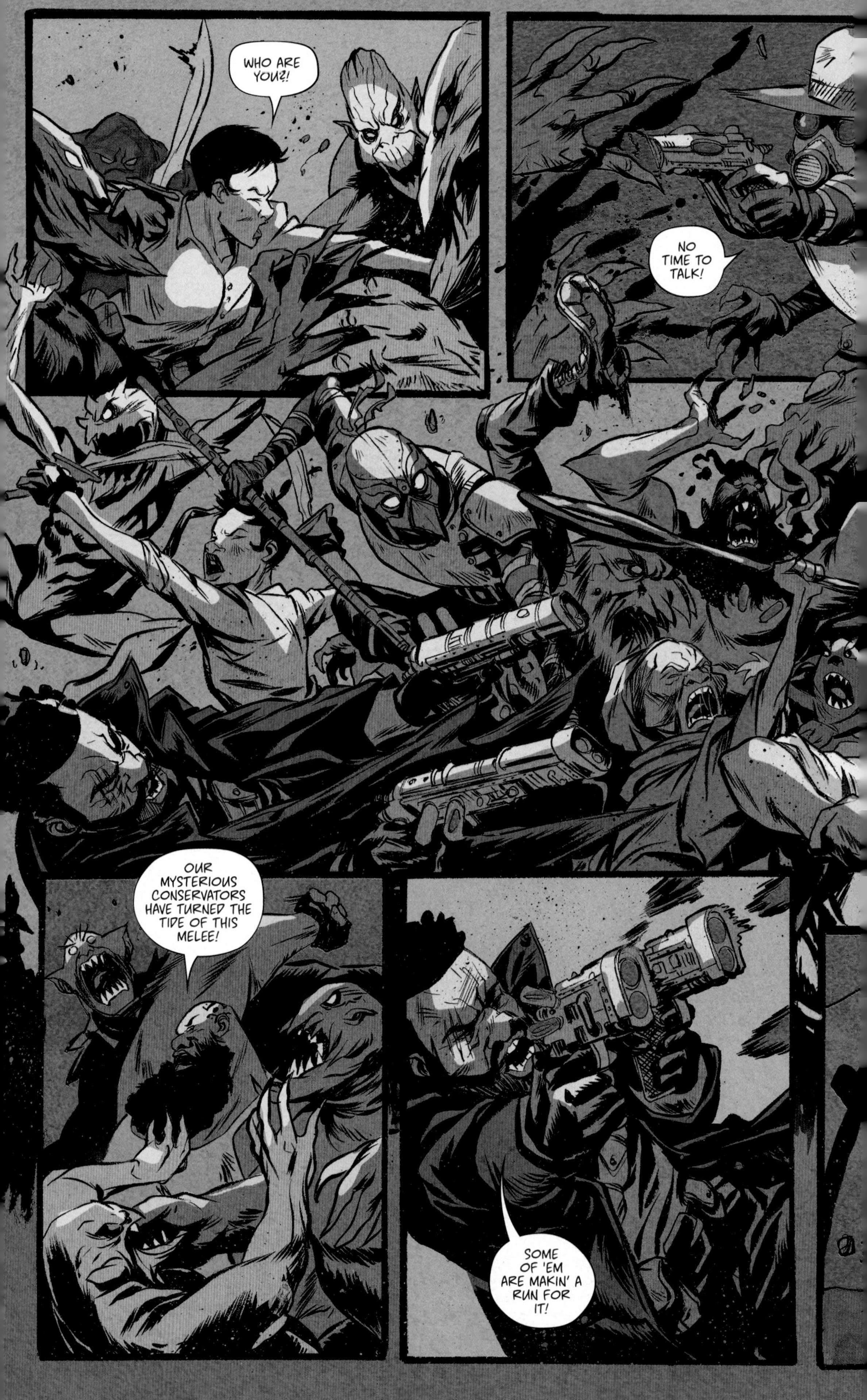
WHO ARE YOU?!
NO TIME TO TALK!
OUR MYSTERIOUS CONSERVATORS HAVE TURNED THE TIDE OF THIS MELEE!
SOME OF 'EM ARE MAKIN' A RUN FOR IT!

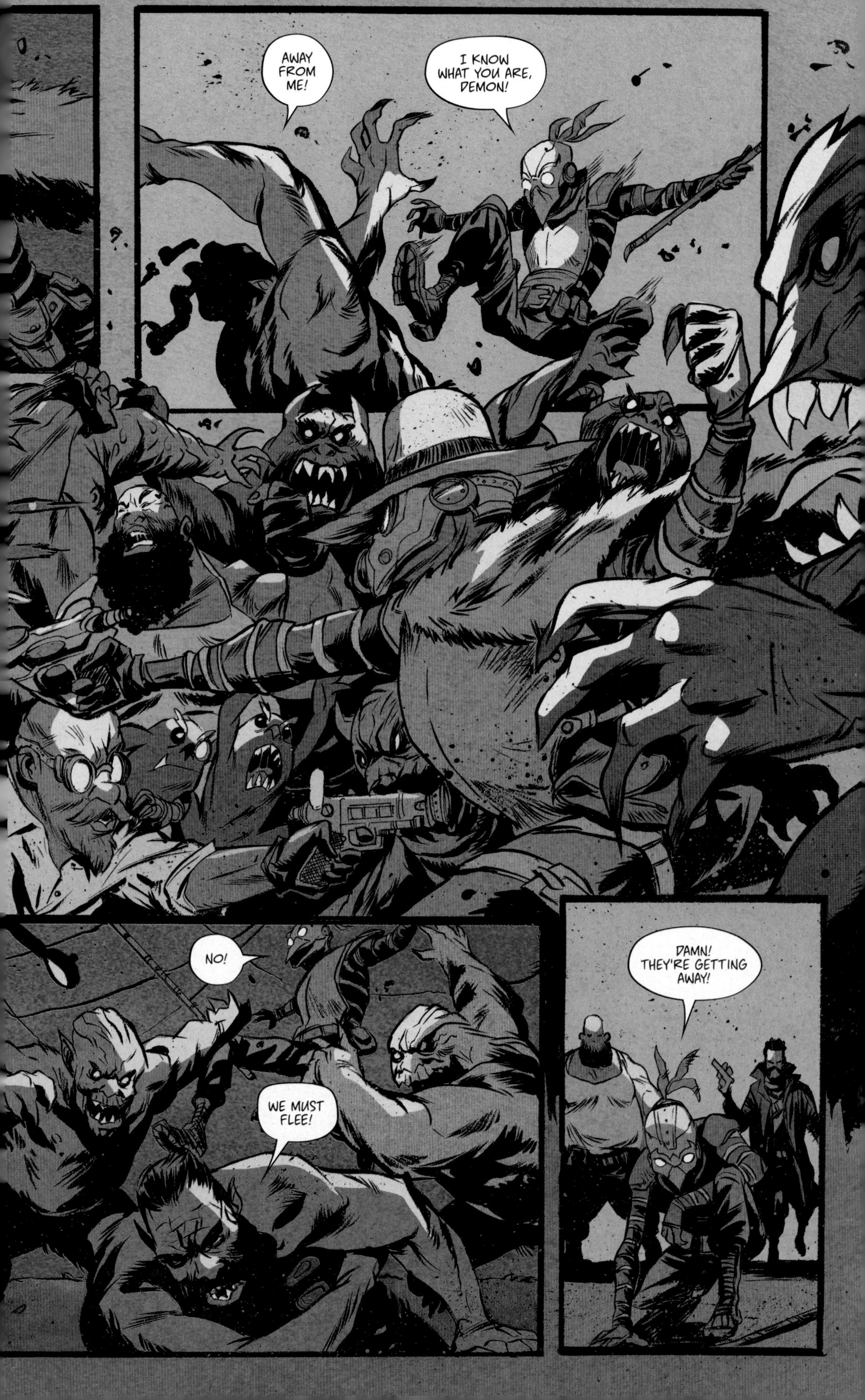
AWAY FROM ME!
I KNOW WHAT YOU ARE, DEMON!
NO!
WE MUST FLEE!
DAMN! THEY'RE GETTING AWAY!

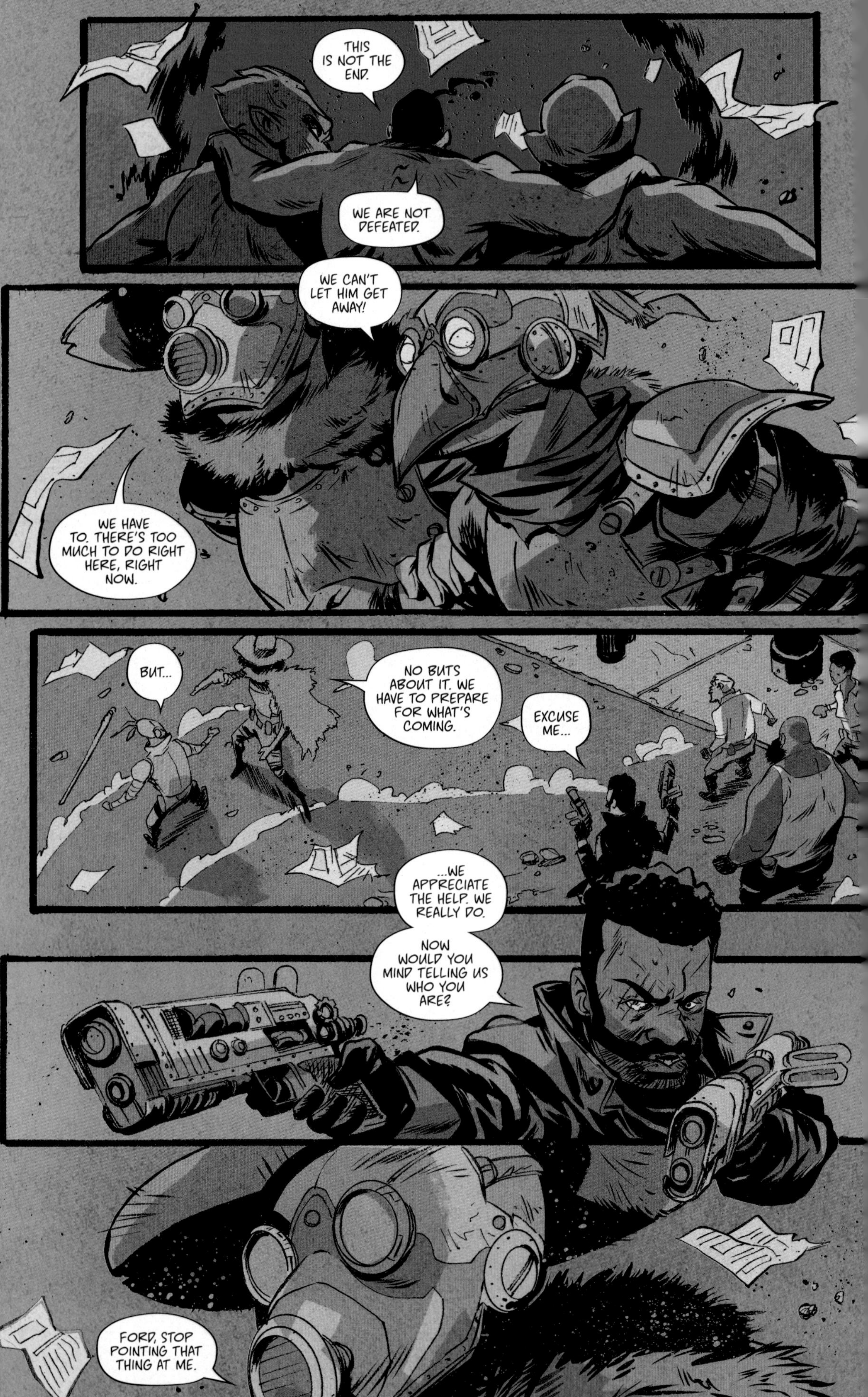
THIS IS NOT THE END.
WE ARE NOT DEFEATED.
WE CAN'T LET HIM GET AWAY!
WE HAVE TO. THERE'S TOO MUCH TO DO RIGHT HERE, RIGHT NOW.
BUT...
NO BUTS ABOUT IT. WE HAVE TO PREPARE FOR WHAT'S COMING.
EXCUSE ME...
...WE APPRECIATE THE HELP. WE REALLY DO.
NOW WOULD YOU MIND TELLING US WHO YOU ARE?
FORD, STOP POINTING THAT THING AT ME.

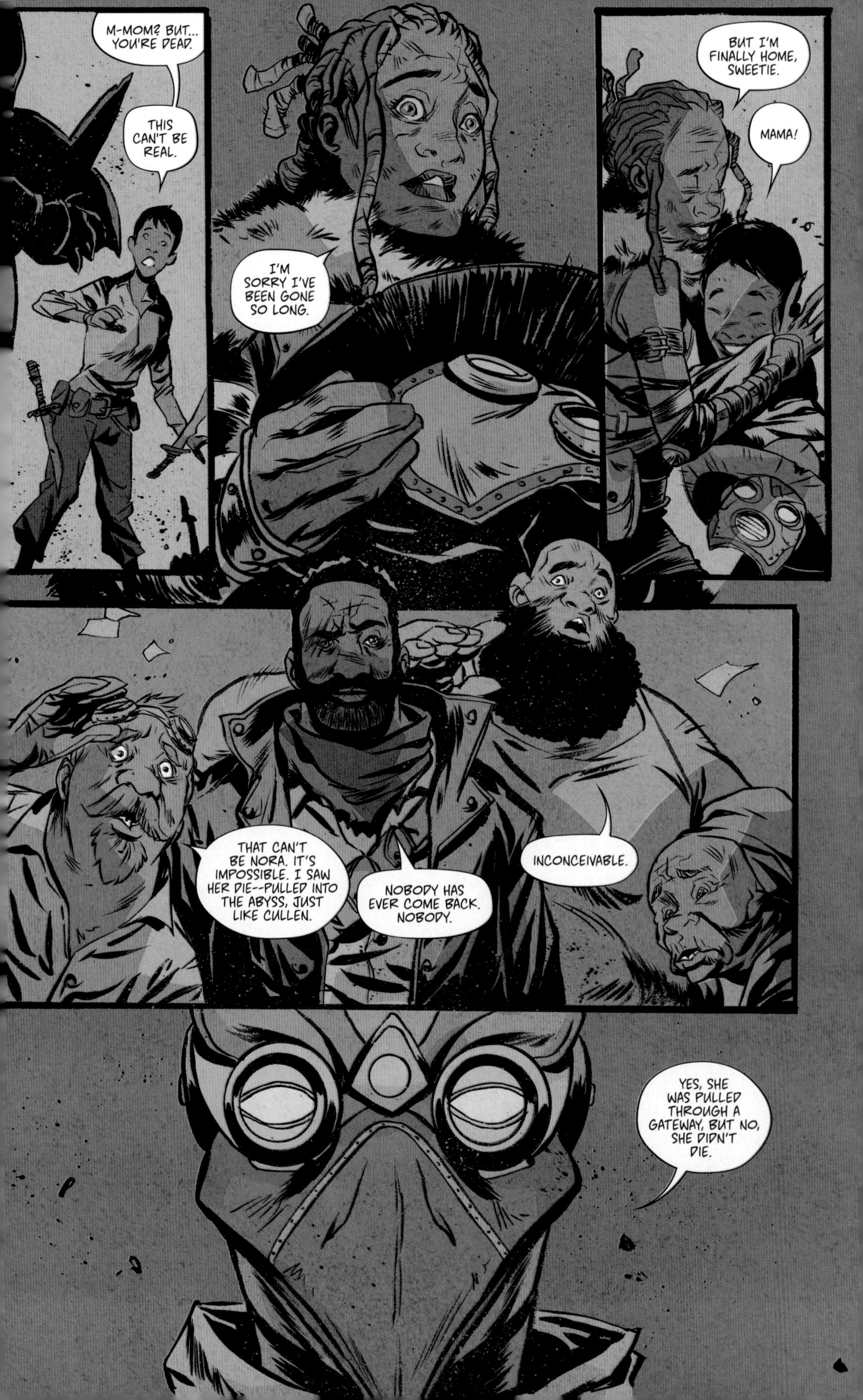
M-MOM? BUT... YOU'RE DEAD.
THIS CAN'T BE REAL.
I'M SORRY I'VE BEEN GONE SO LONG.
BUT I'M FINALLY HOME, SWEETIE.
MAMA!
THAT CAN'T BE NORA. IT'S IMPOSSIBLE. I SAW HER DIE--PULLED INTO THE ABYSS, JUST LIKE CULLEN.
NOBODY HAS EVER COME BACK. NOBODY.
INCONCEIVABLE.
YES, SHE WAS PULLED THROUGH A GATEWAY, BUT NO, SHE DIDN'T DIE.

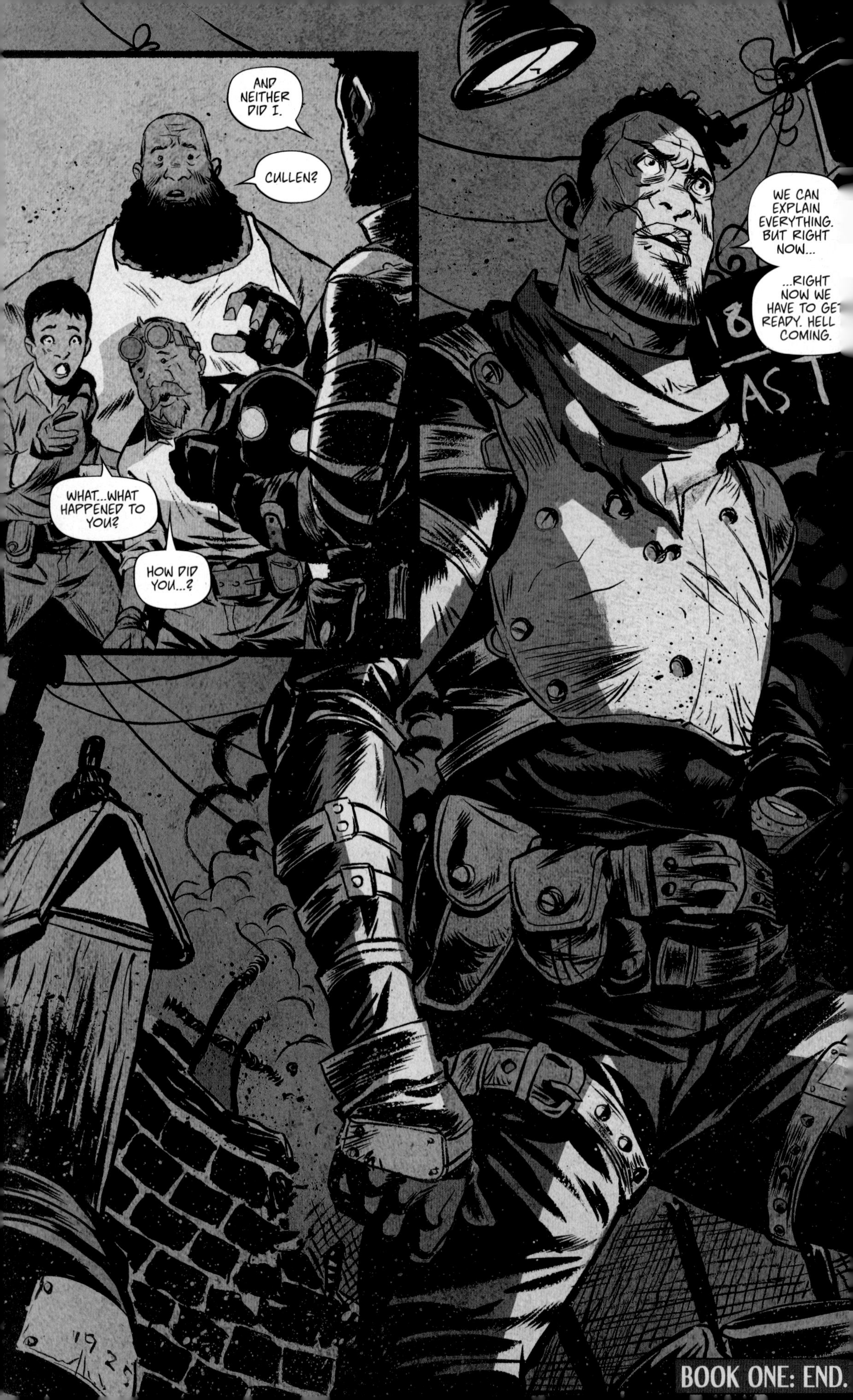
AND NEITHER DID I.
CULLEN?
WHAT...WHAT HAPPENED TO YOU?
HOW DID YOU...?
WE CAN EXPLAIN EVERYTHING. BUT RIGHT NOW...
...RIGHT NOW WE HAVE TO GET READY. HELL COMING.
BOOK ONE: END.

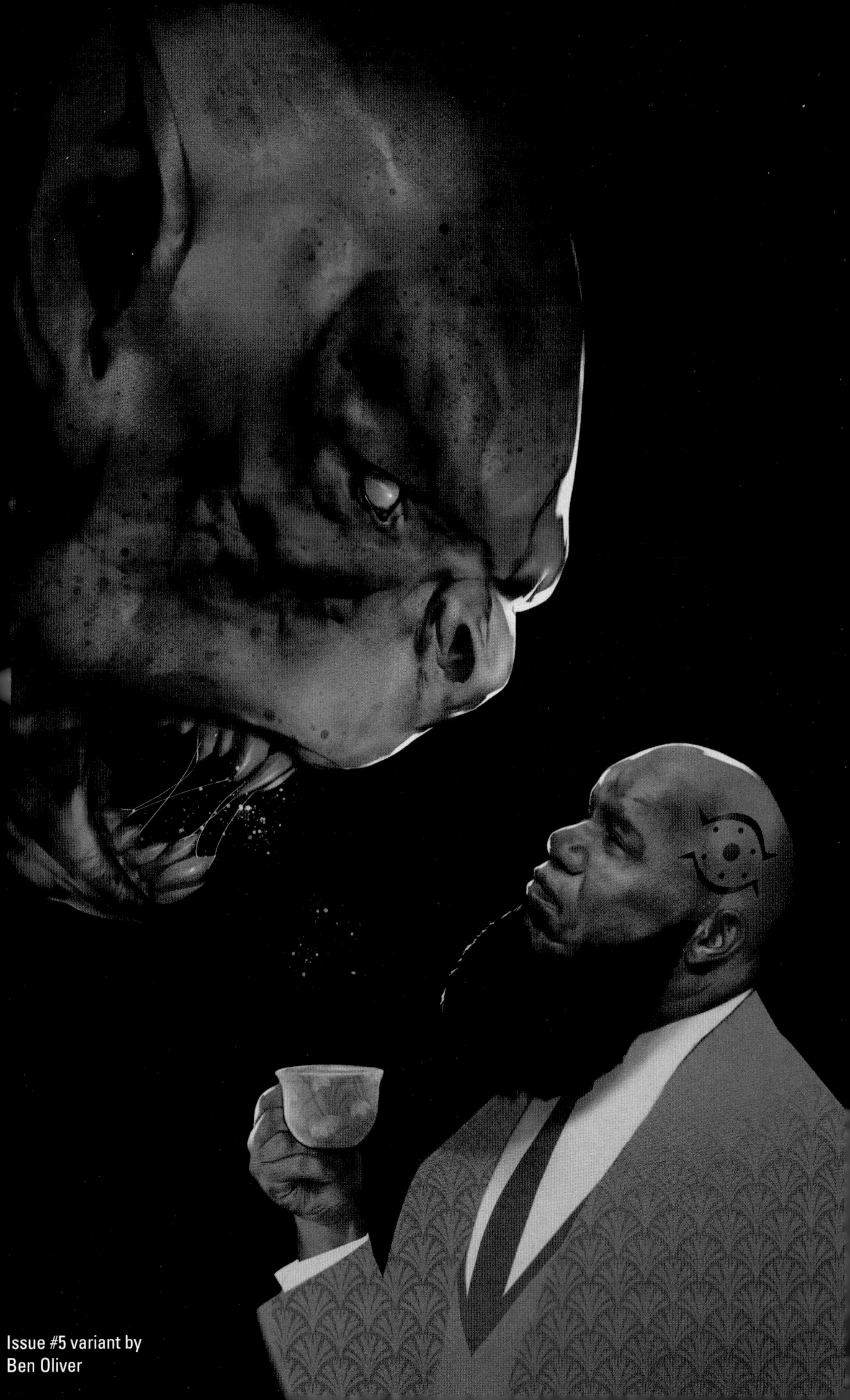

Issue #5 variant by
Ben Oliver

BITTER TRUTHS

"That ain't nothing but the Devil!"

Sometimes horrific events come into our lives. We get fired from our jobs. We become ill. A loved one dies. Scrolling through the news we are overwhelmed with murder and natural disasters, as Mother Nature and our fellow humans seem to be in a race to see who can kill us off first. Hate surrounds us.

It is only human to look at these things and wonder "why"? Why do they hate us? Why do we hate them? Why does so much horror have to happen in the world?

The "why" is the origin of fear. The "why" is the unknown, and people fear the unknown. This fear of the unknown, of the things that lurk in the dark, that threaten our existence…

it is where horror is born.

Some people will look at the horrors of the world—the hate and the violence, the indifference and pestilence—and say,

"That ain't nothing but the Devil!"

Perhaps a red guy with horns and a tail is just a bit easier to process. It is easier, after all, to lay the blame for human misery at the cloven feet of the Devil than it is to take personal accountability. The same is true for vampires and werewolves—they are mythological constructs meant to explain the horrors we face.

One of the greatest horrors we face is racism. It is an ignorant, vile, vicious monster that lurks in humanity's past, present, and, sadly, in our future. *Bitter Root* takes this monster and gives it a face and a body and an uncontrollable desire to kill. But this series also gives hope in fighting this vicious monster, and that hope comes in the form of the Sangerye family. The Sangeryes are fighting a never-ending battle to combat and extinguish the monster born out of racism, intolerance, and hate. *Bitter Root* is filled with action, drama, laughs, and amazing artwork. But at its core, this series is a call to combat the bitter root of racism and hate.

Chuck Brown and
David F. Walker.
October 2018

BITTER TWITTER:

@BITTERROOT18 | @Cbrown803 | @sanfordgreene | @DavidWalker1201

BITTER TRUTHS curated and designed by **John Jennings** / tw @JIJennings
Research Assistant: **Edgardo Delgadillo-Aguilera**

"White people believed that whatever the manners, under every dark skin was a jungle. Swift unnavigable waters, swinging screaming baboons, sleeping snakes, red gums ready for their sweet white blood. In a way, he thought, they were right. The more colored people spent their strength trying to convince them how gentle they were, how clever and loving, how human, the more they used themselves up to persuade whites of something Negroes believed could not be questioned, the deeper and more tangled the jungle grew inside. But it wasn't the jungle blacks brought with them to this place from the other (livable) place. It was the jungle white folks planted in them. And it grew. It spread. In, through and after life, it spread, until it invaded the whites who had made it. Touched them every one. Changed and altered them. Made them bloody, silly, worse than even they wanted to be, so scared were they of the jungle they had made. The screaming baboon lived under their own white skin; the red gums were their own."

- from *Beloved* by Toni Morrison

"Ma Etta" **character desgin by Sanford Greene**

DEEP ROOTS / RICH SOIL:
RACE, HORROR AND THE ETHNOGOTHIC

John Jennings

It's hard to ignore the resurgence of the cultural production form called Afrofuturism. Coined by media scholar Mark Dery in 1993, the term was a moniker used to theorize the use of speculative narratives to deal with real world issues faced by African Americans. Now, there is a new energy around the term. This version, called "Afrofuturism 2.0" by media scholar Reynaldo Anderson, is the new wave of this notion regarding the utility of the speculative for social justice issues. Scholars and artists like Ytasha Womack, Adrienne Marie Brown, Nnedi Okorafor, Stacey Robinson, Clint Fluker, and Adilifu Nama are now dealing with this old notion via this new lens. Race has always been a fiction and, thus, so have blackness and whiteness. How do you unmake the harmful stories of race and "difference"?

By making our own.

Like any movement or cultural phenomenon, there are always exceptions and potential problems. My friend Stanford Carpenter and I became interested in how genre affects these movements. For instance, how does a novel like Octavia E. Butler's *Kindred* fit into notions of a black future? It has elements of the supernatural and the spectral within its narrative. Films like *Candyman* or *Get Out* have decidedly surrealistic elements that can also fall into the horror genre. Were these Afrofuturist? We weren't sure at the time. So, Stanford and I postulated a term that we dubbed "EthnoGothic" because what we now see as mere conventions of a cultural form we once saw as limitations.

To us the EthnoGothic deals with primarily speculative narratives that actively engage with negatively affective and racially oriented psychological traumas via the traditions of Gothic tropes and technologies. These tropes include the grotesque other, body horror, haunted spaces, the hungry ghost, the uncanny, the doppelgänger, fictional historical artifacts, and multivalent disruptive tensions between the constructions of memory, history, the present, and the self.

It can be said that horror, the Gothic, and the uncanny are very much a part of the overarching narratives surrounding how non-whites are treated as inferior, grotesque, and monstrous. This demonization of systemically othered bodies is a core connotation of the horror genre and how it plays upon internal fears and desires. It also gives us a speculative map to interpret or postulate how these projected narrative systems disrupt, entrap, and otherwise displace "the other" into extremely negative life-altering situations. The body that is not "normal" is forced to become an artifact and index of the abject. This state of abjection deals with perception of the other as grotesque and inhuman. This imagined body then becomes a surrogate for all manner of horrific connotations that are seen as aberrant, deviant, surreal, dangerous and unwanted. It is in opposition to the heteronormative body and, therefore, does not fit well into the well-oiled systems that signify what is proper. Despite the negative meanings that these narratives represent, these spaces also carry an equally as potent allure for the repulsive, the gothic, the unseemly, and the freakish. This is because horror is also about the desires that we hide in the shadows of a culture as well. The affordances of comics allow us to graphically explore these complex interactions in our society and give us a safe space in which to exorcise our societal demons. *Bitter Root* is a prime example of this phenomenon.

Three major points excited me about *Bitter Root* as a scholar. The first thing was that the three creators of this series were tapping into the

same allegorical power that previous black creators have when dealing with race and social justice. They decided to deal with how monstrous racism and its associated violence really are. That tradition includes writers and auteurs like Henry Dumas, Rusty Cundief, Toni Morrison, Nalo Hopkinson, Tananarive Due, Jordan Peele and more recently Boots Riley with his new film *Sorry to Bother You*. The *Bitter Root* team has tapped into the zeitgeist of the intersections of race and horror and have done their ancestors proud.

Secondly, I was excited for this book because it is set during one of the most important American cultural movements in our country's history: The Harlem Renaissance. The Harlem Renaissance spanned the 1920s and was a blossoming of black creativity, political thought, and social progress. The speculative was used quite a bit by writers and artists to talk about the strangeness of this thing called "race". One of the most important figures of the movement was W.E.B. DuBois who also used supernatural and speculative elements to talk about race. In his seminal book *The Souls of Black Folks,* he uses the metaphor of "the veil" to talk about how black Americans see themselves, their white counterparts, and their own worth in relation to America. This term "the veil" comes from Hoodoo culture. It refers to a fleshy membrane that sometimes drapes over the faces of certain newborn infants. This "caul," as some root-workers and conjure-folk call it, was said to be a symbol of that child's "second sight": the ability to see into other worlds. DuBois states that due to the uncanny state in which black people find themselves in this country, they are born with this otherworldly power; a power which manifests itself is both a blessing and a curse. Our consciousness, like the Sangerye family, is split into two warring halves. This "one dark body" is always struggling to survive in spite of the pain heaped upon its collective soul.

Finally, *Bitter Root* uses all of this history, creativity, and thirst for justice to turn how black people are sometimes seen by society on its ear. What if black people aren't the grotesque, hungry monsters they are depicted as being? What if white people have a sickness that makes them into monstrous demons that lurk just beneath the skin? Racism and hatred are caustic diseases that must either be exorcised or destroyed. Think of what that metaphor means during this current political moment. Stories are powerful and can be used to explore difficult conversations because it can distance us from them and sometimes give much needed perspective.

The *Bitter Root* team should be very proud. Not just because they've created this "cool" cultural artifact but because they've created a new thread in the ever growing and evolving tapestry of the American story, as told through the veiled and weary eyes of the black American citizen.

Without the bitter, the sweet ain't as sweet.

JOHN JENNINGS is a Professor of Media and Cultural Studies at the University of California at Riverside. Jennings is co-editor of the Eisner Award-winning collection *The Blacker the Ink: Constructions of Black Identity in Comics and Sequential Art.* Jennings is also a 2016 Nasir Jones Hip Hop Studies Fellow with the Hutchins Center at Harvard University. Jennings' current projects include the horror anthology *Box of Bones,* the coffee table book *Black Comix Returns* (with Damian Duffy), and the Eisner-winning, Bram Stoker Award-winning, *New York Times* best-selling graphic novel adaptation of Octavia Butler's classic dark fantasy novel *Kindred.* Jennings is also founder and curator of the ABRAMS Megascope line of graphic novels.

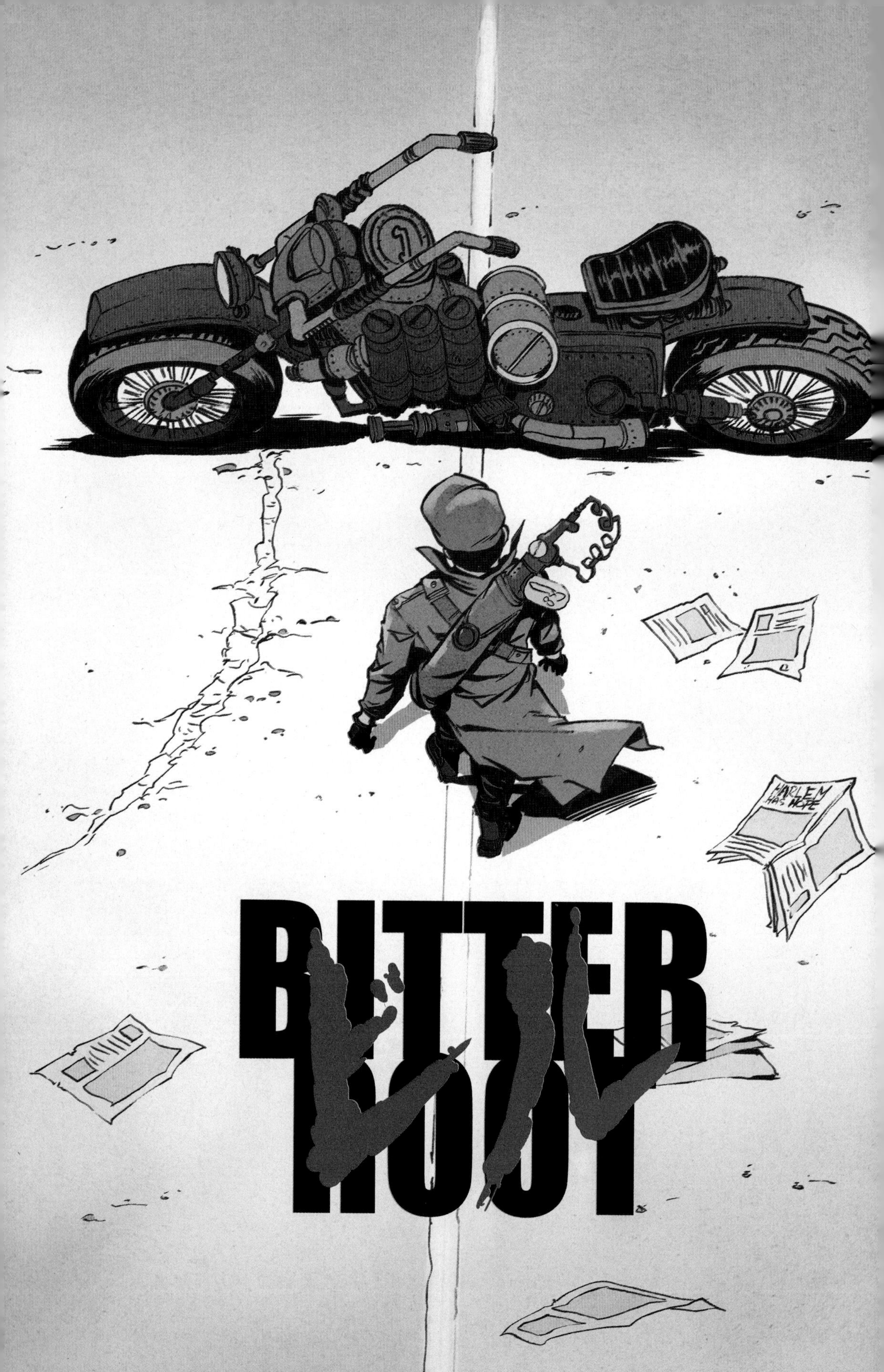
BITTER
ROOT
HARLEM HAS HOPE

Issue #1 eBay variant
by Sanford Greene

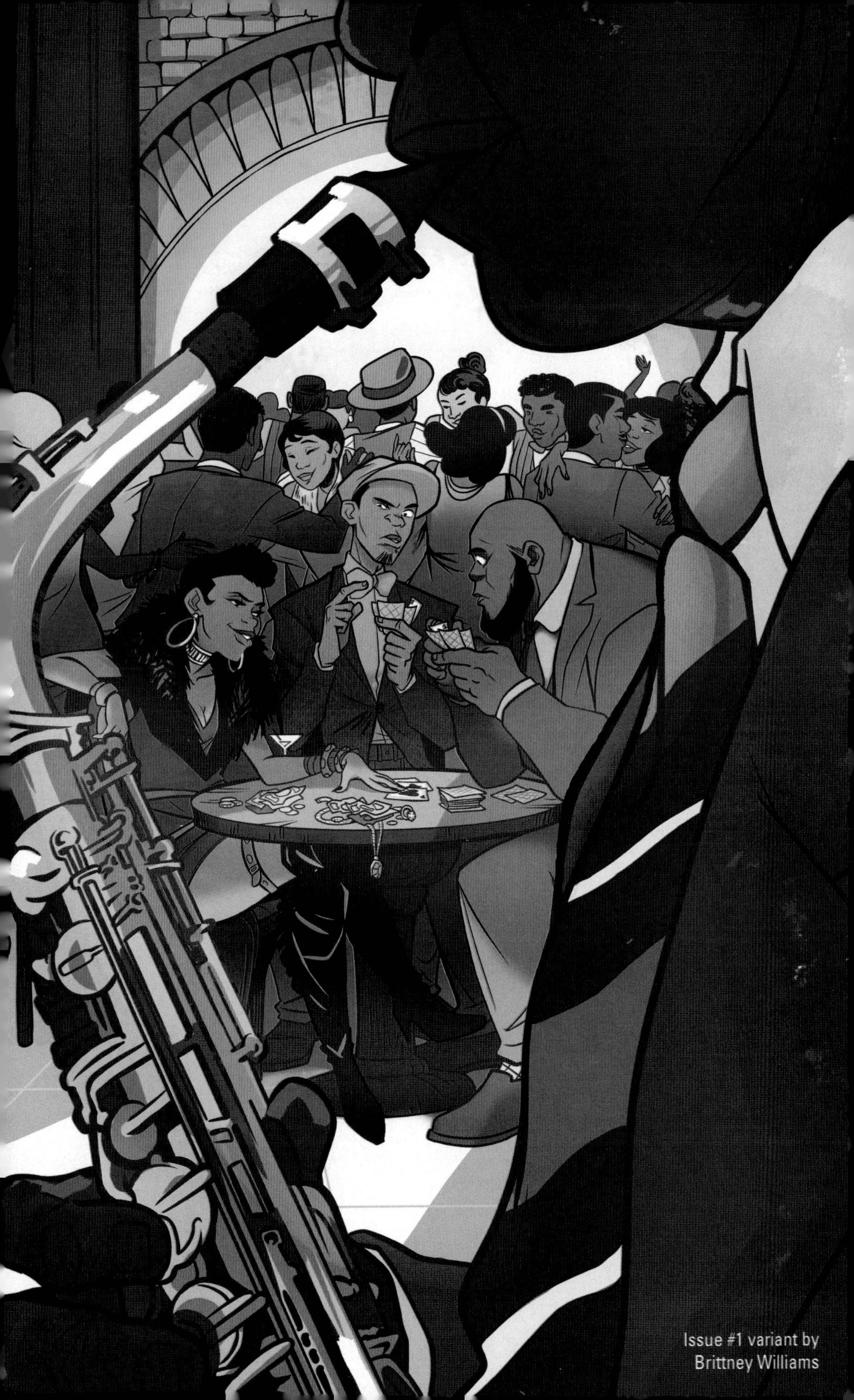

Issue #1 variant by
Brittney Williams

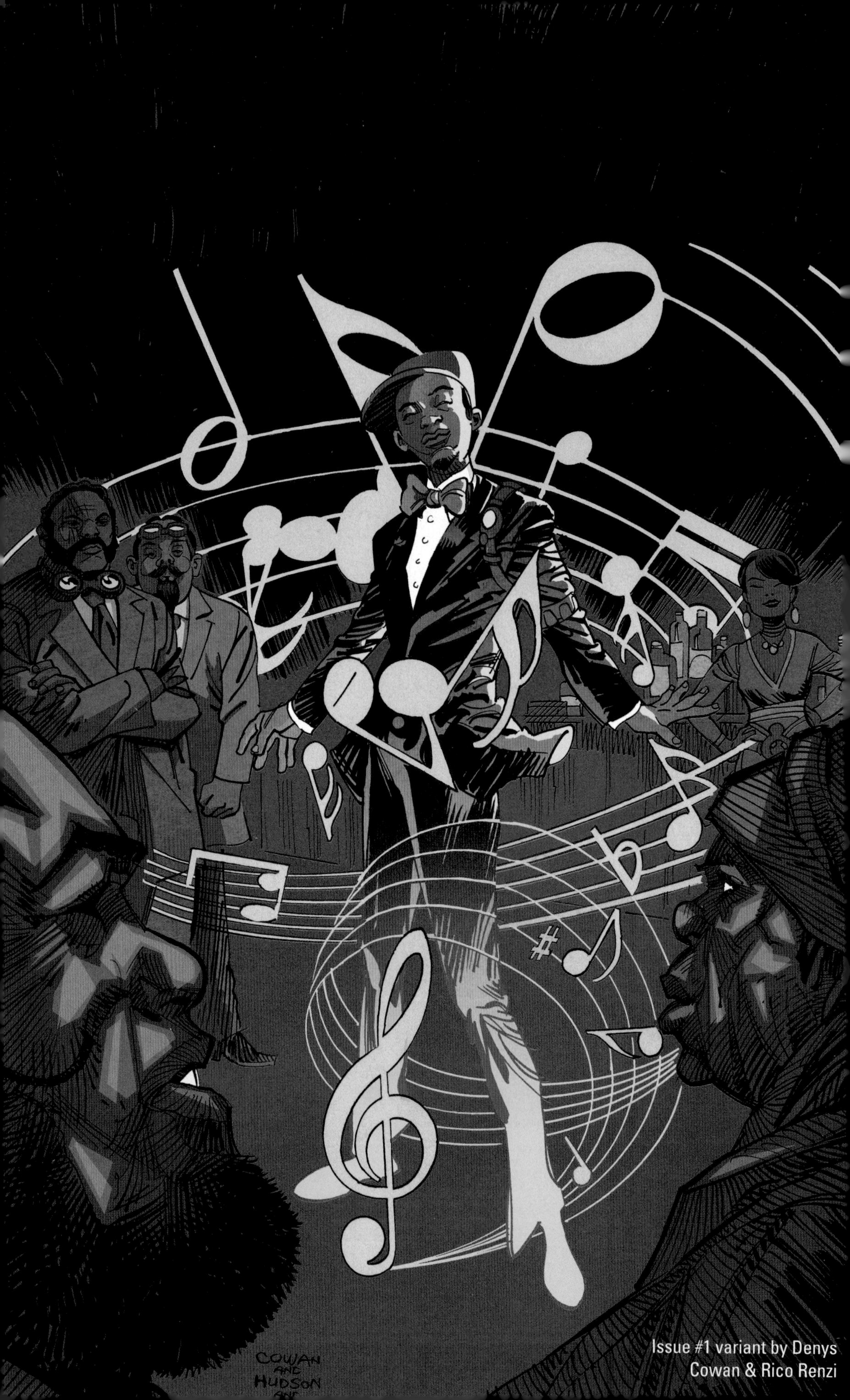
COWAN
AND
HUDSON

Issue #1 variant by Denys Cowan & Rico Renzi

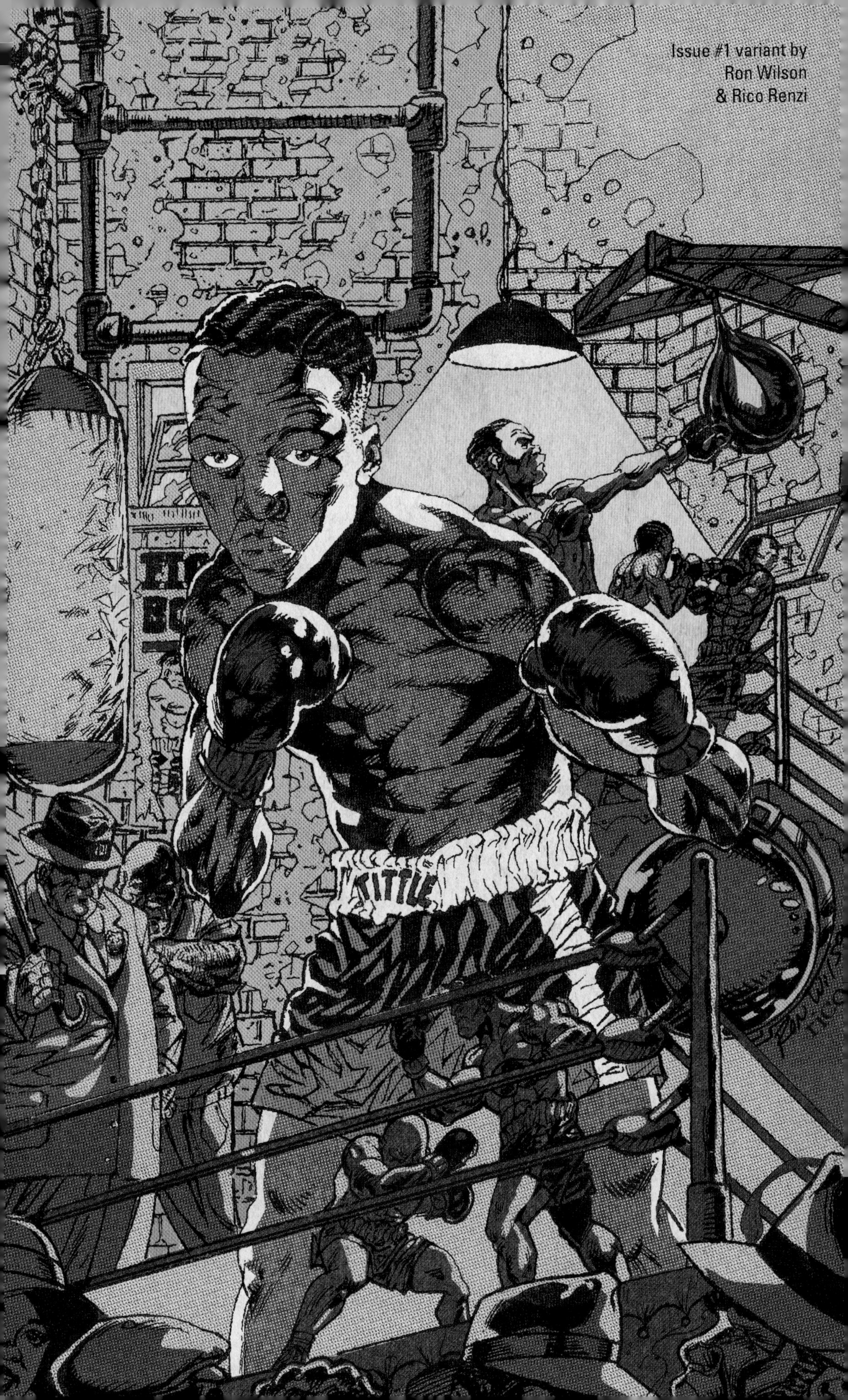

Issue #1 variant by
Ron Wilson
& Rico Renzi

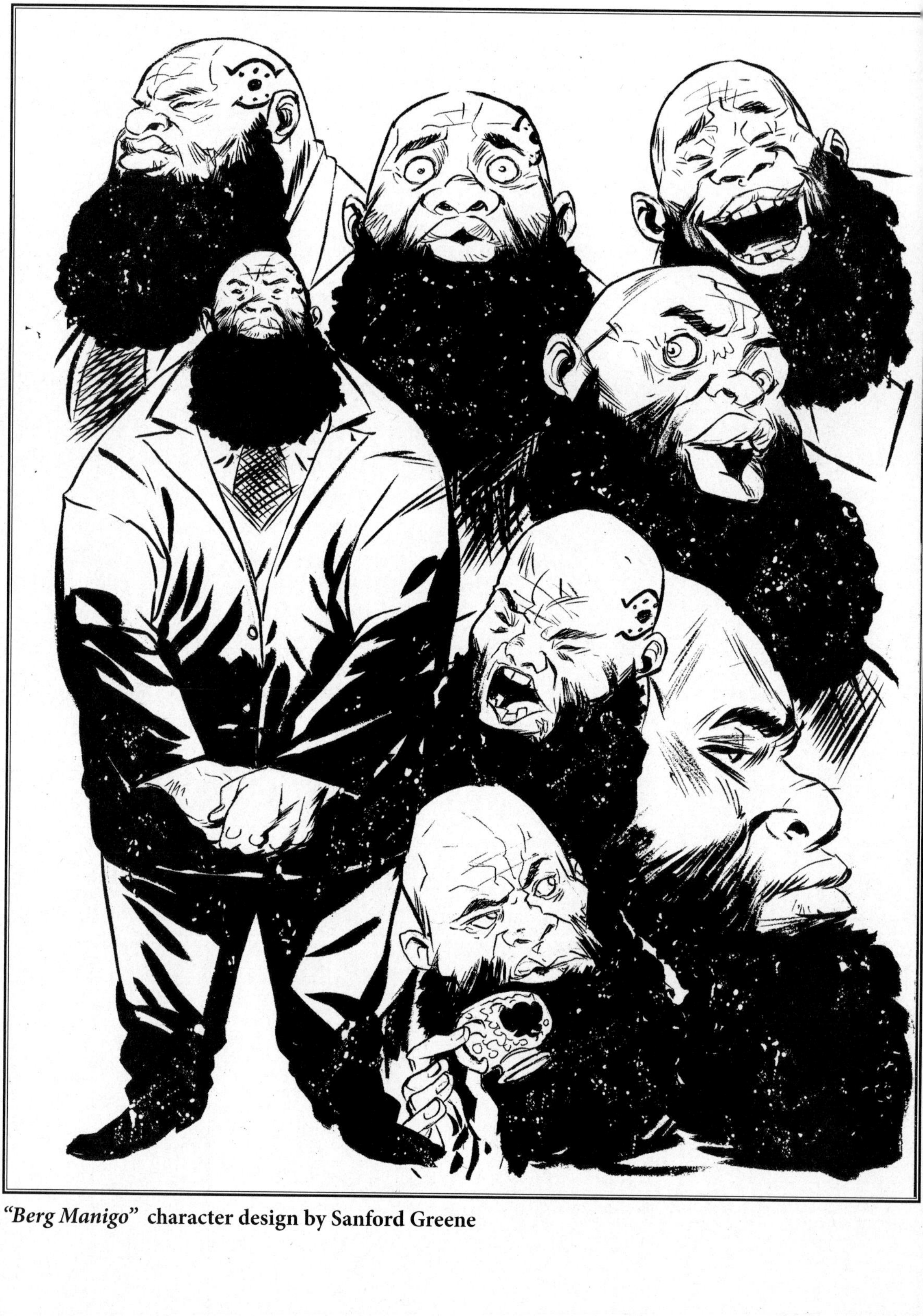

"Berg Manigo" **character design by Sanford Greene**

"Thus all Art is propaganda and ever must be, despite the wailing of the purists. I stand in utter shamelessness and say that whatever art I have for writing has been used always for propaganda for gaining the right of black folk to love and enjoy. I do not care a damn for any art that is not used for propaganda. But I do care when propaganda is confined to one side while the other is stripped and silent."

- from *Criteria of Negro Art*
by WEB DuBois (1926)

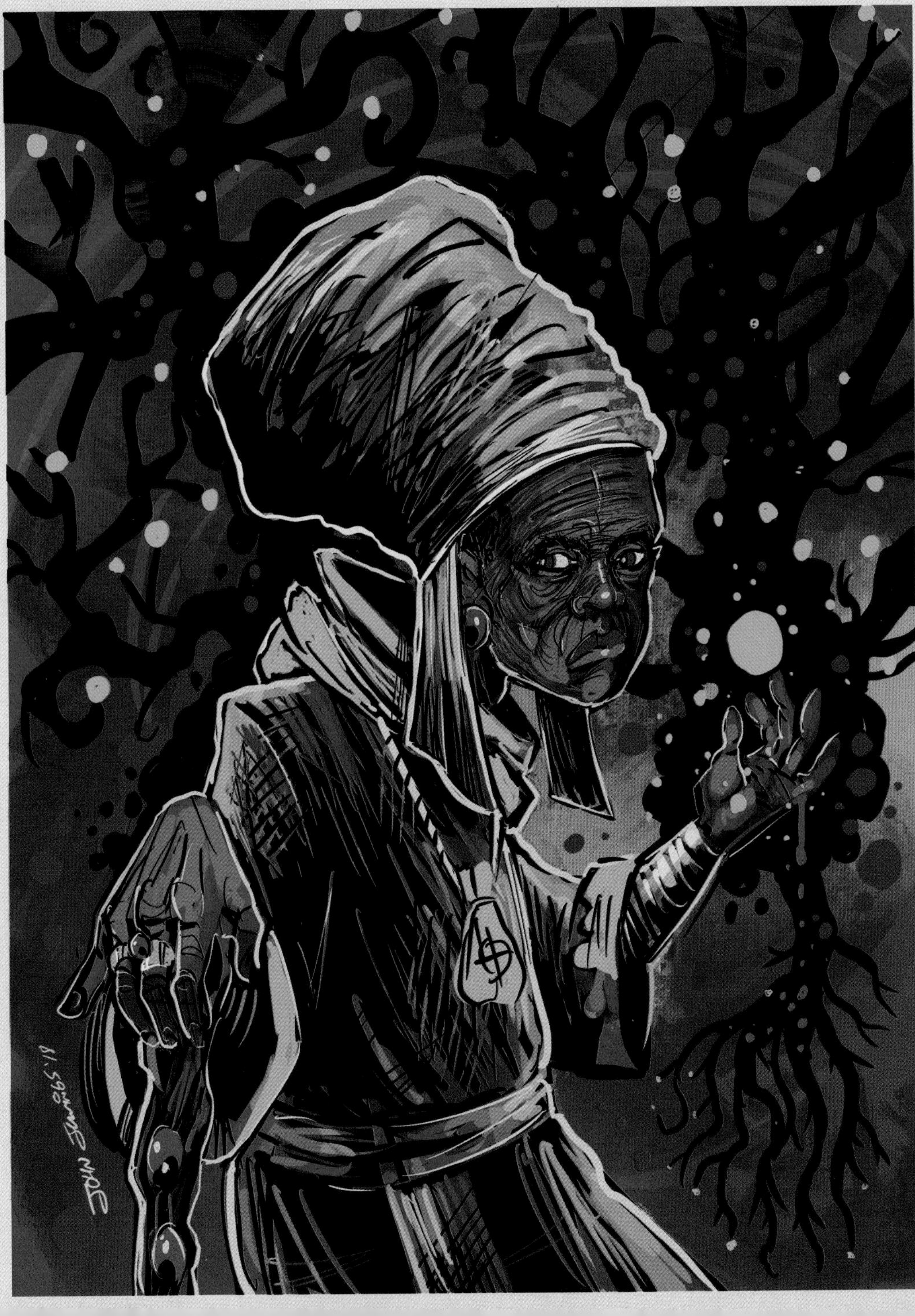

art by JOHN JENNINGS / @JJJennings

THE ROOT OF THE MATTTER

ROOTWORK AND CONJURE IN BLACK POPULAR CULTURE

Kinitra Brooks

> *Conjure studies are capable of linking magical and supernatural elements with medicinal practices and natural processes on the other.*
> – *Theophus H. Smith*

DR. KINITRA BROOKS is the Audrey and John Leslie Endowed Chair in Literary Studies in the Department of English at Michigan State University. Dr. Brooks specializes in the study of black women, genre fiction, and popular culture. She currently has two books in print: *Searching for Sycorax: Black Women's Hauntings of Contemporary Horror* (Rutgers UP 2017), a critical treatment of black women in science fiction, fantasy, and horror and *Sycorax's Daughters* (Cedar Grove Publishing 2017), an edited volume of short horror fiction written by black women. Her current research focuses on portrayals of the Conjure Woman in popular culture. Dr. Brooks will serve as the Advancing Equity Through Research Fellow at the Hutchins Center for African & African American Research at Harvard University for the 2018-2019 academic year.

Rootwork and Conjure are intellectual traditions created, sustained, and practiced by black women the world over. Rootwork is a semi-formal manifestation of black folks' practical need for healing through the making of medicines intertwined with the highly theoretical process of world-building and creating an inheritance of knowledge steeped in spirituality. Literally, rootwork is the foundation of pharmaceutical science as black women have ground up roots to put in salves and steeped leaves to make healing teas. Figuratively, rootwork is an active part of the spirit work that informs black women's knowledge practices, used to both heal and harm as a part of systems of belief threaded through with traditional African religious practices which I often refer to as **Conjure**. Professor Yvonne P. Chireau defines Conjure as "a magical tradition in which spiritual power is invoked for various purposes, such as healing, protection, and self-defense."

We meet the Sangerye Family at their apothecary, a small shop that serves as their home-base in their fight against the Jinoos. But what we don't see is that the apothecary is also a communal hub, serving soothing teas, tonics, and healthful biscuits along with a heavy dose of community news and gossip. Ms. Johnson, picking up a bit of goose grease and honey for her grandbabies' congestion noted to Ma Etta a possible Jinoo sighting by her son, Curtis, in a dark alley last night. As she left, she stopped by a small cafe table to congratulate the young Ms. Hurston, a former clerk of Dr. Carter G. Woodson, on beginning her graduate studies at Barnard. Ms. Hurston sipped delicately on a large mug of horsemint tea as she began to sweat out her fever.

Ma Etta is a Conjurewoman, a woman learned in the pharmaceutical art of rootwork. The Conjurewoman was simultaneously seen as a healer, midwife, herbalist/rootworker, fortune-teller, relationship counselor, and a spiritual advisor. These women had knowledge practices that reached beyond the enslavement of Africans upon our shores to the complex herb-based pharmaceutics practiced in West and Central Africa. Our first popular culture contact with the Conjurewoman occurred in 1899 with the publication of Charles W. Chesnutt's short story collection, **The Conjure Woman**. But the Conjurewoman had long existed in African American folklore as seen in the oral stories collected by scholars of the American South such as Zora Neale Hurston and found in her collection, **Every Tongue Got to Confess: Negro Folk-Tales from the Gulf States** (2001). The tradition of the Conjurewoman was resurrected in popular culture by Beyoncé in her audiovisual album, **Lemonade** (2017), as she celebrated the spiritual and herbalist practices of her Southern maternal ancestors by grounding the second half of the film on a Louisiana plantation full to brimming with black women, both living and occupying the ancestral plane.

Unfortunately, much of the arcane knowledge of the Conjurewoman has been lost to the understandable but sometimes misguided respectability politics of post-Emancipation blackness and spiritual work. As black folks longed to prove that they were worthy of their hard-earned American identities, much of our complex African knowledge and spiritual practices began to be eschewed and treated with disdain. Alas, some of us are doing the work to recover the knowledge and diligently bring its liberatory healing potential back to the forefront of Black life and culture. **Bitter Root** is doing this work with the characterization of Ma Etta, a woman with the knowledge and the confidence to heal, protect, and defend the Sangerye Family. Representation matters and the efficiency and directness of the graphic image is a powerful conjuring tool. Thanks to this series, we can now add Ma Etta to this canon of literary matriarchs that embody both the struggles and triumphs of the Conjurewoman and her beautiful complexity and humanity.

BITTER TWITTER
Root Report

@Julian Chambliss
Just finished the first issue of #BitterRoot. Great to see the world-building in this issue. A great job from @Cbrown803 @sanfordgreene & @DavidWalker1201.

@Kephus
Read this book! EthnoGothic (thanks @JIJennings) 1920's demon hunting family with just stunning art and layouts from Sanford Greene & David F. Walker (*Power Man & Iron Fist*) and Chuck Brown.

@TheNerdsofColor
"This comic is the reason that the comic book form exists," says @reallovepunk in his endorsement of 'Bitter Root" from @ImageComics https://wp.me/p3MnPm-97V

@AshCanPress
All these books are gonna be cool but if you aren't excited for BITTER ROOT #1 by @DavidWalker1201, @Cbrown803, & @sanfordgreene this week, you aren't paying attention.

@BigComicPage
"Strikes up the beat, hits all the right notes, and plonks you right in the middle of the story." **FOUR STARS**

@fojazz
Got to read BITTER ROOT #1 before it hits stores tomorrow. I already love these characters and can't wait to follow their story. Congrats @DavidWalker1201 Chuck Brown & @sanfordgreene ! (and @JIJennings essay on the Ethno-Gothic was icing on the cake!)

"The New Negro" by Winold Reiss from the National Portrait Gallery, Smithsonian Institution

WHEN LOCKE WAS KEY

John Jennings

The word "renaissance" means "rebirth" or "reawakening" and The Harlem Renaissance was exactly that. It was an artistic and intellectual rebellion against the negative mythologies around black people. **The New Negro Movement**, as it was called, was a tactical strike against every attempt to not only take away the citizenship of black Americans but also their very humanity. It wasn't just a wake-up call for black people in America. It was also a clarion for white audiences. Imagine what it would feel like if your **shadow,** this thing that defines you, started to have its own politics, stories, and art? What actions would you take to make sure that your shadow stayed in its place and simply performed its task of only proving you exist? Surely that would be terrifying.

The United States seems to eat its own history in order to protect itself from the truth its origins. The amount of self-delusion it must take to create something as fictitious as the technology of race, and its indexes, is nothing short of herculean. In order to enslave your fellow human being, you must create a system of stories that affirm they ***aren't*** human, that they have no purpose, that they are better as slaves, that they cannot ever be **more** than the thing that you say they are. That's a great deal of storytelling. In a lot of black American homes, particularly in the American South, the word *"story"* is a synonym for the word *"lie."* The story that someone's skin color, hair texture, and nose width makes them less than human is one aspect of the illusion that we call **race.** So, how do we **unmake** this lie? We have to tell the truth. ***We have to shame the devil.***

Alain LeRoy Locke believed this wholeheartedly. He believed that stories of black people and the art of black people were symbols of their humanity. He held to the idea that a **radical subjectivity** would help to end the mistreatment of African Americans in the country they built on their backs – a country that was founded on the principles of freedom. Locke believed in the power of the imagination as a cooling balm against the searing banality of indifference and hate. Alain LeRoy Locke was born in Philadelphia, Pennsylvania. His father, the first black employee of the U.S. Postal Service, died when we was six and his mother was a teacher. She helped foster his interest in literature and the power of education. He was the first African American Rhodes Scholar. Locke was also a staunch proponent of the creation of African American cultural expressions and taught at Howard University until his retirement. He died in 1968 of heart disease. Locke left a legacy of social protest, philosophy and art. He was a proud black gay man who was one of the architects of the Harlem Renaissance. Locke's seminal anthology ***The New Negro*** was published in 1925. It was, in some ways, a collection of "evidence"–not only to the inherent beauty of black thought but its normality. The dream of equality, of course, is the dream of the ordinary. It's the dream to be mediocre and for that to be totally fine. This notion of the normal is something that white people in America take for granted. Their whole race is never judged by the actions of the one. To be black in America is to be an index for **all blackness.** What ***The New Negro*** attempted to do was to show a **spectrum** of black experiences and to show that suffering was not the only thing that defined African American existence. **You see, black *joy* is a radical notion too.**

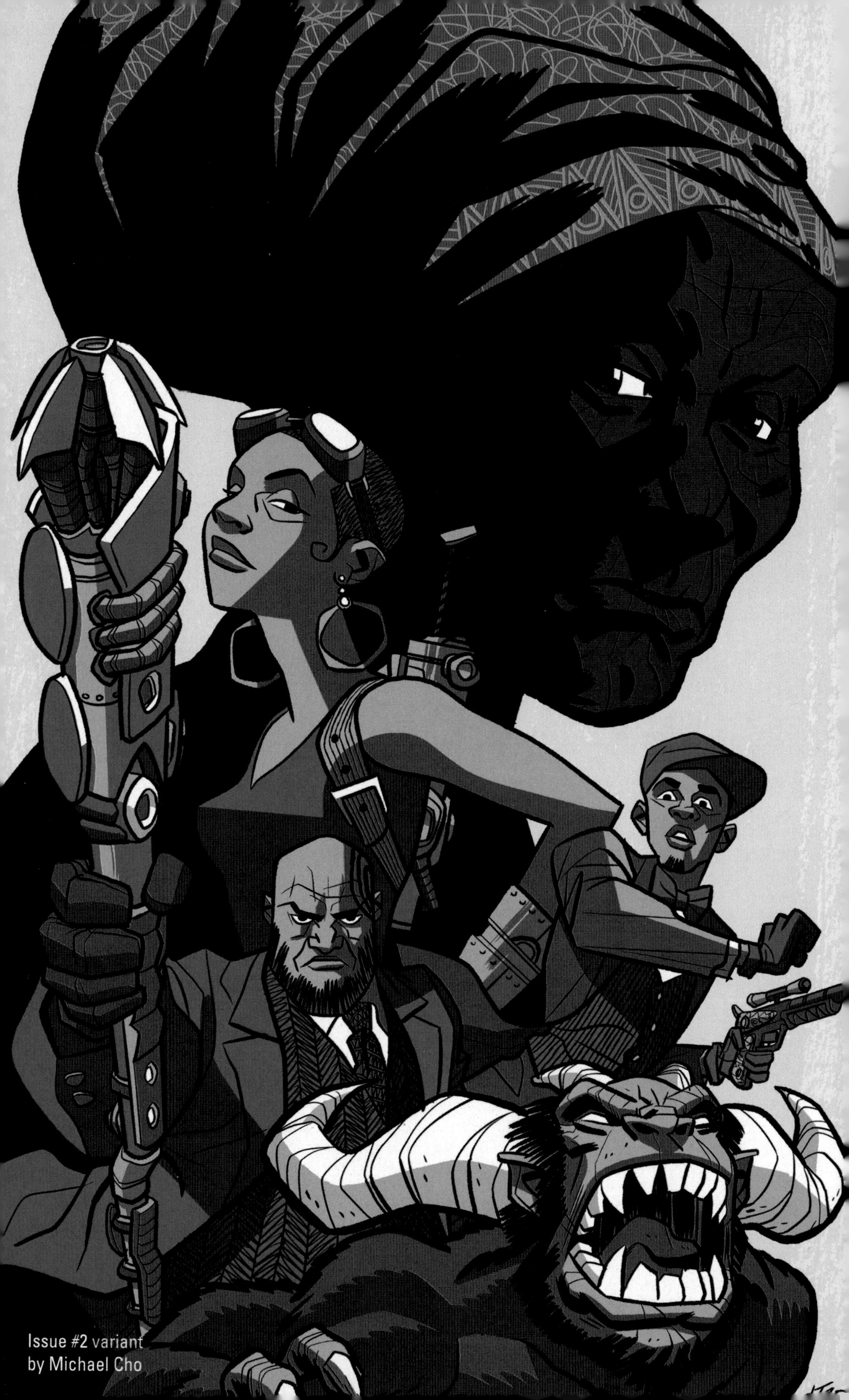

Issue #2 variant
by Michael Cho

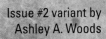

Issue #2 variant by
Ashley A. Woods

BITTER TRUTHS

"I started writing because there's an absence of things I was familiar with or that I dreamed about. One of my senses of anger is related to this vacancy - a yearning I had as a teenager... and when I get ready to write, I think I'm trying to fill that."

- Ntozake Shange

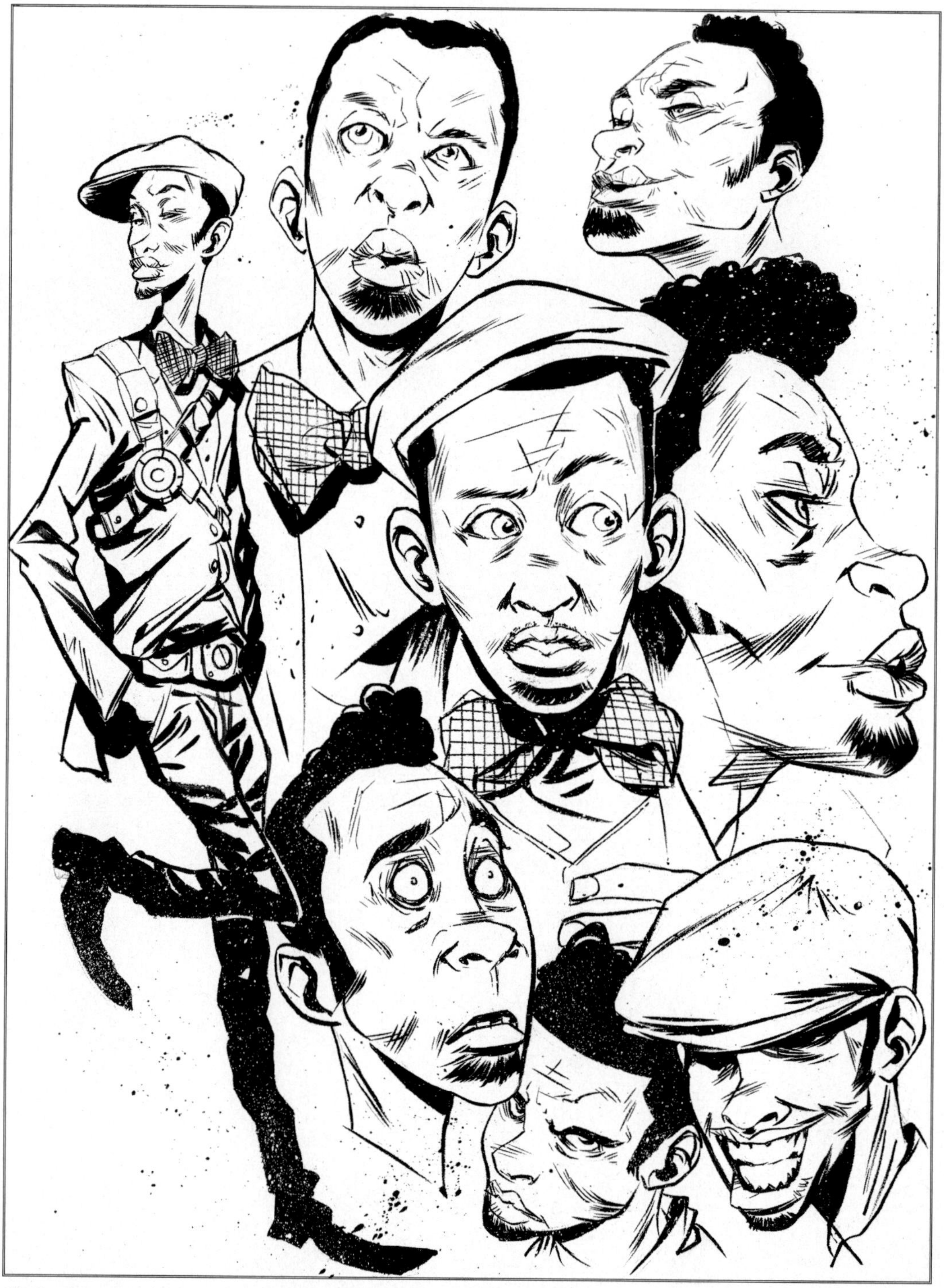

"Cullen" character design and sketch by SANFORD GREENE

BLOOD AND THE RUT

Regina N. Bradley

DR. REGINA N. BRADLEY is a writer and researcher of southern African American life and culture. She is an alumna Nasir Jones Hiphop fellow at Harvard University and Assistant Professor of English and African Diaspora Studies at Kennesaw State University. Dr. Bradley is also the author of *Boondock Kollage: Stories from the Hip Hop South*. She can be reached at www.redclay-scholar.com.

Editor's note: In celebration and honor of Zora Neale Hurston and other southern ancestral griots, this piece is written partially in a Black southern dialect.

A phrase that frequently floats around my head when thinking about the American South, especially the Black South – issa thing – is the phrase **"blood at the rut."** As a southerner, I'm honoring dialect here, pulling from the Zora Neale Hurston school of thought to represent for my people 'nem by sounding like dem. For the uninitiated, **"ruts"** is **"roots"**– or the common practice of applying a little bit of everyday magic, ancestral power, and prayer that connects to the land. It's way more than herbs and a little gardening. As so many southern Black folks have iterated over the years, the land for us is not just a tool or a tomb; the land and the dirt are an archive–a constant reminder of what and who were lost and what is held dear. Ruts reach deep, way past the easily digestible pages of history, down further past what's comfortable and legible, into the very marrow of why and how Black lives matter in a space and place that continually tries to take us out. Blood at the rut is a signifier of the debt paid for Black folks to keep pressing forward. Like the gospel song, the blood travels, reaching from the highest mountain to the lowest valley.

We take the blood and the ruts with us.

But can we talk about how the blood at the rut travels just like its carriers? Folks like to contextualize and argue up and down how bad the South was–is?—for Black people, 'specially during the early 1900s. They like to herald the Great Migration as a sign of progressive thinking, that black folks wanted to move away from the trauma and terror of the South. They were so quick to point and focus on the plank of white supremacy in the South's eye that they were going blind with the plank in their own eye. Further, it does a great disservice to the southern folks who moved "Up South," physically moving their bodies while also moving their trauma and terror with them. See, that's when the blood pulsated, reminding folks that trauma is like a family heirloom;…where you go, I go. I'll tell you this, too: them same mannerisms and missions of bloating white folks' heads so they ain't feel threatened, ain't feel charged to act against Black flesh, take rut in the North, too. The soil might be colder but the trauma of being Black – just being Black – still digs in deep.

Chile, Black folk trauma got a half-life in the United States. That half-life seems to move a helluva lot slower in the southern region. Sometimes trauma runs. Other times trauma crawls. All times it hollers, forcefully motioning to the world that it ain't going nowhere. That's the thing about ruts; they are a response to the trauma. Think of it like this: if trauma is the action, the response is cultural reckoning like horror.

BITTER ROOT is particularly good at showing the blood at the rut traveling between the South and Harlem, no renaissance of knowing required. The Sangeryes got all kind of ruts in their apothecary. Ma Etta be knowing the extent to how deep them ruts got. She be conjuring: Conjuring her own memories – for true, this may be irritating to her grandbaby Blink – but conjure sticks in her bones the way plain ole sight doesn't. Ma Etta understands that Black women and their bodies are sites of reckoning. She sees her ruts as necessities that she needs to pass down so we don't forget. Blink, true to her name, is quick to overlook how Ma Etta is setting her up with this legacy. Blink ready to leap and Ma Etta tryna make sure she don't fall.

Dare I say it, ruts and they blood is a sign of love. Not the sappy and diabetically sweet crap we try and get sold on. Naw, naw. BITTER ROOT shows love as a tense thing, the act of making the illegible visible and a thing that takes its time loving us back. Love is crispy around the edges with generational angst and tinged with the pain of multi-tasking as a gift and as a curse. Love sits at the root like the blood of the past, present, and future. Even when ruts summon the everyday monstrosities of just tryna be, the blood is there, quickening and settling like final breaths from lungs. You can't lose the power of memory, hard truths, and love. That's why the blood is there.

art by **CM DYER** / **@dyertek**

FAN ART

art by **RYAN OAKLEY** / **@ryanoakleyart**

GENIUS OF THE SOUTH:
THINKING OF MOTHER ZORA

John Jennings

"If you are silent about your pain,
they will kill you and say you enjoyed it."
- Zora Neale Hurston

The saying above is one of my favorite quotes by Zora Neale Hurston. Mother Zora didn't know how to be quiet. Her curiosity, talent, and spirit were just too much to not celebrate. The quote always resonates with me because it speaks so plainly about agency, power, and the subjectivity of history. History is just that–a story. The narrative of this story that we take as pure fact is highly flexible. The winner, of course, gets to write the history books. So, like Mother Zora, we have to remember to not be silent and make sure that our pain is heard but also that it teaches future generations to avoid the same traumas.

Zora Neale Hurston was an anthropologist, educator, activist, poet, and fiction writer. She was born in Notasulga, Alabama on January 7, 1891. She was the daughter of Lucy and John Hurston. Early in her life, the family moved to Eatonville, Florida. They lived a wonderful life there until Lucy passed away suddenly creating a massive hole in young Zora's life. She began to fill that space with stories, travel, and a longing to collect other experiences of her people. Zora was an outgoing, magnetic woman with an engaging wit and intense intellect. By the early 1920s, Zora Neale Hurston was part of the amazing collection of black luminaries of the Harlem Renaissance. She became close friends with Ethel Waters, Langston Hughes, and Sterling Brown. By the late 1930s she had written a collection of southern folklore called **Mules and Men, Tell My Horse: a study of Caribbean Voodoo,** and her masterpiece *Their Eyes Were Watching God.* Again, she was never silent. She spent her life with her hands in the dirt of her ancestors. She reverently recorded the folklore, tall tales, and yes, pain of everyday black folks in America. She gave voice to the invisible and would not let them fall silent either. Zora Neale Hurston died in 1960. She was 69 years old. Though she'd become a critically acclaimed writer and scholar, she did not garner a great deal of economic success. There was not enough money for her gravestone and it lay unmarked for many years.

In May of 2018, a never-before-published Hurston interview with a man named Kossola Cudjoe Lewis was released to great fanfare. This man was the last survivor of the last slave ship which brought him and 115 African slaves to Alabama illegally. Although Zora Neale Hurston conducted this landmark interview in 1927, she was never able to get it published. How amazingly sad that this story is still so relevant in a still racially divided United States of America. She is still giving voice to the voiceless. She is still not silent about her pain or the pain and shame of an entire nation. **She's still teaching us.**

The Kossola interview is called **Barracoon: The Story of the Last "Black Cargo"**. It was edited by **Deborah G. Plant** with a foreword by the incredible **Alice Walker**, author of *The Color Purple*. Walker was highly inspired by Zora Neale Hurston which is why she did the foreword and also why she made sure Zora's grave had a marker in 1973. Alice Walker chose a few words from a Jean Toomer poem for her epitaph. It reads **"Zora Neale Hurston: A Genius of the South"**. No truer words have been spoken. Mother Zora gave us back our stories and our ghosts. Both are needed to endure the trials ahead. Thank you, Zora. Your root work is the **best** work.

Special thanks to: zoranealehurston.com and Valerie Boyd regarding research for this piece.

art by JOHN JENNINGS

Issue #3 variant
Larry Stroma

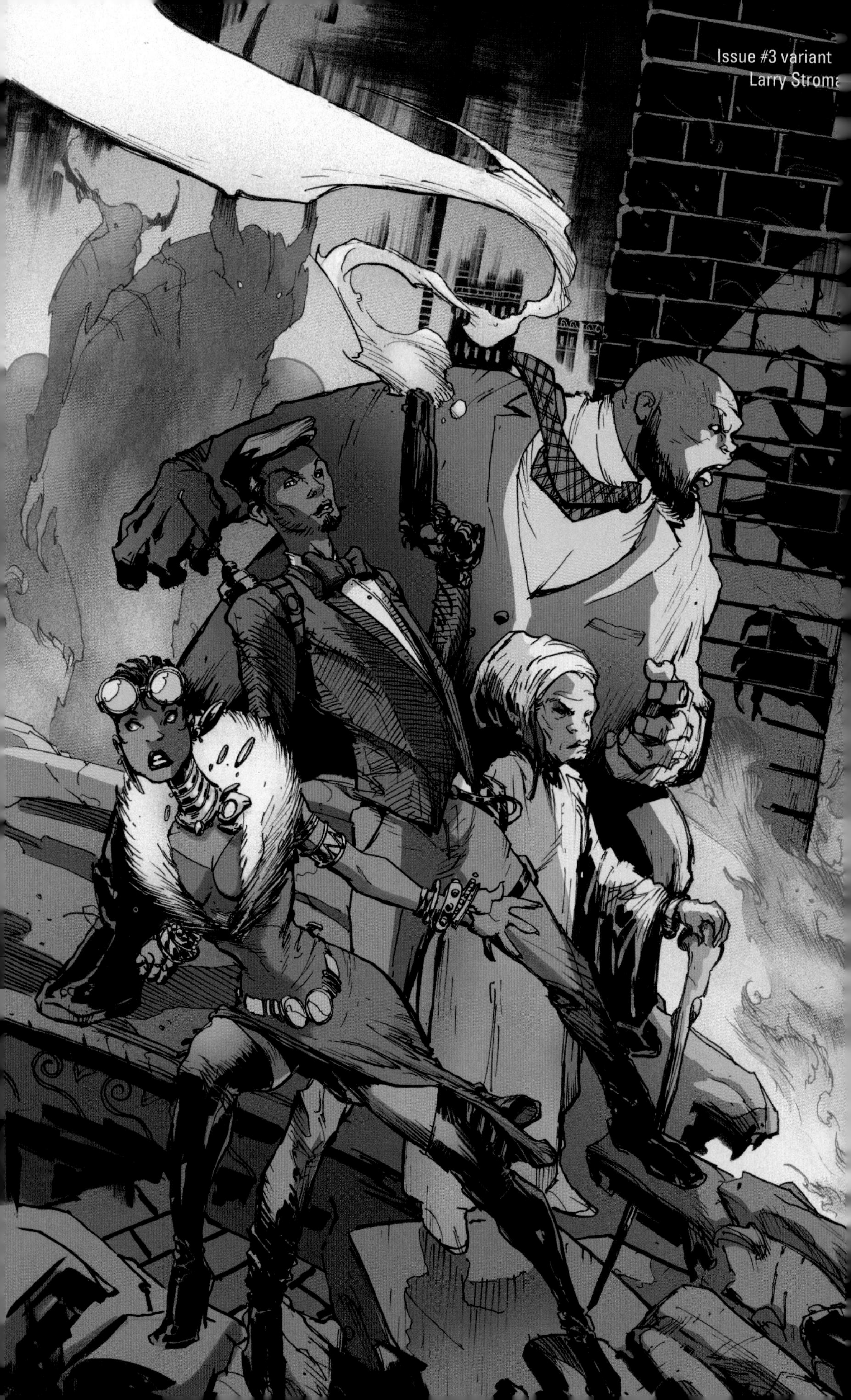

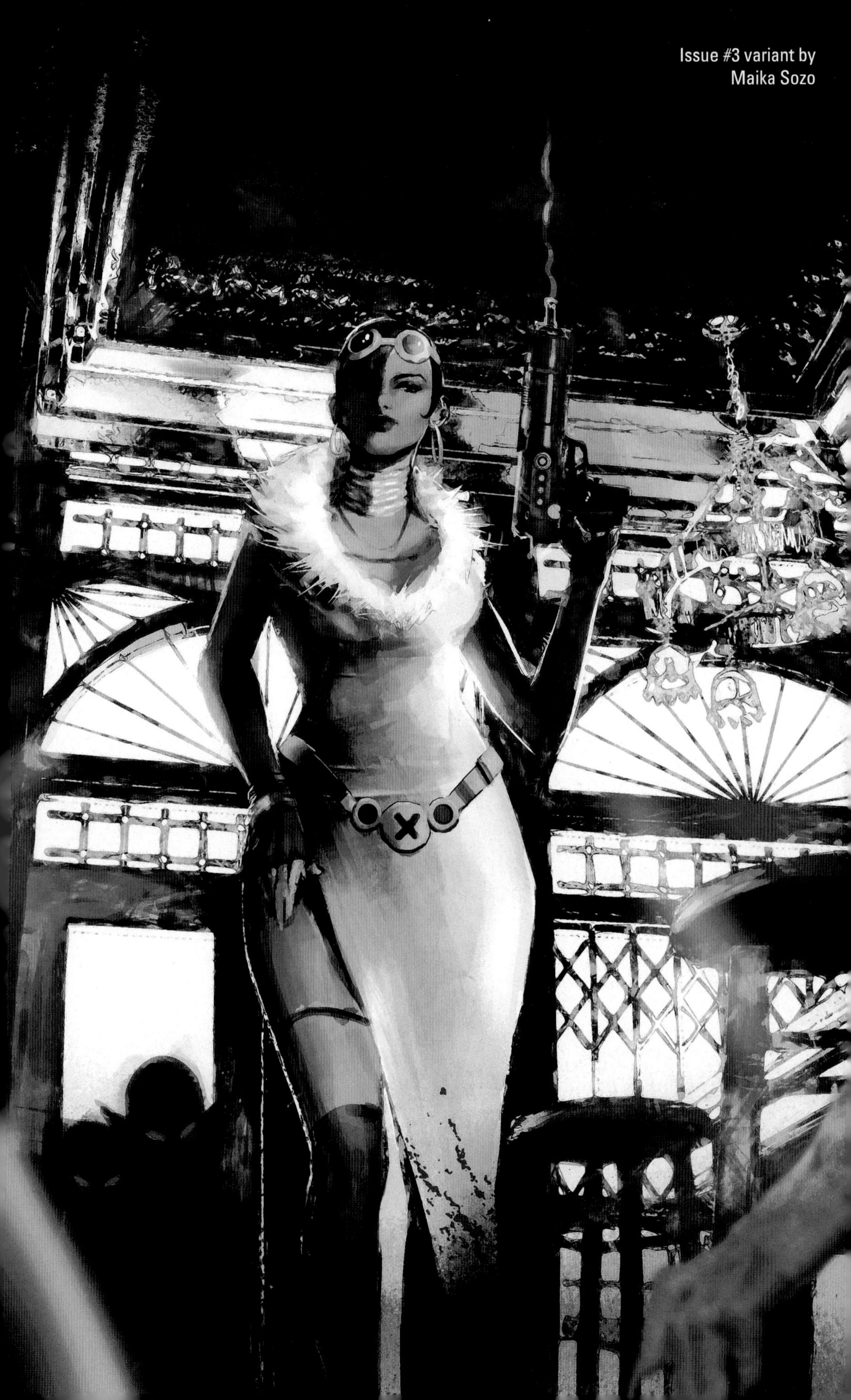

Issue #3 variant by
Maika Sozo

BITTER TRUTHS

SKIN, SKIN DON'T YOU KNOW ME?

Qiana Whitted

DR. QIANA WHITTED is a Professor of English and African American Studies at the University of South Carolina and author of the forthcoming book, *EC Comics: Race, Shock, and Social Protest*. She is also the editor of *Inks: The Journal of the Comics Studies Society* and chair of the International Comic Arts Forum.

Gullah folklore tells the story of the Boo Hag, a soucouyant figure that draws its life force from a sleeping person's breath. Often described as a skinless woman, the Boo Hag can fly unseen in the night, but to survive during the day, she must disguise herself in skin stolen from another.

Variations of this supernatural hag exist throughout European, West African, and Caribbean cultural traditions. Yet the tales that emerge in the United States from the black communities of the Carolina low country use the figure to embody nightmarish images of possession, control, and theft. Thought-pictures mark the Gullah's distinctive telling of the Boo Hag's demise: from the ocean-colored "haint blue" painted on porch ceilings and around windows to keep evil away, to the grainy texture and smell of the salt that must be sprinkled inside the folds of skin that she leaves behind after dark.

And then there is the eerie whine of the trapped Boo Hag's voice when she returns to find her flesh too itchy to wear: **Skin, skin, don't you know me?**

Southern horrors such as the Boo Hag are the foundation of the world that *Bitter Root* inhabits. Chuck Brown and David Walker's speculative plot transforms these expressive folktales and their multi-sensory language – what Zora Neale Hurston described as the "hieroglyphics" of black thought – into the narrative drawings of the comics form. At the heart of the comic's weird fantasy are vicious shapeshifting monsters. Keeping watch are generations of hunters and conjurers with retrofuturistic technologies that combine the skills of the medical practitioner, the priest, and the exterminator. On the streets of Harlem, in the Mississippi woods, the Sangerye family battles creatures whose once-human forms are uncontained by their skin; they even burst free from the panels on Sanford Greene's pages.

As a result, the therianthropic monsters of *Bitter Root* mirror a reality where racism transforms the body and spirit in devastating ways– from the undead Klansmen to those who have been the victims of hate crimes themselves. Whether or not such transformations can truly be undone is the *Bitter Root's* fundamental question.

In Giselle Liza Anatol's analysis of black female vampires and other soucouyant characters, she explains that "skin ostensibly carries the clearest signs of racial identity and evidence of racial belonging (or nonbelonging), and a removable skin suggest that fixed racial identities are, in fact, quite unstable." *Bitter Root* proposes a similar kind of instability through monsters such as the Jinoo, turning visual metonyms of infection and healing serums into an opportunity for anti-racist redemption. If white supremacy is a plague, spread through violent deeds, then can it be eradicated? Perhaps those who are afflicted can be cured – or else "amputated," if Ford Sangerye has his way. Meanwhile, Doctor Sylvester and Miss Knightsdale – the mysterious Jekyll and Hyde of San Juan Hill – scramble to steal the secrets of the Fiif'no root and reclaim a sense of agency in their own recovery from racial trauma.

The social dynamics of these representations have a difficult history in American comics. Blackness has often been central to problematic depictions of the monstrous Other, in keeping with the centuries-old traditions of racist caricature that comics shared with other forms of popular culture. Not surprisingly, then, the editorial cartoons and comic strips published in mid-twentieth century African American newspapers tended to avoid horror and science fiction when grappling with issues such as lynching and political disenfranchisement. (Though to be fair, these concerns didn't keep the stories in the full-color comics supplement of the Pittsburgh Courier from occasionally tackling aliens.)

During the 1950s, EC Comics was particularly successful in developing a brand of empathetic horror in *Tales from the Crypt* and other titles that compelled readers to identify with the ideas that they most feared. Such strategies carried over into EC's social protest comics that dramatize the absurdity of assigning arbitrary characteristics and biological traits to race, often through plots that conceal the skin color of black characters and leave white racists outraged upon the reveal (see "In Gratitude…" or "Blood Brothers" from *Shock SuspenStories*). The most memorable of EC's progressive stories, *"Judgment Day!"* features a black astronaut from the future whose unforeseen racial identity stunned fans too. The legacy of these experimental genre comics endures today among black speculative writers and artists of the medium, including Jeremy Love, John Jennings, Taneka Stotts, Victor LaValle, Shawneé and Shawnelle Gibbs, and Ezra Claytan Daniels.

It is invigorating to see *Bitter Root* take part in such a dynamic range of cultural traditions and histories. As a motley of black southern folklore and the Ethno-Gothic, urban steampunk, and comic book horror, the tales of the Sangeryes give rise to a new boundary-breaking, skin-stealing storytelling experience.

"What a world this will be when human possibilities are freed, when we discover each other, when the stranger is no longer the potential criminal and the certain inferior!"
— W.E.B. DuBois

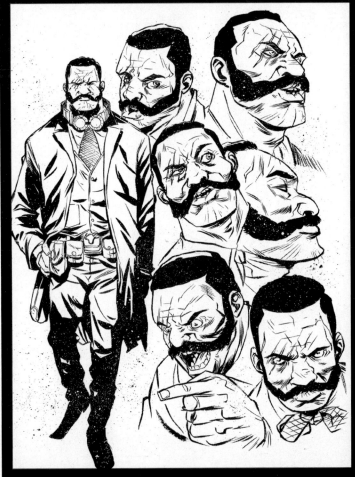

"Ford" character design and sketch by SANFORD GREENE

SOURCES:

Anatol, Giselle Liza. *The Things That Fly in the Night: Female Vampires in Literature of the Circum-Caribbean and African Diaspora*. Rutgers University Press, 2015.

Hurston, Zora Neale. "Characteristics of Negro Expression," *The Sanctified Church*. New York: Marlowe & Company, 1934.

Jackson, Tim. *Pioneering Cartoonists of Color*. Jackson: University Press of Mississippi, 2016.

Morris, Nicole M. "Boo Hag" *American Myths, Legends, and Tall Tales: An Encyclopedia of American Folklore*. Eds. Christopher R. Fee and Jeffrey B. Webb. Santa Barbara: ABC-CLIO, 2016, 149-150.

Pollitzer, William S. *The Gullah People and Their African Heritage*. Athens: University of Georgia Press, 1999.

Issue #4 variant by
Kevin Nowlan

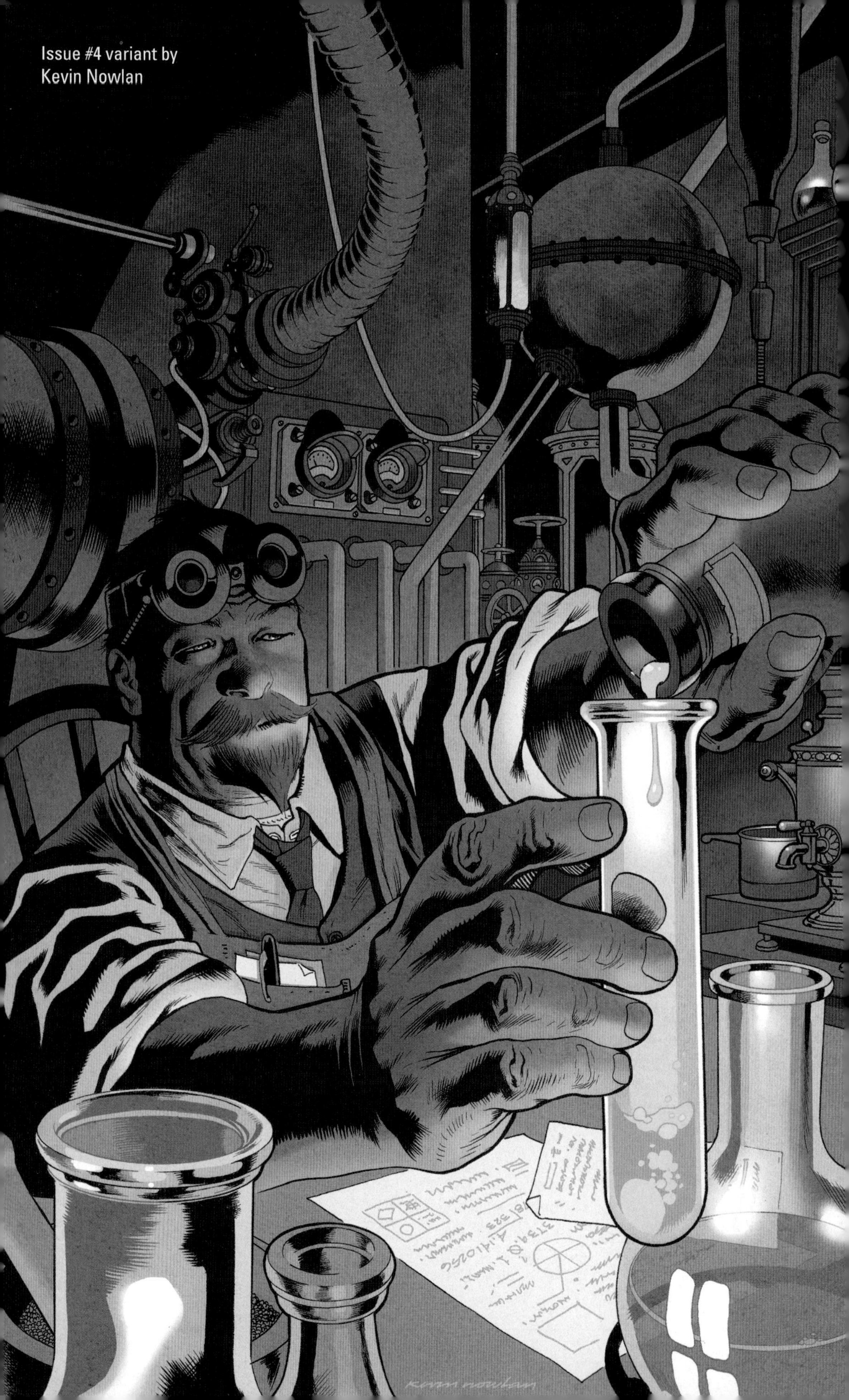

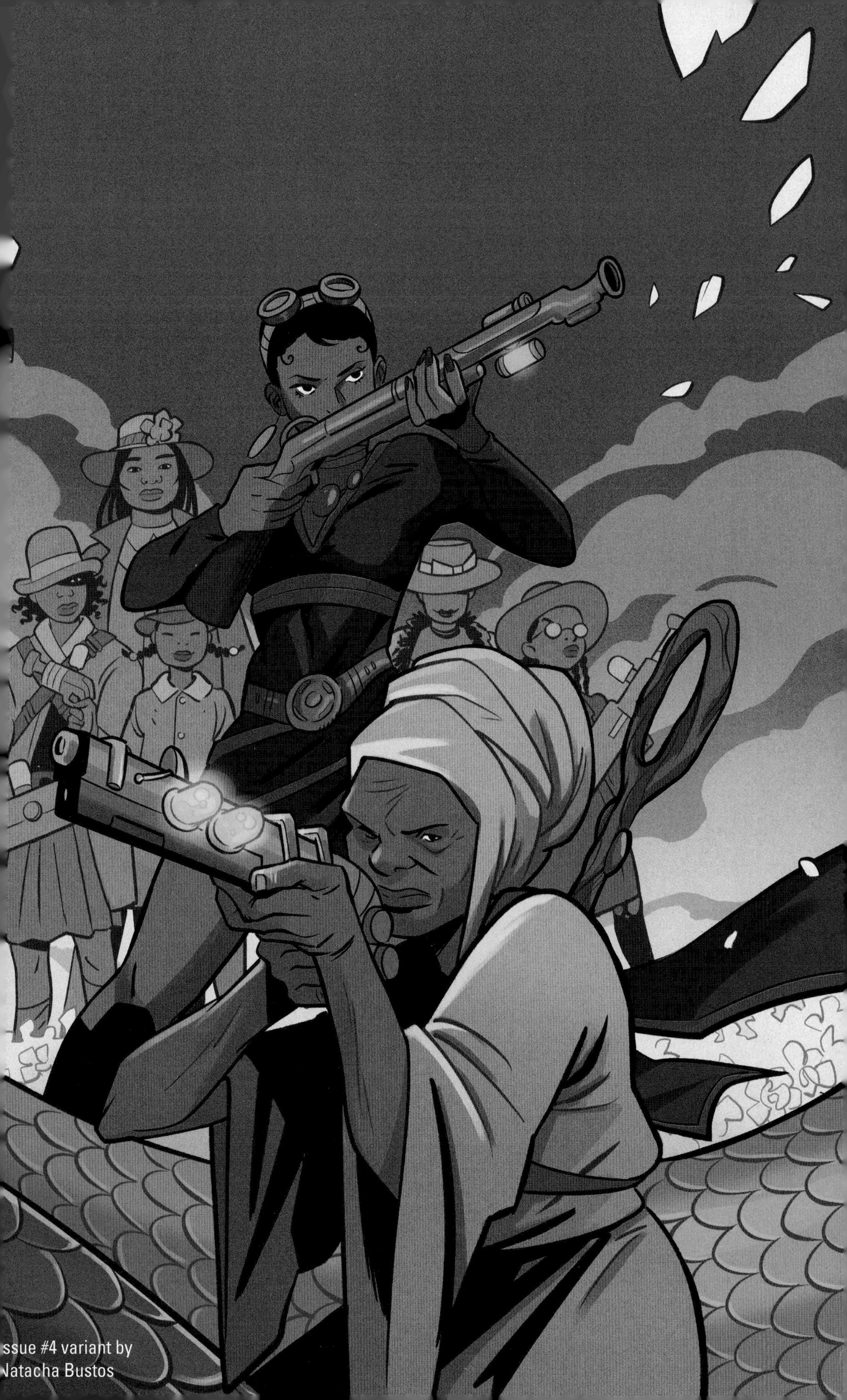

ssue #4 variant by
Natacha Bustos

BUILDING BLACK UTOPIA

Stacey Robinson

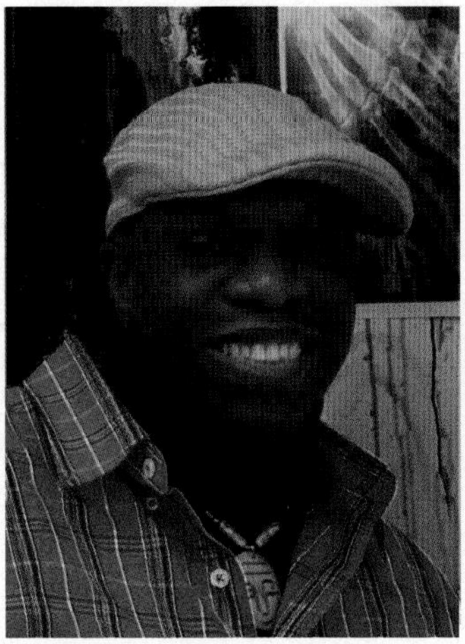

STACEY ROBINSON, is an Assistant Professor of graphic design at the University of Illinois is an Arturo Schomburg fellow who completed his Masters of Fine Art at the University at Buffalo. His multimedia work discusses ideas of "Black Utopias" as decolonized spaces of peace by considering Black affluent, self-sustaining communities, Black protest movements and the art that document(ed) them.

His recent exhibition *'Binary Con-Science'* explores ideas of W.E.B. DuBois' "double consciousness" as a Black cultural adaptation, and a means of colonial survival. His exhibition ***'Branding the AfroFuture'*** looks at designing, and constructing Black futures through various cultural, collage aesthetics.

His latest graphic novel, ***'I Am Alfonso Jones'*** with writer Tony Medina and John Jennings is available from Lee & Low books.

Imagine an affluent and ever-growing Black community, self-sufficient in more regards than any Black American neighborhood today. Imagine the possiblities of social growth, no police brutality, driving/walking/smiling-while-Black harrassment moments. Imagine the potential of a Black bubble in the middle of America that was the pull-yourself-up-by-your-bootstraps manifestation. Then imagine that this sustaining Black community, forced into segregation, flourished to become the brightest example of collective Black wealth inside of colonial America and was then destroyed, for those very same reasons.

Dubbed "Black Wall Street," the Greenwood district of Tulsa, Oklahoma has become forgotten by many, rarely mentioned in documentaries and history books, and never visualized in film. Greenwood was Wakanda in real-time, but was then burned to ashes by the neighboring White Tulsa community, including reports of airplanes dropping bombs on the affluent town. Fake news has been around a long time in American history and was the catalyst for the attack when the Tulsa Tribune published an article titled ***"Nab Negro for Attacking Girl in Elevator"*** with an accompanying back page editorial. The result was the worst of what happens when Black people unify under forced segregation, colonialism, and fear. This too, as Childish Gambino said, "is America."

2018 broadened our collective imaginations with Marvel Studio's ***Black Panther.*** We saw a Black futuristic city set in the backdrop of the present, one month after President Trump's multi-flawed comments about "shit-hole countries like Africa, and Haiti." I argue that the most inspirational aspect of the 1-billion-plus-dollar grossing box office film still is the globally inspired conversations that are still taking place surrounding ideas of Black liberation, peace, and justice through reconnecting with ancient African history, education, religions, sciences, art, etc.

Originally imagined in 1966 by second-generation Jewish immigrants, Stan Lee and Jack Kirby, the world of Wakanda became something different, something more in the 2018 imagining. Marvel Studio's ***Black Panther*** inspired many of us with a long period of hope we rarely get to experience. However, the euphoria of a speculative African nation unaffected by colonialism can't measure to the real flourishing unified 11,000-plus Black Greenwood community consisting of 108 Black-owned businesses, 2 theaters, 2 schools, 15 doctors' offices, a bank, churches, a taxi service, and more.

Almost 100 years after the incidents called the ***"Tulsa Race Riot,"*** the Greenwood district still remains one of the most celebrated examples and a shining contradiction to a narrative that says Black people can't unify, govern ourselves, and prosper. To see the pictures of the beautiful homes, businesses, cars, and smiling residents in the historical photographs is to time travel, and see the history of a destroyed dream that was not deferred.

After viewing the film, many people said that they are leaving America, that they are going to Wakanda. One of my favorite things to say to people in response to this is that "Wakanda is not a resort" – it's a tangible space that we can only experience temporarily until we as a Black diaspora collectively mature enough to create, value, maintain, and preserve it. It has to be built, for a future generation that we will not see, and it has already begun, inside the Black speculative imagination.

Collectively, Black people have never lacked the ability to see ourselves free from colonialism. Just as many Black Americans, the Sangeryes of *Bitter Root* have this foresight. Their family, as a secret society, safeguard the world from the onslaught of a literal "hell on Earth." Ma Etta's, Ford's, and Dr. Sylvester's methods are different, inspirational, and effective in their respects as they serve society with an idealism for a better tomorrow.

Our Wakanda, whatever we choose to call it, will be to us as Rev. Dr. Martin Luther King saw the "Mountain Top," where he said, "I may not get there with you, but I've looked over and have seen the promised land." Tulsa, like a pre-gentrified Harlem, and many other Black communities, was a space where Black ideas, culture, and wealth became commonplace. We are building that again through various modes of creative planning, and taking our agency through imagination. Comic books are only one part of a multi-medium series of Black resistance networks used for disseminating ideas to build Black creative safe-spaces. Today there are a wide range of creative outlets including Black comic book conventions, social media spaces, conferences, exhibitions, television/film stories, and more that center Black creativity. We have that potential for Tulsa again and more, but it first begins in the Black radical imagination.

"Not everything that is faced can be changed, but nothing can be changed until it is faced. Love takes off masks that we fear we cannot live without and know we cannot live within. People are trapped in history and history is trapped in them."

- James Baldwin

"Blink" character design and sketch by SANFORD GREENE

BITTER TWITTER:

@BITTERROOT18 | @Cbrown803 | @sanfordgreene | @DavidWalker1201

BITTER TRUTHS curated and designed by **John Jennings** / tw @JIJennings
Research Assistant: **Edgardo Delgadillo-Aguilera**

ROOTS, RISK, AND RESILIENCE

Ceeon D. Quiett Smith

CEEON D. QUIETT SMITH, PhD is Chief of Staff at Benedict College in Columbus, South Carolina. She has taught courses in Homeland Security, Emergency Management, Crisis Communications and Public Relations.

Research areas involve investigations of the federal governments communications policies and applications of new technology in responding to crisis and disasters. She has juried papers and conference presentations that include: *"Crisis Communication in the Public and Private Sector: A Content Analysis of the Gulf Oil Spill Pinpointing Rupture and Capping "* (2014); *"Media and Policy Framing During Disasters: Which Frame Dominates?"* (June 2015); *"Citizen Framing of Ferguson: Visual Representations on Twitter and Tumblr."* (August 2015); *"Citizen Framing of #Ferguson on Twitter." The Journal of Social Media in Society* (November 2016).

The historical context of *Bitter Root* in the Harlem Renaissance introduces exploration in the dialectic of migration, crisis, risk, and resilience. From these theoretical views are tenets that crisis and risks are ineluctable links in the social fabric of contemporary society; and that migration is both informed by and generates risk and uncertainty. *Bitter Root* sets the stage for the convergence of these theories in the historical context of the migration of African Americans from the rural south to urban cities in the north.

As a native of New Orleans, I experienced firsthand the impact on families and communities by Hurricanes Katrina and Rita. As a result, I was driven to the study of crisis, risk, and response to correct inaccuracies found in the literature by researchers who were not familiar with the city, its geography, history, or culture. As I became more immersed, the impact of crisis and the capacity to recover and respond specifically by African American communities in New Orleans, was either oversimplified or absent from the literature. Similarly, the significant impact and theoretical exploration of the largest migration in American history, that of African Americans from the South to the North, has yet to be fully appreciated in risk and resilience research. However, through the journey of the Sangerye family — in New York and Mississippi — readers can experience the family's fight against racism, violence, greed and other evils, the uncertainty and risk of African American families during The Great Migration.

Uncertainties in migration literature as discussed in economic studies of African Americans who migrated from the rural areas of the south, reveal that although they increased their earnings, significant economic disparities remained when compared to the earnings of their white counterparts. Researchers contend that one reason for this, if not the primary reason, were racist northern labor practices. As a result, African Americans from the rural south were face-to-face again with the racism and inequality that initiated the migration.

The convergence of migration and risk is where the creators of *Bitter Root* have created additional avenues for exploration. For example, in addition to facing the same disparities of racism, African Americans from the rural South also faced isolation and criticism among African Americans in the North. In the first issue, the behavior is demonstrated in the police officer, who quickly separates himself from the Sangerye family, and as a result from other African Americans who migrated to Harlem, in his exclamation that the Sangerye people are not "his people" and that "my people don't mess with no mumbo jumbo!" Although the police officer's expressed reasoning was the practice of the families roots and spirits, this is an example of the critique many families experienced and the resulting isolation they experienced from others of which whom they shared the same history, socioeconomic status and social context as African Americans in America. The burden Ma Etta carries in her spirit is palpable: *"Like I said – Too old to run... and too stubborn to quit."* Similarly, the rebel attitude of Ford magnifies his deeper feelings: *"I don't purify; I amputate."*

Although the context of Ford's statement refers to his method and approach to the monsters **(amputation)** that stands in conflict with his family's approach **(purification)**, his sharpness and isolation convey his sense of being 'left behind' that underlies his uncertainty and risk as he continues to fight in Mississippi without his family.

ConjurePunk Aesthetic at the Root
in Jennings

omics are a primarily visual storytelling method. a result, style and visual aesthetics are very important in the medium. One can say that a style is system of decisions. These decisions are usually ated to the artist's influences, training, choice of ols, and artistic philosophy. ***Bitter Root*** has three eators who are highly eclectic in their influences. om Hip Hop to Blaxploitation and Horror Sci-fi historical fiction, this trio of conjure men have ven us a hybrid form that I feel falls into what nave dubbed a ConjurePunk aesthetic. I define is visual language as:

eculative stylistic forms that are situated and eated within or related to Black Southern spaces merging the cultural practices, aesthetics, and lkloric technologies of rootwork and conjure ith the tropes and world-building affordances of ack cyberpunk (cyberfunk), black steampunk teamfunk), or black dieselpunk (dieselfunk).

, if the EthnoGothic provides the abstract and iritually political underpinnings of ***Bitter Root*** en ConjurePunk can be considered an explanaon of the formal style. You can see this reflected the striking ***Bitter Root*** logo. It's a large powerl gear intersected with an elegant and ominous ot. Rootwork is a type of technology. It is folkased hacking. It is an older method of problem lving that is not based on a Western idea of scice. So, what happens when this older and often isunderstood technology is in a wonderful tenon with a current more "modern" tech? Whether s digital, steam-based, or diesel-powered appaatuses, conjure and rootwork stands the test of me because of its oral and culturally situated asis. This mode represents the remixing of ideas om the African Diaspora, arcane practices of Euope, and the wild mixture of what happens when nose cultures meet the age-old ceremonies of Nave American shamans. ConjurePunk, like ***Bitter oot*** is this multi-layered visual gumbo and, boy, oes it taste good.

would say that the work of Jamaican-born, anadian-bred speculative fiction writer Nalo opkinson is the godmother of this form. Her culurally centered techno-mixes and writer-scholr Ishmael Reed's notions around what he called NeoHoodoo" are the blueprints for the hex-mahine that makes this type of expression. Both Hopkinson and Reed speak about a cultural equivlence between hoodoo practices and modern chnology. One is not better than the other and ecause of that, they can be mixed together or even xchanged. So, at the root of this aesthetic expreson is a basic understanding that the best stories nd expressions are usually somewhere at the interection of these ideas.

Bitter Root underscores the uncertainty and the risks of migration as conceptualized in literature. Risk is theoretically conceived as a situation or event in which something of human value and/or humans have been put at stake and where the outcome is uncertain (Tierney, 2014). Researchers also contend that an individual's perception and response to risk can only be understood against the background of their connection in a sociocultural background and identity as a member of a social group. Mary Douglas positions that risk should be considered "a social construction in a particular historical and cultural context".

Resilience, like risk, has its origins in the social order. The ability to be resilient in the face of crisis is often associated with economic prosperity and the protections it buys. Further, resilience is also framed as a creative response to a crisis or risk. Risk researchers contend that the capacity to be resilient also involves economic advantages that are often not available to vulnerable, under-resourced, poor populations. And that resilience is an individual or community's capacity to creatively respond to a crisis or risk.

The Harlem Renaissance is an example of a community's resilience – a creative response to the risk and uncertainties of migration. History reveals that by 1910, African Americans had become the majority group in the Harlem. By 1920, Harlem had emerged as the capital of black America. As poor southern farmers and sharecroppers made their way northward, they joined African American northerners and intellectuals such as W. E. B. Du Bois and James Weldon Johnson. One historian notes that although Harlem did not have a college or university, Harlem became the arts and cultural center — a Mecca — for its aspiring young African Americans.

I applaud, personally and professionally, the creators of *Bitter Root* for revitalizing this important time in our history and for challenging all of us to dig deeper into our past in order to learn more about our future.

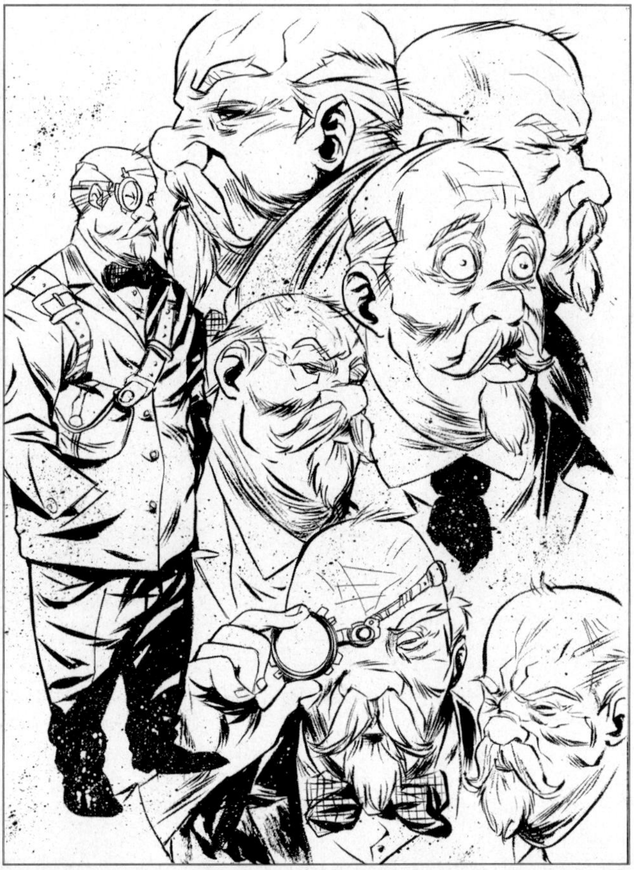

"Uncle E" character design and sketch by SANFORD GREENE

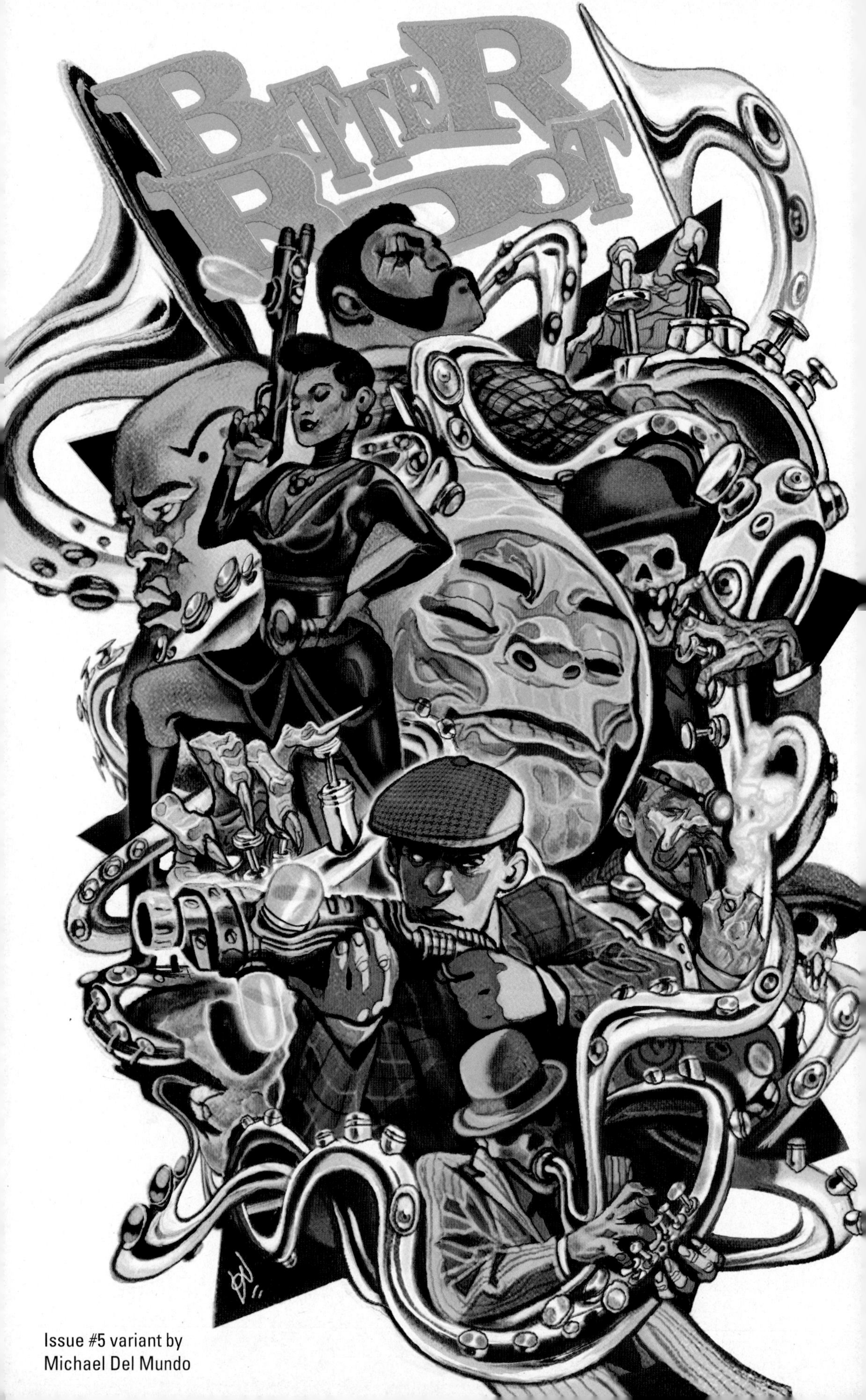

Issue #5 variant by
Michael Del Mundo

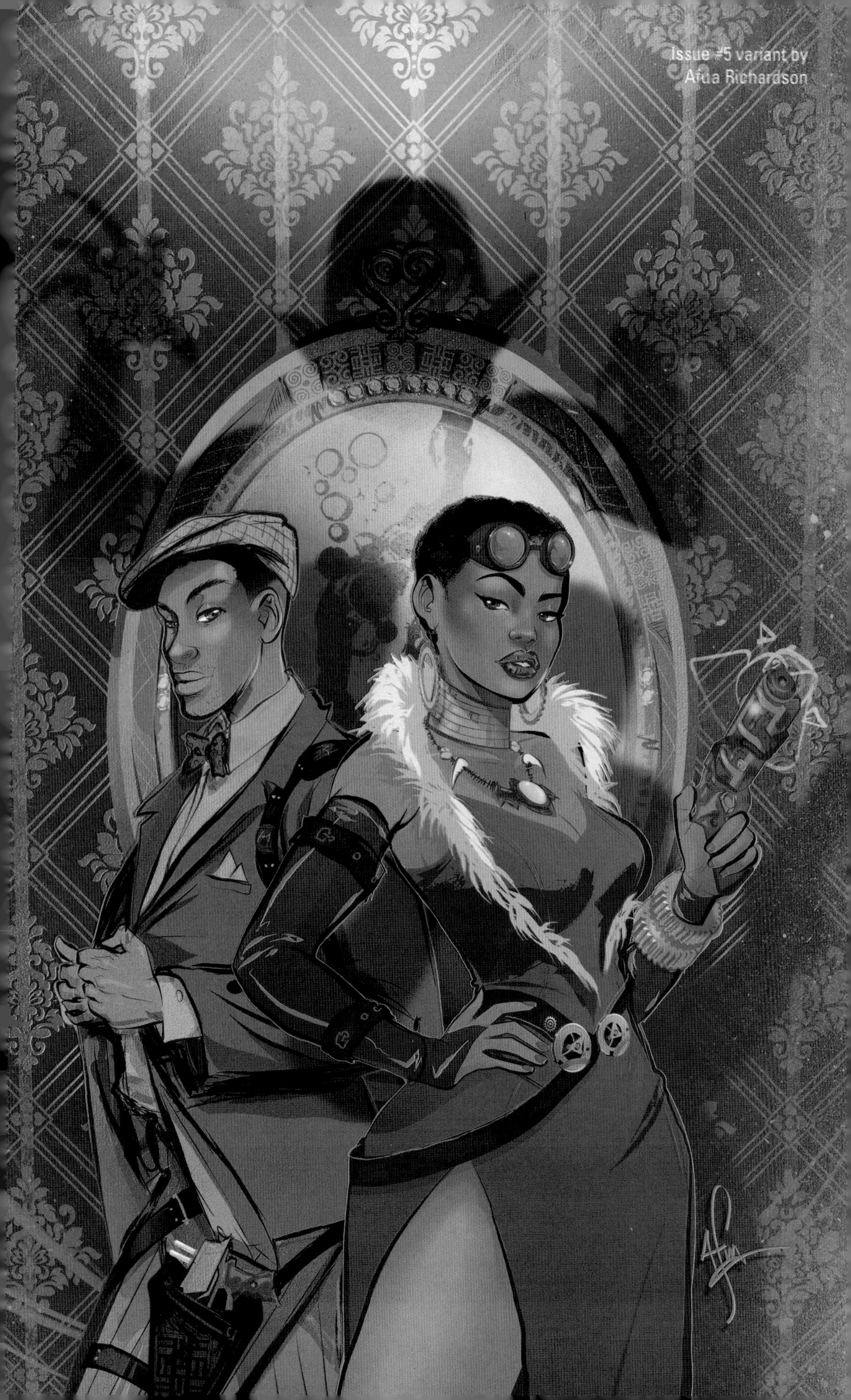

Issue #5 variant by
Afua Richardson

DAVID F. WALKER is a writer, filmmaker, and award-winning journalist. He teaches Writing for Comics at Portland State University.

CHUCK BROWN has written *The Punisher* and *Black Panther* comics for Marvel. He is the writer and co-creator of *Rotten Apple* for Dark Horse Comics and the co-writer and co-creator of BITTER ROOT at Image Comics.

SANFORD GREENE has been a successful cartoonist for over 17 years and is a sequential art instructor at his alma mater, Benedict College.

RICO RENZI is an artist and designer from Washington DC. His work has appeared in the Academy Award-winning *Spider-Man: Into The Spider-Verse,* WIRED and Fast Company Magazines, and various publications from D.C., Marvel, Image, Dark Horse, Scholastic, Boom Studios, Oni Press and IDW. Best known for his work on Marvel's *Spider-Gwen* and *Unbeatable Squirrel Girl,* he resides in Charlotte, North Carolina with his wife and daughter. NoLongerMint.com

CLAYTON COWLES is a 2009 graduate of the Joe Kubert School. He has lettered numerous books for Marvel, DC, and Image Comics. He lives in upstate New York in a house with two cats.